JUVENILE OSTEOLOGY

JUVENILE OSTEOLOGY: A LABORATORY AND FIELD MANUAL

Maureen Schaefer
University of Dundee, College of Life Sciences, Centre for Anatomy and Human Identification, Dundee, United Kingdom

Sue Black
University of Dundee, College of Life Sciences, Centre for Anatomy and Human Identification, Dundee, United Kingdom

Louise Scheuer
University College London, Department of Anatomy and Developmental Biology, London, United Kingdom
University of Dundee, College of Life Sciences, Centre for Anatomy and Human Identification, Dundee, United Kingdom

Illustrations by
Angela Christie

AMSTERDAM • BOSTON • HEIDELBERG • LONDON
NEW YORK • OXFORD • PARIS • SAN DIEGO
SAN FRANCISCO • SINGAPORE • SYDNEY • TOKYO
Academic Press is an imprint of Elsevier

Academic Press is an imprint of Elsevier

30 Corporate Drive, Suite 400, Burlington, MA 01803, USA
525 B Street, Suite 1900, San Diego, California 92101-4495, USA
84 Theobald's Road, London WC1X 8RR, UK

Library of Congress Cataloging-in-Publication Data
APPLICATION SUBMITTED

British Library Cataloguing-in-Publication Data
A catalogue record for this book is available from the British Library.

ISBN: 978-0-12-374635-1

For information on all Academic Press publications
visit our Web site at www.elsevierdirect.com

Dedication

"To my son Bryce, whose conception and delivery coincided with the development of this book."

Maureen Schaefer

Table of Contents

3. The Vertebral Column

4. The Thorax

5. The Pectoral Girdle

6. The Upper Limb

7. The Pelvic Girdle

8. The Lower Limb

9. Summaries, Recording Forms, and Practical Sequencing Information

Preface

In response to the lack of a suitable text, in 1990 we began to plan and write a laboratory and field manual of fetal and juvenile osteology that would aid our diagnoses in the mortuary and in the lab. By 1992 it was clear that what we were writing was not suitable for its original purpose and in 1994 we set about a complete re-organisation and rewrite of our text and our thoughts. We had learned so much in those four years from the work of others that it was clear that a reference text was required that would bring together the widely scattered literature that not only spanned hundreds of years but also hundreds of academic publications—and so the foundations of *Developmental Juvenile Osteology* were laid. The text was published in 2000 and was exceptionally well received, gaining a prize from the Society of Authors and Royal Society of Medicine book awards. However it was large and expensive and can truthfully be described as a major academic reference. Elsevier wanted to produce a student version of the text and in 2004 *The Juvenile Skeleton* was published. This book received a 'Highly Commended' award from the BMA Medical Book Competition. It was aimed almost exclusively at the postgraduate student audience and was not designed for the experienced practitioner. Whilst it retained much of the basic information of its predecessor, tables and raw data were removed leaving only summary information that outlined significant milestone events in the maturation of the human skeleton.

Personal and professional issues took their toll and our drive and commitment to finally produce a laboratory manual were severely challenged. In 2004 Maureen Schaefer commenced her PhD studies at the University of Dundee working on a re-evaluation of epiphyseal closure for age evaluation, utilising data recovered from the deceased following the fall of Srebrenica. She not only completed her degree in the prescribed 3 years, but was responsible for new and stimulating research in age evaluation in the juvenile skeleton and she brought the enthusiasm and drive that was required to see the laboratory and field manual come to fruition—18 years after the original idea.

This text is not designed as an instructor's manual, nor is it for the amateur. It is solely and directly aimed at those who work in the field of age evaluation from the juvenile skeleton, whether in the archaeological or the forensic arena. In the UK, we would call it a 'ready reckoner' —something that facilitates analysis and computation for the expert who already is experienced in this area. This is a resource for the practitioner who needs little in the way of academic prose or anatomical explanation, but requires the basic numerical and morphological tools to assist them to undertake their job in a practical environment.

We have requested that it be produced in a format that is directly aimed to meet the needs of the average working environment.

The spiral bound presentation is to ensure that it can be opened without pages having to be weighted down; these are in a glossy format to be as resistant to dirt as possible; the format is laid out in a variety of ways to ensure that the practitioner can find one that is most suited to their requirements and we have added some datasheet suggestions.

We have only quoted publications that have utilised material of documented origin or is sourced from material where age has been reliably determined and thereby we have attempted to avoid the circular arguments associated with age estimation in archaeological material. We have given wide ranges for developmental stages and some may differ marginally from those published in *Developmental Juvenile Osteology* or *The Juvenile Skeleton*, but they represent the incorporation of the most recent research available. There is no doubt that there are some anatomical regions that are sparse in information but hopefully with time, these will become fewer as the areas are duly addressed where more research urgently needs to be undertaken.

We have now come full circle with a trilogy of texts and other than alterations to new editions—we finally feel that our contribution is complete.

Sue Black and Louise Scheuer

CHAPTER

1

The Head and Neck

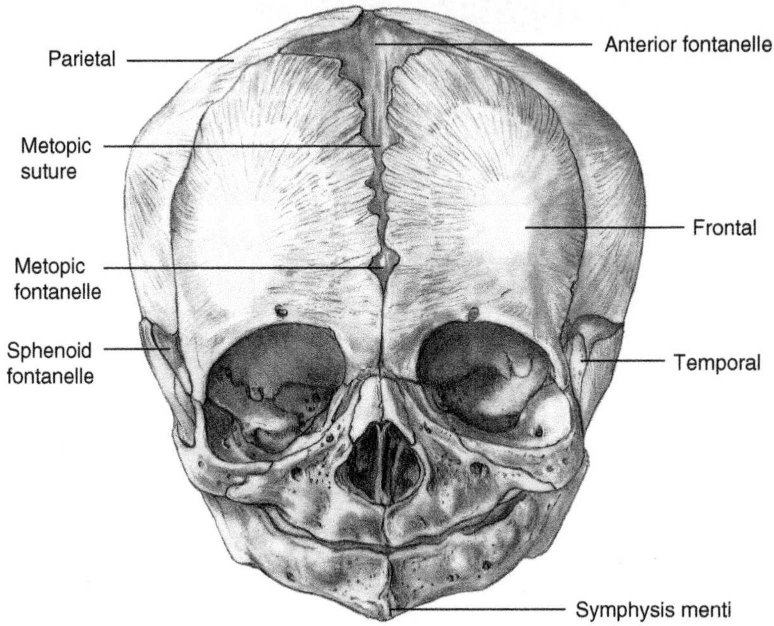

Anterior view of fetal skull and mandible

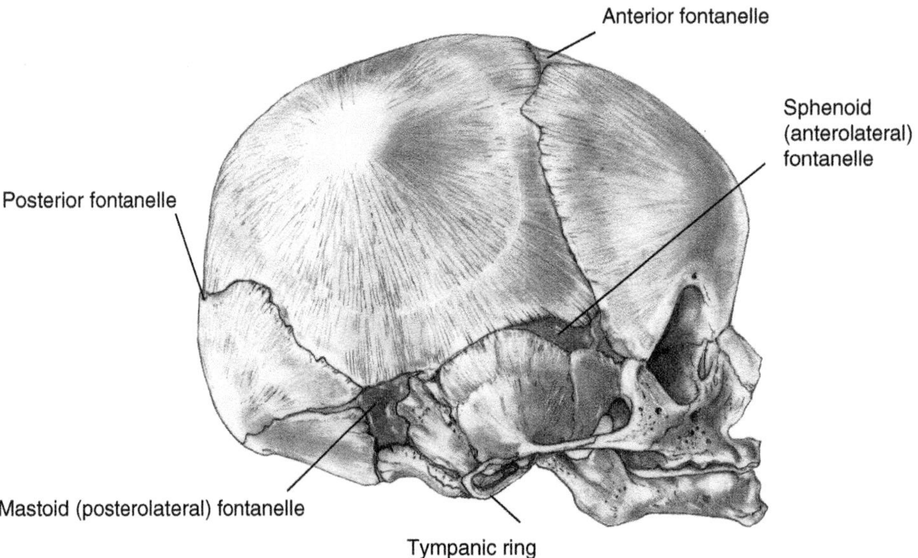

Lateral view of fetal skull and mandible

THE FETAL SKULL

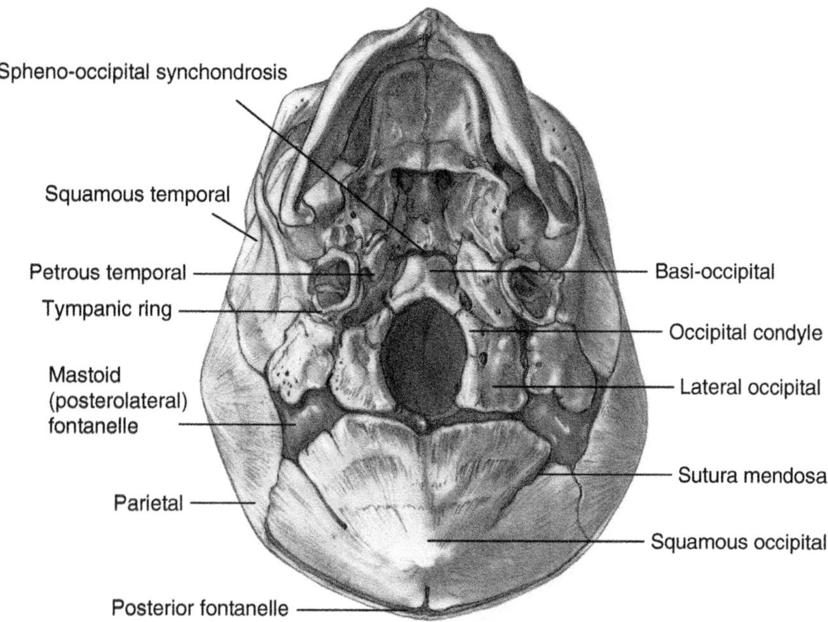

Basal view of fetal skull and mandible

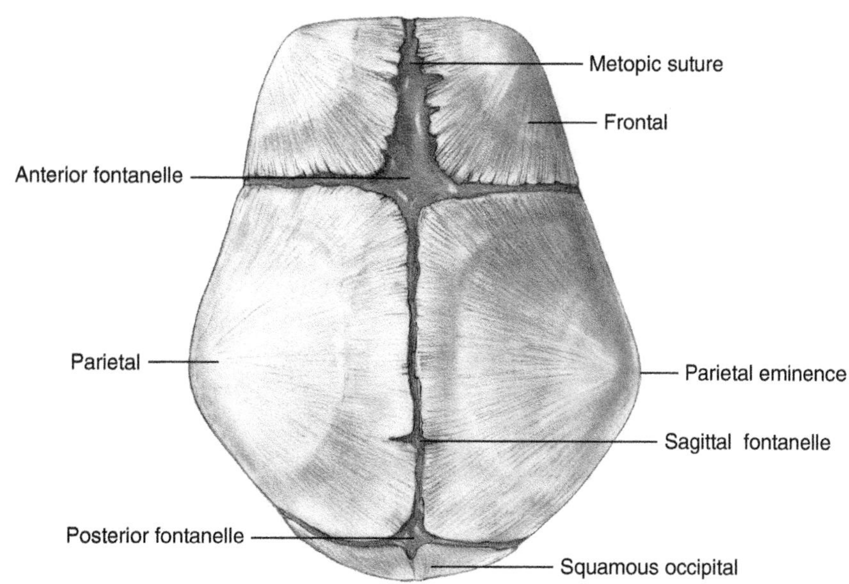

Superior view of fetal skull

THE OCCIPITAL

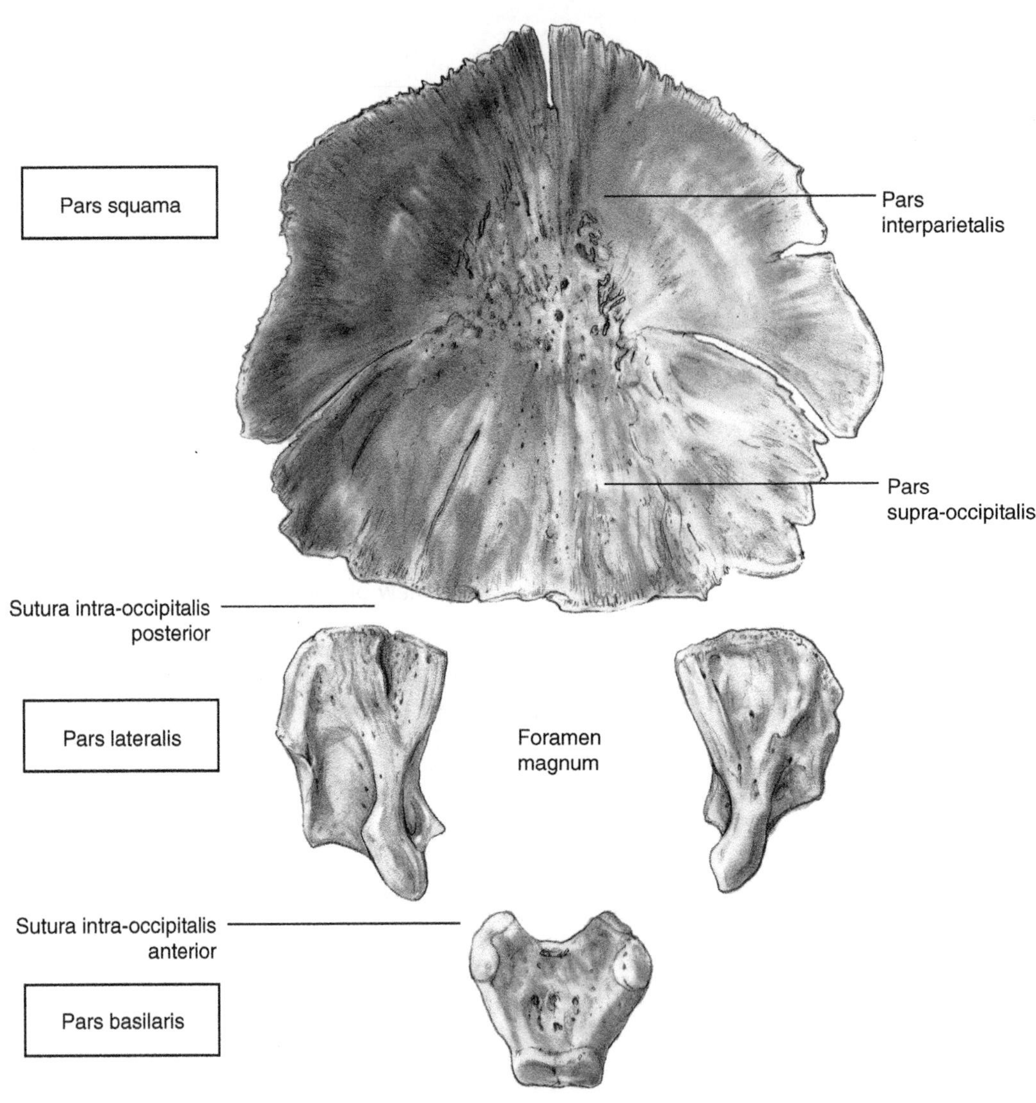

Intracranial view of the perinatal occipital

Pars Squama

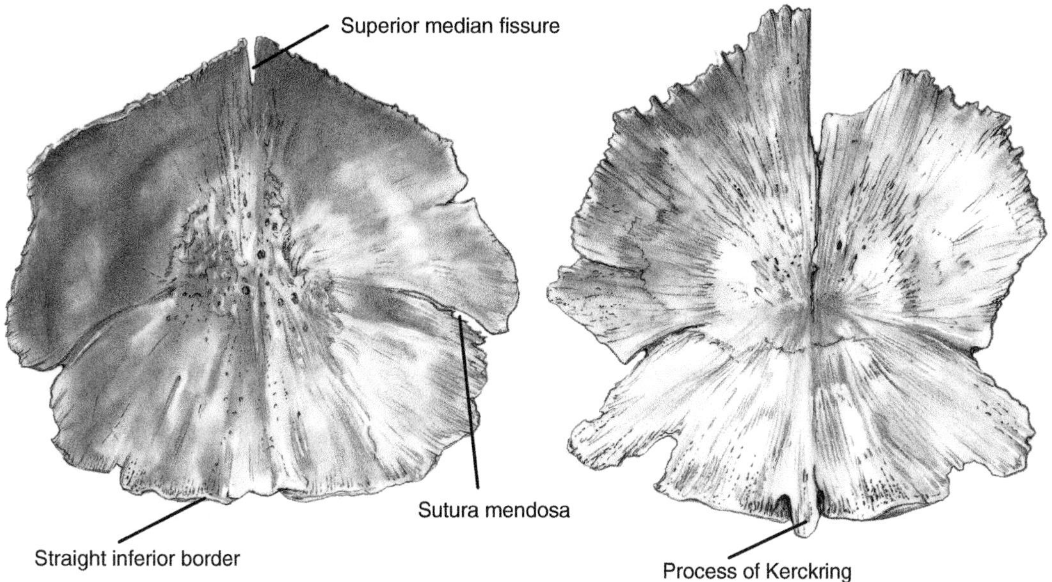

Perinatal pars squama

Identification

- Probably indistinguishable from fragments of other vault bones unless a characteristic part, such as the process of Kerckring, is present.
- More robust in the region of the foramen magnum than other vault bones.

Orientation

- Superior border is angled, inferior border is straight.
- Mendosal sutures are obliquely oriented in an inferolateral direction.

Pars Lateralis

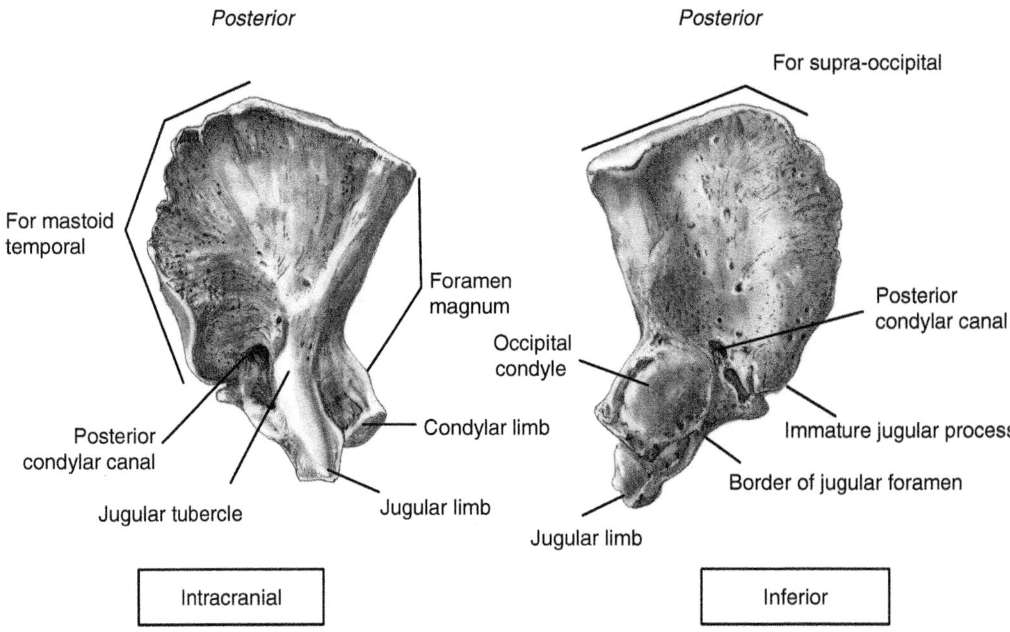

Right perinatal pars lateralis

Identification – During perinatal life, the inferior surface resembles that of the scapula (see page 7).

- Within a single skeleton, the scapula is much larger and its blade is more extensive than the body of the pars lateralis.
- Presence of the occipital condyles easily distinguishes the pars lateralis.

Siding

- The condylar and jugular limbs are orientated anteromedially.
- The condylar limb, as identified by the partial presence of the occipital condyle, is situated inferiorly or ectocranially.

Similar Morphology

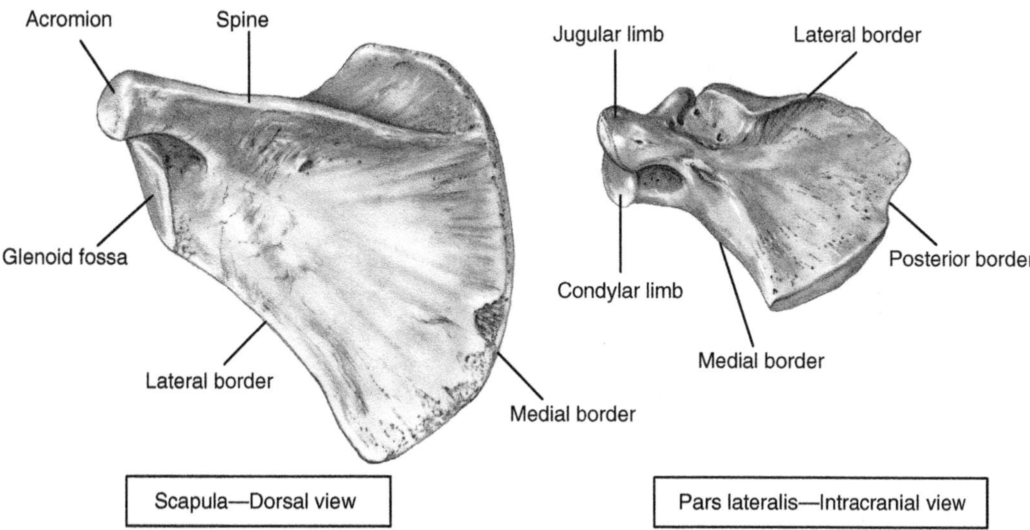

Comparison between the left perinatal scapula and the right pars lateralis from the same skeleton

Pars Basilaris

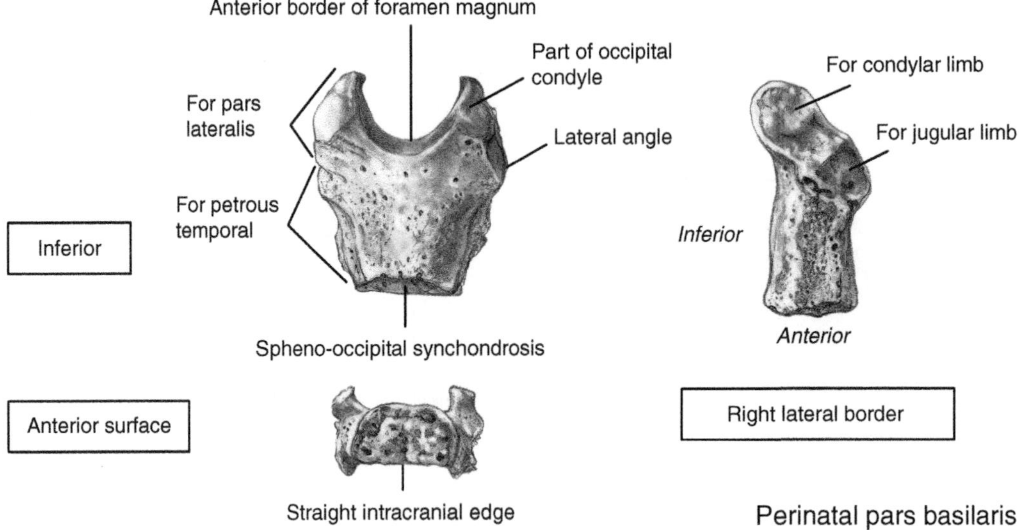

Perinatal pars basilaris

Identification – The prenatal pars basilaris is longer and displays a smaller lateral angle when compared to its postnatal appearance. Similar in shape to the manubrium sterni.

- During the perinatal period, the pars basilaris is much more substantial than the manubrium sterni, which is barely more than a thin disc.
- Following perinatal life, the manubrium remains smaller and thinner with less well-defined borders.

Siding/Orientation

- Intracranial surface is slightly concave.
- The ectocranial or inferior surface is slightly convex, and parts of the occipital condyles can usually be seen at the tips of the posterior curve.
- Anterior border is flat, whereas the posterior border curves to form the foramen magnum.
- When viewed anteriorly, the intracranial edge is straight.

Metrics

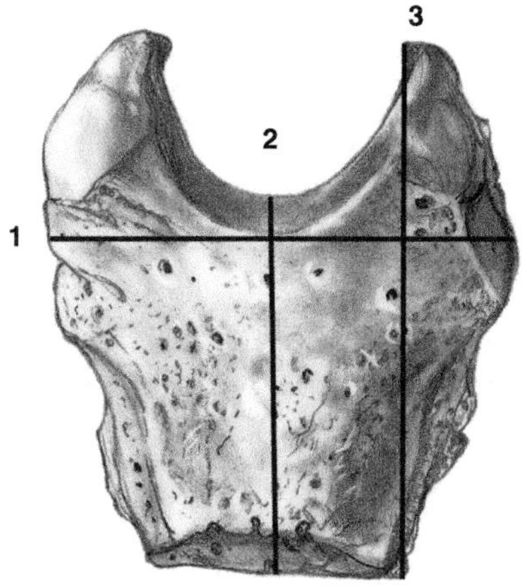

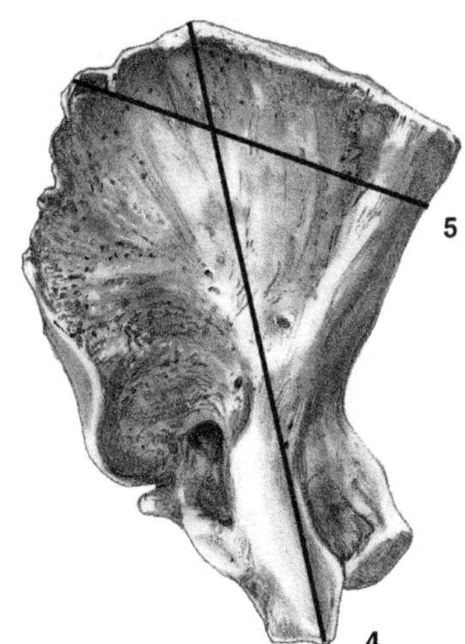

Reference landmarks for occipital measurements

Notes

1. Maximum width basilaris: Greatest distance measured in the line of the lateral angles
2. Sagittal length basilaris: Midline distance between the foramen magnum and synchondrosis sphenooccipitalis
3. Maximum length basilaris: Maximum distance between the posterior edge of the lateral condyle and the synchondrosis sphenooccipitalis
4. Maximum length lateralis: Greatest distance between the anterior and posterior interoccipital synchondroses
5. Maximum width lateralis: Greatest distance between the medial and lateral margins of the posterior interoccipital synchondrosis

Fazekas and Kósa

Dry Bone Fatal Measurements—Occipital Squama (mm)										
		Chord				Arc				
		Height		Width		Height		Width		
Prenatal Age (wks)	*n*	Mean	Range	Mean	Range	Mean	Range	Mean	Range
12	2	7.5	7.0–8.0	12.0	11.0–13.0	7.5	7.0–8.0	12.0	11.0–13.0
14	3	10.6	9.0–13.5	14.4	13.2–15.0	10.6	9.0–13.5	14.4	13.2–15.0
16	9	15.0	13.0–19.5	18.6	14.0–23.4	15.7	14.0–20.0	19.6	15.0–24.0
18	15	18.8	16.0–23.0	22.5	17.5–29.0	19.9	17.0–24.0	23.8	19.0–29.0
20	13	23.7	21.0–27.0	27.5	24.0–32.6	24.7	22.5–28.0	29.4	25.0–33.0
22	11	27.3	25.0–30.2	31.2	28.0–32.5	28.9	27.0–33.0	34.2	33.0–36.0
24	12	28.7	24.0–32.2	32.9	29.0–36.1	32.1	28.0–36.0	39.0	36.0–42.0
26	12	32.8	27.0–36.5	36.5	30.5–40.0	36.0	32.0–40.0	40.9	36.0–52.0
28	12	35.4	32.0–37.8	39.6	37.0–42.6	40.8	36.0–45.0	45.9	42.0–48.0
30	12	39.0	33.0–45.0	43.0	39.0–48.0	44.4	41.0–48.0	49.0	46.0–53.0
32	8	42.5	41.0–43.5	47.6	43.0–52.0	47.7	47.0–49.0	55.9	53.0–60.0
34	7	49.4	48.1–50.0	50.0	46.0–56.0	59.2	57.0–62.0	60.0	59.0–65.0
36	5	50.3	46.0–53.0	51.6	47.0–58.0	61.3	57.0–64.0	63.1	60.0–70.0
38	7	53.5	48.5–56.5	56.3	53.0–62.0	63.8	60.0–66.0	67.0	64.0–71.0
40	10	55.2	51.5–59.0	59.3	56.0–66.5	68.8	65.0–74.0	70.5	65.0–76.0

Notes

Height (chord): Straight line distance from the posterior border of the foramen magnum to the tip of the squama in the midline

Height (arc): Same landmarks as described above taken along the convexity of the occipital bone

Width (chord): Straight line distance from the greatest width of the occipital squama in line of the sutura mendosa

Width (arc): Same landmarks as described above taken along the convexity of the occipital bone

Source

Dry bone measurements on mid twentieth century Hungarian fetal remains from autopsy—males and females combined. Age was estimated based on fetal crown heel length.

Reference

Fazekas, I.Gy. and Kósa, F. (1978). *Forensic Fetal Osteology*. Budapest: Akadémiai Kiadó.

Dry Bone Fetal Measurements-Pars Basilaris (mm)

Prenatal Age (wks)	*n*	Sagittal Length		Maximum Width	
		Mean	Range	Mean	Range
12	2	2.8	2.5–3.0	1.8	1.5–2.0
14	3	4.0	3.5–4.5	2.6	1.8–3.1
16	9	5.5	4.5–6.4	3.9	2.2–5.0
18	15	6.9	6.0–8.0	5.1	4.0–6.4
20	13	8.0	7.3–9.0	6.1	5.5–6.5
22	11	8.3	7.4–9.0	6.8	5.5–7.8
24	12	8.7	8.0–9.6	8.0	6.5–8.9
26	12	9.1	8.5–9.6	8.4	8.0–9.4
28	12	9.6	9.0–10.5	9.1	8.0–9.8
30	12	10.1	9.4–11.0	10.0	8.5–11.5
32	8	10.5	10.0–11.1	10.9	9.2–12.0
34	7	11.0	10.4–11.7	12.0	11.5–12.5
36	5	11.8	11.5–12.0	12.4	12.0–13.0
38	7	12.4	12.0–13.0	13.4	12.5–14.0
40	10	13.1	12.2–13.6	15.2	13.4–17.7

Dry Bone Fetal Measurements-Pars lateralis (mm)

Prenatal Age (wks)	*n*	Max Length		Max Width	
		Mean	Range	Mean	Range
12	2	2.7	2.5–3.0	1.4	1.2–1.5
14	3	4.0	3.5–4.6	1.8	1.5–2.2
16	9	5.9	5.0–6.9	2.9	2.2–4.0
18	15	7.7	6.6–8.7	4.1	3.0–4.8
20	13	9.5	9.0–10.2	5.1	4.4–5.7
22	11	10.6	9.0–11.9	5.8	5.0–6.5
24	12	11.8	10.0–13.2	6.7	5.5–7.3
26	12	13.1	12.2–14.5	7.1	6.8–7.5
28	12	14.1	13.0–15.0	7.9	7.5–8.5
30	12	14.7	13.0–16.0	8.5	7.0–10.0
32	8	17.0	15.0–18.2	8.9	8.0–10.5
34	7	19.3	18.0–20.2	10.9	9.0–12.1
36	5	20.8	20.0–22.5	11.6	11.0–12.0
38	7	23.4	20.0–26.6	13.2	11.0–15.0
40	10	26.5	22.0–29.0	14.0	11.0–16.0

Scheuer and MacLaughlin-Black

Dry Bone Prenatal Measurements-Pars Basilaris (mm)

	Age*	*n*	Mean MW	Mean SL	Mean ML
MW<SL	26 fetal wks	1	8.7	9.4	11.4
	28 fetal wks	1	9.6	10.3	12.1
MW>SL	30 fetal wks	1	10.9	10.4	12.8
	38 fetal wks	2	13.7	11.9	15.3
	40 fetal wks	5	15.5	12.7	16.5
	40+ fetal wks	4	15.6	13.0	16.6

*Fetal age determined through use of Fazekas and Kosa data

Notes

MW = Maximum width
SL = Sagittal length
ML = Maximum length

Source

Spitalfields and St. Bride's collection: Dry bone measurements on early eighteenth to mid nineteenth century documented remains.

Reference

Scheuer, L., and MacLaughlin-Black, S. (1994). Age estimation from the pars basilaris of the fetal and juvenile occipital bone. *The International Journal of Osteoarchaeology* **4**: 377–380. Copyright John Wiley & Sons Limited. Reproduced with permission.

Scheuer and MacLaughlin-Black

	Dry Bone Postnatal Measurements-Pars basilaris (mm)				
	Age	***n***	**Mean MW**	**Mean SL**	**Mean ML**
MW<SL	2 wks	3	14.5	11.3	15.6
	3 wks	1	16.9	12.7	17.0
	4 wks	1	15.6	12.6	16.8
	7 wks	1	15.5	11.6	15.9
	3 mths	1	15.4	13.8	16.7
MW>SL	5 mths	1	18.4	13.4	18.1
	8 mths	2	21.0	13.8	20.5
	9 mths	3	20.5	13.9	19.6
	11 mths	1	22.3	14.0	19.7
	1 yr	1	18.3	13.9	17.9
	1 yr 1 mth	2	22.1	14.8	19.8
	1 yr 2 mths	3	22.7	15.8	21.3
	1 yr 3 mths	1	23.6	16.8	22.7
	1 yr 4 mths	1	18.6	14.0	18.6
	1 yr 6 mths	3	21.9	15.5	20.8
	1 yr 8 mths	1	22.8	15.7	21.7
	1 yr 9 mths	1	22.7	16.8	21.3
	2 yrs 3 mths	2	24.4	18.1	23.5
	2 yrs 5 mths	2	25.8	17.5	24.2
	2 yrs 6 mths	1	24.6	17.5	22.4
	2 yrs 7 mths	4	25.9	17.4	24.2
	2 yrs 9 mths	2	24.2	16.4	23.3
	3 yrs 2 mths	1	23.2	16.6	22.7
	3 yrs 4 mths	1	27.6	16.6	24.6
	3 yrs 5 mths	1	26.1	18.1	24.1
	3 yrs 7 mths	1	27.8	17.5	24.8
	3 yrs 8 mths	1	27.3	15.5	24.0
	4 yrs 3 mths	2	25.9	16.4	24.2
	4 yrs 7 mths	1	26.2	15.3	23.9

Union Timings

Compilation Research

Occipital Sutures
Lateral sections of Sutura Mendosa
1. Fuses between 1-4 mths (closed but not obliterated)
2. Persists until 3 or 4 yrs
3. Fuses between 5-11 mths
Sutura Intra-Occipitalis Posterior
1. Obliterated in about half of the specimens by 5 yrs of age
3. Fuses between 2-4 yrs
4. Begins as early as 2 yrs, completes between 3-6 yrs
Sutura Intra-Occipitalis Anterior
3. Begins after 24 mths
4. Begins as early as 2-4 yrs, completes between 7-10 yrs
5. Begins as early as 3-4 yrs, completes between 5-8 yrs

Sources

1. Dry bone inspection of undocumented medieval remains from Mistihalj, in southern Yugoslavia
2. Dry bone inspection of mid twentieth century Hungarian fetal remains from autopsy
3. Dry bone inspection of early eighteenth to mid nineteenth century documented remains from Spitalfields, London
4. CT scans of American patients between 1991 and 1994
5. Dry bone inspection of known-aged skulls, albeit their provenance and time period were not disclosed

References

1. Redfield, A. (1970). A new aid to aging immature skeletons: Development of the occipital bone. *American Journal of Physical Anthropology* **33**: 207–220.
2. Fazekas, I.Gy. and Kósa, F. (1978). *Forensic Fetal Osteology*. Budapest: Akadémiai Kiadó.
3. Molleson, T. and Cox, M. (1993). The Spitalfields Project. *Volume 2 – The Anthropology – The Middling Sort*, Research Report 86. London: Council for British Archaeology.
4. Madeline, L. and Elster, A. (1995). Suture closure in the human chondrocranium: CT assessment. *Radiology* **196**: 747–756.
5. Tillman, B. and Lorenz, R. (1978). The stress at the human atlanto-occipital joint: The development of the occipital condyle. *Anatomy and Embryology* **153**: 269–277.

Spheno-Occipital Synchondrosis								
	Males				Females			
Method	n	Open	Fusing	Complete	n	Open	Fusing	Complete
1. Dry bone	68	≤16	–	19≤	69	≤12	–	14≤
2. Dry bone	50	≤16	13–18	15≤	34	≤16	12–16	13≤
3. Radiographic	205	≤15	10–17	13≤	193	≤13	9–13	10≤
4. Radiographic	152	≤15	9–16	12≤	162	≤13	9–14	10≤

Sources

1. The Coimbra collection: Documented Portuguese material from the mid to late nineteenth and early twentieth century
2. Northwest Indian autopsy subjects
3. Radiographs from American orthodontic patients during the mid twentieth century
4. Radiographs from American patients during the mid twentieth century

References

1. Coqueugniot, H. and Weaver, T. (2007). Infracranial maturation in the skeletal collection from Coimbra, Portugal: New aging standards for epiphyseal union. *American Journal of Physical Anthropology,* DOI: 10.1002/ajpa.20696.
2. Sahni, D., Jit, I., Neelam and Suri, S. (1998). Time of fusion of the basisphenoid with the basilar part of the occipital bone in northwest Indian subjects. *Forensic Science International* **98**(1–2): 41–45.
3. Powell, T. and Brodie, A. (1963). Closure of the spheno-occipital synchondrosis. *Anatomical Record* **147**: 15–23.
4. Konie, J. (1964). Comparative value of x-rays of the spheno-occipital synchondrosis and of the wrist for skeletal age assessment. *Angle Orthodontist* **34**: 303–313.

Morphological Summary

Prenatal	
Wks 8–10	Ossification centers for supra-occipital, interparietal and pars lateralis appear in that order
Wks 11–12	Ossification center for pars basilaris appears
By mth 5	Supra-occipital and interparietal parts of squama fused
By mth 7	Pars basilaris develops lateral angle
By mth 8	Pars lateralis longer than pars basilaris
Birth	Represented by pars basilaris, two partes laterales, pars squama
By mth 6	Pars basilaris width always greater than length
During yr 1	Median sagittal suture and remains of sutura mendosa close
	Jugular process develops on pars lateralis
	Vascular and neural markings become apparent
1–3 yrs	Fusion of pars lateralis to squama
2–4 yrs	Hypoglossal canal complete excluding pars basilaris
5–7 yrs	Fusion of pars basilaris and pars lateralis
11–16 yrs (f)	Fusion of spheno-occipital synchondrosis
13–18 yrs (m)	Fusion of spheno-occipital synchondrosis
22–34 yrs	Closure of jugular growth plate

THE TEMPORAL

Pars Squama

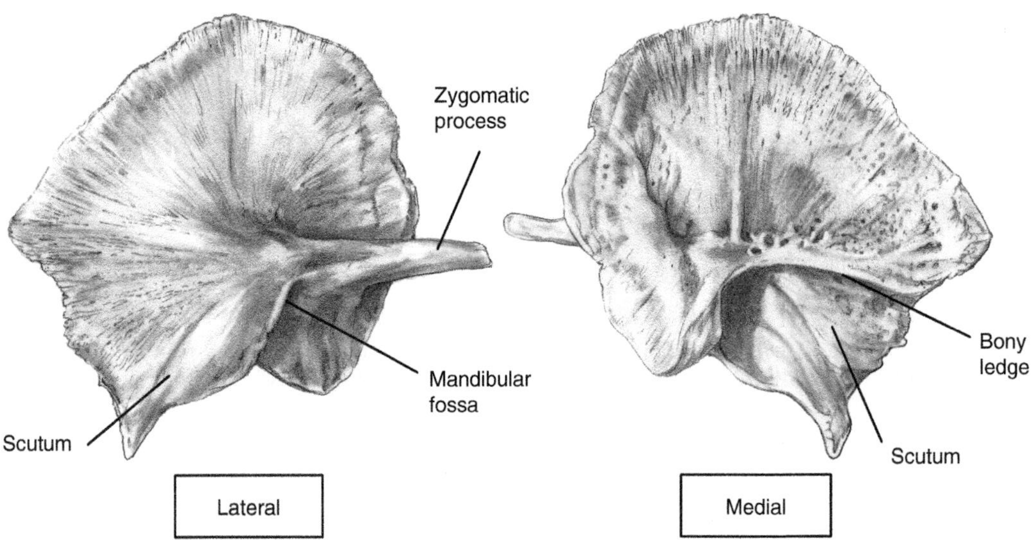

Right perinatal pars squama

Identification

- Fragments of the squama are probably indistinguishable from other cavarial fragments unless containing part of the zygomatic process or the scutum.
- An isolated zygomatic process could be mistaken for an incomplete posterior arch of the atlas.

Orientation

- The zygomatic process points anteriorly from the lateral surface.
- The triangular scutum lies posterior and below a bony ledge on the intracranial surface.

Pars Tympani

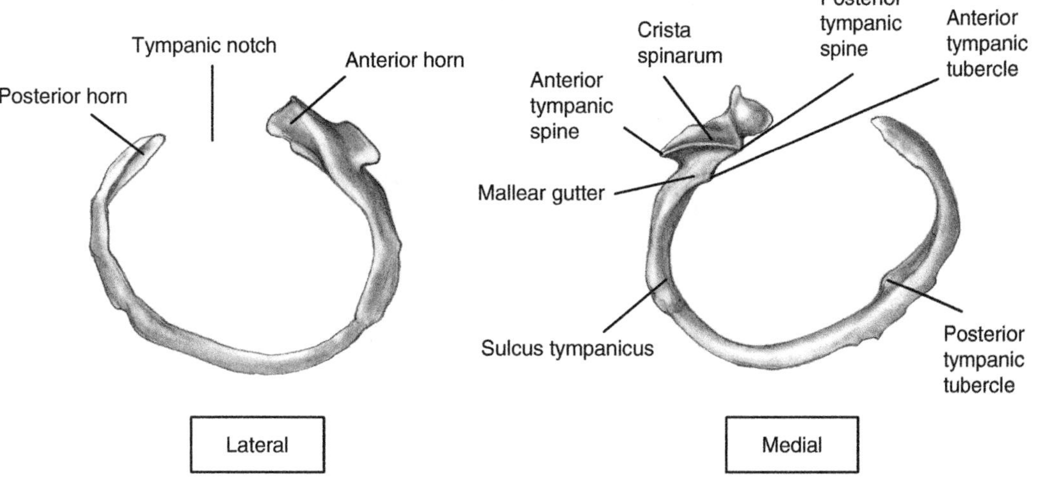

Right perinatal tympanic ring

Siding/Orientation

- Difficult to side until late fetal life when the sulcus for the tympanic membrane has developed on the medial side.
- By birth, the ring is usually partly fused to the pars squama.
- The anterior horn is more robust than the posterior horn, which tapers to a point.

Pars Petrosa

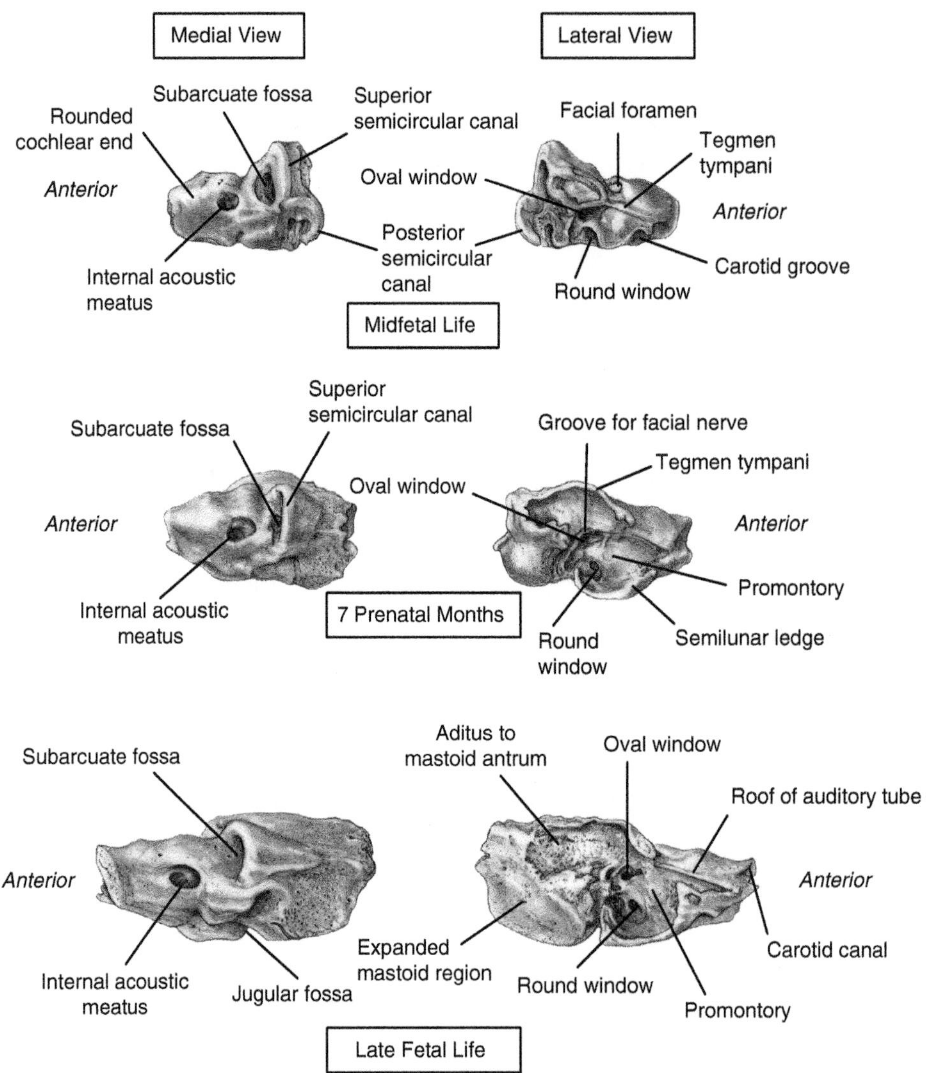

Ossification of the right pars petrosa

Siding/Orientation

- In early stages, rounded cochlear end is anterior and prominent posterior semi-circular canal is posterior.
- Middle ear cavity lies laterally and the intracranial surface is medial.
- On the lateral surface, the smooth mastoid part of the bone lies posterior.
- On the intracranial surface, the anteriorly pointing subarcuate fossa lies superior to the oval internal auditory meatus.

Postnatal Growth and Fusion

Humphrey and Scheuer

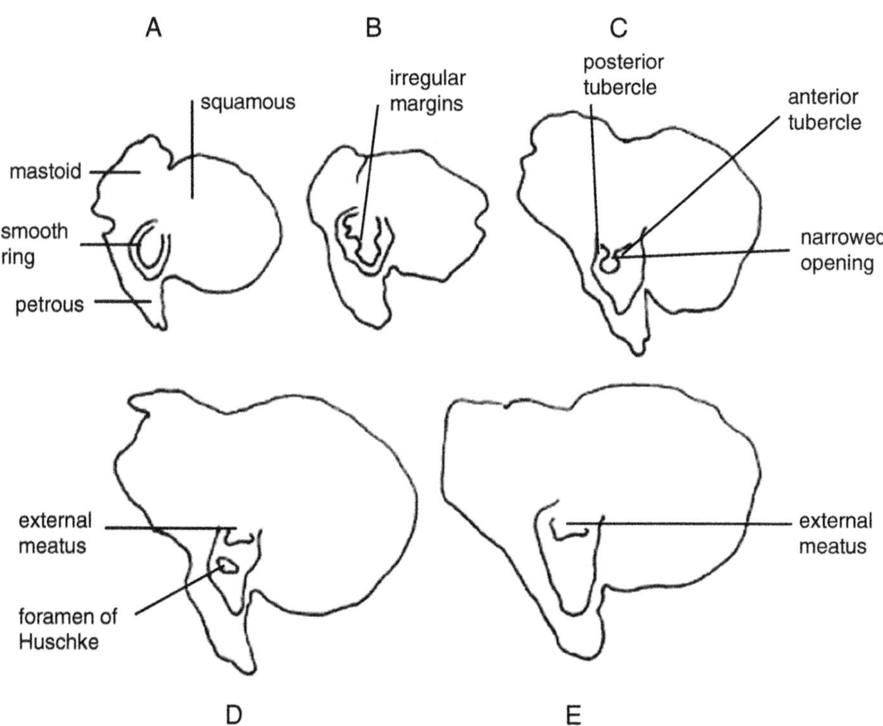

Stages in the development of the tympanic plate

Notes

Stage A (Smooth): The interior walls of the tympanic ring are smooth.
Stage B (Irregular): The interior walls of the tympanic ring are irregular, but the ring remains narrow and the overall dimensions are not markedly reduced.
Stage C (Tubercles): The anterior and posterior tubercles have approached each other but remain unconnected.
Stage D (Foramen): The anterior and posterior tubercles have bridged over, creating a foramen.
Stage E (Closed): The foramen of Huschke has closed.

Dry Bone Assessment-Tympanic Plate							
			Stage of Development (%)				
Age Range	No. of Individuals	No. of Bones	Smooth Stage A	Irregular Stage B	Tubercles Stage C	Foramen Stage D	Closed Stage E
Birth-5 mths	13	23	17.4	60.9	21.7	–	–
5-11 mths	10	16	–	–	93.8	6.2	–
11-18 mths	19	33	–	–	30.3	66.7	3.0
18-30 mths	18	32	–	–	–	100.0	–
30-39 mths	24	42	–	–	–	64.3	35.7
39-54 mths	22	41	–	–	–	65.9	34.1
4.5-7 yrs	15	30	–	–	–	56.7	43.3
7-8 yrs	12	24	–	–	–	37.5	62.5
8-10 yrs	10	20	–	–	–	50.0	50.0
10-15 yrs	25	46	–	–	–	21.7	78.3
15-20 yrs	26	45	–	–	–	31.1	68.9
Adult	128	240	–	–	–	19.6	80.4

Source

Dry bone observations on London remains from the early eighteenth to mid nineteenth century (Spitalfields collection) and medieval remains from Oxfordshire (Abingdon collection). Age was documented in some remains and estimated in others using dental analysis.

Reference

Humphrey, L.T. and Scheuer, L. (2006). Age of closure of the foramen of Huschke: An osteological study. *International Journal of Osteoarchaeology* **16**: 47–60. Copyright John Wiley & Sons Limited. Reproduced with permission.

Metrics

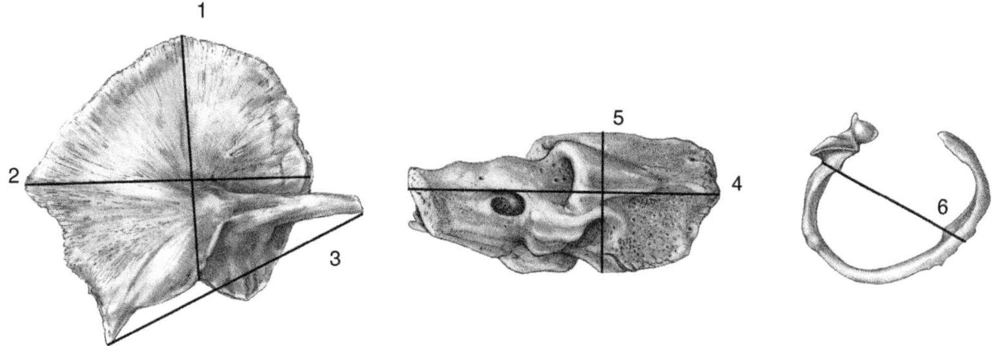

Reference landmarks for temporal measurements

Notes

1. Temporal squama height: Distance from center of tympanic notch to superior border of bone
2. Temporal squama width: Distance from the posterior arch of the squamomastoid suture to the anterior border of the squamous part
3. Temporal squama length: Maximum distance from tip of scutum to anterior end of zygomatic process
4. Pars petrosa length: Maximum anteroposterior distance across bone
5. Pars petrosa width: Maximum distance at right angles to length across arcuate eminence
6. Tympanic ring diameter: Maximum distance across ring from anterior tympanic process

Fazekas and Kósa

Dry Bone Fetal Measurements-Squamous Part (mm)							
		Height		Width		Length	
Prenatal Age (wks)	*n*	Mean	Range	Mean	Range	Mean	Range
12	1	2.8	–	2.8	–	7.0	–
14	3	3.6	2.8–5.0	3.6	2.8–5.0	9.3	7.5–12.6
16	9	6.7	5.0–9.0	10.1	9.0–11.0	11.5	10.0–14.0
18	15	9.0	7.5–13.0	12.4	11.5–14.0	15.0	14.3–19.0
20	13	10.6	9.8–12.5	14.0	13.5–14.5	17.4	16.5–18.0
22	11	11.8	10.0–12.8	15.4	14.5–16.0	18.8	17.0–20.5
24	12	13.0	12.0–13.9	16.9	16.0–18.0	20.5	18.0–22.0
26	12	14.3	12.4–16.0	18.6	17.0–20.5	21.0	18.0–22.9
28	12	16.0	14.5–16.9	20.2	19.0–21.0	22.2	20.5–23.0
30	12	17.7	16.0–20.0	21.5	20.0–23.0	23.6	20.0–26.5
32	8	19.8	18.0–22.4	24.1	23.0–25.0	26.5	25.0–28.5
34	7	22.4	21.0–24.2	26.1	26.0–26.6	28.3	27.0–30.4
36	5	22.9	22.4–23.0	26.9	26.5–27.0	29.6	29.0–29.9
38	7	24.1	22.0–26.1	29.9	27.0–32.0	31.6	28.0–35.0
40	10	25.4	22.0–30.8	32.6	29.5–38.0	34.2	30.0–39.6

Dry Bone Fetal Measurements-Petrosa Part (mm)					
		Length		Width	
Prenatal Age (wks)	*n*	Mean	Range	Mean	Range
16	7	10.5	9.0–12.0	5.3	5.0–6.0
18	15	12.3	10.0–15.8	5.7	5.0–6.0
20	13	14.4	11.0–17.0	8.7	7.0–10.1
22	11	17.3	15.0–18.5	9.7	8.7–10.5
24	12	18.8	17.0–20.0	10.2	9.5–11.2
26	12	19.9	18.5–22.2	10.6	10.0–12.0
28	12	21.4	20.0–22.7	10.9	10.0–12.0
30	12	22.5	19.1–25.0	13.1	10.8–14.7
32	8	27.7	26.0–30.0	13.5	12.0–14.0
34	7	29.7	28.0–31.0	15.4	14.5–16.8
36	5	33.0	31.5–34.0	16.1	15.7–16.7
38	7	35.1	32.0–38.0	17.0	15.0–18.3
40	10	38.1	37.0–40.4	17.5	16.0–18.5

Dry Bone Fetal Measurements-Tympanic Ring (mm)			
		Diameter	
Prenatal Age (wks)	*n*	Mean	Range
14	1	4.0	–
16	9	5.7	4.5–7.3
18	15	7.5	7.0–8.4
20	13	8.0	7.5–8.8
22	11	8.5	7.7–10.0
24	12	9.0	8.5–9.8
26	12	9.5	8.0–10.3
28	12	9.9	9.0–10.5
30	12	10.5	9.9–11.0
32	8	10.8	10.0–12.0
34	7	11.5	11.0–12.1
36	5	11.8	11.5–12.0
38	7	12.0	11.0–13.5
40	10	12.5	12.0–13.5

Source

Dry bone measurements on mid twentieth century Hungarian fetal remains from autopsy—males and females combined. Age was estimated based on fetal crown heel length.

Reference

Fazekas, I.Gy. and Kósa, F. (1978). *Forensic Fetal Osteology.* Budapest: Akadémiai Kiadó.

Morphological Summary

Prenatal	
Wks 7–8	Ossification center for squamous part appear
Wk 9	First ossification center for tympanic ring appears
Wk 12	Centers for tympanic ring joined together
Wk 16	First ossification center for petrous part appears
	Ossification center for incus appears
Wks 16–17	Ossification center for malleus appears
Wk 18	Ossification center(s) for stapes appear(s)
Wk 19	Goniale fuses to malleus
Wk 30	Tympanic cavity complete except for lateral wall
Wk 35	Epitympanum complete
	Pnuematisation of petromastoid starts
	Posterior segment of ring fuses to squamous part
Birth	Usually represented by two parts: petromastoid and squamotympanic
During yr 1	Petromastoid and squamotympanic parts fuse
	Anterior and posterior tympanic tubercles commence growth
1–5 yrs	Growth of tympanic plate and formation of foramen of Huschke
	Mastoid process forming

THE SPHENOID

Principal Components

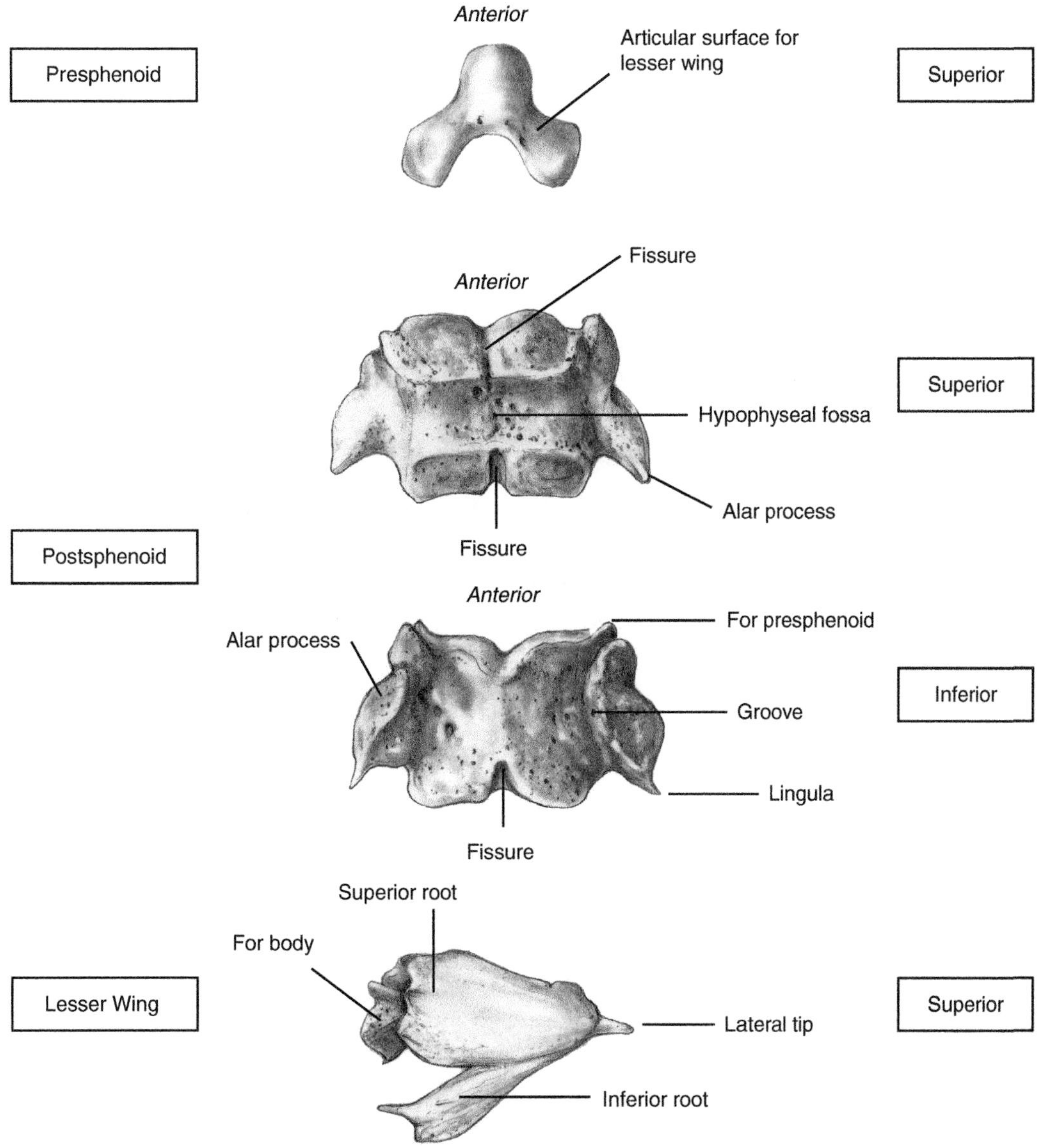

Fetal presphenoid, postsphenoid, and right lesser wing

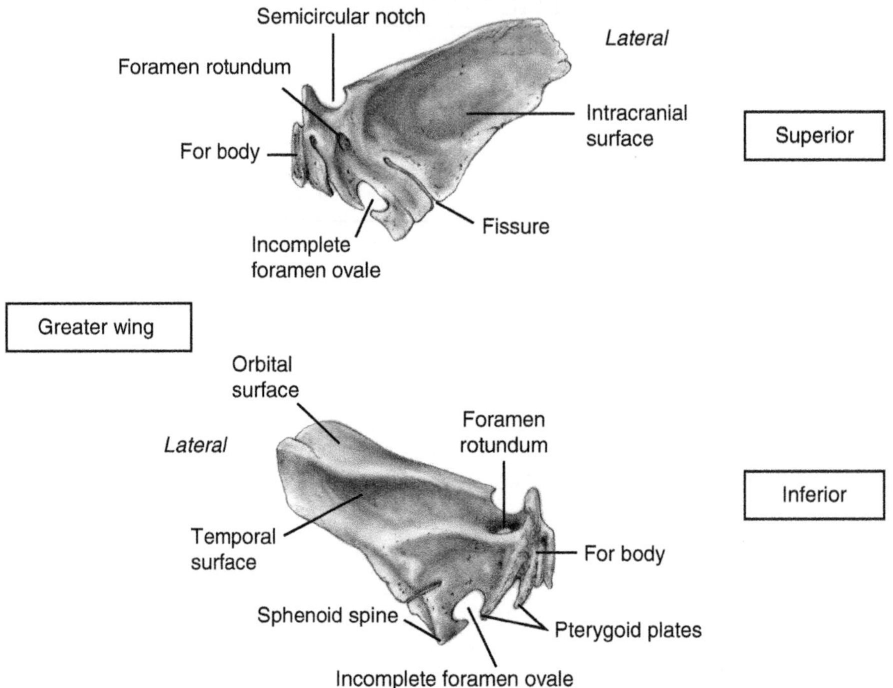

Right greater wing of the perinatal sphenoid

Siding/Orientation

Body (pre- and postsphenoid)

- The hypophyseal fossa is located on the intracranial (superior) surface
- The alar projections extend postero-laterally

Lesser wing

- Resembles an arrowhead with the flatter superior root positioned anteriorly and the narrower inferior root positioned posteriorly
- The superior surface of the superior root is slightly concave whereas its inferior surface is more convex

Greater wing

- Intracranial surface is concave
- Foramen rotundum points anteriorly
- Pterygoid plates are attached inferiorly
- The external cranial surface is angled anteriorly, differentiating its two (temporal and orbital) surfaces

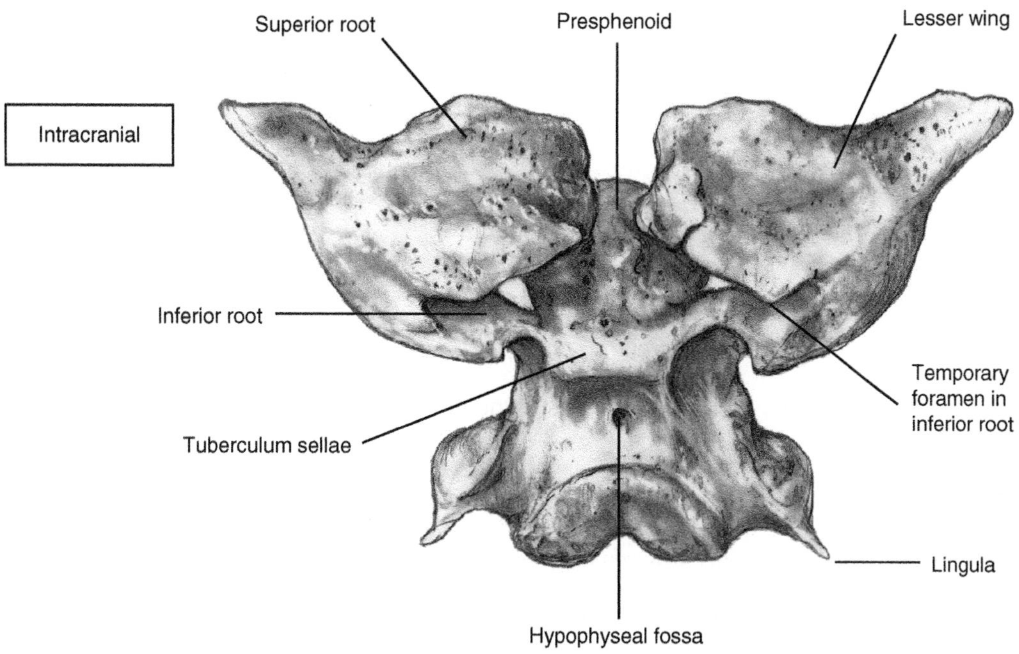

Perinatal sphenoid with lesser wings fused to body

Identification – Recognition of the body will depend on its state of fusion (pre- and post-sphenoid parts normally are fused by late fetal life), whereas the lesser and greater wings are recognizable from midfetal life. The lesser wings usually fuse to the body before birth, whereas the greater wings will normally undergo fusion soon after birth. Each component has a characteristic shape and is unlikely to be confused with other bony material.

Metrics

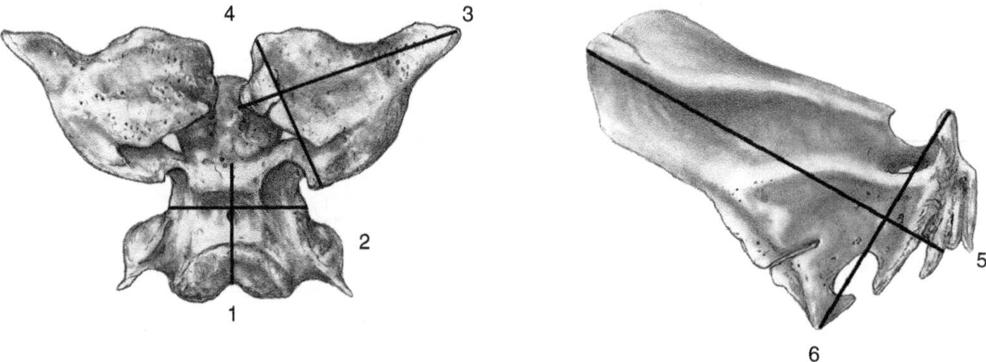

Reference landmarks for measurements of the sphenoid

Notes

1. Body length: Midline distance between the synchondrosis intrasphenoidalis and spheno-occipitalis
2. Body width: Maximum transverse distance in the mid-hypophyseal fossa
3. Lesser wing length: Lateral tip of lesser wing to midline of synchondrosis intrasphenoidalis (lateral tip of wing to medial end of wing in younger fetuses)
4. Lesser wing width: Maximum distance of lesser wing across optic canal
5. Greater wing length: Maximum distance between medial pterygoid plate and the lateral tip of the greater wing
6. Greater wing width: Maximum distance between the sphenoidal spine and the anterior end of the medial pterygoid plate

Fazekas and Kósa

Dry Bone Fetal Measurements-Body (postsphenoid) (mm)					
		Length		Width	
Prenatal Age (wks)	*n*	Mean	Range	Mean	Range
16	4	2.7	2.0–3.0	4.5	4.0–5.0
18	11	3.7	3.0–5.0	5.5	4.0–6.0
20	13	5.1	4.0–6.0	9.6	9.0–10.3
22	11	5.9	5.0–7.0	10.6	9.8–11.5
24	12	6.1	5.4–7.0	11.7	10.0–12.2
26	12	7.4	6.5–8.0	12.2	12.0–13.0
28	12	7.9	7.2–8.5	12.5	12.0–13.2
30	12	8.1	7.2–9.0	13.5	12.0–14.5
32	8	8.6	8.3–9.0	14.6	13.5–15.1
34	7	9.1	8.5–10.0	15.0	14.0–15.5
36	5	9.5	9.0–9.8	16.0	15.5–16.5
38	7	10.9	10.0–12.0	17.2	16.0–18.5
40	10	11.7	11.0–12.0	17.9	16.0–19.0

Dry Bone Fetal Measurements-Lesser wing (mm)					
		Length		Width	
Prenatal Age (wks)	*n*	Mean	Range	Mean	Range
16	5	4.7	3.0–6.0	4.0	3.0–5.0
18	12	5.9	5.0–7.0	4.8	4.0–5.0
20	13	6.3	5.5–7.0	5.2	4.5–6.0
22	11	7.9	6.5–9.5	6.0	5.0–7.0
24	12	9.0	8.0–10.2	6.4	5.6–7.0
26	12	10.7	10.0–12.5	7.0	6.5–8.5
28	12	12.5	11.5–13.0	7.6	6.5–8.0
30	12	13.7	12.2–15.0	8.2	7.0–9.0
32	8	14.7	14.0–15.5	8.5	8.0–9.0
34	7	15.1	14.0–15.6	9.3	8.5–10.0
36	5	15.8	15.0–16.1	10.3	9.8–10.9
38	7	17.1	17.0–18.0	11.0	10.5–12.0
40	10	19.4	18.0–20.0	12.4	12.0–13.0

Dry Bone Fetal Measurements-Greater wing (mm)					
		Length		Width	
Prenatal Age (wks)	*n*	Mean	Range	Mean	Range
12	1	5.0	–	1.5	–
14	3	5.1	4.5–6.0	2.3	2.1–2.5
16	7	10.3	8.0–13.2	5.7	4.5–7.0
18	15	13.1	11.0–15.0	7.0	6.0–8.0
20	13	15.3	13.2–16.5	8.5	*
22	11	17.1	15.5–19.1	9.2	7.4–10.0
24	12	19.0	17.0–20.5	10.1	9.5–11.2
26	12	19.7	18.3–21.5	10.5	9.8–11.1
28	12	21.6	20.0–23.2	11.7	10.4–12.7
30	12	22.0	20.0–25.0	12.6	10.0–14.0
32	8	24.5	23.0–26.1	13.7	12.0–15.0
34	7	25.4	21.6–27.5	14.8	14.0–16.0
36	5	26.4	25.5–27.0	15.4	15.0–16.0
38	7	28.7	27.0–30.5	16.1	14.0–18.5
40	10	31.0	27.5–34.5	17.4	14.1–22.0

*Misprinted within original text.

Source

Dry bone measurements on mid twentieth century Hungarian fetal remains from autopsy—males and females combined. Age was estimated based on fetal crown heel length.

Reference

Fazekas, I.Gy. and Kósa, F. (1978). *Forensic Fetal Osteology*. Budapest: Akadémiai Kiadó.

Morphological Summary

Prenatal	
Wks 9–10	Medial pterygoid plates and lateral part of greater wings commence ossification in membrane
Wks 12–14	Endochondral centers for postsphenoid part of body and lesser wings appear
Early mth 3	Lateral pterygoid plate commences ossification in membrane
	Endochondral center for hamulus appears
Wk 13	Endochondral center for medial part of greater wing appears
Mths 4–6	First ossification centers for sphenoidal conchae appear
Mth 5	Ossification center for lingula appears
	Lesser wings usually fused to body
By mth 8	Pterygoid plates fused to greater wings
	Pre- and postsphenoid parts of body usually fused together
Birth	Usually represented by body with lesser wings and two separate greater wings with attached pterygoid plates
During yr 1	Greater wings fuse to body
	Foramen ovale is completed
	Sinus commences pneumatization
By yr 2	Foramen spinosum is completed
By yr 5	Dorsum sellae ossified
Yr 4-puberty	Sphenoidal conchae fuse to ethmoid

THE PARIETAL

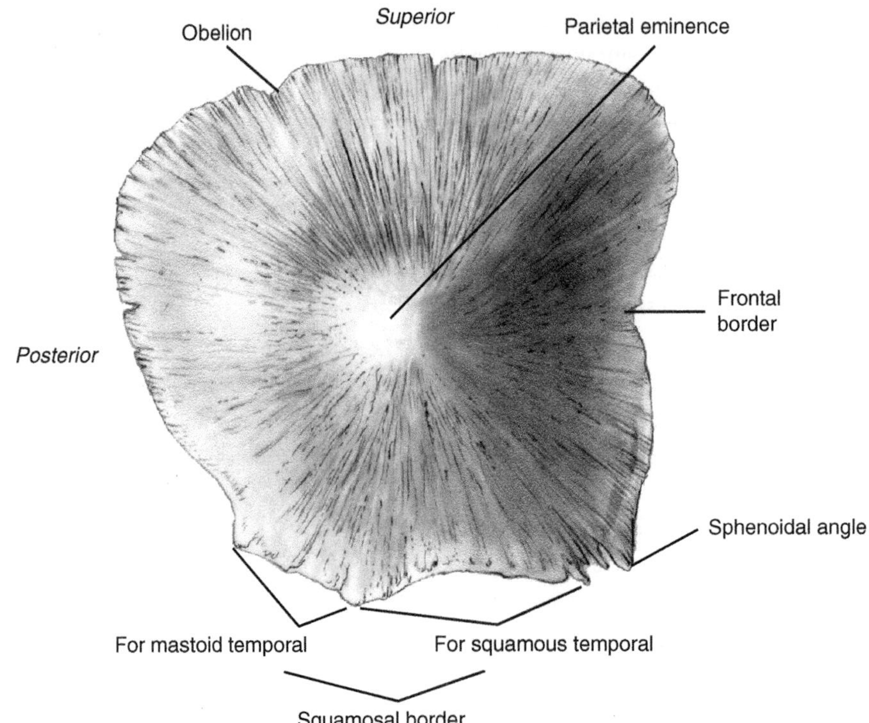

Right perinatal parietal

Identification – Small fragments are probably indistinguishable from other vault fragments unless one of the following characteristic markings is present:

- Groove for the sagittal sinus.
- Granular foveolae along the sagittal border.
- Grooves for meningeal vessels.
- A distinct parietal foramen near a serrated border.
- Temporal lines.
- Characteristic bevelling on the squamosal border.

Siding/Orientation

- The sharp, protruding sphenoidal angle lies at the antero-inferior corner.
- The frontal border is gently concave and finely serrated.
- A parietal notch or foramen may be present near the posterior end of the sagittal border.
- The squamosal border is divided into two sections, a posterior blunt portion and an anterior concave part.
- The squamosal border becomes characteristically bevelled soon after birth.

Metrics

Fazekas and Kósa

Dry Bone Fetal Measurements-Parietal (mm)

		Chord				Arc			
		Height		Width		Height		Width	
Prenatal Age (wks)	*n*	Mean	Range	Mean	Range	Mean	Range	Mean	Range
12	1	10.0	–	14.0	–	10.0	–	14.0	–
14	3	12.3	10.0–15.0	16.0	13.0–20.0	12.3	10.0–15.0	16.0	13.0–20.0
16	9	22.1	16.0–30.0	25.3	20.0–31.7	26.1	22.0–32.0	26.7	22.0–32.0
18	15	28.4	25.0–32.5	30.7	29.0–34.6	31.6	28.0–37.0	32.6	30.0–35.0
20	13	33.8	29.0–35.1	36.9	32.0–40.0	38.0	36.0–40.0	37.0	34.0–40.0
22	11	36.6	34.5–39.0	39.7	38.5–41.7	44.4	42.0–47.0	43.0	41.0–46.0
24	12	38.1	35.0–42.2	43.0	39.0–46.3	49.1	46.0–54.0	49.6	48.0–53.0
26	12	41.6	36.0–46.5	46.0	44.0–47.5	50.7	46.0–57.0	51.6	47.0–57.0
28	12	45.2	42.0–47.0	50.4	48.4–52.2	58.2	55.0–61.0	55.9	53.0–59.0
30	12	48.8	43.0–55.0	56.0	50.0–62.0	61.6	55.0–69.0	61.7	55.0–66.0
32	8	52.6	48.0–61.5	58.5	56.0–62.8	66.9	62.0–72.0	64.8	62.0–70.0
34	7	56.0	54.0–57.0	63.3	60.0–73.0	73.9	70.0–79.0	71.6	68.0–76.0
36	5	57.1	52.0–62.0	66.9	64.0–70.0	78.4	76.0–82.0	78.6	75.0–80.0
38	7	63.5	61.5–65.0	70.5	67.0–75.0	84.4	81.0–91.0	79.5	76.0–87.0
40	10	65.8	62.3–70.5	72.4	64.0–78.0	86.8	81.0–92.0	82.0	75.0–90.0

Source

Dry bone measurements on mid twentieth century Hungarian fetal remains from autopsy—males and females combined. Age was estimated based on fetal crown heel length.

Notes

Height (chord): Straight line distance from midsquamous border to midsagittal border across parietal eminence parallel to coronal suture

Height (arc): Same landmarks as described above, taken along the convexity of the frontal bone

Width (chord): Straight line distance from frontal to occipital borders across parietal eminence, parallel to sagittal suture

Width (arc): Same landmarks as described above, taken along the convexity of the frontal bone

Reference

Fazekas, I.Gy. and Kósa, F. (1978). *Forensic Fetal Osteology.* Budapest: Akadémiai Kiadó.

Young

Radiographic Postnatal Measurements-Parietal (mm)					
Males		**Arc**		**Chord**	
Age	***n***	**Mean**	**Range**	**Mean**	**Range**
1 mth	15	107.1	95–135	94.3	84–109
3 mth	13	120.2	104–149	104.3	94–119
6 mth	15	127.2	117–159	111.1	104–130
9 mth	15	131.2	122–165	114.7	107–135
1 yr	18	135.8	124–170	119.6	112–139
2 yr	19	143.0	129–179	127.8	118–146
3 yr	19	143.8	127–179	128.1	117–147
4 yr*	19	146.1	134–182	129.8	122–150

*Growth is essentially completed by age 4.

Source

Longitudinal radiographic study on 20 mid-century American boys from the Fels growth study.

Notes

Parietal arc: The distance from bregma to lambda along the outer table of the bone
Parietal chord: The straight-line distance from bregma to lambda

Reference

Young, R. (1957). Postnatal growth of the frontal and parietal bones in white males. *American Journal of Physical Anthropology* **15**: 367–386.

Morphological Summary

Prenatal	
Wks 7–8	Two centers of ossification form which rapidly fuse
By mth 6	Borders and angles become definitive
	There may be a sagittal fontanelle
Birth	Single bone with prominent eminence
	Sagittal fontanelle usually is obliterated
Childhood	Gradually takes on the appearance of the adult bone as the eminence becomes less obvious

THE FRONTAL

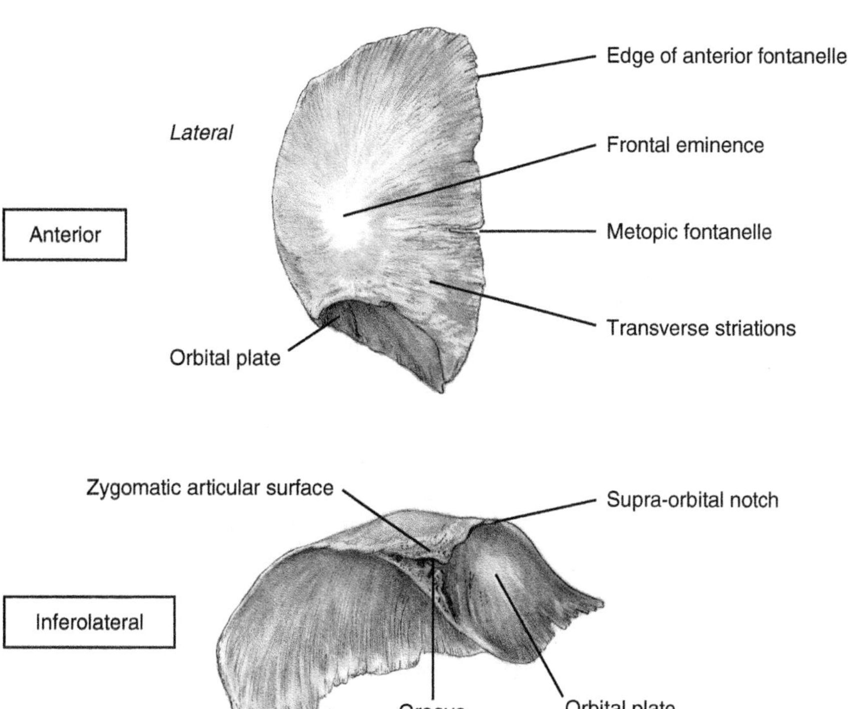

Right perinatal frontal

Identification – Small fragments are probably indistinguishable from other vault fragments unless a characteristic part of the bone is present.

- Orbital rims and orbital plates are set at an angle to the rest of the bone.
- Traces of the frontal air sinuses.
- Traces of the crista frontalis (the mid sagittal crest that is present on the intracranial surface).

Siding/Orientation – Unlikely to recover an isolated frontal bone that is complete as most bones of the vault are damaged.

- The orbital margin is thickened and forms the anteroinferior border.
- The inferolateral margin displays a triangular thickening, which forms the articular surface for the zygomatic bone.

Metrics

Fazekas and Kósa

Dry Bone Fetal Measurements-Frontal (mm)

		Chord				Arc			
		Height		Width		Height		Width	
Prenatal Age (wks)	*n*	Mean	Range	Mean	Range	Mean	Range	Mean	Range
12	2	7.0	6.0–8.0	11.5	9.0–14.0	7.0	6.0–8.0	11.5	9.0–14.0
14	3	10.1	8.8–12.0	13.8	13.0–14.5	10.1	8.8–12.0	13.8	13.0–14.5
16	9	21.5	18.0–26.4	17.9	15.0–21.0	21.6	19.0–23.0	18.8	17.0–22.0
18	15	24.5	22.0–28.0	21.3	19.0–23.0	26.5	24.0–30.0	23.2	22.0–25.0
20	13	28.7	25.0–33.0	24.4	23.8–25.0	30.3	27.0–34.0	26.3	25.0–28.0
22	11	30.5	28.4–32.0	26.1	24.0–28.3	31.8	30.0–35.0	27.5	26.0–30.0
24	12	32.8	31.0–36.0	29.1	27.1–32.8	36.4	34.0–40.0	32.6	31.0–35.0
26	12	35.0	31.0–39.1	31.0	28.0–33.0	40.0	36.0–45.0	33.7	31.0–36.0
28	12	37.8	35.7–41.0	33.0	32.0–34.2	42.9	40.0–46.0	37.4	35.0–39.0
30	12	40.8	36.3–45.0	34.6	31.0–38.0	46.5	42.0–49.0	38.5	37.0–43.0
32	8	43.7	40.0–49.0	37.8	37.0–38.4	49.6	48.0–51.0	41.3	40.0–43.0
34	7	47.0	43.5–51.2	39.7	37.5–45.0	54.0	48.0–59.0	45.0	43.0–50.0
36	5	50.4	47.0–52.0	41.3	36.0–47.0	58.0	50.0–61.0	49.2	45.0–55.0
38	7	53.1	50.7–56.1	43.6	39.6–45.5	61.8	58.0–69.0	52.0	50.0–55.0
40	10	54.8	52.5–57.4	45.2	42.0–50.2	64.5	62.0–67.0	54.1	51.0–59.0

Source

Dry bone measurements on mid twentieth century Hungarian fetal remains from autopsy—males and females combined. Age was estimated based on fetal crown heel length.

Notes

Height (chord): Straight-line distance from middle of the superior margin of the orbit to superior peak of bone across frontal eminence

Height (arc): Same landmarks as described above, taken along the convexity of the frontal bone

Width (chord): Straight-line distance from width across frontal eminence at right angles to length (width at superior border of orbit in younger fetuses)

Width (arc): Same landmarks as described above, taken along the convexity of the frontal bone

Reference

Fazekas, I.Gy. and Kósa, F. (1978). *Forensic Fetal Osteology*. Budapest: Akadémiai Kiadó.

Young

Radiographic Postnatal Measurements-Frontal (mm)					
Males		Arc		Chord	
Age	*n*	Mean	Range	Mean	Range
1 mth	13	81.2	72–90	73.0	67–80
3 mth	13	93.3	80–106	81.9	74–92
6 mth	15	103.6	91–115	89.3	82–96
9 mth	15	107.5	98–113	93.4	86–99
1 yr	18	114.8	100–125	99.6	90–109
2 yr	19	127.6	110–137	109.2	97–115
3 yr	20	128.4	113–140	110.0	101–117
4 yr	19	130.1	114–142	111.5	99–118
6 yr	20	130.9	114–147	113.2	103–123
8 yr	18	131.2	118–142	114.2	104–120
10 yr	20	133.5	118–149	116.3	104–125
12 yr	20	134.6	119–149	117.9	105–128
14 yr	20	134.9	118–149	118.8	105–129
16 yr	12	135.4	121–145	120.0	107–126

Source

Longitudinal radiographic study on 20 mid-century American boys from the Fels growth study.

Notes

Frontal arc: The distance from nasion to bregma along the outer table of the bone
Frontal chord: The straight-line distance from nasion to bregma

Reference

Young, R. (1957). Postnatal growth of the frontal and parietal bones in white males. *American Journal of Physical Anthropology* **15**: 367–386.

Morphological Summary

Prenatal	
Wks 6–7	Primary center of ossification appears
Wks 10–13	Zygomatic process and medial angular processes start ossifying
By mth 5	Anteroposterior longer than mediolateral length
Birth	Represented by right and left halves
1–2 yrs	Anterior fontanelle closed
2–4 yrs	Metopic suture normally closed

THE NASAL

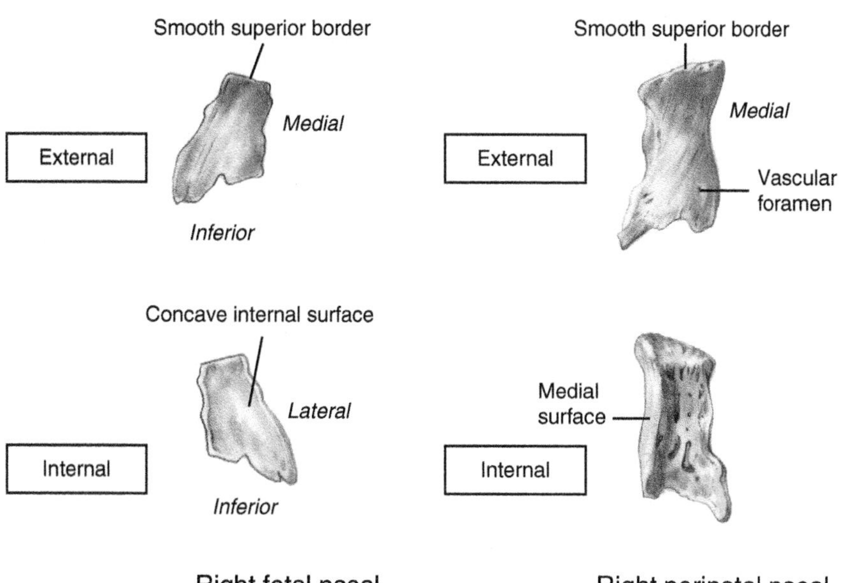

Identification – Does not become recognizable in isolation until late fetal life as it is small and fairly fragile, but by birth it is more robust.

Siding/Orientation

- The superior border is narrower than the inferior border.
- The medial border is shorter than the lateral border and bears the thickened articular surface for articulation with the bone of the opposite side.

Metrics

Fazekas and Kósa

Dry Bone Fetal Measurements-Nasal bone (mm)					
		Length		Width	
Prenatal Age (wks)	*n*	Mean	Range	Mean	Range
16	8	4.5	4.0–4.6	2.5	2.2–2.6
18	15	5.1	4.8–5.5	3.0	2.7–3.3
20	13	5.9	5.5–6.2	3.3	2.6–3.8
22	11	6.1	5.0–7.0	3.9	3.0–4.5
24	12	6.8	6.5–7.2	4.0	3.7–4.8
26	12	7.3	7.0–7.8	4.2	3.5–4.5
28	12	7.9	7.0–8.5	4.2	3.5–4.8
30	12	8.6	8.2–9.2	4.3	3.2–4.9
32	8	9.6	8.5–10.0	5.2	4.5–5.6
34	7	10.6	10.0–11.0	5.3	5.0–5.5
36	5	11.6	11.0–12.0	5.9	5.6–6.2
38	7	11.8	11.0–12.0	6.6	6.0–7.0
40	10	12.3	11.8–13.0	7.4	6.2–8.0

Source

Dry bone measurements on mid twentieth century Hungarian fetal remains from autopsy—males and females combined. Age was estimated based on fetal crown heel length.

Notes

Length: Superior to inferior margin in midline
Width: Maximum distance across the inferior border

Reference

Fazekas, I.Gy. and Kósa, F. (1978). *Forensic Fetal Osteology*. Budapest: Akadémiai Kiadó.

Lang

Postnatal Measurements-Nasal aperture (mm)						
	Height		Superior Width		Maximum width	
Age	Mean	Range	Mean	Range	Mean	Range
Neonate	11.3	10.13	9.8	7–11	12.4	11–13.5
1 yr	17.4	15–19	11.9	11–13	16.5	16–18
5 yrs	22.6	20–33	13.3	11–18	18.2	14–20
13 yrs	26.0	25–27	14.0	13–15	19.7	19–21
Adult	29.1	21–37	16.3	10–22	23.6	20–28

Notes

Height: Maximum height from superior to inferior nasal aperture
Superior width: Width across aperture at level of inferior lateral border of nasal bones
Maximum width: Maximum width across aperture

Postnatal Measurements-Nasal Bone (mm)				
	Height		Breadth	
Age	Mean	Range	Mean	Range
Neonate	8.3	7.9–9	8.4	6–10
1 yr	12.8	11–14	11.2	9–15
5 yrs	16.2	13–19	11.4	9–18
13 yrs	22.8	22–24	12.0	11–15
Adult	24.9	18–31	13.0	7–18

Notes

Height: Maximum length of internasal suture
Breadth: Distance across both nasal bones at point at which frontal process of maxilla meets lateral border of nasal bones

Source

Not stated.

Reference

Lang, J. (1989). *Clinical Anatomy of the Nose, Nasal Cavity and Paranasal Sinuses,* trans. P.M. Stell. New York: Thieme.

Morphological Summary

Prenatal	
Wks 9–10	Intramembranous ossification center appears for each bone
Mths 9–10	Medial articular border develops
Birth	Morphology similar to adult, except length-to-width proportion differs, borders are smooth, and vascular foramen is in lower half of the bone
About yr 3	Superior border becomes serrated
Puberty	Adopts adult morphology and size

THE ETHMOID

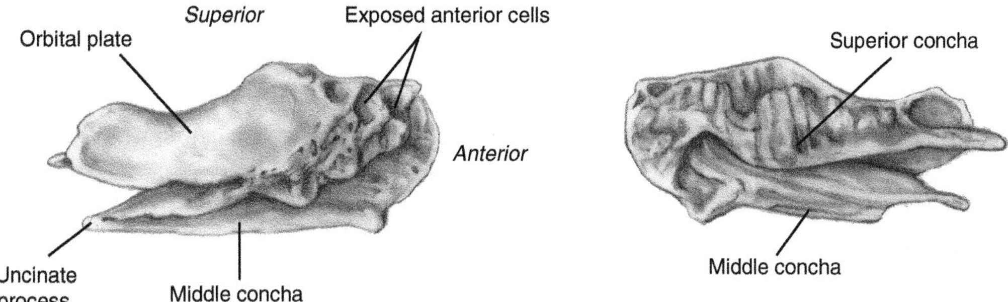

Right perinatal ethmoidal labyrinth

Identification – The perinatal ethmoid is represented by two labyrinths held together by the cartilaginous cribriform and perpendicular plates, a complete ethmoid bone is not recognizable until about the second year as the cribriform plate does not start to ossify until after birth. Small fragments of any of the pneumatised bones could be mistaken for the ethmoidal labyrinth. Recognizable parts of the ethmoid, which do not appear until late juvenile life, include:

- The crista galli
- The nasal septum

Siding/Orientation

- The smooth orbital plate lies laterally
- The wrinkled conchal surface is medial
- The free edge of the middle concha is inferior
- The uncinate process lies posteriorly
- Air sinuses can usually be seen anteriorly on the superior surface

Morphological Summary

Prenatal	
Mth 5	Ossification centers appear in the cartilage of the conchal regions of the labyrinth
Birth	Represented by two labyrinths joined by cartilage
1–2 yrs	Cribriform plate and crista galli ossify and fuse with labyrinths
3–10 yrs	Ossified perpendicular plate reaches vomer and "sphenoidal tail" usually visible posteriorly
10 yrs–puberty	Progressive expansion of ossification into nasal septum
20–30 yrs	Ethmoid and vomer fuse

THE INFERIOR NASAL CONCHA

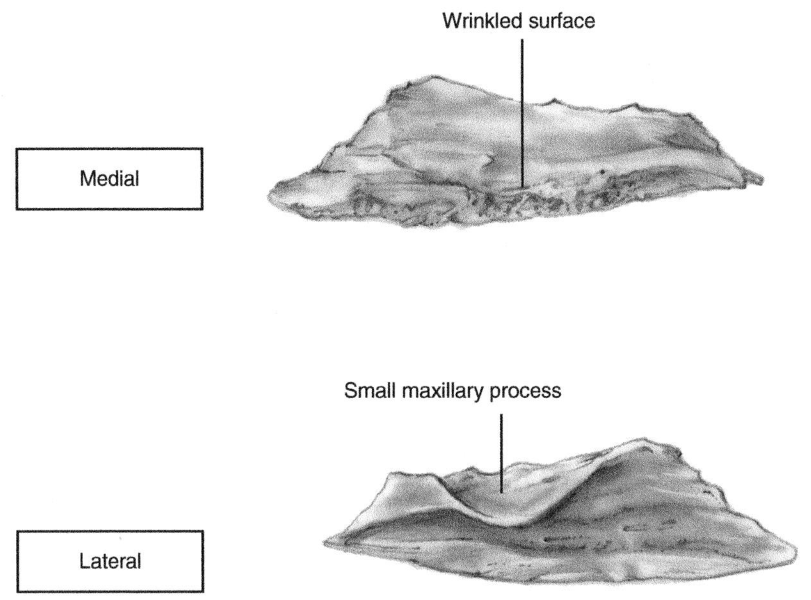

Right perinatal inferior concha

Identification – Part of an inferior concha would be very difficult to distinguish from fragments of the labyrinths of the ethmoid bone.

Siding/Orientation – Unlikely to recover an isolated and complete juvenile inferior concha. Correct sideing ultimately depends on the completeness of the specimen.

- Medial surface is wrinkled and convex.
- Lateral surface is smoother and concave.
- The posterior end is more pointed than the anterior end.
- The inferior border is curved under and thickened.

Metrics

Fazekas and Kósa

Dry Bone Fetal Measurements-Inferior Nasal Concha (mm)

Prenatal Age (wks)	*n*	Length	
		Mean	Range
16	7	4.0	3.0–5.1
18	11	4.8	4.5–5.1
20	10	5.5	5.0–5.8
22	10	6.0	5.5–6.5
24	11	6.3	4.5–7.0
26	12	7.9	6.2–9.1
28	12	9.3	7.5–10.3
30	12	10.2	7.3–12.5
32	8	11.9	10.5–13.0
34	7	14.2	14.0–16.0
36	5	15.0	14.0–16.0
38	7	18.7	17.0–20.0
40	10	19.9	17.0–22.0

Source

Dry bone measurements on mid twentieth century Hungarian fetal remains from autopsy—males and females combined. Age was estimated based on fetal crown heel length.

Reference

Fazekas, I.Gy. and Kósa, F. (1978). *Forensic Fetal Osteology*. Budapest: Akadémiai Kiadó.

Morphological Summary

Prenatal

Wk 16	Single intramembranous ossification center appears
Mth 7	Maxillary process develops
Mth 8	Ethmoidal and lacrimal processes develop
Birth	Adult morphology, except more wrinkled and lacrimal, maxillary and ethmoid processes are less well developed

THE LACRIMAL

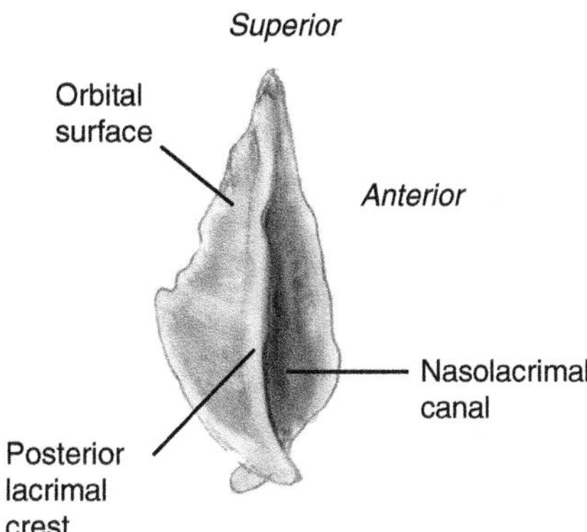

Right perinatal lacrimal

Identification – Fragments of the orbital plate of the ethmoid bone could be confused with that of the lacrimal.

Siding/Orientation

- Unlikely to recover a lacrimal bone in isolation.
- Position the lacrimal canal anteriorly with the hamulus directed inferiorly, the side to which the lacrimal crest or hamulus lies is the opposite side from which the bone comes.
- The orbital surface is lateral.

Morphological Summary

Prenatal	
Wk 10	Single intramembranous ossification center appears
Birth	Long, slim bone with narrow section posterior to crest
2–3 yrs	Adult morphology

THE VOMER

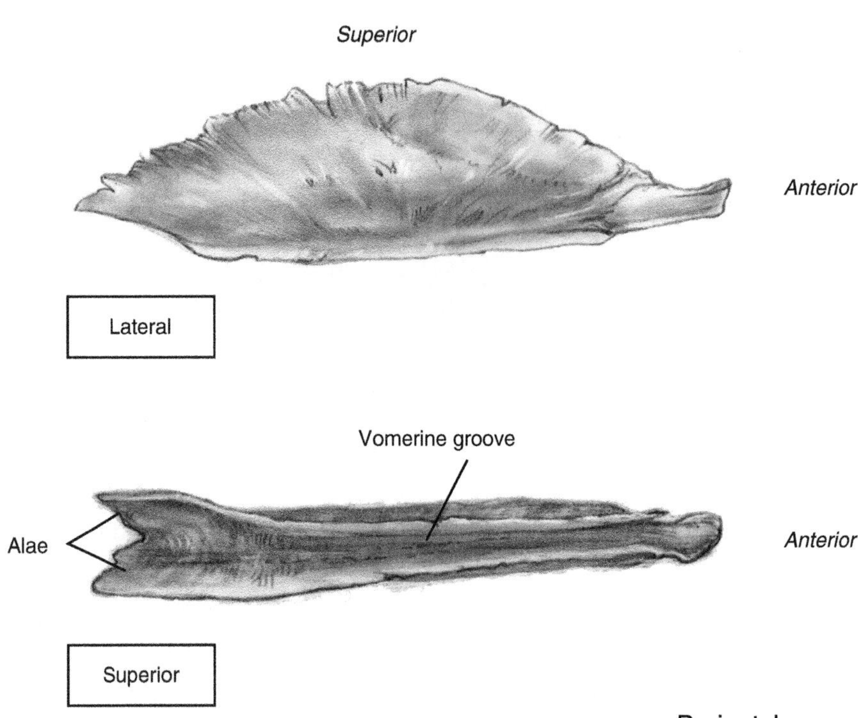

Perinatal vomer

Identification – Unlikely to misidentify a complete vomer with any other element due to its characteristic shape. Fragments, however, are likely to be indistinguishable from other delicate nasal and facial fragments.

Siding/Orientation

- Composed of two laminae that are fused inferiorly, but separated superiorly
- The spread between laminae is greater posteriorly than anteriorly

Metrics

Fazekas and Kósa

Dry Bone Fetal Measurements-Vomer (mm)			
		Length	
Prenatal Age (wks)	*n*	Mean	Range
12	1	4.0	–
14	3	5.6	5.1–6.5
16	9	9.9	8.2–11.0
18	15	11.9	10.0–14.0
20	13	14.1	13.0–15.5
22	11	15.9	14.1–17.0
24	12	17.5	15.7–18.8
26	12	18.2	16.5–20.0
28	12	20.1	19.0–20.9
30	12	21.3	19.0–23.0
32	8	23.1	20.0–24.3
34	7	23.8	22.5–25.0
36	5	28.3	28.0–29.0
38	7	28.7	27.0–29.5
40	10	30.6	29.0–33.3

Source

Dry bone measurements on mid twentieth century Hungarian fetal remains from autopsy—males and females combined. Age was estimated based on fetal crown heel length.

Notes

Length: Maximum length from anterior end to posterior end of alae

Reference

Fazekas, I.Gy. and Kósa, F. (1978). *Forensic Fetal Osteology*. Budapest: Akadémiai Kiadó.

Morphological Summary

Prenatal	
Wks 9–10	Two intramembranous ossification centers appear
Wks 11–12	Fusion at the lower edges of the two leaves of bone
Mths 3–5	Change from U-shaped to Y-shaped base
Birth	Boat-shaped bone composed of two laminae
3–10 yrs	Ossification of perpendicular plate of ethmoid toward vomer
10 yrs–puberty	Edges of vomerine groove fuse to form canal
20–30 yrs	Vomer normally fuses with perpendicular plate of ethmoid

THE ZYGOMATIC

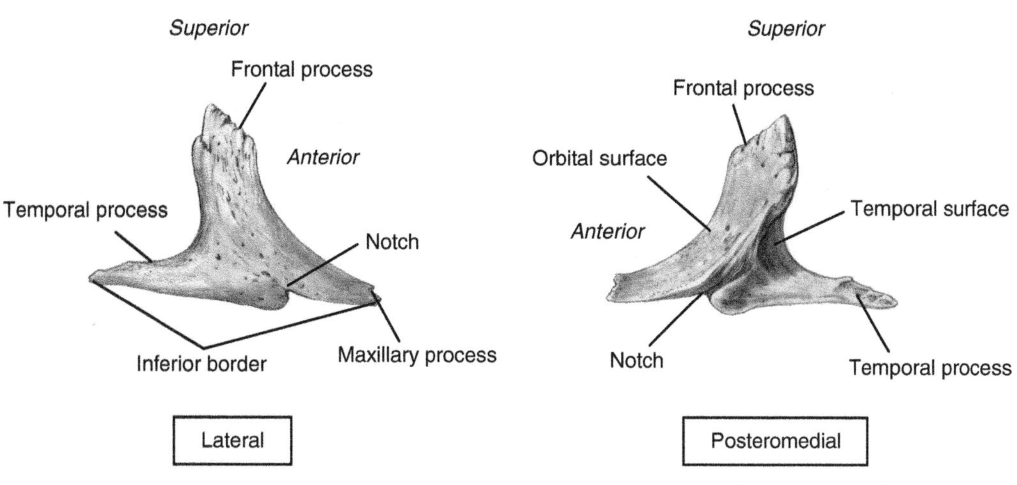

Right perinatal zygomatic

Identification – Recognizable in isolation from mid-fetal life. Fragments of one of its processes could be confused with pointed parts of other cranial bones, such as the zygomatic process of the temporal or lesser wing of sphenoid.

Siding/Orientation

- Depends on correct orientation of the external convex triradiate surface.
- The curved orbital surface lies anteromedially (when viewed anteriorly, it extends to point to the side from which the bone comes).
- The notched border is inferior.
- The concave temporal surface and the slender temporal process point posteriorly.
- With the rapid growth of the face in the first years of life, the site of the notch on the inferior surface becomes the site of angulation between the lateral end of the maxillary suture and the free lower edge of the zygomatic arch.

Metrics

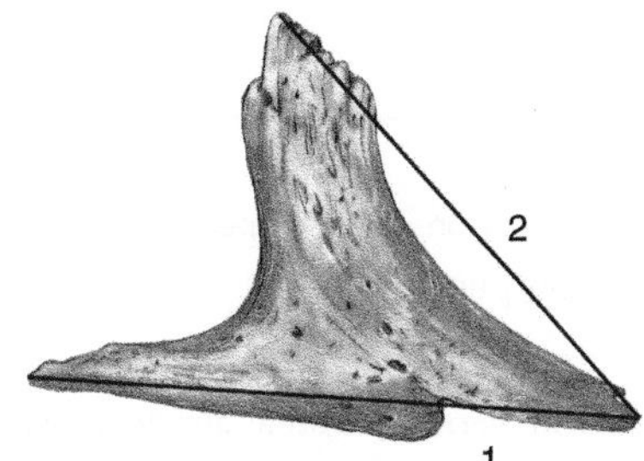

Reference landmarks for zygomatic measurements

Notes

1. Length: Anterior end of maxillary process to posterior end of temporal process
2. Oblique height: Anterior end of maxillary process to superior end of frontal process

Dry Bone Fetal Measurements-Zygomatic (mm)

Prenatal Age (wks)	*n*	Length		Oblique height	
		Mean	Range	Mean	Range
12	2	4.0	–	4.5	4.0–5.0
14	3	4.9	4.8–5.1	5.8	5.5–6.0
16	9	9.0	7.0–11.0	7.1	5.5–8.3
18	15	11.5	10.0–13.5	9.6	8.0–11.0
20	13	13.5	12.0–16.0	10.3	9.0–11.5
22	11	14.2	13.5–14.6	11.2	10.0–12.0
24	12	15.0	14.0–16.0	12.1	10.0–13.0
26	12	16.5	16.0–17.0	13.4	12.5–14.6
28	12	17.5	16.5–18.0	14.1	13.0–14.5
30	12	18.5	16.0–20.0	14.8	13.0–16.0
32	8	19.5	18.0–21.0	15.6	15.0–16.1
34	7	20.9	19.4–22.0	16.6	15.0–17.5
36	5	21.8	20.5–22.2	17.2	17.0–17.7
38	7	24.6	24.0–25.0	18.4	16.7–20.6
40	10	25.8	24.0–28.5	20.2	18.0–22.7

Source

Dry bone measurements on mid twentieth century Hungarian fetal remains from autopsy—males and females combined. Age was estimated based on fetal crown heel length.

Reference

Fazekas, I.Gy. and Kósa, F. (1978). *Forensic Fetal Osteology*. Budapest: Akadémiai Kiadó.

Morphological Summary

Prenatal	
Wk 8	Single intramembranous ossification center appears
Mth 6	Adopts recognizable adult morphology
Birth	Slender triradiate bone with notched inferior border
2–3 yrs	Adopts adult proportions with serrated frontal and temporal processes
	The tuberculum marginale (tubercle on the posterosuperior border just below the articulation for the frontal bone) and the eminentia orbitalis (tubercle on the anterosuperior margin of the bone along the orbital margin) are palpable
Puberty	Malar tubercle may be obvious in males

THE MAXILLA

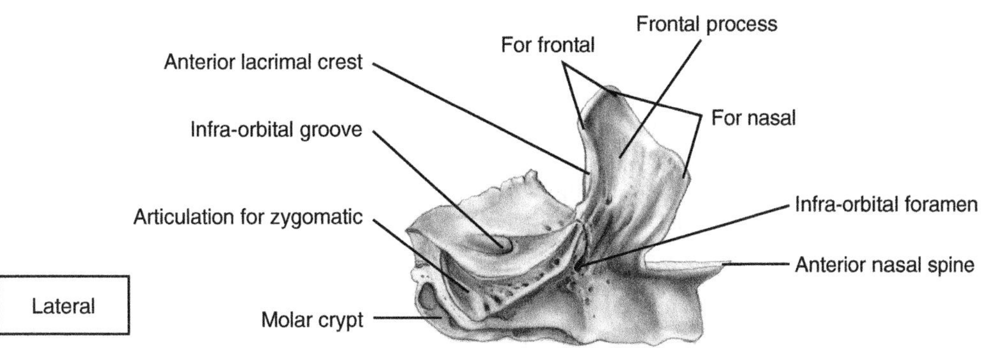
Lateral
Anterior lacrimal crest
Infra-orbital groove
Articulation for zygomatic
Molar crypt
For frontal
Frontal process
For nasal
Infra-orbital foramen
Anterior nasal spine

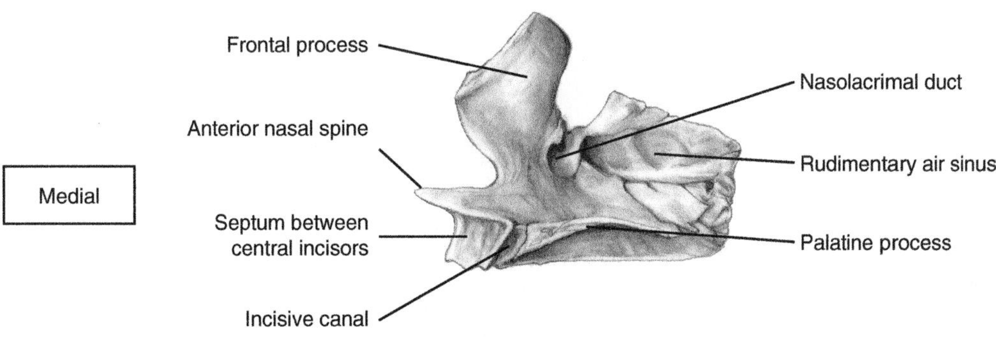
Medial
Frontal process
Anterior nasal spine
Septum between central incisors
Incisive canal
Nasolacrimal duct
Rudimentary air sinus
Palatine process

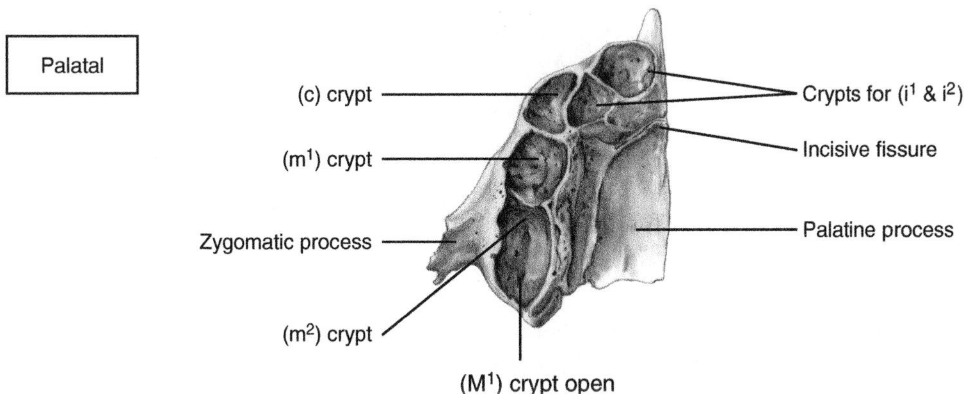
Palatal
(c) crypt
(m1) crypt
Zygomatic process
(m2) crypt
(M1) crypt open
Crypts for (i1 & i2)
Incisive fissure
Palatine process

Right perinatal maxilla

Identification

- Fragments of the maxillary alveolar processes may resemble fragments of the mandibular alveolar processes.
- The supporting bone in the mandible has a dense cortex whereas the bone above the maxillary crypts is the thin nasal or orbital floor.

Siding/Orientation

- Does not ossify completely until late fetal life.
- The dental crypts lie inferiorly.
- The frontal process extends anterosuperiorly.
- The palatal process points medially.

Metrics

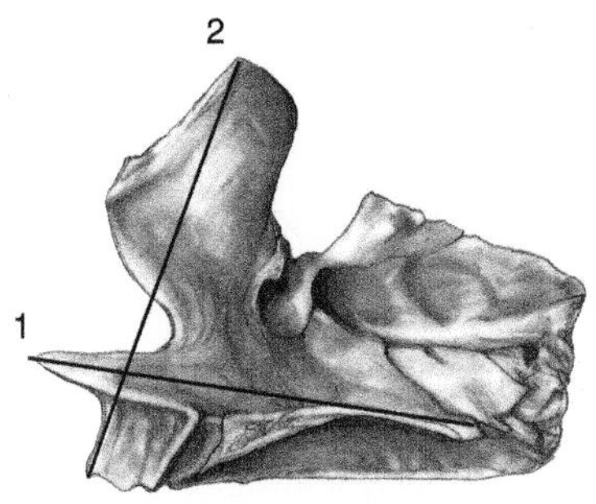

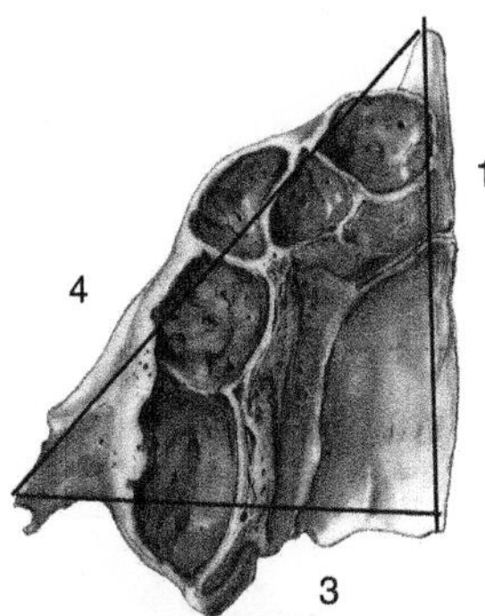

Reference landmarks for maxillary measurements

Notes

1. Length: Anterior nasal spine to posterior border of palatal process in sagittal plane
2. Height: Alveolar process to tip of frontal process in vertical plane
3. Width: Posterior border of the palatal process to the lateral end of zygomatic process
4. Longest oblique length: Anterior nasal spine to lateral end of zygomatic process in oblique plane

Fazekas and Kósa

Dry Bone Fetal Measurements-Maxilla (mm)										
Prenatal Age (wks)	n	Length		Width		Height		Oblique Length	
		Mean	Range	Mean	Range	Mean	Range	Mean	Range
12	2	4.2	3.0–5.5	–	–	3.1	3.0–3.2	6.0	5.0–7.0
14	3	6.3	6.0–7.0	5.6	5.5–5.8	5.6	5.4–5.8	9.3	9.0–10.0
16	9	8.9	8.0–10.0	9.8	9.4–10.2	8.9	8.0–9.5	14.0	12.0–16.0
18	15	10.6	9.2–12.0	11.6	11.0–12.5	10.0	9.0–11.0	15.4	10.0–18.0
20	13	12.6	12.0–13.5	13.0	12.4–13.5	12.3	11.2–12.8	18.7	17.3–20.0
22	11	13.5	12.5–14.5	14.2	13.1–15.0	13.5	12.5–14.5	20.0	19.0–21.6
24	12	15.1	14.0–16.0	15.4	15.0–16.7	14.1	13.6–15.0	21.6	19.3–23.4
26	12	15.9	14.5–16.5	15.9	14.5–16.5	15.6	15.0–16.0	22.3	20.0–23.6
28	12	17.3	16.0–18.5	17.7	17.0–18.5	17.1	16.0–18.0	23.4	22.0–24.4
30	12	17.8	16.3–19.0	18.7	18.0–20.0	18.2	17.0–20.0	23.8	22.5–25.0
32	8	19.4	18.0–20.3	20.0	19.6–20.5	19.6	19.0–21.0	26.0	24.0–28.5
34	7	20.0	19.0–20.9	21.2	20.0–22.3	20.9	19.5–22.0	28.2	26.6–29.1
36	5	22.0	21.0–23.0	22.3	22.0–23.0	21.9	21.0–22.5	28.9	28.0–30.0
38	7	24.1	23.3–25.0	24.2	23.5–24.5	24.1	23.5–25.2	32.1	29.5–35.0
40	10	24.1	23.7–25.0	25.1	24.1–25.6	24.5	23.0–26.0	34.3	34.0–35.6

Source

Dry bone measurements on mid twentieth century Hungarian fetal remains from autopsy—males and females combined. Age was estimated based on fetal crown heel length.

Reference

Fazekas, I.Gy. and Kósa, F. (1978). *Forensic Fetal Osteology*. Budapest: Akadémiai Kiadó.

Morphological Summary

Prenatal	
Wk 6	Intramembranous ossification center appears
By wk 8	Body and four processes (frontal, zygomatic, alveolar, and palatine) identifiable
Wks 10–12	Maxillary sinus starts to develop
Wk 11	Formation of crypts for deciduous dentition
Wks 14–16	Deciduous tooth germs start to form
Wks 17–18	All deciduous crypts completed
Birth	Main parts of bone present
	Sinus rudimentary
	Crowns of deciduous teeth in crypts
	Calcification of first permanent molar commenced
Infancy and Childhood	Gradual increase in size of body of bone
	Increase in size of sinus
	Eruption and replacement of deciduous teeth
By 12–14 yrs	All permanent teeth emerged except third molars (further details of teeth in chapter on dentition)

THE PALATINE

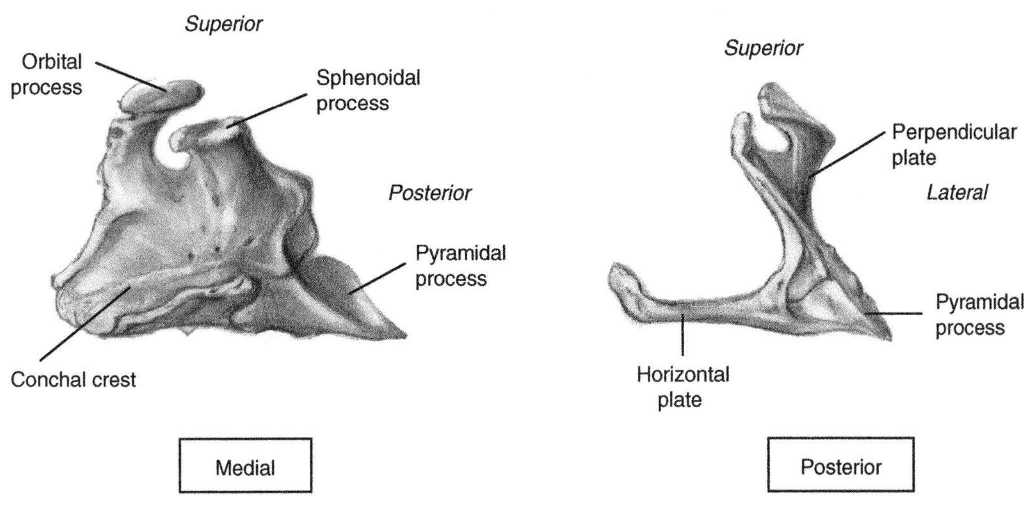

Right perinatal palatine

Identification – An intact bone is unlikely to be confused with any other element due to its distinct shape. Fragments of the palatine are unlikely to be identified, except perhaps the pyramidal process, which bears some similarity to the pointed lateral end of the lesser wing of the sphenoid or the pointed end of the medial pterygoid of the sphenoid. However, the fine structures of each are characteristic.

Siding/Orientation

- Place the horizontal plate in a horizontal position.
- Position the perpendicular plate vertical (the perpendicular plate has two processes extending superiorly).
- The pyramidal process is relatively robust and extends posterolaterally (when viewed posteriorly, it points to the side from which the bone belongs).

Metrics

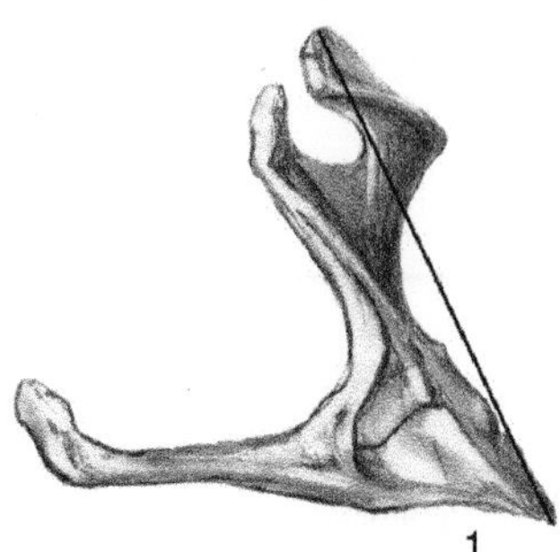

Reference landmarks for palatine measurements

Notes

Oblique height: Oblique distance from tip of pyramidal process to maximum height of orbital process

Fazekas and Kósa

Dry Bone Fetal Measurements-Palatine (mm)			
Prenatal Age (wks)	*n*	Oblique Height	
		Mean	Range
12	2	2.2	2.0–2.5
14	3	2.9	2.0–4.0
16	9	5.8	5.0–6.5
18	15	6.7	6.0–8.0
20	13	7.7	6.8–8.1
22	11	8.4	7.5–9.0
24	12	8.9	8.5–9.6
26	12	9.7	8.3–11.1
28	12	9.9	8.9–10.9
30	12	10.5	9.0–11.5
32	8	11.5	10.0–13.0
34	7	12.1	11.6–12.5
36	5	12.7	11.0–13.5
38	7	13.7	12.0–15.4
40	10	15.3	14.0–16.5

Source

Dry bone measurements on mid twentieth century Hungarian fetal remains from autopsy—males and females combined. Age was estimated based on fetal crown heel length.

Reference

Fazekas, I.Gy. and Kósa, F. (1978). *Forensic Fetal Osteology*. Budapest: Akadémiai Kiadó.

Morphological Summary

Prenatal	
Wks 7–8	Ossification center for perpendicular plate appears
Wk 10	Orbital and sphenoidal processes start to develop
Wk 18	Palatal processes fuse
Mid-fetal life	Has adopted adult morphology, but not proportions
Birth	Adult morphology except horizontal and perpendicular plates are of equal width and height
	Orbital process does not contain air cells
From yr 3	Perpendicular plate starts to increase in height
Puberty	Adult morphology and proportions

THE MANDIBLE

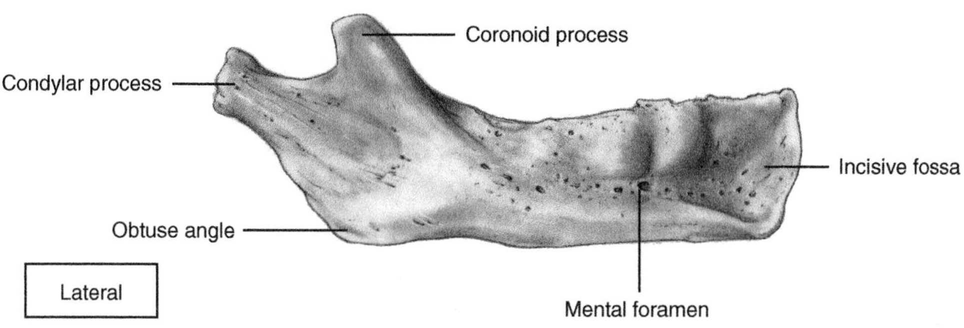

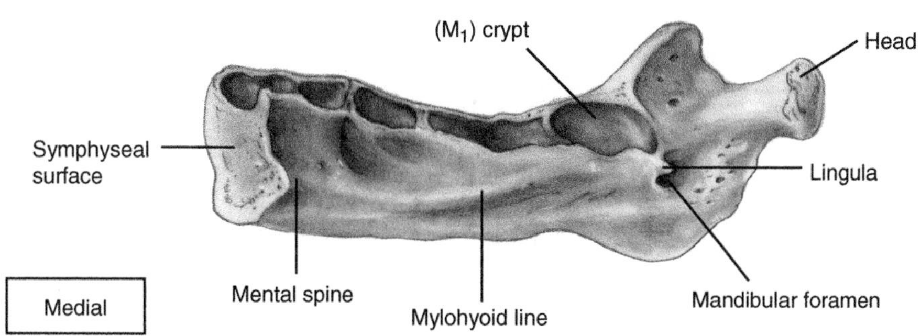

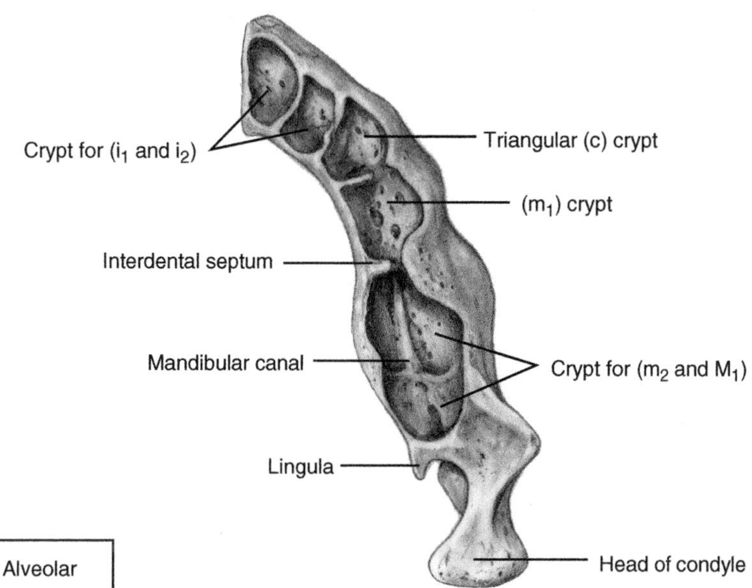

Right perinatal hemi-mandible

Identification – The mandible is identifiable in isolation by mid-fetal life. Fragments of the alveolar area may appear similar to those of the maxilla.

- The condyle bears similarities to the acromial end of a scapular spine, the acetabular end of a perinatal pubis, and to the pedicle end of vertebral half arches.
- The body of bone beneath the crypts of the mandible is thick and rounded, whereas the bone related to the crypts of the maxilla is part of the thin nasal or orbital floor.

Siding/Orientations

- The coronoid and condylar processes extend posterosuperiorly and the anterior end of the body curves medially.

Metrics

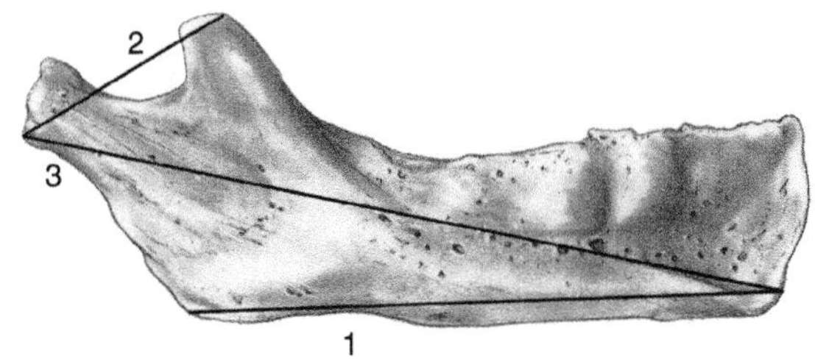

Reference landmarks for mandibular measurements

Notes

1. Body length: From tuberculum mentale to mandibular angle
2. Width: Posterior border of condyle to tip of coronoid process
3. Oblique length: From tuberculum mentale to posterior border of condyle

Dry Bone Fetal Measurements-Mandible (mm)							
		Body Length		Width		Oblique Length	
Prenatal Age (wks)	n	Mean	Range	Mean	Range	Mean	Range
12	2	8.0	7.5–8.5	–	–	10.7	10.0–11.5
14	3	9.6	9.3–10.0	3.2	3.0–3.5	12.6	12.2–13.5
16	9	13.0	12.3–14.5	6.5	5.8–7.2	17.9	15.6–20.6
18	15	14.2	13.3–17.0	6.9	6.1–7.5	21.6	20.0–23.0
20	13	17.6	16.8–18.2	8.0	7.2–8.5	25.6	24.0–28.0
22	11	19.2	18.0–22.0	9.0	8.0–10.0	27.3	26.0–28.5
24	12	21.5	20.0–23.0	10.2	9.0–11.5	30.1	28.0–31.7
26	12	22.6	21.0–24.0	10.9	10.0–12.1	31.9	30.0–33.5
28	12	24.2	22.2–25.5	11.3	10.5–12.5	34.0	33.0–35.0
30	12	26.0	24.5–27.5	13.0	12.0–14.0	35.9	34.5–37.5
32	8	27.7	26.5–29.0	14.1	13.5–15.0	39.0	37.0–40.5
34	7	30.0	29.0–31.2	15.1	14.5–16.0	40.2	39.0–42.0
36	5	31.7	31.0–32.3	16.4	16.0–16.5	42.7	41.2–45.0
38	7	34.7	34.0–37.0	17.0	16.0–18.5	47.5	46.0–50.6
40	10	36.5	35.0–38.0	18.0	16.0–21.0	49.7	48.0–52.0

Source

Dry bone measurements on mid twentieth century Hungarian fetal remains from autopsy—males and females combined. Age was estimated based on fetal crown heel length.

Reference

Fazekas, I.Gy. and Kósa, F. (1978). *Forensic Fetal Osteology.* Budapest: Akadémiai Kiadó.

Morphological Summary

Prenatal	
Wk 6	Intramembranous ossification center develops lateral to Meckel's cartilage
Wk 7	Coronoid process differentiating
Wk 8	Coronoid fuses with main mass
About wk 10	Condylar and coronoid processes recognizable
	Anterior part of Meckel's cartilage starting to ossify
Wks 12–14	Secondary cartilages for condyle, coronoid, and symphysis appear
Wks 14–16	Deciduous tooth germs start to form
Birth	Mandible consists of separate right and left halves
During yr 1	Fusion at symphysis
Infancy and childhood	Increase in size and shape of bone
	Eruption and replacement of teeth
By 12–14 yrs	All permanent teeth emerged except third molars

THE HYOID

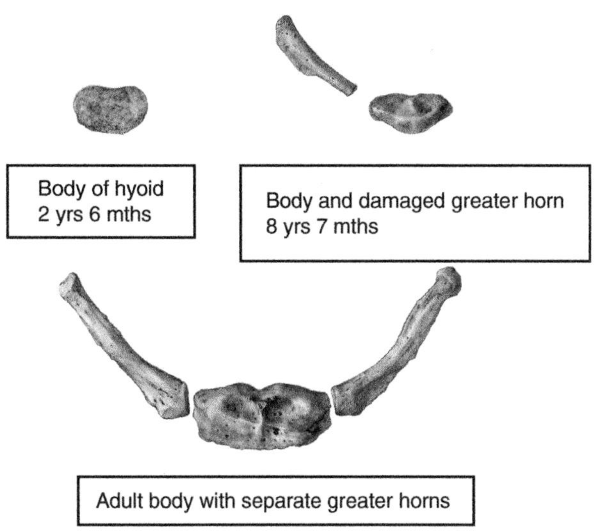

Development of the hyoid bone

Identification – An isolated body may be confused with an unfused anterior arch of the atlas as both have a concave posterior surface; isolated fragments of the greater horn may look like ossified horns of the laryngeal thyroid cartilage.

- The anterior arch has a tubercle in the middle of its anterior surface.
- The hyoid body is divided into two horizontal sections set at an angle to each other.
- Within a single skeleton, the atlas is more robust and about twice the size of the hyoid.

Orientation/Siding – In the complete hyoid, the body faces anteriorly and the greater horns extend superoposteriorly.

- An isolated body is convex anteriorly and the smaller biconcave section of the anterior surface faces superiorly.
- Isolated horns are difficult to side: the anterior end is wide whereas the posterior end is marked by a tubercle; the inferior surface tends to be smoother than the superior surface, which has muscle markings.

Morphological Summary

Prenatal	
Wk 5	Cartilaginous center for body appears
Wk 7	Body, greater and lesser horns chondrified
Birth	Ossification centers may be present in the upper half of body and ventral ends of greater horns
By yr 2	Body usually completely ossified
Puberty	Body and most of greater horns ossified

CHAPTER

2

The Dentition

DENTAL RECORDING SYSTEMS

Quadrants

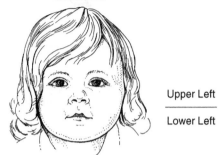

Upper Right / Lower Right — Upper Left / Lower Left

Systems

System	Dentition	Upper Right / Lower Right	Upper Left / Lower Left
Zsigmondy Palmer	Permanent	8 7 6 5 4 3 2 1	1 2 3 4 5 6 7 8
		8 7 6 5 4 3 2 1	1 2 3 4 5 6 7 8
	Deciduous	e d c b a	a b c d e
		e d c b a	a b c d e
FDI	Permanent	18 17 16 15 14 13 12 11	21 22 23 24 25 26 27 28
		48 47 46 45 44 43 42 41	31 32 33 34 35 36 37 38
	Deciduous	55 54 53 52 51	61 62 63 64 65
		85 84 83 82 81	71 72 73 74 75
Universal	Permanent	1 2 3 4 5 6 7 8	9 10 11 12 13 14 15 16
		32 31 30 29 28 27 26 25	24 23 22 21 20 19 18 17
	Deciduous	A B C D E	F G H I J
		T S R Q P	O N M L K

A compilation of various dental recording systems

Example of Recording System

Recording the First Right Mandibular Molar		
System	**Permanent**	**Deciduous**
Zsigmondy	6⌉	d⌉
FDI	46	84
Universal	30	S

Cusp Terminology

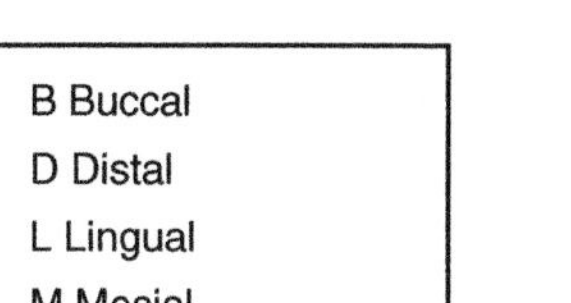

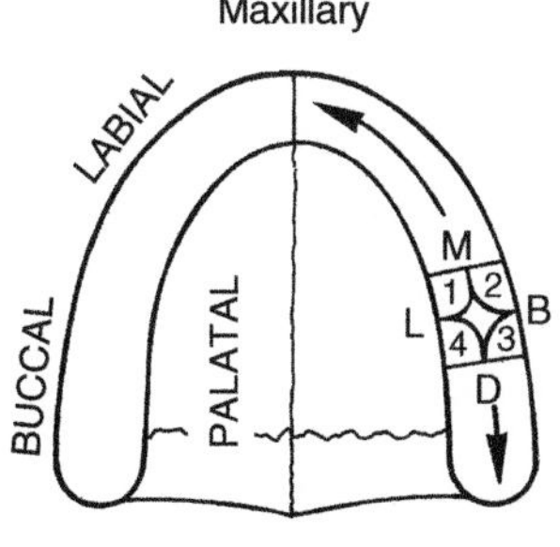

1 Mesiolingual
2 Mesiobuccal
3 Distobuccal
4 Distolingual

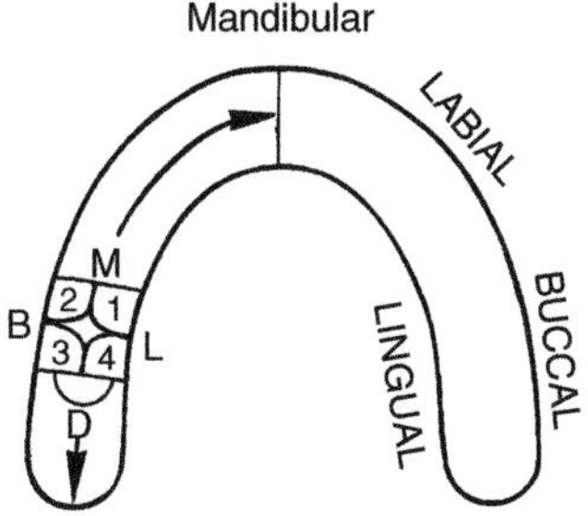

Dental arcades and molar cusp terminology

Deciduous Dentition

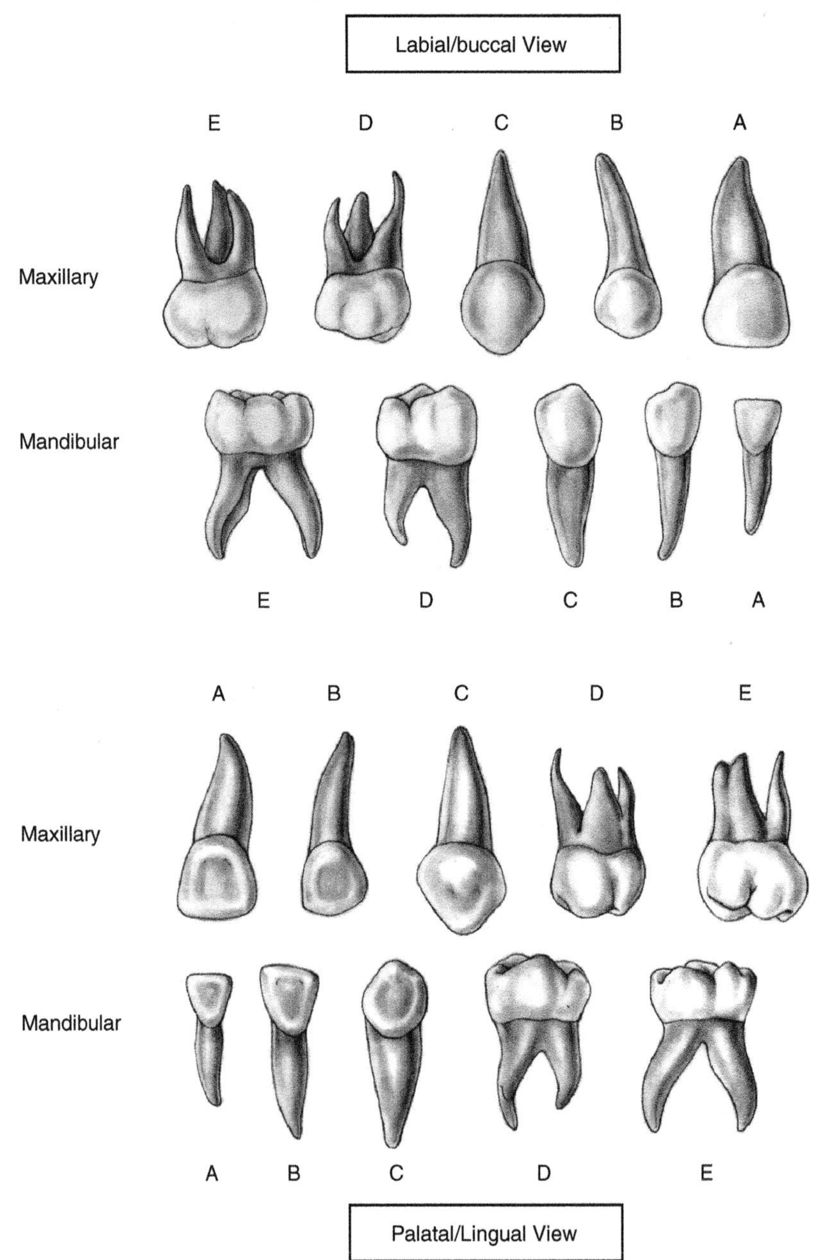

Deciduous teeth

Permanent Dentition

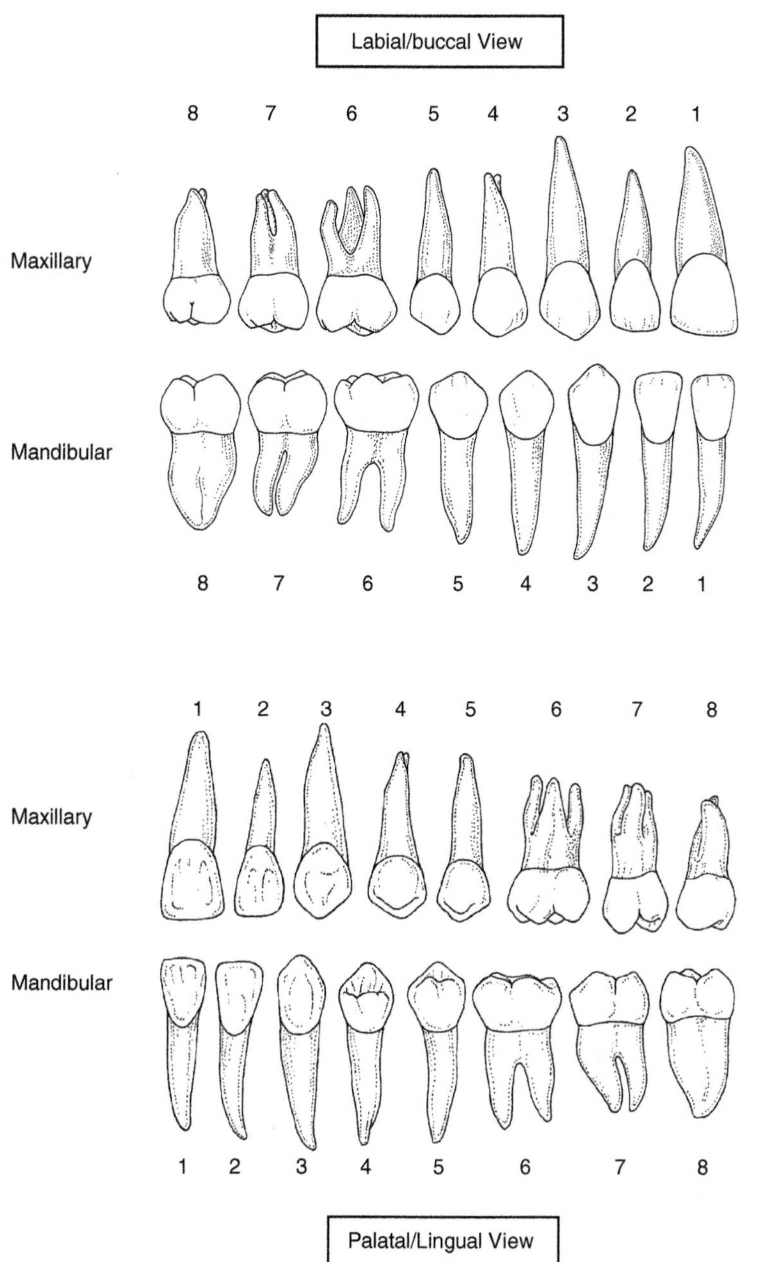

Permanent teeth

INCISORS

Deciduous versus Permanent

- Deciduous incisors have smaller crowns and roots compared to permanent incisors but are similar in shape.
- Deciduous incisors are characterized by a prominent cervical enamel margin.
- Deciduous incisors appear rounder and more bulbous due to their short crown height and proportionally longer roots.

Maxillary versus Mandibular

- The maxillary incisor crowns are wider in the mesiodistal dimension than mandibular incisors.
- Maxillary incisors have a more prominent cingulum (bulge on the lingual surface near the cervical region of the tooth).
- Occasionally the marginal ridges of maxillary incisors may be rounded along with displaying a cingulum pit, thus creating a shovel shape.
- The roots of maxillary incisors are somewhat triangular in cross section, whereas the roots of the mandibular incisors are flattened mesiodistally.
- The roots of maxillary central incisors are straight and robust, whereas the root apices of most other permanent incisors tend to angle distally.

Central versus Lateral

Maxillary

- Central incisors are larger than lateral incisors in both permanent and deciduous dentition.
- Viewed from the buccal aspect, the incisal (cutting) edge of central incisors are straight, whereas the incisal edge of lateral incisors slope toward the distal side, giving them a shorter distal crown height.
- The root of the central incisor is considerably stouter than the lateral incisor.

Mandibular

- Central incisors are smaller than lateral incisors in both permanent and deciduous dentition.
- The deciduous central incisor root is considerably shorter than the lateral incisor root.
- In permanent dentition, the lateral incisor may have a slightly longer root and longitudinal grooves may be more marked than on the central incisor.
- The central incisal (cutting) edge is straight; the incisal edge of lateral incisors slopes toward the distal side. This is especially prominent in deciduous dentition.

- The lateral incisor crown is slightly off-center with the root when viewed from the occlusal surface; that is, the medial marginal ridge on the lingual side is slightly longer and more curved than that of the distal marginal ridge.

Left versus Right

- The mesial incisal angle of all incisors forms a right angle compared to the rounded distal angle.
- The curvature of the enamel margin is more sinuous (extends further into the crown) on the mesial surface than on the distal surface, thus resulting in a shorter mesial than distal crown height.
- Curvature of root apices is usually distal.

CANINES

Deciduous versus Permanent

- The deciduous canines are smaller than the permanent canines, with proportionally longer roots.
- The tooth at the crown margin is considerably thicker in the deciduous canine crown, making the crown appear short and stout and the neck constricted.

Maxillary versus Mandibular

- Maxillary canines display greater mesiodistal width than mandibular canines in both deciduous and permanent dentition.
- The maxillary cingulum (bulge on the lingual surface near the cervical region of the tooth) is more substantial than the mandibular cingulum (particularly in the permanent canines).
- A maxillary canine usually displays a central strengthening ridge extending from the cingulum to the cusp.
- The mandibular canine does not display a central lingual ridge, thus the lingual surface is flatter.
- The maxillary canine root is the longest and strongest of the whole dentition.
- The mandibular canine root is flattened and grooved distally.

Left versus Right

- The distal crown surface of all canines is markedly convex compared to the flatter mesial surface.
- The mesial slope from cusp tip to contact area (location where contact is made with its neighboring tooth) is shorter than the distal slope, except in the deciduous maxillary

canine, which exhibits the opposite effect (however, the effect can be reversed after 6 months of wear).
- The mesial contact area occurs further along the crown edge (toward the tip of the cusp) than the distal contact area, which occurs in a more central location, except in the deciduous maxillary canine, which exhibits contact points at similar levels on both sides.
- The curvature of the enamel margin is more sinuous (extends further into the crown) on the mesial surface than on the distal surface, thus resulting in a shorter mesial than distal crown height.
- The large root often inclines distally and may display a distal groove.

PREMOLARS

Maxillary versus Mandibular Premolars

- Viewed from the occlusal surface, the maxillary crowns are oval in shape, consisting of two distinct cusps, whereas the outline of the mandibular crowns is circular.
- Viewed from the occlusal surface, maxillary premolars have two cusps of similar size divided by a central fissure; mandibular premolars are dominated by a larger buccal cusp and smaller lingual cusp(s).
- Mandibular lingual cusps tend to be offset toward the mesial side; if the second premolar displays two lingual cusps the mesial one is larger.
- The first maxillary premolar is distinct in that it usually has two roots as opposed to the single root displayed by the other premolars.

First versus Second Premolars

Maxillary

- The first premolar will normally have two roots; other premolars are single rooted.
- The first premolar displays sharper, more prominent cusps with the buccal cusp being significantly larger than the palatal cusp; the second premolar has more rounded, shorter cusps that are similar in size and height.
- The mesial crown surface of the first premolar has a concavity that extends into the root trunk surface (referred to as the canine fossa); the mesial crown surface of the second premolar is convex.
- The second premolar may have a longer root than the first premolar.

Mandibular

- The first premolar has a large, pointed buccal cusp and a much smaller lingual cusp; the second premolar displays rounded cusps that are more equal in size and height.
- Viewed occlusally, the buccal cusp of the first premolar is placed centrally over the root.

- Both premolars display two pits on their occlusal surface (mesial and distal); on the first premolar, the two pits lie on either side of a central enamel ridge whereas those on the second premolar are connected by a fissure that curves around the larger buccal cusp.
- The root of the first premolar may be deeply grooved on its mesial surface.
- The lingual cusp of the second premolar is commonly subdivided into two cusps, the mesial cusp being larger.

Left versus Right Premolars

Maxillary

- In the first premolar, the occlusal fissure extends across the mesial marginal ridge onto the mesial crown surface.
- The mesial crown and root surface of the first premolar is slightly concave (canine fossa).
- Viewed from the lingual surface, the lingual cusp is more medially oriented; that is, the distal slope of the lingual cusp is longer than its mesial slope.
- Viewed from the buccal surface, the buccal cusp of the first premolar has a longer mesial slope as compared to its distal slope; the second premolar displays the opposite effect with a longer distal slope (just as in the canine).

Mandibular

- The distal occlusal pit is larger than the mesial pit. The mesial pit of the first premolar may extend into a mesiolingual groove.
- Viewed from the buccal or lingual surface, the mesial marginal ridge is higher than the distal marginal ridge in the second premolar.
- May show some distal curving of the root apices.

MOLARS

Deciduous versus Permanent Molars

- Both the crowns and roots of deciduous molars are smaller than those of permanent molars.
- Deciduous molars have a prominent cervical enamel margin making the cervix appear narrow and the crown bulbous.
- The first deciduous molar bears a distinguishing enamel tubercle (named after Zuckerkandl) on its mesiobuccal crown margin that often extends onto the root surface.
- The roots of deciduous molars are slimmer and more curved than those of permanent molars.
- Deciduous molar roots arise from a very short root trunk and show marked divergence, allowing space for the developing premolar crowns.
- Deciduous molar roots converge apically, although this feature is not apparent if the root is partly resorbed during exfoliation.
- Roots of permanent molars are longer and more robust than deciduous molar roots.

Maxillary versus Mandibular Molars

Deciduous

- The maxillary molars are quadrilateral in outline and the mandibular molars tend to be more rectangular with soft rounded edges.
- Maxillary molars display three roots whereas mandibular molars display two roots.

Permanent

- Maxillary crowns consist of three or more cusps and are wider in a buccolingual than mesiodistal direction, whereas mandibular crowns have four or more cusps and display longer mesiodistal than buccolingual dimensions.
- The crown of maxillary molars is rhombic in shape, whereas mandibular crowns are more squared or rectangular.
- Maxillary molars display three roots; mandibular molars display two roots.

First versus Second Deciduous Molars

Maxillary (three roots—two buccal and one palatal)

- The first deciduous molar is quadrilateral in shape with unparallel mesial and distal borders, whereas the second is more rhombic in shape; that is, it displays more parallel mesial and distal edges.
- Both first and second molars consist of four cusps (two buccal and two palatal cusps), however the palatal cusps may not be as clearly separated in the first maxillary molar.
- Viewed from the occlusal surface, the buccal cusps of the first molar are considerably wider mesiodistally than the palatal cusps; in the second molar these dimensions are more similar.
- The crown of the second molar is larger than the first.
- An oblique ridge runs through the second molar from the mesiopalatal cusp to the distobuccal cusp.
- Occasionally an extra cusp (Carabelli) is present on the mesiopalatal surface of the same cusp; may also be present on the maxillary permanent first molar.

Mandibular (two roots—one mesial, one distal)

- The first deciduous mandibular molar is considerably smaller than the second.
- The second mandibular molar consists of three buccal and two lingual cusps.
- The second deciduous molar is smaller than but similar in shape to the permanent mandibular first molar.

First, Second, or Third Permanent Molar

Maxillary

- The first two maxillary molars are similarly rhomboid in shape, however the crown of the first is much larger than the second.
- The first molar tends to have four cusps (two buccal, two palatal), however the mesial palatal surface may display an additional Carabelli's cusp.
- The second molar will have either three or four cusps, depending on the presence or absence of the distopalatal cusp.
- The second molar displays distal cusp(s) of reduced size in relation to the first molar.
- The roots of the second molar are less divergent and closer together than those of the first molar (may even be fused).
- The third molar is highly variable but is usually smaller than the other two molars.
- The third molar is triangular in outline and made up of three or more cusps (one palatal, two buccal); the distopalatal cusp is small or absent.
- The roots of the third molar are shorter than those of other molars and often are fused.

Mandibular

- The first molar is the largest and has five cusps (three buccal, two lingual); the second and third buccal cusps are reduced in size, helping to retain its rectangular shape.
- The second molar has four equal-sized cusps, having lost the distal cusp.
- The second molar displays two central fissures that form a cross on the occlusal surface; the fissures on the first molar are more stellate in their pattern due to the extra cusp.
- The roots of the second molar are less divergent and less curved than those of the first.
- The third molar consists of four or more cusps.
- The mesial crown margin of the third molar may have a contact area showing interproximal wear whereas the distal margin would not.
- The two roots of the third molar tend to be shorter and less divergent, or fused, compared to the other mandibular molars.

Left versus Right Molars

Deciduous First Molars (Maxillary and Mandibular)

- The buccal cusps are considerably wider in a mesiodistal direction than the palatal cusps in both mandibular and maxillary first molars.
- The mesiobuccal crown margin of both mandibular and maxillary first molars may show a pronounced bulge.
- The distal margin of the tooth is flatter in both mandibular and maxillary molars, making a wider contact area with the crown of the second deciduous molar; this is opposed to the mesial margin, which is angled in the area where contact is made with the canine tooth.

Deciduous Second Maxillary Molar

- The maxillary second molar consists of four cusps: the largest is the mesiopalatal followed by the mesiobuccal, and the distopalatal cusp is the smallest.
- The maxillary second molar is rhombic in shape with its two acute angles occurring in the mesiobuccal and distopalatal corners and its obtuse angles occurring in the remaining corners.
- An oblique ridge runs from mesiopalatal to the distobuccal cusp.

Deciduous Mandibular Molars

- The medial cusps of the first mandibular molar are larger and higher than the distal cusps with the mesiobuccal cusp being the largest.
- An enamel ridge separates the occlusal surface of the first mandibular molar into a small mesial and larger distal fossa.
- The buccal cusps of the first mandibular molar are not well defined but the lingual cusps are separate and sharper.
- The second molar has three buccal cusps and two palatal cusps; the smallest is the most distal buccal cusp.

Permanent Maxillary Molars

- An oblique ridge runs from mesiopalatal to distobuccal with a distinct fissure between the larger mesiopalatal cusp and the distopalatal cusp.
- The largest cusp of the permanent first molar crown is the mesiopalatal, but the mesiobuccal is the highest.
- The crown is rhomboid in outline consisting of obtuse angles along its mesiopalatal and distobuccal edges and acute angles along the mesiobuccal and distopalatal edges.
- The mesial cusps are wider buccolingually than the distal cusps (may be less noticeable on second and third molars).
- Maxillary molars have two buccal roots and one palatal root.
- Roots tend to curve distally in all maxillary molars.
- The third molar has three or more cusps, the largest being the palatal and the distopalatal cusp being small or absent.

Permanent Mandibular Molars

- These molars tend to display a flattened mesial border and a rounded distal border.
- The buccal surface is rounded compared to the flatter lingual surface.
- Larger mesial cusps make the tooth wider buccolingually than at the distal cusps.
- In the first molar, the mesial marginal ridge is higher than the distal marginal ridge viewed from the buccal aspect.
- Roots tend to display some degree of distal curvature.
- The mesial root is always broader than the distal root.

Metrics

Liversidge et al.

Dental Measurements-Deciduous tooth length (mm)	
Tooth*	**Regression Equation for estimating age (yrs)**
i1	Age = $-0.653 + 0.144 \times$ length ± 0.19
i2	Age = $-0.581 + 0.153 \times$ length ± 0.17
c	Age = $-0.648 + 0.209 \times$ length ± 0.22
m1	Age = $-0.814 + 0.222 \times$ length ± 0.25
m2	Age = $-0.904 + 0.292 \times$ length ± 0.26

*Results from maxillary and mandibular teeth were combined.

Dental Measurements-Permanent tooth length (mm)		
Tooth*	**Regression Equation**	**Max t/I****
I1	Age = $0.237 - 0.018 \times$ length $+ 0.042 \times$ (length)$^2 \pm 0.21$	<11.3
I^2	Age = $-0.173 + 0.538 \times$ length $+ 0.003 \times$ (length)$^2 \pm 0.14$	<9.9
I_2	Age = $0.921 - 0.281 \times$ length $+ 0.075 \times$ (length)$^2 \pm 0.12$	<9.8
C	Age = $-0.163 + 0.294 \times$ length $+ 0.028 \times$ (length)$^2 \pm 0.25$	<9.8
M1	Age = $-0.942 + 0.441 \times$ length $+ 0.010 \times$ (length)$^2 \pm 0.25$	<11.5

*Measurements from mandibular and maxillary dentition were combined with exception of the lateral incissors.
**Maximum tooth length on which the data is based.

Source

Dry tooth measurements from children interred between the years 1729 and 1859 and excavated from the crypt of Christ Church, Spitalfields, London. Males and females combined.

Notes

Tooth length: The distance from the cusp-tip or mid-incisal edge to the developing edge of crown or root in the midline; only appropriate if root is incomplete, i.e. tooth is still growing.

Reference

Liversidge, H.M., Herdeg, B. and Rosing, F.W. (1998). Dental age estimation of non-adults. A review of methods and principles. In: *Dental Anthropology, Fundamentals, Limits and Prospects* (K.W. Alt F.W. Rosing and M. Teschler-Nicola (Eds.), (pp. 419–442). Vienna: Springer.

Development

Moorrees et al.

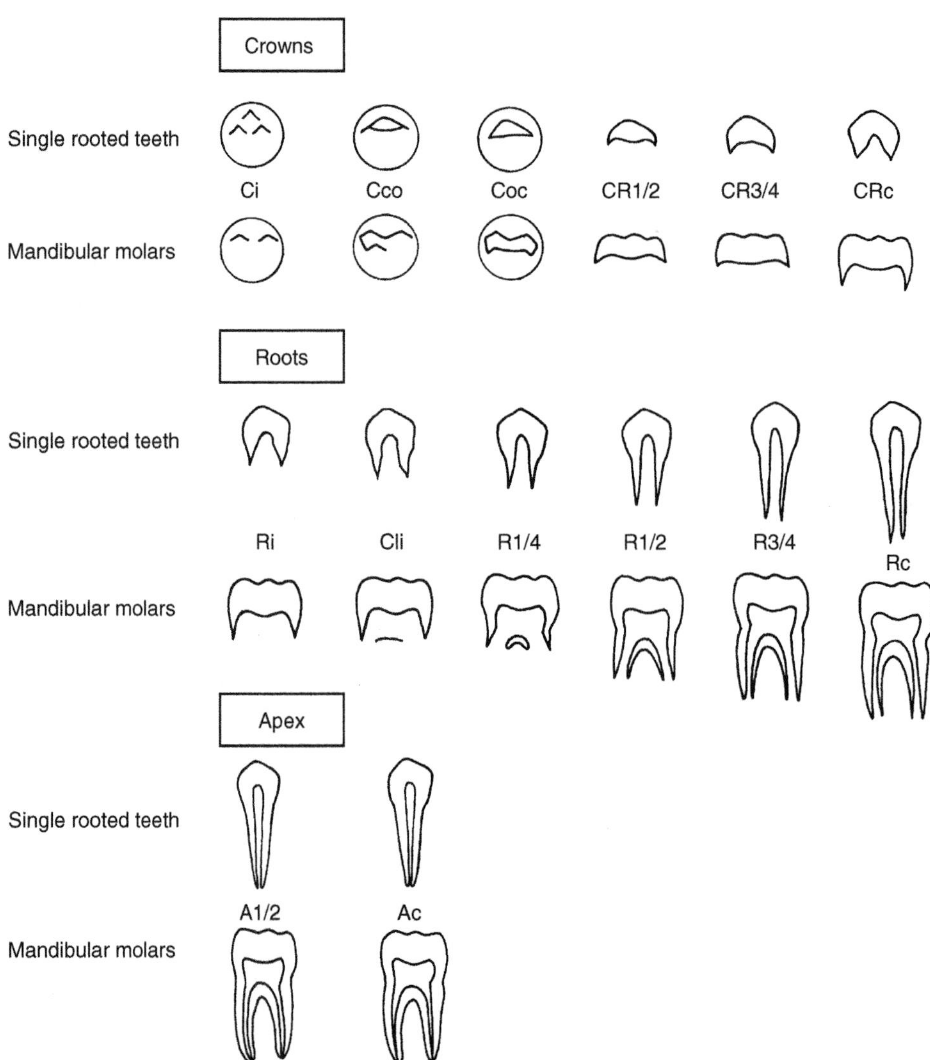

Mineralization stages of the crown, roots and apex

Definition of Tooth Formation Stages	
C_i	Initial cusp formation
C_{co}	Coalescence of cusps
C_{oc}	Cusp outline complete
$CR_{1/2}$	Crown half complete
$CR_{3/4}$	Crown three-quarters complete
CR_c	Crown complete
R_i	Initial root formation
Ci_i	Initial cleft formation
$R_{1/4}$	Root length quarter
$R_{1/2}$	Root length half
$R_{3/4}$	Root length three-quarters
R_c	Root length complete
$A_{1/2}$	Apex half closed
A_c	Apical closure complete

Notes

This method considers the developmental maturity of each tooth independently from that of the other teeth to derive an age estimate. Each tooth is staged and an age is assigned to each stage.

Source

Intraoral radiographs of 134 Boston children (48 males and 51 females) as well as radiographs from 136 boys and 110 girls included in the longitudinal study from the Fels Research Institute program in Yellowsprings, Ohio.

Reference

Moorrees, C., Fanning, E., and Hunt, E. (1963). Age variation of formation stages for ten permanent teeth. *Dental Research* **42**(6): 1490–1502.

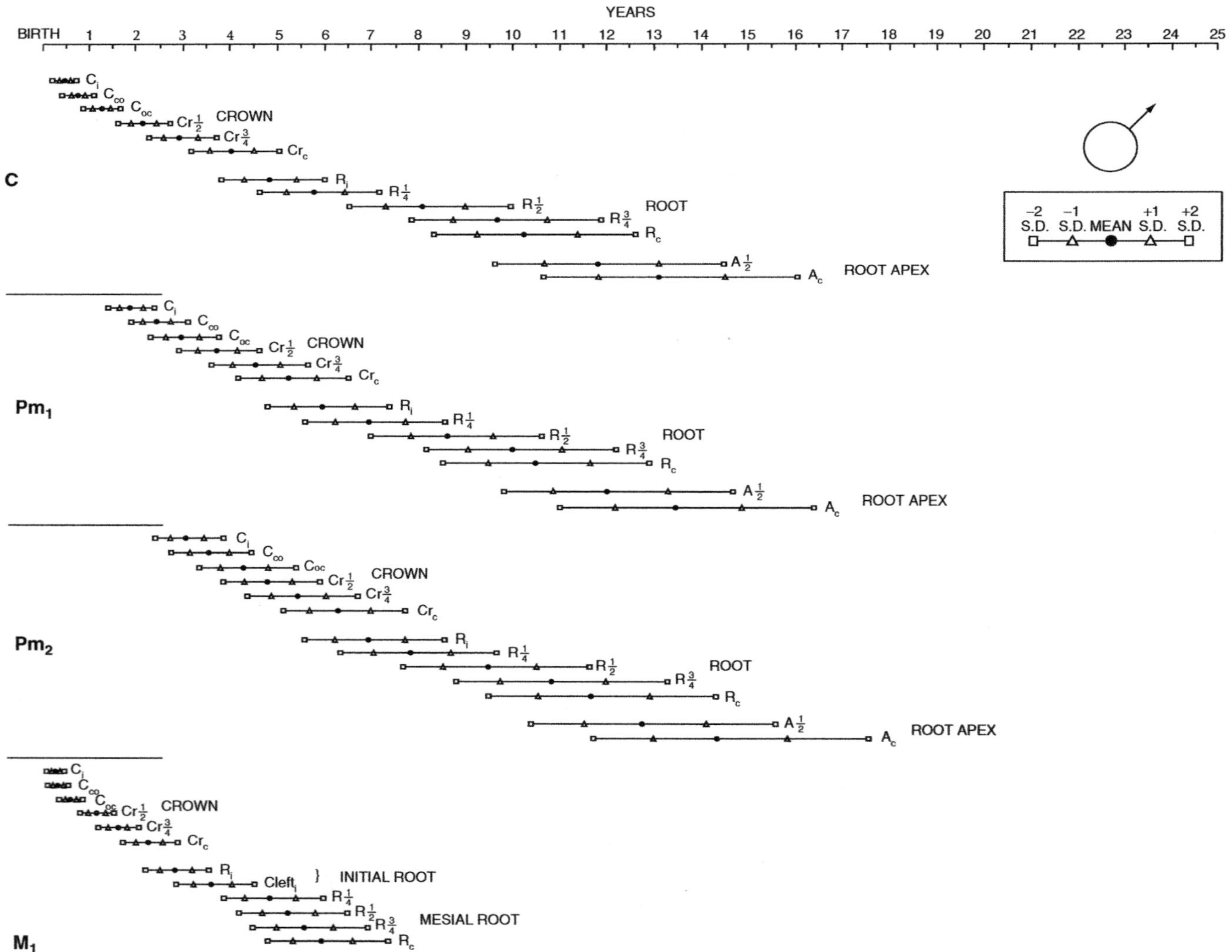
YEARS
BIRTH 1 2 3 4 5 6 7 8 9 10 11 12 13 14 15 16 17 18 19 20 21 22 23 24 25
C
Ci
Cco
Coc
Cr½ CROWN
Cr¾
Crc
Ri
R¼
R½ ROOT
R¾
Rc
A½
Ac ROOT APEX
−2 S.D.
−1 S.D.
MEAN
+1 S.D.
+2 S.D.
Pm1
Ci
Cco
Coc
Cr½ CROWN
Cr¾
Crc
Ri
R¼
R½ ROOT
R¾
Rc
A½
Ac ROOT APEX
Pm2
Ci
Cco
Coc
Cr½ CROWN
Cr¾
Crc
Ri
R¼
R½ ROOT
R¾
Rc
A½
Ac ROOT APEX
M1
Ci
Cco
Coc
Cr½ CROWN
Cr¾
Crc
Ri
Cleft_i } INITIAL ROOT
R¼
R½
R¾ MESIAL ROOT
Rc

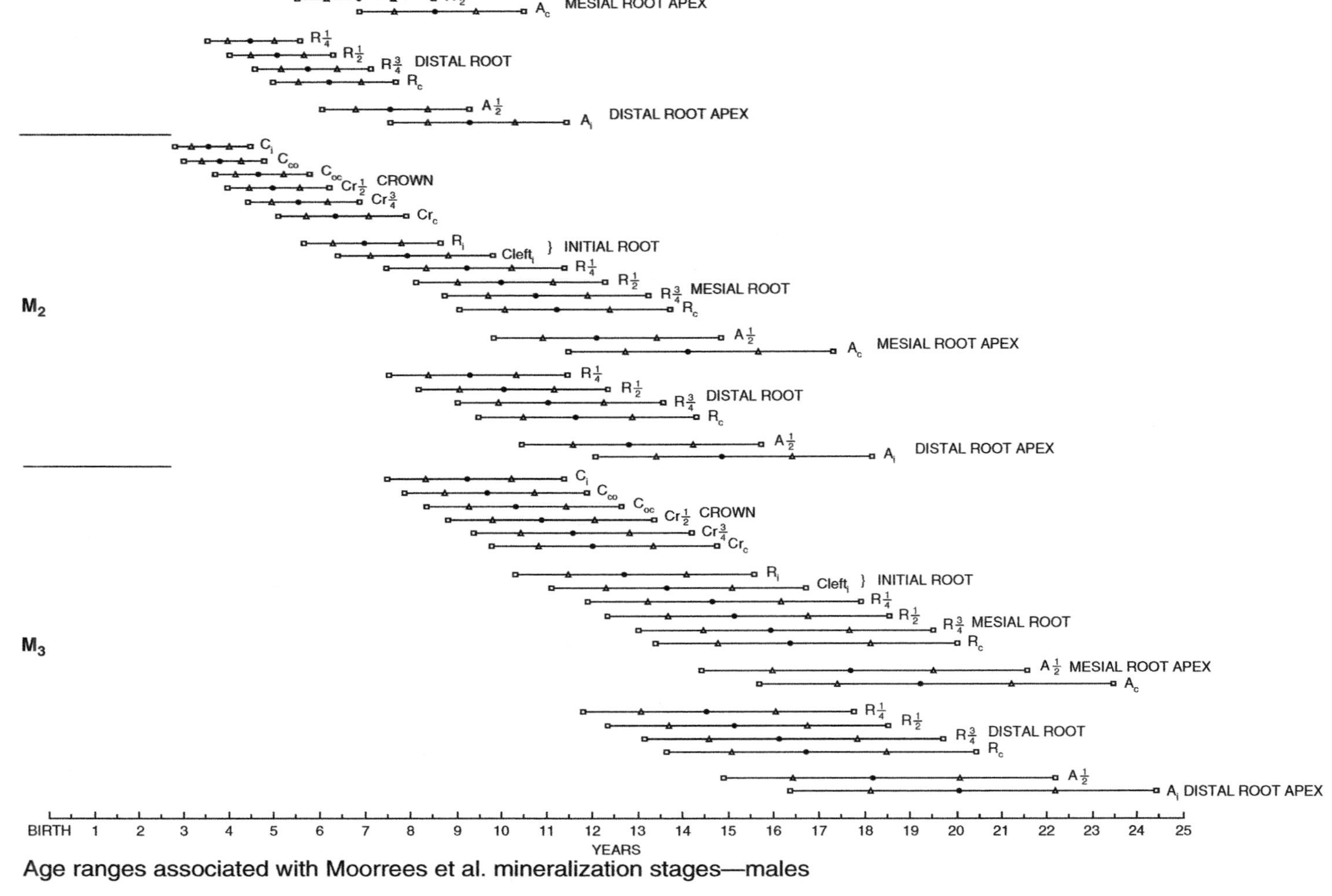

Age ranges associated with Moorrees et al. mineralization stages—males

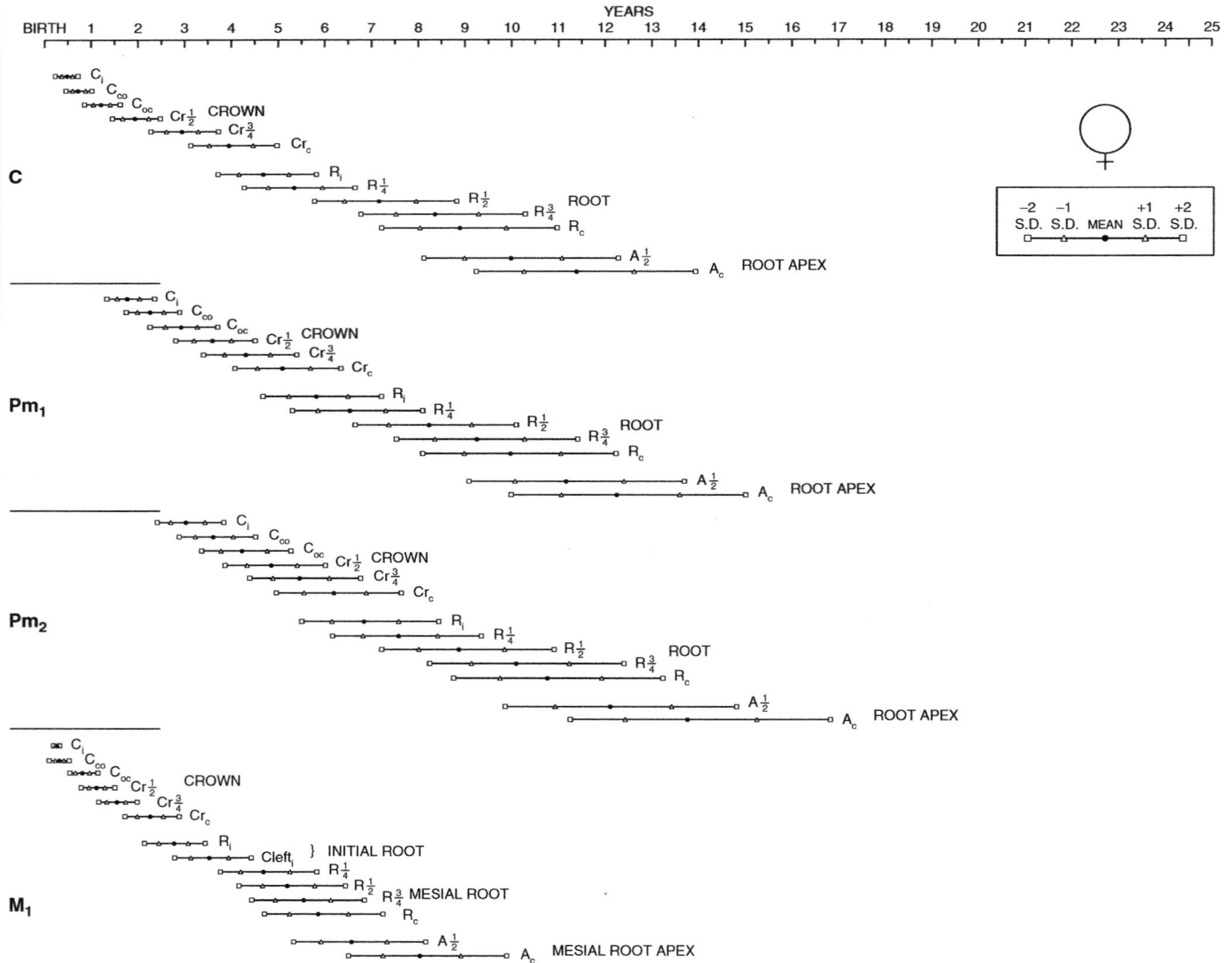
YEARS
BIRTH 1 2 3 4 5 6 7 8 9 10 11 12 13 14 15 16 17 18 19 20 21 22 23 24 25
−2 S.D. −1 S.D. MEAN +1 S.D. +2 S.D.
C
C_i
C_{co}
C_{oc}
$Cr\frac{1}{2}$ CROWN
$Cr\frac{3}{4}$
Cr_c
R_i
$R\frac{1}{4}$
$R\frac{1}{2}$ ROOT
$R\frac{3}{4}$
R_c
$A\frac{1}{2}$
A_c ROOT APEX
Pm1
C_i
C_{co}
C_{oc}
$Cr\frac{1}{2}$ CROWN
$Cr\frac{3}{4}$
Cr_c
R_i
$R\frac{1}{4}$
$R\frac{1}{2}$ ROOT
$R\frac{3}{4}$
R_c
$A\frac{1}{2}$
A_c ROOT APEX
Pm2
C_i
C_{co}
C_{oc}
$Cr\frac{1}{2}$ CROWN
$Cr\frac{3}{4}$
Cr_c
R_i
$R\frac{1}{4}$
$R\frac{1}{2}$ ROOT
$R\frac{3}{4}$
R_c
$A\frac{1}{2}$
A_c ROOT APEX
M1
C_i
C_{co}
C_{oc}
$Cr\frac{1}{2}$ CROWN
$Cr\frac{3}{4}$
Cr_c
R_i
$Cleft_i$ } INITIAL ROOT
$R\frac{1}{4}$
$R\frac{1}{2}$
$R\frac{3}{4}$ MESIAL ROOT
R_c
$A\frac{1}{2}$
A_c MESIAL ROOT APEX

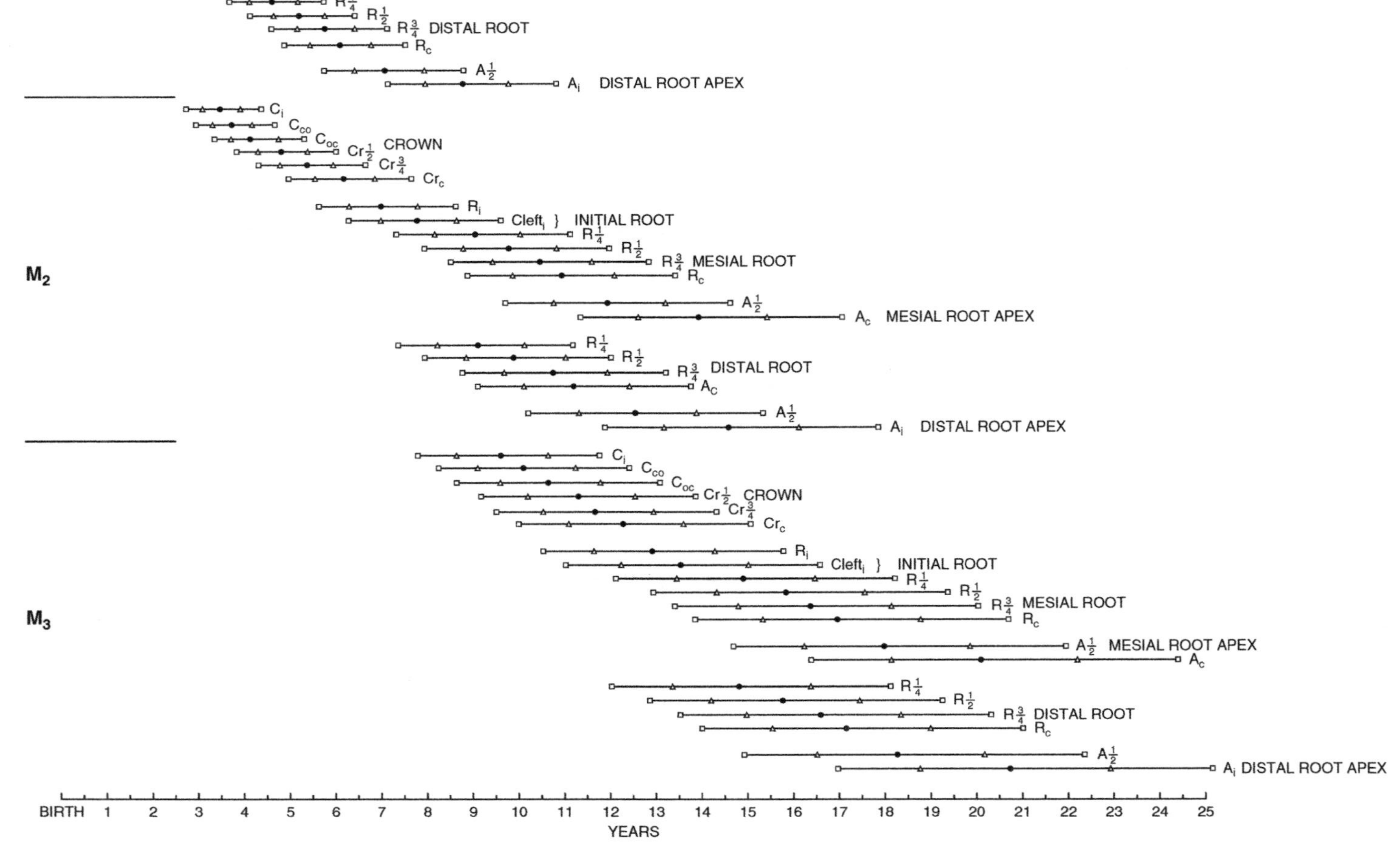

Age ranges associated with Moorrees et al. mineralization stages—females

Demirjian et al.

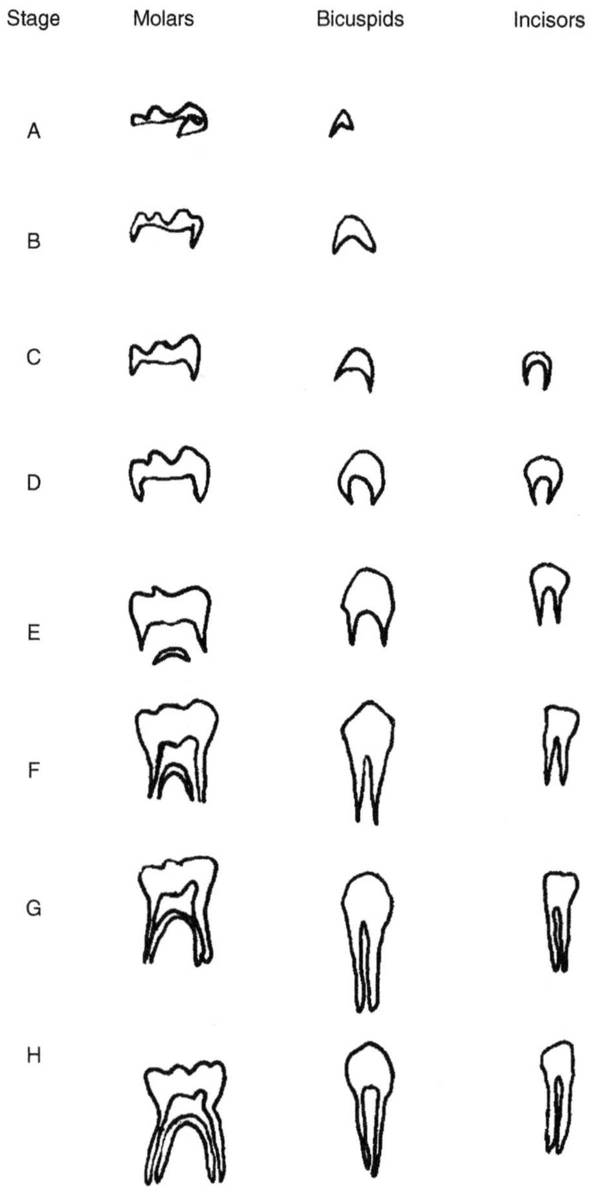

Stage Molars Bicuspids Incisors

A

B

C

D

E

F

G

H

Stages of tooth formation

	Definition of tooth formation stages
A	Calcification of the cusp tips have initialized, however have not yet united in multiradicular teeth
B	Cusp tips unite to form a regularly outlined coronal surface
C	Crown formation extends towards cervical region; dentinal deposition and pulp chamber are observable
D	Crown formation is complete; pulp chamber is curved in uniradicular teeth and exhibits a trapezoidal form in molars
E	Walls of pulp chamber exhibit straight lines in uniradicular teeth; initial formation of radicular bifurcation in molars; root length is less than the crown height in all teeth
F	Walls of pulp chamber form isosceles triangles in uniradicular teeth; molar roots are more definite and funnel shaped; root length is equal to or greater than the crown height in all teeth
G	Root length is nearly complete; however its apical end remains open
H	Apical end of the root is closed; the periodontal membrane has a uniform width around the root and apex

Notes

This method was originally intended to be used as a means to derive a composite estimate based on the development of all permanent teeth (with exception of the third molar). Each tooth was staged according to its most recent developmental achievement and then assigned a value rating according to the defined stage for that tooth. The scores of all seven teeth then were summed to derive a composite score that was plotted against age.

Source

Panoramic radiographs taken from 2928 mid twentieth century children of French-Canadian descent.

Reference

Demirjian, A., Goldstein, H., and Tanner, J.M. (1973). A new system of dental age assessment. *Human Biology* **45**(2): 211–227.

Rated value assigned to tooth stages									
Males									
Tooth	**0**	**A**	**B**	**C**	**D**	**E**	**F**	**G**	**H**
M_2	0.0	2.1	3.5	5.9	10.1	12.5	13.2	13.6	15.4
M_1				0.0	8.0	9.6	12.3	17.0	19.3
P_2	0.0	1.7	3.1	5.4	9.7	12.0	12.8	13.2	14.4
P_1			0.0	3.4	7.0	11.0	12.3	12.7	13.5
C_1				0.0	3.5	7.9	10.0	11.0	11.9
I_2				0.0	3.2	5.2	7.8	11.7	13.7
I_1					0.0	1.9	4.1	8.2	11.8

Male Age Assessment in Relation to Composite Dental Scores (7 teeth-mandible only)

Age	Estimated* 50th Percentile Score	Estimated* 10th-90th Percentile Score Range
3	15.0	6.0–26.0
4	21.5	11.0–33.0
5	29.5	18.0–42.0
6	39.0	26.0–59.0
7	55.0	36.0–79.0
8	78.5	52.0–89.0
9	86.5	72.0–92.0
10	90.5	82.0–94.0
11	93.5	87.0–96.0
12	95.5	90.0–97.0
13	96.0	92.0–98.0
14	97.0	94.0–99.0
15	98.0	95.0–100.0

*Values estimated from a centile growth curve.

Rated value assigned to tooths									
Females									
Tooth	**0**	**A**	**B**	**C**	**D**	**E**	**F**	**G**	**H**
M_2	0.0	2.7	3.9	6.9	11.1	13.5	14.2	14.5	15.6
M_1				0.0	4.5	6.2	9.0	14.0	16.2
P_2	0.0	1.8	3.4	6.5	10.6	12.7	13.5	13.8	14.6
P_1			0.0	3.7	7.5	11.8	13.1	13.4	14.1
C_1				0.0	3.8	7.3	10.3	11.6	12.4
I_2				0.0	3.2	5.6	8.0	12.2	14.2
I_1					0.0	2.4	5.1	9.3	12.9

Female Age Assessment in Relation to Composite Dental Scores (7 teeth-mandible only)

Age	Estimated* 50th percentile Score	Estimated* 10th-90th percentile Score Range
3	17.5	5.0–31.0
4	25.0	12.0–39.0
5	33.0	19.0–49.0
6	44.0	28.0–69.0
7	64.0	39.0–85.0
8	73.0	57.0–92.0
9	84.0	80.0–95.0
10	93.0	87.0–97.0
11	95.5	91.0–98.0
12	97.0	94.0–99.0
13	98.0	95.0–100.0
14	99.0	96.0–100.0
15	99.5	97.0–100.0

*Values estimated from a centile growth curve.

Radiographic and Direct Assessment-Deciduous Tooth Development according to Demirjian Stages						
	Postnatal Age of Attainment of Crown and Root Stages (mean ± SD in years)					
	C	D	E	F	G	H
i^1		0.12 ± 0.24	0.42 ± 0.31	0.98 ± 0.23	1.42 ± 0.35	2.26 ± 0.15
i_1		0.10 ± 0.20	0.32 ± 0.13	0.83 ± 0.27	1.2 ± 0.11	1.98 ± 0.11
i^2		0.28 ± 0.24	0.52 ± 0.19	0.96 ± 0.32	1.49 ± 0.04	2.58 ± 0.49
i_2		0.32 ± 0.07	0.47 ± 0.17	1.0 ± 0.28	1.60 ± 0.30	2.39 ± 0.40
c^1	0.34 ± 0.20	0.83 ± 0.26	1.07 ± 0.30	1.94 ± 0.18	2.47 ± 0.36	3.33 ± 0.13
c_1	0.38 ± 0.18	0.81 ± 0.12	1.02 ± 0.26	1.75 ± 0.13	2.38 ± 0.42	3.51 ± 0.35
m^1	0.18 ± 0.26	0.35 ± 0.11	0.70 ± 0.12	1.29 ± 0.12	2.30 ± 0.41	2.87 ± 0.53
m_1	0.13 ± 0.25	0.48 ± 0.18	0.78 ± 0.25	1.29 ± 0.12	2.49 ± 0.35	2.91 ± 0.35
m^2	0.29 ± 0.14	0.78 ± 0.26	1.23 ± 0.27	2.32 ± 0.47	3.05 ± 0.28	3.92 ± 0.60
m_2	0.39 ± 0.21	0.92 ± 0.26	1.34 ± 0.11	2.28 ± 0.51	2.78 ± 0.45	3.54 ± 0.74

Source

121 documented and undocumented remains interred between 1729 and 1852 and excavated from the crypt of Christ Church, Spitalfields, London. Age was estimated in undocumented remains using tooth length equations.

Notes

Mean ages were calculated for each tooth separately according to each stage of development. Development of the dentition was not considered as a whole.

Reference

Liversidge, H.M. and Molleson, T. (2004). Variation in crown and root formation and eruption of human deciduous teeth. *American Journal of Physical Anthropology* **123**: 172–180. Reprinted with permission of Wiley-Liss, Inc., a subsidiary of John Wiley & Sons, Inc.

Emergence

Liversidge and Molleson

Radiographic and Direct Assessment Postnatal-Eruption times			
Mean ± SD in years			
Tooth	Alveolar Level	Midpoint	Occlusal Level
i^1	0.34 ± 0.11	0.72 ± 0.12	0.85 ± 0.12
i_1	0.27 ± 0.14	0.66 ± 0.12	0.90 ± 0.33
i^2	0.62 ± 0.11	0.83 ± 0.12	1.13 ± 0.30
i_2	0.66 ± 0.36	1.03 ± 0.34	1.27 ± 0.12
c^1	1.05 ± 0.26	1.49 ± 0.44	2.19 ± 0.15
c_1	1.05 ± 0.30	1.32 ± 0.11	1.93 ± 0.38
m^1	0.81 ± 0.12	1.22 ± 0.34	1.36 ± 0.11
m_1	0.89 ± 0.23	1.21 ± 0.11	1.65 ± 0.25
m^2	1.29 ± 0.32	1.95 ± 0.45	2.56 ± 0.40
m_2	1.38 ± 0.11	2.06 ± 0.48	2.49 ± 0.51

Source

121 documented and undocumented remains interred between 1729 and 1852 and excavated from the crypt of Christ Church, Spitalfields, London. Age was estimated in undocumented remains using tooth length equations.

Reference

Liversidge, H.M. and Molleson, T. (2004). Variation in crown and root formation and eruption of human deciduous teeth. *American Journal of Physical Anthropology* **123**: 172–180. Reprinted with permission of Wiley-Liss, Inc., a subsidiary of John Wiley & Sons, Inc.

Hurme

Direct Assessment-Gingival Emergence Times		
Averaged Median Ages ± S.E.*		
Tooth	Females	Males
M^1	6.25 ± 0.06	6.43 ± 0.05
M_1	5.98 ± 0.06	6.23 ± 0.06
I^1	7.13 ± 0.05	7.40 ± 0.04
I_1	6.18 ± 0.06	6.44 ± 0.06
I^2	8.11 ± 0.06	8.58 ± 0.06
I_2	7.23 ± 0.05	7.61 ± 0.05

*Values represent a compilation of data on the median age of emergence from multiple sources, those values were then averaged.

Source

Compilation of data from multiple sources representing almost entirely western and northern European ethnic groups.

Reference

Hurme, V.O. (1948). Standards of variation in the eruption of the first six permanent teeth. *Child Development* **19**: 213–231.

Haavikko

Permanent Dentition Eruption Times-Median age in yrs ± SD					
		Males		Females	
Tooth	Stage	Maxillary	Mandibular	Maxillary	Mandibular
I1	alveolar	6.2 ± 0.86	5.9 ± 0.74	6.1 ± 0.35	5.8 ± 0.43
	clinical	6.9 ± 0.86	6.3 ± 0.70	6.7 ± 0.66	6.2 ± 0.55
I2	alveolar	7.3 ± 1.29	6.9 ± 0.78	7.0 ± 0.90	6.5 ± 0.55
	clinical	8.3 ± 1.25	7.3 ± 0.70	7.8 ± 0.86	6.8 ± 0.70
C	alveolar	11.2 ± 1.21	9.8 ± 1.09	9.3 ± 1.25	8.8 ± 0.63
	clinical	12.1 ± 1.41	10.4 ± 1.17	10.6 ± 1.45	9.2 ± 1.06
PM1	alveolar	9.8 ± 1.41	9.6 ± 1.29	9.0 ± 1.09	9.1 ± 0.90
	clinical	10.2 ± 1.41	10.3 ± 1.80	9.6 ± 1.37	9.6 ± 1.48
PM2	alveolar	11.1 ± 1.60	10.3 ± 1.72	9.5 ± 1.37	9.2 ± 1.64
	clinical	11.4 ± 1.48	11.1 ± 1.72	10.2 ± 1.60	10.1 ± 0.67
M1	alveolar	5.3 ± 0.74	5.3 ± 0.35	5.3 ± 0.47	5.0 ± 0.39
	clinical	6.4 ± 0.63	6.3 ± 0.55	6.4 ± 0.55	6.3 ± 0.55
M2	alveolar	11.4 ± 1.09	10.8 ± 1.02	10.3 ± 0.90	9.9 ± 1.06
	clinical	12.8 ± 1.25	12.2 ± 1.41	12.4 ± 1.17	11.4 ± 1.41
M3	alveolar	17.7 ± 1.52	18.1 ± 2.15	17.2 ± 2.46	17.7 ± 2.34

References

Data from Haavikko, K. (1970). The formation and the alveolar and clinical eruption of the permanent teeth. An orthopantographic study. *Proceedings of the Finnish Dental Society* **66**: 101–170.

Table from Liversidge, H.M., Herdeg, B. and Rösing, F.W. (1998). Dental estimation of nonadults. A review of methods and principles. In: *Dental Anthropology, Fundamentals, Limits and Prospects* (K.W. Alt, F.W. Rösing and M. Teschler-Nicola. (Eds.), (pp. 419–442). Vienna: Springer.

Combined Methods

Ubelaker

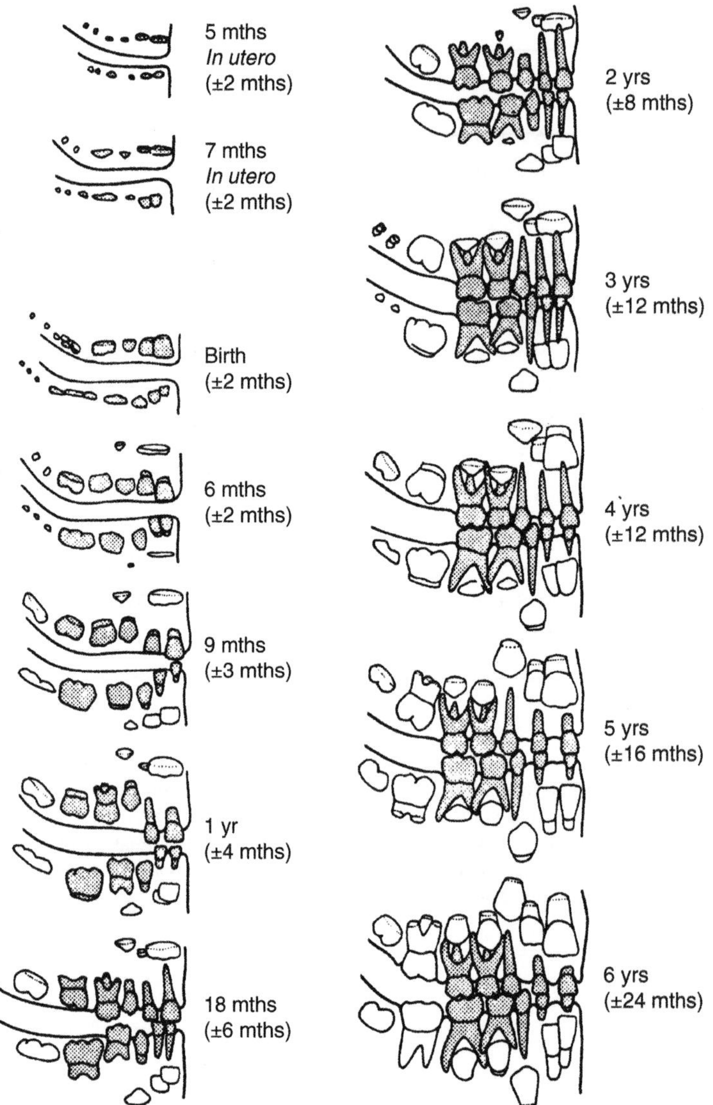

Source

Compilation of data from multiple sources. Data from the "early" end of the published variation was used in preparing the chart to represent suggested earlier development among Native American Indians.

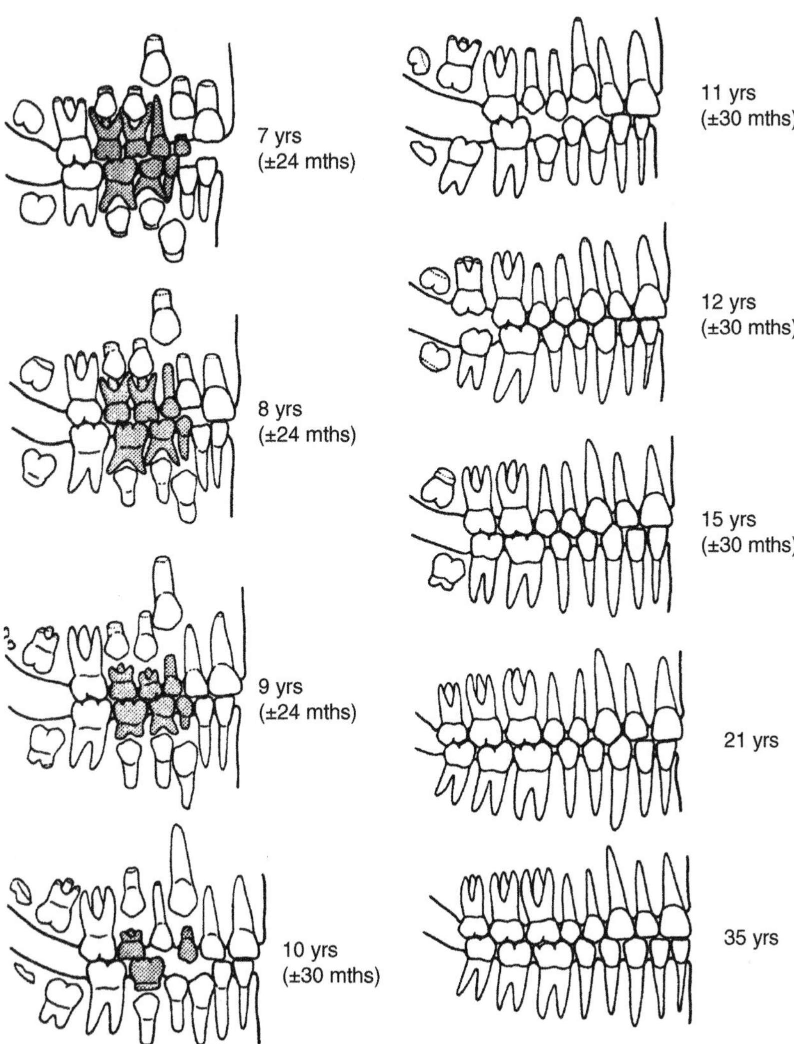

Development of the teeth from 5 months *in utero* to 35 years

Notes

Eruption refers to emergence through the gum, not the alveolar bone.

Reference

Ubelaker, D.H. (1979). *Human Skeletal Remains: Excavation, Analysis and Interpretation.* Washington, DC: Smithsonian Institute Press.

CHAPTER

3

The Vertebral Column

THE TYPICAL VERTEBRAE

Primary Centers

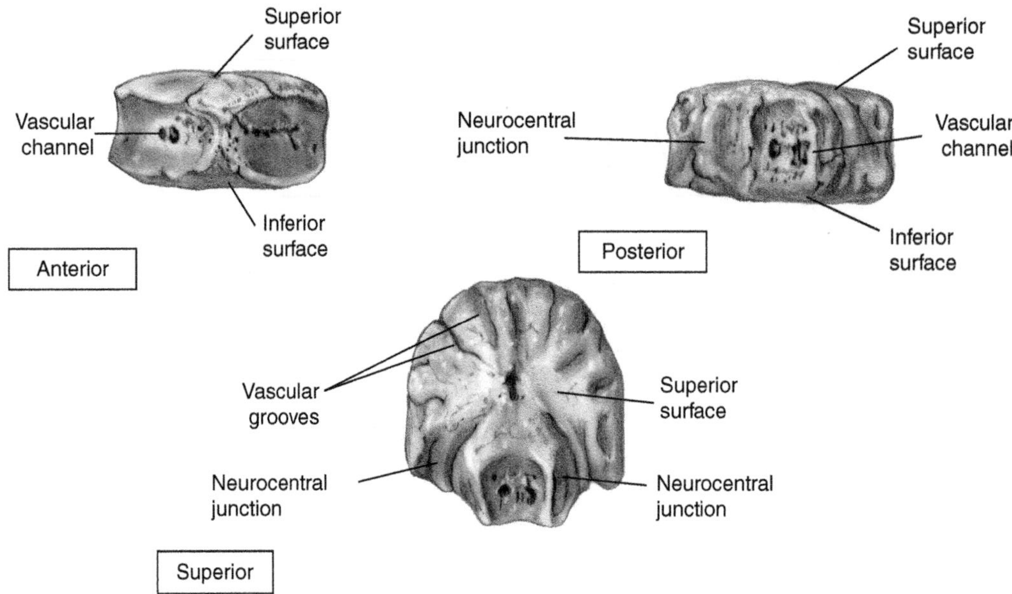

Vertebral centrum (T 8) from a child of approximately 4 years

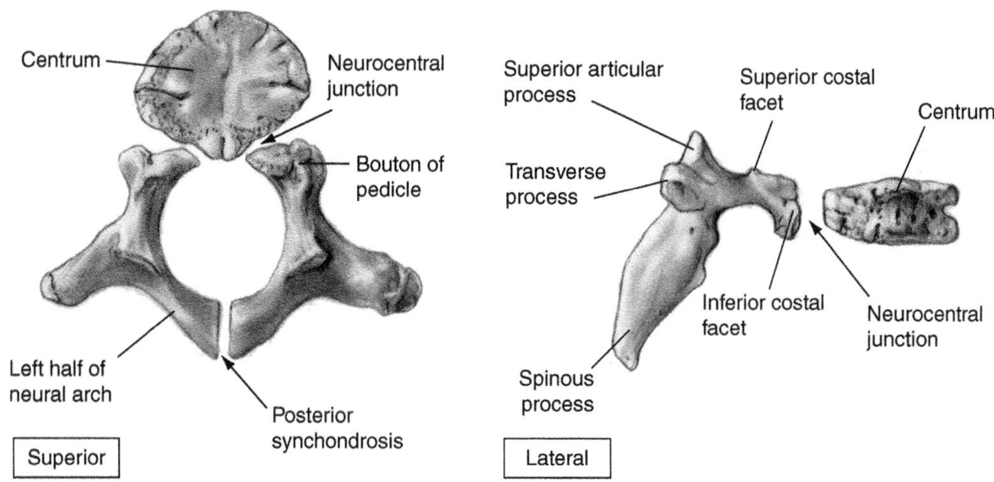

Thoracic vertebra including centrum and half neural arches from a child of approximately 1.5 years

Identification – Typical vertebrae consist of three primary ossification centers: one centrum and two half-neural arches. Centra can be confused with developing sternebrae and half-neural arches may be confused with rib fragments.

- Vascular grooves are present on vertebral centra, and not on sternebrae.
- Vertebral centra are thicker and more regular in shape than the sternebrae.
- Neural arches have metaphyseal edges, whereas a rib fragment will have at least one fractured edge.

Comparison of Typical Vertebrae

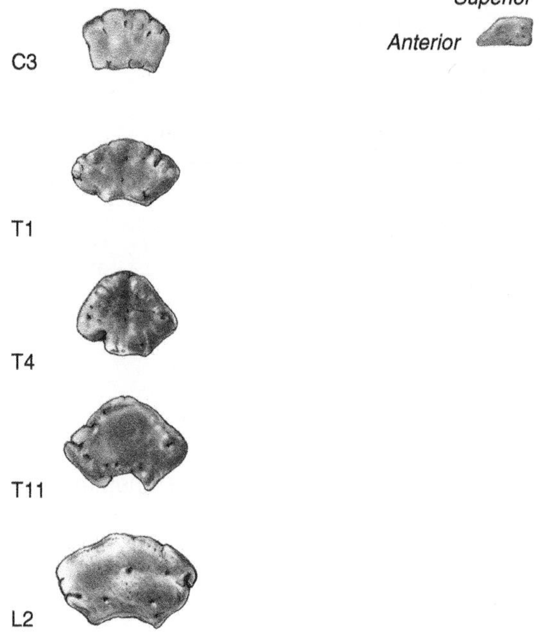

Regional perinatal centra

Interregional Identification of Centra

- The centra increase in size and thickness as the column descends.
- Cervical centra are thin wedge-shaped pieces of bone with pinched anterior borders.
- Thoracic centra will vary in shape, with the first and last few resembling those of cervical and lumbar centra, respectively, and those in the middle assuming more of a triangular outline.
- Lumbar centra are thicker and their transverse diameter far exceeds that of their anteroposterior diameter.

Orientation of Centra

Cervical

- Cervical centra have larger inferior surfaces as their superior surfaces form the downward slope that faces anteriorly.

Thoracic and Lumbar

- Anterior margin is convex; posterior margin is concave.
- Neurocentral junctions are more dorsally located.
- Superior/inferior orientation is not possible.

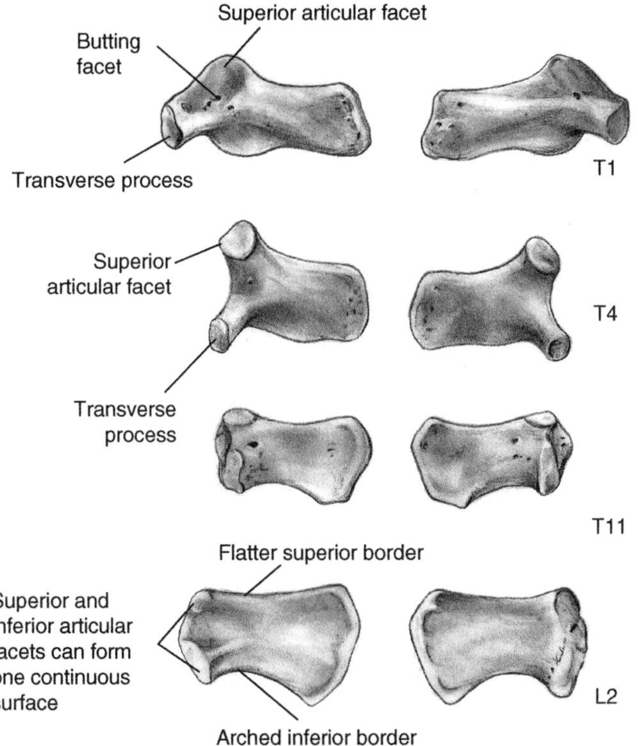

Perinatal thoracic and lumbar neural arches

Interregional Identification of Neural Arches

- Cervical neural arches carry the foramen transversarium.
- Thoracic neural arches have well-defined transverse processes.
- Lumbar neural arches look similar to the blade of an axe; their superior and inferior articular facets merge together to form one continuous surface in the perinate.

Siding Neural Arches

Cervical

- Superior articular facet faces posterolaterally; inferior facet faces anteromedially.
- Lamina is obliquely oriented, sloping infero-laterally.

Thoracic

- The transverse processes generally slope downward.
- The superior articular facets tend to be perched on the superior border, whereas the inferior articular facets are located on the inner aspect of the laminae.

Lumbar

- Inferior border of lamina is arched; superior border is more flat.

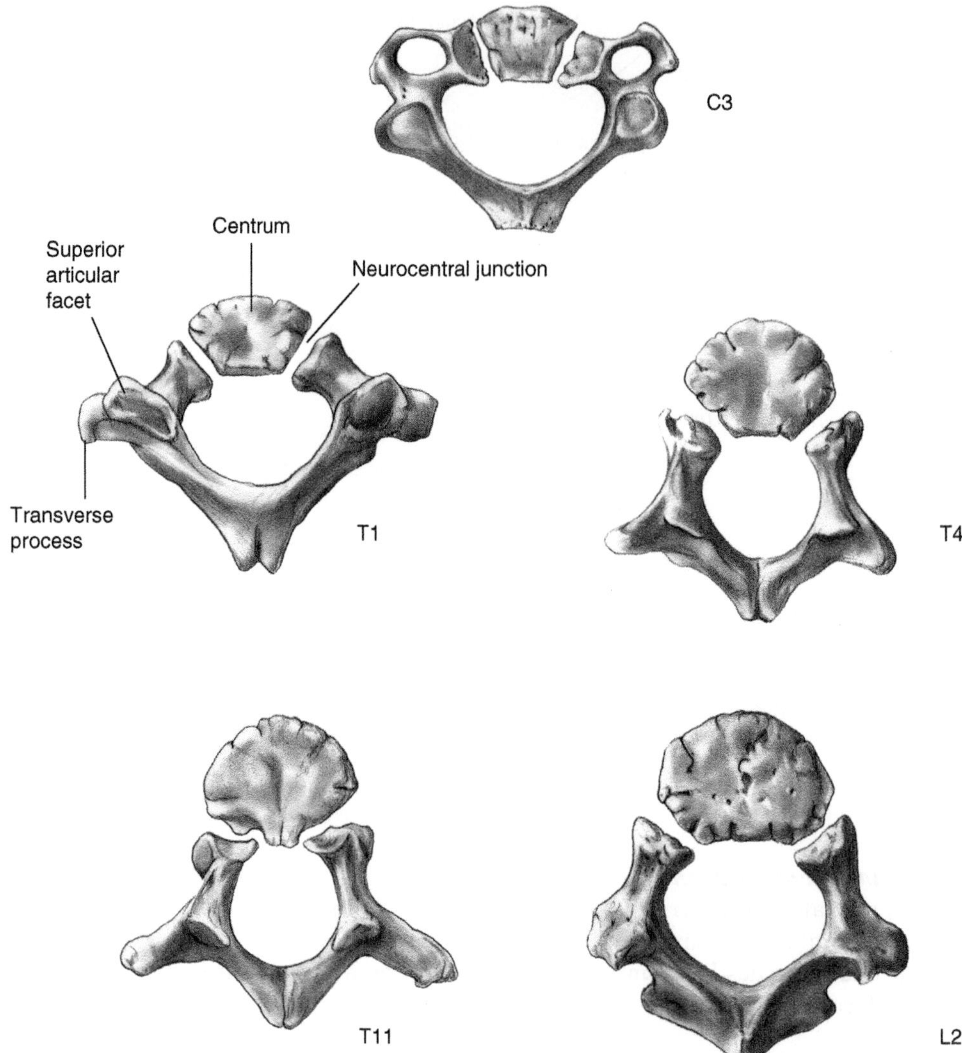

Comparison of two part vertebrae in a 2-3 year old

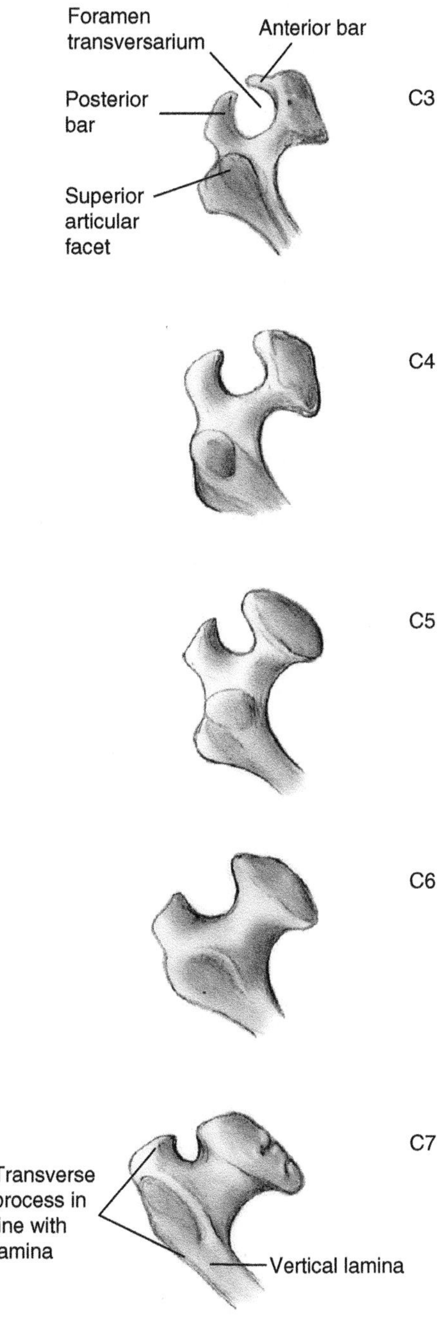

Perinatal cervical neural arches

Intraregional Identification of Neural Arches – Virtually impossible to identify a specific level unless the entire column is present for comparison.

Cervical

- Posterior bar increases in robusticity and becomes more square in shape as the column is descended.
- Laminae of C7 stands almost vertical as in thoracic vertebrae.
- The robust transverse process of C7 is located in line with the lamina.

Thoracic

- T1 displays the longest and most slender lamina.
- T3–10 are roughly T-shaped when viewed from above.
- T11–12 display reduced transverse processes and lamina that are more square in shape.
- T12 displays thoracic-like superior articular facets, whereas the inferior facets take on lumbar morphology; the superior and inferior articular facets remain separated from one another (unlike that of the lumbar arches).

Lumbar

- Cannot detect any defining features.

Secondary Centers

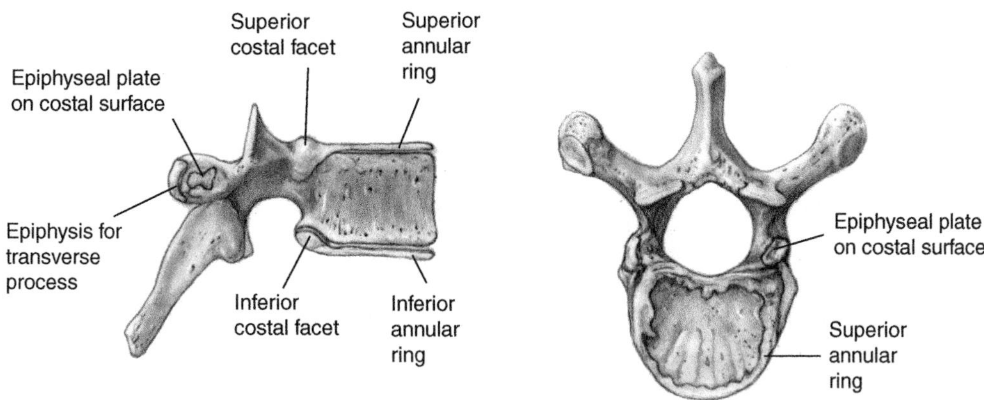

Epiphyses of the annular rings and transverse processes fusing to a thoracic vertebra (female 16-18 yrs)

Identification – Typical cervical, thoracic, and lumbar vertebrae generally possess five epiphyses:

- Two at the tips of the transverse processes (one for each side)
- One spinous process (the bifid cervical vertebrae possess two)
- Two annular rings associated with the superior and inferior surfaces

C1—THE ATLAS

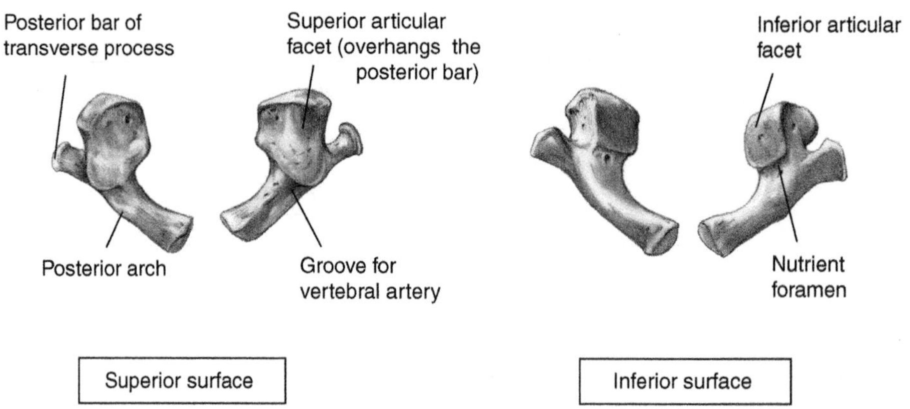

The perinatal atlas

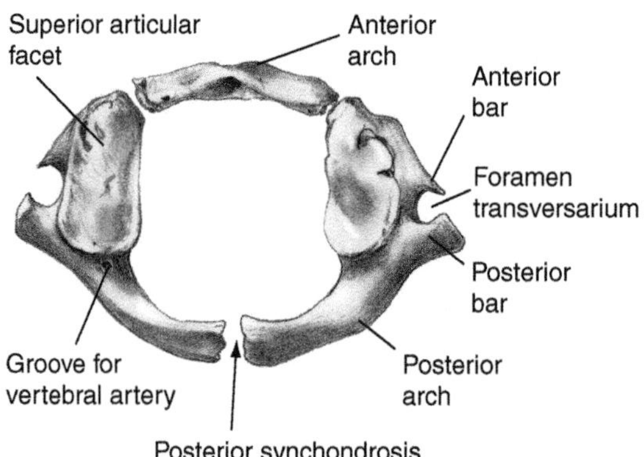

The atlas at 2-3 years

Identification – Usually composed of three primary centers of ossification including one anterior arch and two half-neural arches. The neural components are identifiable in isolation from the fourth prenatal month onward, however, are easily confused with those of the axis. The anterior arch does not ossify until sometime between the first and second year and may be confused with the body of the hyoid bone.

- The body of the hyoid bone displays a more deeply scooped posterior surface.
- The posterior surface of the anterior arch bears the atlanto-axial articulation.
- The posterior bar of the neural arch is bigger in the atlas than in the axis.
- The axis displays posterior arches that are more stout and broad.
- The superior and inferior articular facets of the atlas are positioned directly above and below one another, whereas the inferior articular facet of the axis is positioned more dorsally to that of the superior articular facet.

Siding/Orientation

Anterior Arch

- Anterior surface is slightly convex; posterior surface is slightly concave.
- Downward-projecting tubercle on its anterior surface.
- Smooth articular facet on its posterior surface for articulation with the dens.

Neural Arch

- Superior surface contains the larger and more concave occipital facets.
- Inferior surface contains the smaller and flatter inferior articular facets.
- The superior articular surface overhangs the posterior bar, whereas the inferior articular facet does not.
- A relatively large nutrient foramen can usually be found on the inferior surface at the junction between the limits of the inferior articular facet and the transverse process.
- A groove for the vertebral artery is present behind the superior articular facet.

Secondary Centers

Identification

- Displays two epiphyses at the tips of the transverse processes (one for each side).

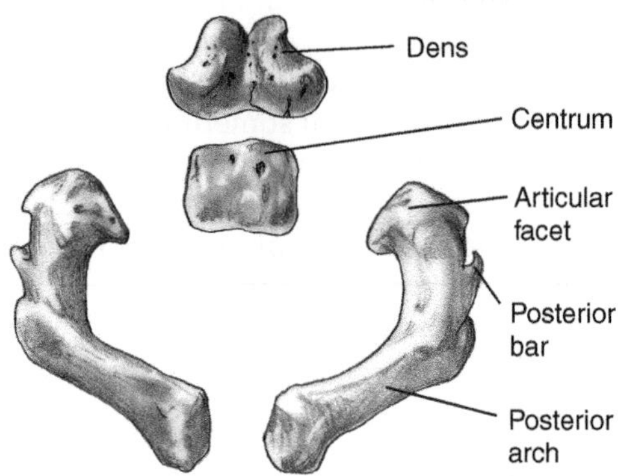

The perinatal axis

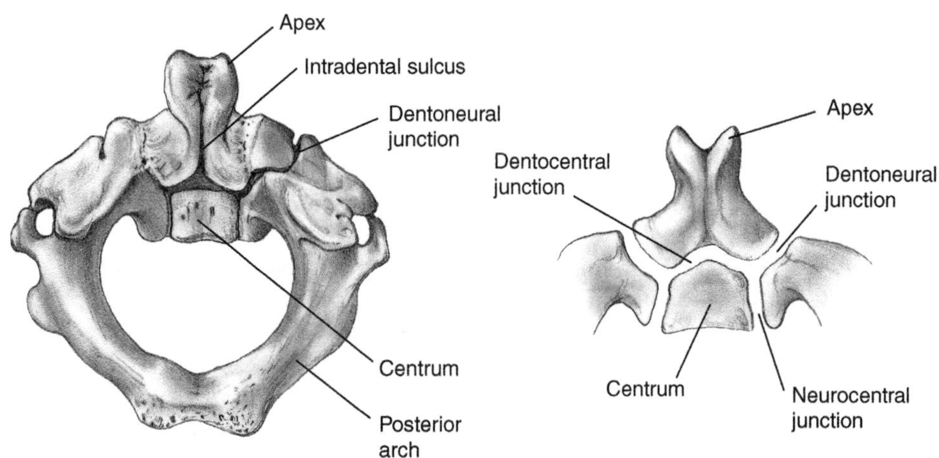

The juvenile axis at 3 years

Identification – Composed of five primary centers of ossification: two half-dens, one centrum, and two half-neural arches. The neural components of the axis are identifiable in isolation from four to five prenatal months, but the centers for the centrum and the dens are clearly recognizable only toward the end of prenatal life.

- Neural arches of the axis are more robust than those of the other cervical arches.
- The inferior articular facet of the axis is positioned more dorsal to that of the superior articular facet. This is unlike the superior and inferior facets of the atlas, which are positioned directly above and below one another.
- The perinatal axis is represented by a very thin posterior bar.
- The centrum of the axis is larger than any of the other cervical centra and is not wedge-shaped.

Orientation

Dens

- The base of the dens is broad and the apex is bifid.
- The intradental sulcus is most obvious on the posterior part of the dens.

Neural Arches

- The neural arch is particularly robust and the superior and inferior articular facets are not in a vertical pillar.
- The posterior bar is located posterior to the superior articular facet and anterior to the inferior articular facet.
- The laminae slope inferolaterally on their outer surface.
- The inferior surface between the inferior articular facet and the articular surface for the centrum is concave.

Centrum

- Orientation is difficult due to its largely square morphology.

Secondary Centers

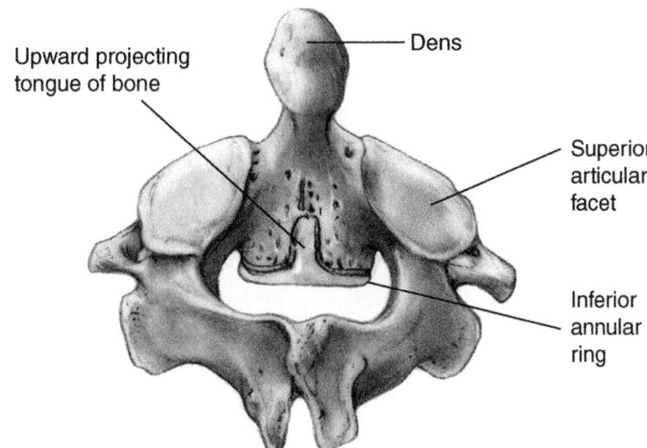

Inferior annular ring fusing to the body of the axis (female 16-18 yrs)

Identification

Displays six epiphyses:

- Two at the tips of the transverse processes (one for each side)
- Two for the bifid spinous process
- One inferior annular ring
- One ossiculum terminale (plug that fills the apical cleft in the dens)

THE SACRUM

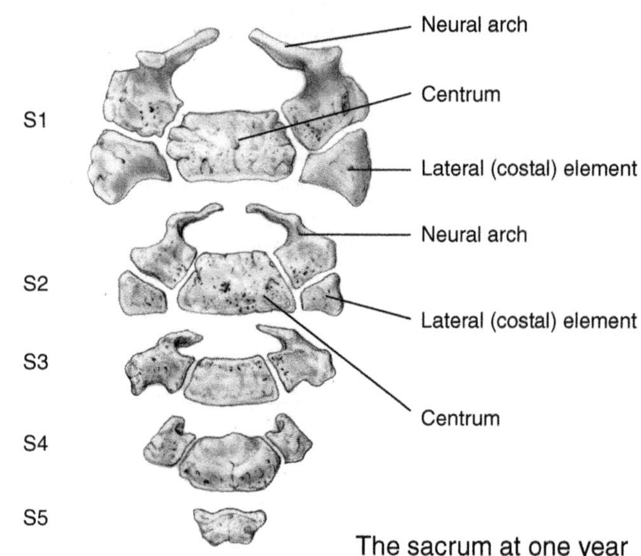

The sacrum at one year

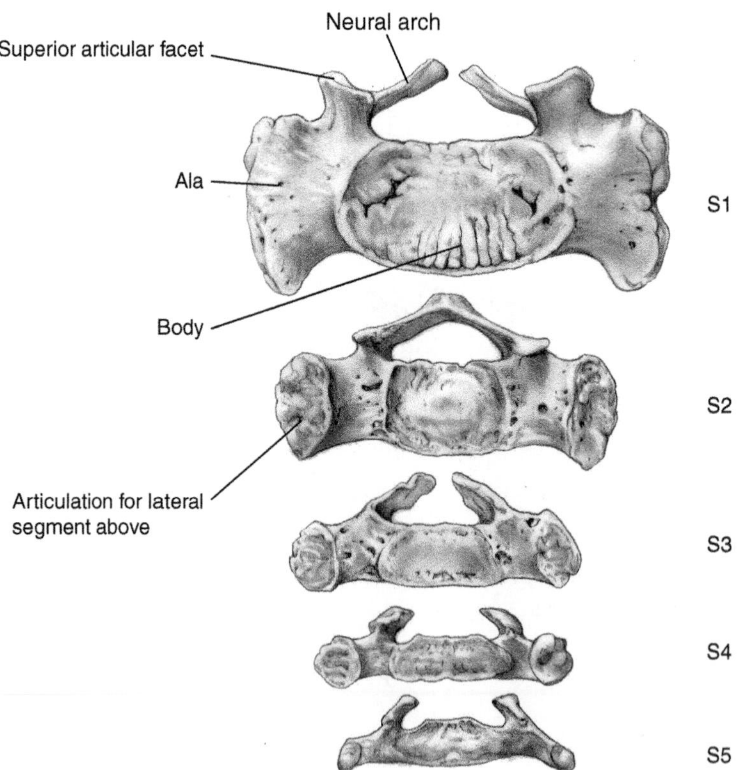

The sacrum at 7-8 years

Identification – Composed of approximately 21 primary elements: five centra, 10 half-neural arches (5 pairs) and six lateral elements (3 pairs).

Neural Arches

- S1 and S2 may be confused with lumbar neural arches in a perinate.
- The inferior articular facets of sacral neural arches are located on the inner surface of the lamina and thus do not form a continuous articular pillar with the superior articular facet as occurs in perinatal lumbar neural arches.
- The sacral neural arches display an articular surface on the inferior aspect of the pedicle that extends anteriorly to connect with the anterior articular surface. As the sacrum develops this surface is displaced laterally and forms the junction site for the lateral element.

Centra

- May be confused with other vertebral centra.
- Sacral centra are more rectangular in shape.

Orientation/Siding

Centra

- The superior metaphyseal surface is larger than the inferior surface and they are wider anteriorly than posteriorly.
- The two flattened surfaces are oriented anterior posteriorly, whereas the billowed surfaces are oriented superior inferiorly. This may seem unnatural in the lower sacral centra as the anterior posterior surfaces are flatter and wider so that the bone naturally lays on one of these two surfaces.
- The upper sacral centra display paired billowed surfaces for articulation with the neural arch posteriorly and the lateral element anteriorly; this becomes more evident during postnatal development.

Neural Arches

- The superior articular facets form bony projections, whereas the inferior articular surfaces are positioned on the inner surface of the laminae.
- Displays two billowed articular surfaces, one for articulation with the lateral element (anteriolateral) and the other with the centrum (anteriomedial)
- Laminae point inferomedially.

Lateral (Costal) Elements

- Pyramidal in shape.
- The anterior surface is concave, forming the identifiable curvature of the sacral alae.
- The inferior surface is concave, forming the upper margin of the sacral foramen. The superior surfaces of 2–3 also form the upper margin of the sacral foramen, however they are much flatter than the inferior surfaces.
- The posterior surface is billowed for articulation with the anterior aspect of the neural element.
- The medial surface (apex of the pyramid) is for articulation with the anterolateral part of centrum.
- The lateral surface forms the articular surface of the sacro-iliac joint.

Secondary Centers

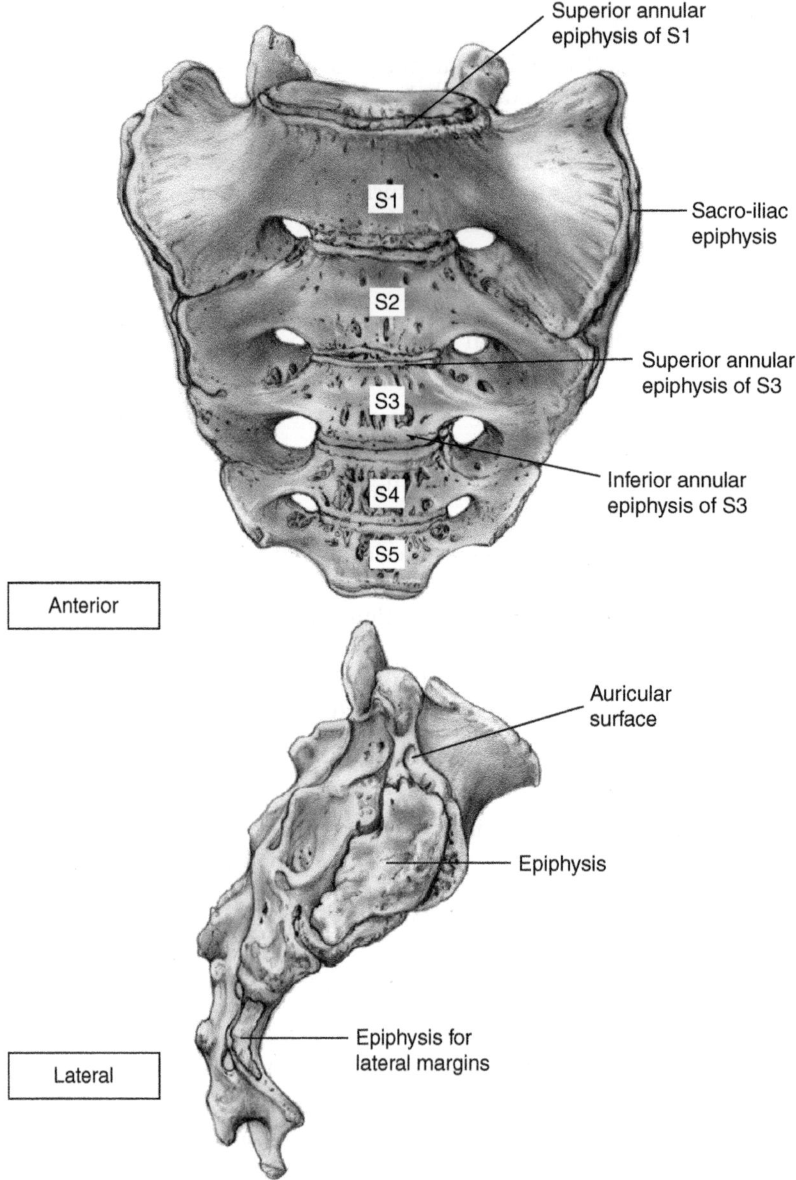

The constant epiphyses of the sacrum (female 16-18 yrs)

Identification – Generally possesses 14 constant secondary centers:

- 10 annular rings for the five sacral bodies (superior and inferior rings for each body)
- Two auricular epiphyses for the sacro-iliac joint (one for each side)
- Two epiphyses for the lateral margins (one for each side)

Metrics

Fazekas and Kósa

Dry Bone Fetal Measurements-Atlas and Axis					
		Max Length- Neural Arches (mm)			
		Atlas		Axis	
Prenatal Age (wks)	*n*	Mean	Range	Mean	Range
16	9	4.2	3.8–5.0	5.0	4.5–5.3
18	15	5.3	4.9–5.9	5.9	5.1–7.0
20	13	6.2	5.5–6.9	7.4	6.8–8.0
22	11	7.0	6.5–7.9	7.7	7.0–8.5
24	12	7.9	6.9–9.1	9.2	8.3–10.2
26	12	8.2	7.0–9.8	9.7	9.0–10.8
28	12	9.0	8.1–9.6	10.3	9.5–11.5
30	12	10.2	9.2–11.0	12.2	11.0–13.0
32	8	11.0	10.5–12.0	13.3	12.5–14.1
34	7	11.4	10.9–12.0	14.7	14.0–15.0
36	5	11.9	11.0–12.4	16.1	15.3–16.5
38	7	13.1	12.0–13.8	17.2	16.3–18.5
40	10	15.0	13.0–16.5	18.2	16.5–20.0

Source

Dry bone measurements on mid twentieth century Hungarian fetal remains from autopsy—males and females combined. Age was estimated based on fetal crown heel length.

Reference

Fazekas, I.Gy. and Kósa, F. (1978). *Forensic Fetal Osteology*. Budapest: Akadémiai Kiadó.

Appearance and Union Times for Primary Centers

Bagnall et al.

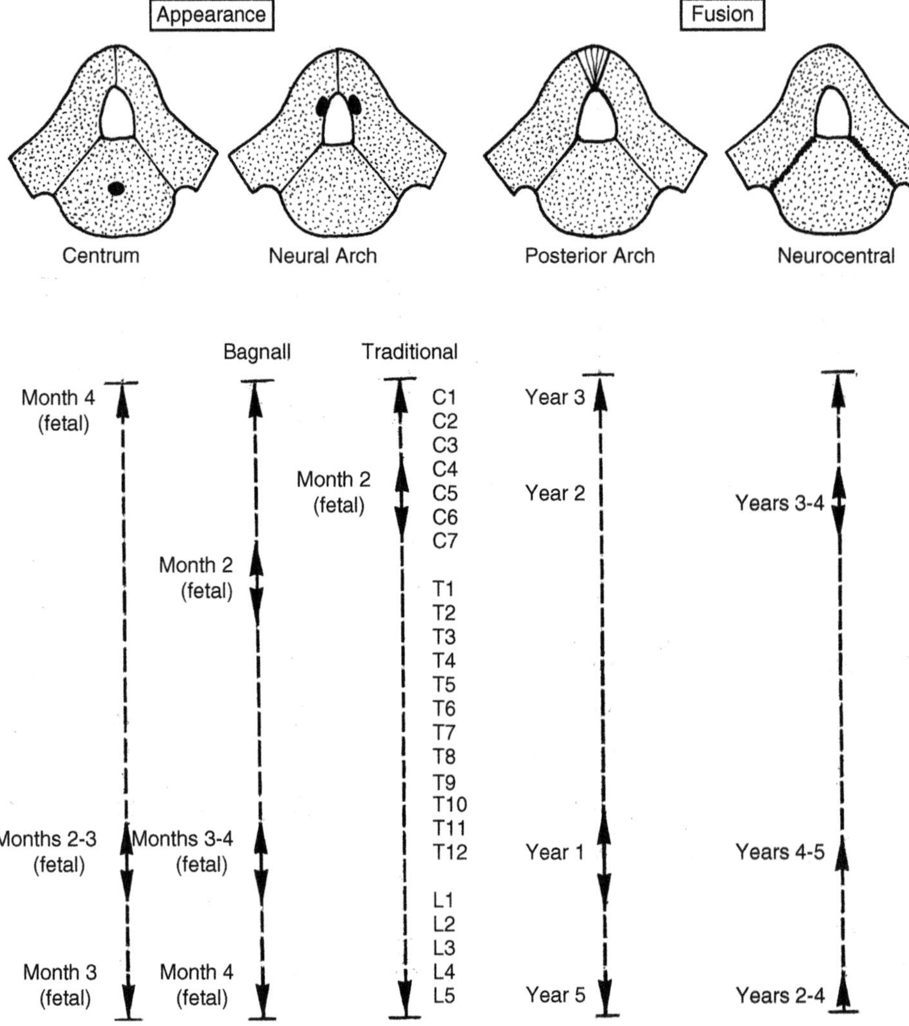

Source

Radiographic assessment of mid twentieth century fetuses obtained from hysterotomies.

Reference

Bagnall, K.M., Harris, P.F., and Jones, P.R.M. (1977). A radiographic study of the human fetal spine. 2. The sequence of development of ossification centers in the vertebral column. *Journal of Anatomy* **124**(3): 791–802.

Epiphyseal Union Times

McKern and Stewart

Dry Bone Assessment-composite rating including general impression of all vertebrae												
	Superior Surface* - % Stage of Union						Vertebral Spines - % Stage of Union					
Age	*n*	**0**	**1**	**2**	**3**	**4**	*n*	**0**	**1**	**2**	**3**	**4**
17–18	54	5	22	37	23	13	52	21	16	20	18	25
19	50		10	30	36	24	51	7	10	15	27	41
20	43		7	14	33	46	42	4	3	7	14	72
21	35			20	27	63	34			11	12	77
22	24			4	8	88	23				4	96
23	26				7	93	26				3	97
24–25	27					100	27					100

*No significant difference in the rate of union between superior and inferior rings.

Notes

Stage 0: Nonunion of epiphysis
Stage 1: ¼ of epiphysis united
Stage 2: ½ of epiphysis united
Stage 3: ¾ of epiphysis united
Stage 4: Complete union of epiphysis

Frequencies Associated with Complete Union of Thoracic Vertebrae T1-T12													
Age	*n*	**1**	**2**	**3**	**4**	**5**	**6**	**7**	**8**	**9**	**10**	**11**	**12**
17–18	54	13	13	13	8	4	4	8	13	13	13	13	13
19	50	24	22	14	6	8	8	22	24	24	24	24	24
20	43	100	86	77	70	68	77	96	100	100	100	100	100
21	35	100	92	83	86	83	89	95	100	100	100	100	100
22	24	100	96	84	67	71	91	96	100	100	100	100	100
23	26	100	97	93	81	85	97	100	100	100	100	100	100
24–25	27	100	100	100	100	100	100	100	100	100	100	100	100

Source

American war dead from Korea (1951–1957)—males only.

Reference

McKern, T.W. and Stewart, T.D. (1957). Skeletal age changes in young American males, analysed from the standpoint of age identification. *Headquarters Quartermaster Research and Development Command, Technical Report*. EP-45. Natick, MA.

Albert and Maples

Dry Bone Assessment-Superior and Inferior Epiphyses of T1-L2						
			% Stages of Union			
Age	**No. of Individuals**	**No. of Epiphyses**	**0**	**1**	**2**	**3**
16 and under	9	232	95	5	0	0
17–18	5	124	6	34	30	30
19–20	8	209	2	17	63	18
21–22	6	143	0	0	78	22
23–24	5	134	0	0	34	66
25–26	7	176	0	0	26	74
27–28	6	164	0	0	74	100
29+	6	163	0	0	0.6	99.4

Source

Mostly late twentieth century American autopsy. Males and females combined.

Notes

Stage 0: Nonunion
Stage 1: Beginning or progressing union; less than 50% union
Stage 2: Almost complete or recent union; more than 50% union
Stage 3: Complete union; obliteration of epiphyseal line (scar may persist)

Reference

Albert, A.M. and Maples, W.R. (1995). Stages of epiphyseal union for thoracic and lumbar vertebral centra as a method of age determination for teenage and young adult skeletons. *Journal of Forensic Sciences* **40**(4): 623–633.

Schaefer

Dry Bone Assessment-Vertebral Rings			
Age Parameters	**Cervical**	**Thoracic**	**Lumbar**
Oldest No Union (1 Vert)	20	21	21
Oldest No Union (all Verts)	19	18	18
Youngest Partial Union (1 Vert)	16	15	14
Oldest Partial Union (1 Vert)	21	23	21
Youngest Complete (1 Vert)	18	20	20
Fusing Range	16–21	15–23	14–21

Source

Bosnian war dead from fall of Srebrenica (1995)—males only.

Notes

Oldest No Union (1 Vert): At least one regional vertebra within the column displays no fusion.
Oldest No Union (all Verts): All regional vertebrae display no union.
Youngest Partial Union (1 Vert): At least one regional vertebra within a column displays partial union while others display no union.
Oldest Partial Union (1 Vert): At least one regional vertebra within a column continues to display partial union while the others display complete union.
Youngest Complete Union (1 Vert): At least one regional vertebra within a column displays complete union.

Reference

Schaefer, M. Unpublished data.

Coqueugnoit and Weaver

Dry Bone Assessment-Sacral Segments						
	Males			Females		
	Open	Partial	Complete	Open	Partial	Complete
Posterior 4–5	≤16	16–27	≥16	≤21	?–28	≥12
Lateral 4–5	–	15–21	≥16	≤19	?–14	≥10
Medial 4–5	≤20	16–27	≥20	≤21	?–23	≥21
Posterior 3–4	≤19	17–20	≥16	≤11	10–19	≥14
Lateral 3–4	≤16	16–21	≥19	≤19	10–21	≥17
Medial 3–4	≤16	16–28	≥20	≤20	12–21	≥19
Posterior 2–3	≤16	16–20	≥16	≤12	10–19	≥11
Lateral 2–3	≤16	16–21	≥19	≤19	11–23	≥20
Medial 2–3	≤16	16–28	≥20	≤20	11–26	≥21
Posterior 1–2	≤27	16–26	≥19	≤19	11–26	≥14
Lateral 1–2	≤20	15–27	≥19	≤19	11–22	≥20
Medial 1–2	≤27	19–?	≥25	≤27	14–?	≥21

Notes

Posterior: Documents the fusion of successive laminae and spinous processes that form the posterior border of the vertebral foramen.

Lateral: Documents the fusion that occurs along the anterior surface of the sacrum, lateral to the sacral foramina, but not including the separate ossification centers for the auricular surfaces and inferior lateral margins.

Medial: Documents the union that occurs on the anterior surface between the bodies of the sacral vertebrae.

Source

Documented Portuguese material born between 1904 and 1938 (Coimbra collection), including 69 females and 68 males between the ages of 7 and 29 years.

Warning

Many ages are poorly represented.

Reference

Coqueugniot, H. and Weaver, T. (2007). Infracranial maturation in the skeletal collection from Coimbra, Portugal: new aging standards for epiphyseal union. *American Journal of Physical* **134**(3): 424–437.

Overall Morphological Summary of the Vertebral Column

Fetal	
Mth 2	Ossification centers appear for lateral masses of C1 and neural arches of C2-T2
Mth 3	Ossification centers appear for centra of C4-S2; neural arches of T3-L2
Mth 4	Ossification centers appear for centra of C2-3 and S3-4; neural arches of L3-5; paired centers for odontoid process
	All primary centers for the presacral vertebrae are present by this age
Mth 5	Ossification centers appear for centrum of S5 and neural arches of S4-5
Mth 6	Ossification centers appear for lateral elements of S1-3 and coastal processes of C7
Mth 7	Intradental fusion
Mth 8	Ossification center for Co1 appears
Birth	All primary centers are present, except the distal coccygeal segments
	Intradental fusion has occurred
Yr 1	Posterior fusion of the laminae commences in the thoracic and lumbar regions
Yr 2	Development of the anterior arch of the atlas
	Ossification commences in ossiculum terminale (tip of the dens)
	Fusion of posterior synchondrosis in C3-7, complete in most thoracic and upper lumbar vertebrae
	Transverse processes starting to develop in lumbar region
	Annular rings may be present
3–4 yrs	Foramen transversarium complete in all cervical vertebrae
	Midline sulcus on posterior surface of dens in process of filling in
	Fusion of posterior synchondrosis of axis and dentoneural synchondrosis
	Neurocentral fusion in C3-7, all thoracic and lumbar vertebrae
	Neurocostal fusion in S1 and S2
	Co2 appears
4–5 yrs	Posterior fusion of the atlas
	Dentocentral fusion commencing in the axis
	Commencement of fusion of neurocostal elements of S1 and S2 to centra
	Laminae unite in L5
5–6 yrs	Neurocentral fusion in the axis
	Axis complete, apart from fusion of ossiculum terminale
	Primary centers fused in all thoracic and lumbar vertebrae
	Primary centers fused in all sacral segments, apart from the region of the posterior synchondrosis
	Anterior arch of atlas fuses

6–8 yrs	Commencing fusion of posterior synchondrosis in sacrum
Yr 10	Continued fusion of posterior synchondrosis in sacral region
	Co3 appears
Yr 12	Dens complete following fusion of ossiculum terminale
	Lateral elements and central regions of the bodies initiate fusion in the lower sacrum
Puberty	All epiphyses appear
	Posterior sacrum is completed
	Co4 appears
Early 20s	Most epiphyses fused and column is virtually complete, except for fusion between bodies of S1 and S2
25+ yrs	Column complete

Morphological Summary C1

At birth	2 parts	Two lateral masses
By yr 2	3 parts	Two lateral masses, anterior arch
4–6 yrs	2 parts	Posterior and anterior arches
6 yrs +	1 part	Fusion of arches

Morphological Summary C2

Late prenatal	5 parts	Two half-neural arches, centrum, two dental centers
Birth	4 parts	Two half-neural arches, centrum, dens
By 3 yrs	4 parts	Neural arch, centrum, dens, ossiculum terminale
3–4 yrs	3 parts	Dentoneural, centrum, ossiculum terminale
By 6 yrs	2 parts	Dentoneurocentral fusion, ossiculum terminale
By 12 yrs	1 part	Fusion of ossiculum terminale
Puberty–early 20s	1 part	Epiphyses appear and fusion completed

Morphological Summary C3-7

Birth	3 parts	Two half neural arches, centrum
By 2 yrs	2 parts	Neural arch, centrum
By 4 yrs	1 part	Neurocentral fusion
Puberty–early 20s	1 part	Epiphyses appear and fusion completed

Morphological Summary T1-T12

Birth	3 parts	Two half neural arches, centrum
By 2 yrs	2 parts	Neural arch, centrum
By 6 yrs	1 part	Neurocentral fusion
Puberty–early 20s	1 part	Epiphyses appear and fusion completed

Morphological Summary L1-L5

Birth	3 parts	Two half-neural arches, centrum
Yrs 1–5	2 parts	Neural fusion (one neural arch*, one centrum)
By yr 5	1 part	Neurocentral fusion
Puberty–early 20s	1 part	Epiphyses appear and fusion complete

*Posterior fusion may not occur in L5.

Morphological Summary Sacrum

Birth	21 parts	All primary centra: S1-S3 in five parts (2 half-neural arches, centrum, 2 lateral elements), S4-S5 in three parts (2 half-neural arches, centrum)
2–6 yrs	5 parts	Elements fuse within each sacral level
12–14 yrs	variable	Lateral elements from different levels fuse, lower sacral segments unite
Puberty	1 part	Epiphyses appear and commence union, lateral and central fusion in a caudocranial direction
25+	1 part	Bodies of S1 and S2 complete fusion along ventral border

CHAPTER

4

The Thorax

THE STERNUM

The Manubrium and Mesosternum

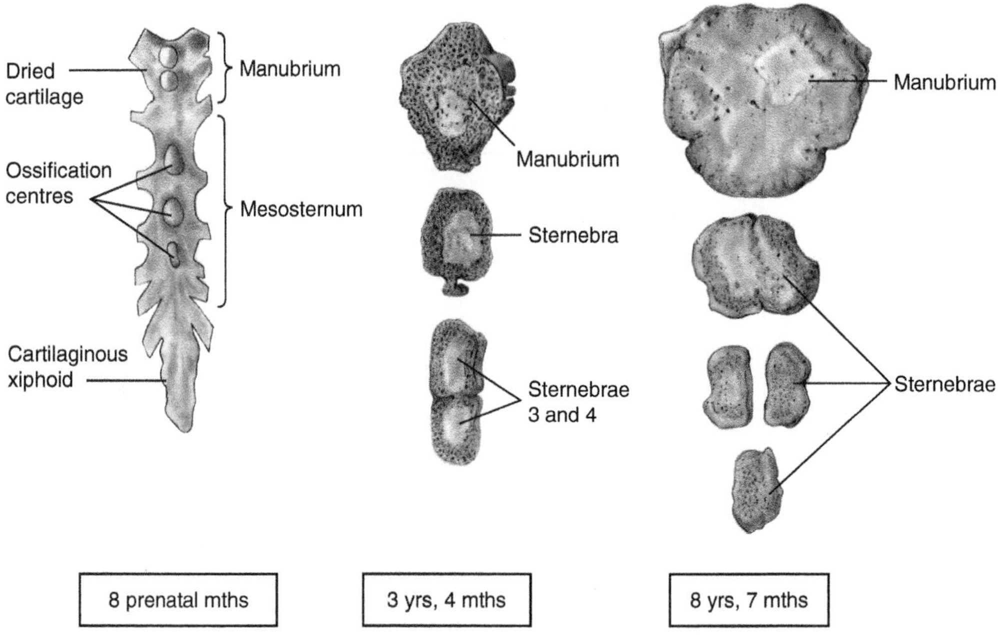

Development of the manubrium and sternum

Identification

- The segments of the sternum can be confused with the pars basilaris of the occipital bone (see page 8).
- Equally they may be confused with the vertebral centra (see page 100), although they tend to be flatter, more irregular in shape and do not show the billowed vascular attributes of the centra.

Orientation

- Reliable orientation of the manubrium is possible by approximately six months *post partum* but does not occur for sternebrae until older than two to three years.

Manubrium

- The bone is flattened in an anteroposterior direction.
- The superior aspect is broader and more robust than the inferior region.
- The superior border is rounded and smooth and may show the concavity of the jugular notch. The inferior border is roughened and more clearly defined as an articular joint.
- The posterior surface is smoother than the anterior surface.
- Vertical facets for articulation with the first costal cartilage can be identified as extending for almost half the length of the bone and tend to be located more toward the superior pole.

Mesosternum

- Positive identification of a specifc sternebra is difficult unless all are present.
- Generally, the more superior the center, the larger it will be.
- The posterior surface is usually flatter than the anterior surface.
- In general, the height of each sternebra exceeds its width.

The Manubrial Flakes

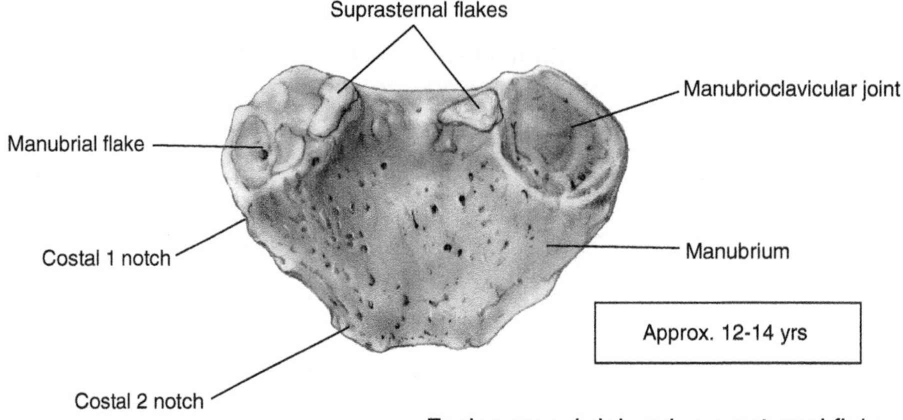

Fusing manubrial and suprasternal flakes

Identification

- Manubrial epiphyses include the suprasternal and articular manubrial flakes, as well as flakes at the first and second costal notches.
- The epiphyses are not identifiable in isolation.

The Mesosternal Flakes

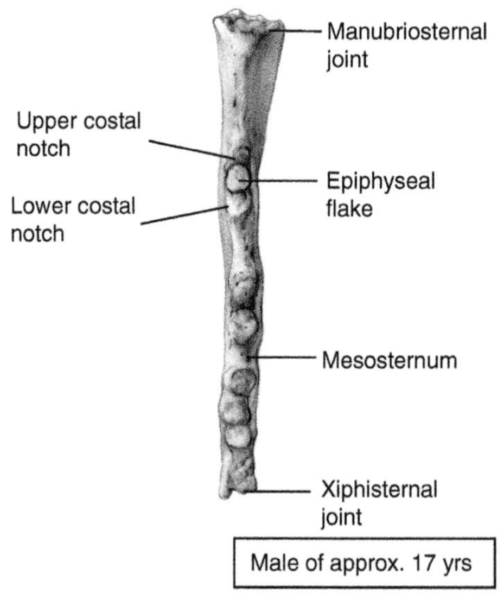

Costal notch flake in the process of fusing

Identification

- The epiphyses are not identifiable in isolation.

Appearance Timings

Odita et al.

Radiographic Assessment-Maunubrium and Sternebrae		
	Absent	**Present**
Manubrium	<35 gw	>30 gw
1st Sternebra	<37 gw	>30 gw
2nd Sternebra	<37 gw	>30 gw
3rd Sternebra	<38 gw	>34 gw
4th Sternebra	–	>37 gw

gw = gestational weeks.

Source

Late twentieth century newborn Nigerian infants—males and females combined.

Reference

Odita, J.C., Okolo, A.A., and Omene, J.A. (1995). Sternal ossification in normal newborn infants. *Pediatric Radiology* **15**: 165–167.

Union Times

Jit and Kaur

Radiographic Assessment-Fusion of Sternebrae 1 and 2										
	Male % - Stage of Union					Female % - Stage of Union				
Age	*n*	0	1	2	3	*n*	0	1	2	3
0--5	5	100	–	–	–	4	100	–	–	–
6-10	14	58	22	22	–	7	100	–	–	–
11-14	24	50	25	25	–	2	100	–	–	–
15-17	23	17	35	26	22	16	50	31	19	–
18-20	61	12	14	20	54	34	71	–	12	17
21-25	152	1	10	17	72	67	6	9	10	75
26-30	118	–	2	4	94	34	–	3	3	94
31-35	101	–	3	7	90	32	–	–	–	100
36+	374	–	1	3	96	45	–	–	–	100

Radiographic Assessment-Fusion of Sternebrae 2 and 3										
	Male % - Stage of Union					Female % - Stage of Union				
Age	*n*	0	1	2	3	*n*	0	1	2	3
0-5	5	60	40	–	–	4	50	50	–	–
6-10	14	57	29	14	–	7	29	71	–	–
11-14	24	21	25	29	25	2	–	–	50	50
15-17	23	13	13	26	48	16	–	19	6	75
18-20	61	3	5	10	82	34	–	3	–	97
21-25	152	–	3	3	94	67	–	2	2	96
26-30	118	–	–	–	100	34	–	–	3	97
31+	475	–	–	–	100	77	–	–	–	100

Radiographic Assessment-Fusion of Sternebrae 3 and 4										
	Male % - Stage of Union					Female % - Stage of Union				
Age	*n*	0	1	2	3	*n*	0	1	2	3
0-5	5	40	60	–	–	4	–	25	75	–
6-10	14	36	21	36	7	7	–	43	14	43
11-14	24	33	13	13	41	2	–	–	50	50
15-17	23	–	–	–	100	16	–	–	–	100
18+	806	–	–	–	100	212	–	–	–	100

Notes

Stage 0: Nonfusion
Stage 1: Less than ½ fusion
Stage 2: More than ½ fusion
Stage 3: Complete fusion

Source

Radiographs of mid to late twentieth century Punjabi Indians taken during autopsy.

Reference

Jit, I., and Kaur, H. (1989). Time of fusion of the human sternebrae with one another in Northwest India. *American Journal of Physical Anthropology* **80**: 195–202.

Schaefer

Dry Bone Assessment-Male %								
	Sternebrae 1-2 - Stages of Union				Sternebrae 2-3 - Stages of Union			
Yrs	*n*	0	1	2	*n*	0	1	2
14	2	100	–	–	2	100	–	–
15	2	100	–	–	2	100	–	–
16	4	100	–	–	5	40	40	20
17	5	80	20	–	4	50	–	50
18	10	80	10	10	10	20	20	60
19	9	56	11	33	10	10	20	70
20	7	14	14	72	8	–	25	75
21	4	–	–	100	5	–	–	100
22	5	–	–	100	5	–	–	100
23	8	12	–	88	8	–	–	100
24	4	–	–	100	4	–	–	100
25	8	–	–	100	8	–	–	100
26	6	–	17	83	6	–	–	100
27	6	–	–	100	6	–	–	100
28+	16	–	–	100	16	–	–	100

Notes

Stage 0: Nonunion
Stage 1: Partial Union
Stage 2: Complete union marked by obliteration of the epiphyseal line (scar may be present)

Dry Bone Assement-Manubrial Centers-Male %								
	Suprasternal Flake - Stages of Union				Manubrial Flake - Stages of Union			
Yrs	*n*	0	1	2	*n*	0	1	2
14	2	100	–	–	2	100	–	–
15	1	100	–	–	1	100	–	–
16	7	86	–	14	7	86	14.3	–
17	5	–	20	80	5	–	20	80
18	8	–	63	38	5	–	40	60
19	10	–	20	80	10	–	20	80
20	8	–	25	75	8	–	25	75
21	6	–	–	100	5	–	–	100
22	5	–	–	100	45	–	–	100
23+	45	–	–	100	45	–	–	100

Notes

Stage 0: Immature surface
Stage 1: Flake present
Stage 2: Mature surface

Source

Bosnian war dead from the fall of Srebrenica (1995)—males only. Age reflects those individuals half a year above and half a year below (e.g., age 18 = 17.5–18.5).

Reference

Schaefer, M. (2008). A summary of epiphyseal union timings in Bosnian males. *International Journal of Osteoarchaeology* DOI: 10.1002/oa.959. Copyright John Wiley & Sons Limited. Reproduced with permission.

McKern and Stewart

Dry Bone Assessment-Sternebrae 1-2						
		Male % - Stage of Union				
Yrs	*n*	**0**	**1**	**2**	**3**	**4**
17-18	46	45.6	2.2	13.0	34.8	4.3
19	43	27.9	–	13.9	51.2	7.0
20	38	13.2	5.3	7.9	52.6	21.0
21	38	13.2	–	7.9	52.6	26.3
22	23	8.7	–	4.3	56.5	30.4
23	24	16.7	–	–	58.3	25.0
24-25	24	–	–	4.2	41.7	54.2
26-27	25	12.0	–	–	36.0	52.0
28-30	29	3.4	–	–	37.9	58.6

Dry Bone Assessment-Sternebrae 2-3						
		Male % - Stage of Union				
Yrs	*n*	**0**	**1**	**2**	**3**	**4**
17-18	44	9.1	9.1	9.1	68.2	4.5
19	42	11.9	–	4.8	69.0	14.3
20	36	5.6	–	–	55.6	38.9
21	37	8.1	2.7	2.7	48.6	37.8
22	22	4.5	–	–	45.4	50.0
23	24	–	–	–	50.0	50.0
24-25	24	–	–	–	8.3	91.7
26-27	–	–	–	–	–	–
28-30	–	–	–	–	–	–

Notes

Stage 0: Nonunion of epiphysis
Stage 1: ¼ of epiphysis united
Stage 2: ½ of epiphysis united
Stage 3: ¾ of epiphysis united
Stage 4: Complete union of epiphysis

Source

American war dead from Korea (1951–1957)—males only.

Dry Bone Assessment-Clavicular Notch				
Male % - Stage of Union				
Yrs	*n*	0	1	2
17	9	33.3	–	66.7
18	35	2.8	5.7	91.4
19	43	–	9.3	90.7
20	42	–	4.8	95.2
21	36	–	2.8	97.2
22	19	–	5.3	94.7
23	23	–	–	100.0

Notes

Stage 0: Epiphysis ununited
Stage 1: Epiphysis uniting
Stage 2: Surface essentially mature

Dry Bone Assessment-Costal Notch 1				
Male % Maturity Stage				
Yrs	*n*	0	1	2
17	5	100.0	–	–
18	21	81.0	19.0	–
19	28	57.1	42.8	–
20	25	44.0	56.0	–
21	24	33.3	37.5	29.2
22	17	17.6	47.0	35.3
23	15	13.3	33.3	53.3
24	9	–	55.6	44.4
25	9	–	11.1	88.9
26	13	–	–	100.0

Notes

Stage 0: Obviously immature
Stage 1: Traces of immaturity
Stage 2: No signs of immaturity

Reference

McKern, T.W. and Stewart, T.D. (1957). Skeletal age changes in young American males, analysed from the standpoint of age identification. *Headquarters Quartermaster Research and Development Command, Technical Report EP-45*. Natick, MA.

Morphological Summary

Prenatal	
Mth 5	Primary center develops for the manubrium
Mths 5–6	Primary center develops for first sternebra
Mth 7–8	Primary centers develop for sternebrae 2 and 3
Birth	The sternum is represented by at least four centers of ossification
Yr 1	Primary center develops for sternebra 4
Yrs 3–6	Ossification can commence in the xiphoid
Yrs 4–15	Sternebrae 3 and 4 fuse
Yrs 11–20	Sternebra 2 fuses to 3 and 4
	Epiphyses appear and commence fusion
Yrs 15–25	Sternebra 1 fuses to rest of mesosternum
	Epiphyses continue to fuse
21+ yrs	Sternum essentially complete, although lines of fusion may persist and anomalous nonunion may be observed
25+ yrs	All epiphyseal plaques in costal notches have fused
40+ yrs	Xiphoid process commences fusion to mesosternum

Warning: Appearance and union times of the sternebrae are highly variable.

THE RIBS

Primary Centers

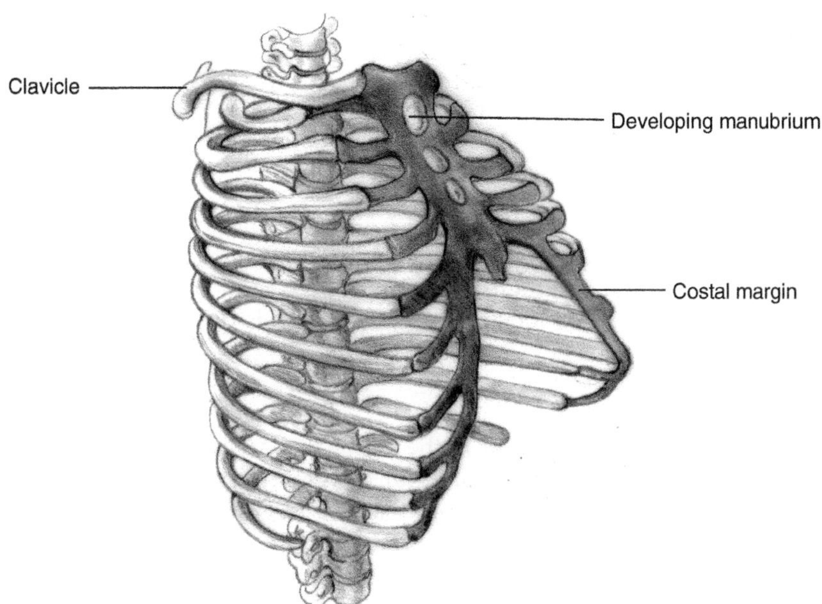

Perinatal thoracic skeleton

Identification – Confusion is not likely but fragments may be misidentified as unfused vertebral arches. Rib fragments will display fractured edges in comparison to the immature edges of unfused vertebral arches.

Fetal and perinatal

- **Rib 1** has the same morphology as the adult.
- **Ribs 2–3** are hooked; this begins to straighten by rib 4 as the shaft takes on a more gentle curve.
- **Ribs 2–6** heads are generally in contact with horizontal plane when placed in the correct orientation.
- **Ribs 7–9** heads rise above the horizontal plane, with rib 7 or 8 showing the greatest elevation.
- **Ribs 10–12** lack definition in the region of the head and are smaller in size.
- **Rib 10** The head and shaft usually lie in contact with the horizontal plane.
- **Ribs 11–12** are markedly more rudimentary in terms of their development.

Young child

- As the thorax descends, the ribs show more torsion.
- The heads of ribs 5 and 6 start to rise from the horizontal plane within the first year so that by the third year, ribs 3 through 9 show significant torsion and head elevation.

Siding/Orientation

First rib

- The superior surface of rib 1 carries grooves for the subclavian vessels.
- When placed on a horizontal surface, if the head of the rib is in contact with the surface then it is in correct superior/inferior orientation.

Typical ribs

- The head is posterior, the cup-shaped costochondral junction is anterior, the inner surface is concave and the outer surface is convex.
- The inferior border carries the subcostal groove, which is deeper posteriorly and more shallow anteriorly.

Floating ribs

- The shaft of rib 11 increases in height in the region just anterior to the posterior angle by an addition of a ledge of bone on the inferior margin.
- The superior border of rib 12 faces more outward, whereas the inferior border faces more inward, thus, when looking at the outer surface, the superior border will overhang the inferior border.

The Epiphyses of the Head and Tubercle

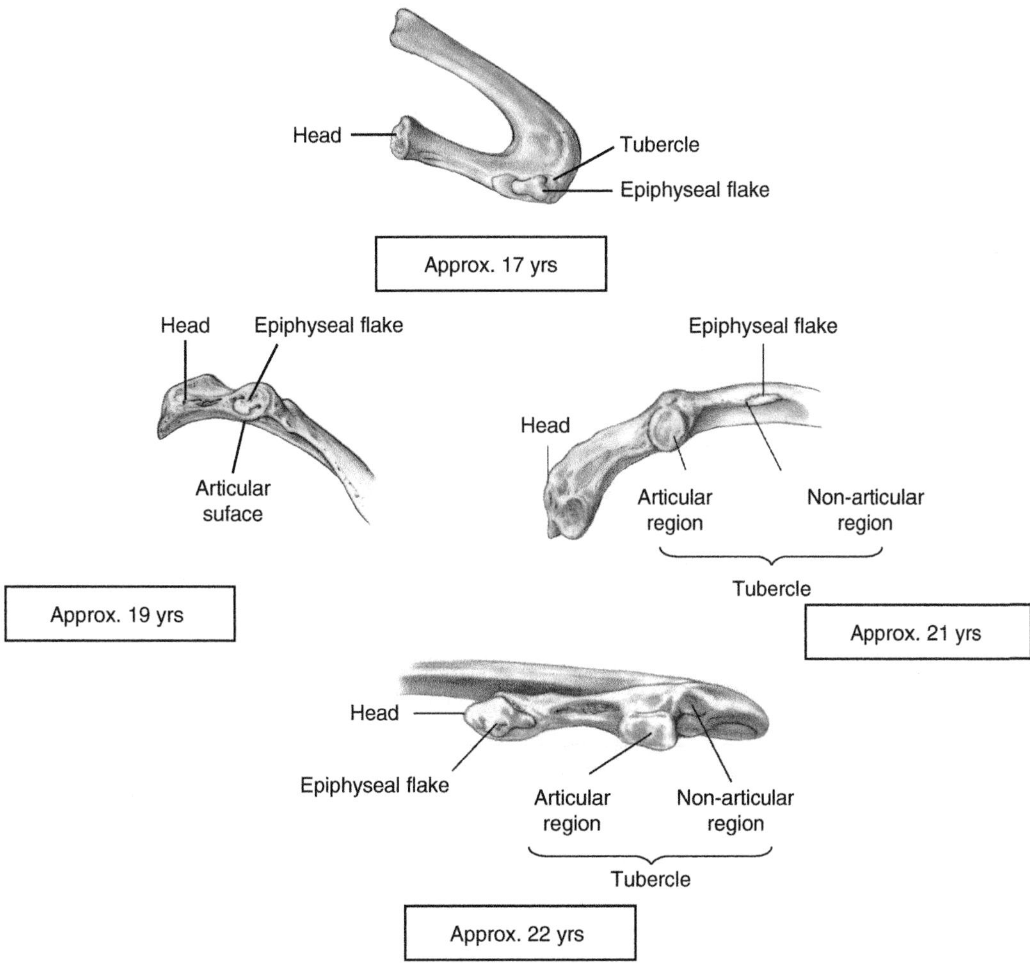

Epiphyseal flakes on the head, articular and non-articular regions of the ribs

Identification

- The epiphyses are not identifiable in isolation.
- **Rib 1** the epiphysis at the nonarticular aspect frequently extends posteriorly also to cover the articular aspect of the tubercle. There is a separate epiphysis for the head.
- **Ribs 2–9** (and sometimes 10) contain epiphyses at the head, and the articular and nonarticular aspects of the tubercle.
- **Ribs 11–12** contain only an epiphysis at the head.

Metrics

Fazekas and Kósa

Dry Bone Fetal Measurements-First Rib			
Prenatal Age (wks)	*n*	Max length (mm) Mean	Max length (mm) Range
14	3	4.2	4.0–4.5
16	9	7.1	6.0–8.7
18	15	9.2	8.0–10.5
20	13	11.6	10.5–14.0
22	11	12.4	10.5–13.5
24	12	14.0	12.0–17.0
26	12	15.3	14.2–17.5
28	12	16.0	13.5–17.3
30	12	16.7	14.6–19.5
32	8	17.7	16.5–19.0
34	7	19.1	16.0-19.5
36	5	20.4	20.0–21.5
38	7	22.1	20.0–23.0
40	10	24.0	22.0–26.0

Source

Dry bone measurements on mid twentieth century Hungarian fetal remains from autopsy—males and females combined. Age was estimated based on fetal crown heel length.

Reference

Fazekas, I.Gy. and Kósa, F. (1978). *Forensic Fetal Osteology*. Budapest: Akadémiai Kiadó.

Morphological Summary

Prenatal	
Wks 8–9	Ossification centers appear for ribs 5-7
Wks 11–12	Ossification centers present in all ribs
Birth	All primary ossification centers present
Yrs 12–14	Epiphyses appear in nonarticular region of the tubercle
Around yr 18	Epiphyses appear for articular region of the tubercle
Yrs 17–25	Epiphyses appear and fuse for head region
21+ yrs	Ossification may be present in the costal cartilages
25+ yrs	Ribs are fully adult

CHAPTER

5

The Pectoral Girdle

THE CLAVICLE

Primary Center

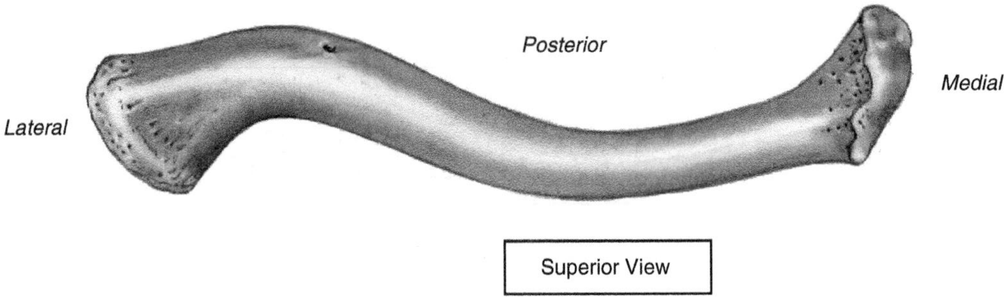

Right perinatal clavicle

Identification – Fragments of the shaft can be confused with those of other long bones although its smaller diameter and the lack of a medullary cavity within the clavicle should prevent confusion. Fragments of the lateral end can be confused with rib fragments or the acromion process.

- Lateral clavicular fragments will display the conoid tubercle.
- Lateral clavicular fragments will not present the same billowy metaphyseal surface as the acromion process.
- Clavicular fragments are more robust, rounded, and have a thicker cortex than rib fragments.

Siding

- Follows the same principles as for the adult.
- The inferior surface is roughened by the conoid tubercle, trapezoid line, and costal facet.
- The lateral end is flattened, whereas the medial end is rounded.
- An anterior medial curvature is followed by a posterior lateral curvature.

The Medial Epiphysis

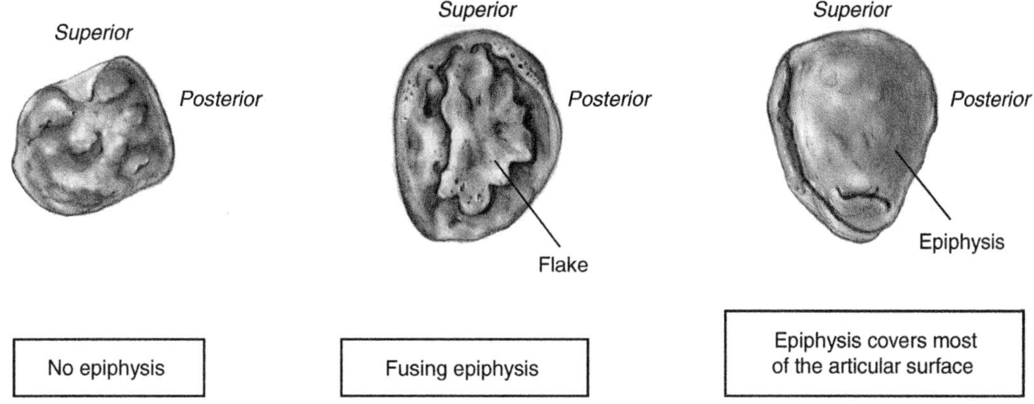

Epiphyseal union at the medial end of a right clavicle

Identification – Unlikely ever to be recognized as a separate center of ossification.

Shaft Metrics

Fazekas and Kósa

Dry Bone Fetal Measurements-Clavicle			
Prenatal Age (wks)	Max Length (mm)		
	n	Mean	Range
12	2	8.2	7.5–9.0
14	3	11.1	10.3–11.5
16	9	16.3	14.3–17.7
18	15	19.4	17.0–21.0
20	13	22.7	21.0–25.5
22	11	24.5	23.0–26.0
24	12	26.9	26.0–30.0
26	12	28.3	27.0–30.1
28	12	30.3	29.0–31.6
30	12	31.3	30.0–33.0
32	8	35.6	34.0–37.3
34	7	37.1	35.6–38.0
36	5	37.7	37.0–39.5
38	7	42.6	38.7–45.0
40	10	44.1	42.0–45.6

Source

Dry bone measurements on mid twentieth century Hungarian fetal remains from autopsy—males and females combined. Age was estimated based on fetal crown heel length.

Reference

Fazekas, I.Gy. and Kósa, F. (1978). *Forensic Fetal Osteology*. Budapest: Akadémiai Kiadó.

Sherer et al.

Sonogram Fetal Measurements-Clavicle				
		Max Length (mm)		
Prenatal Age (wks)	*n*	5th Centile	50th Centile	95th Centile
14	9	9.8	11.0	12.2
15	20	11.9	13.3	14.6
16	14	13.9	15.4	16.9
17	18	15.7	17.3	19.0
18	14	17.4	19.2	21.0
19	24	19.1	21.0	22.9
20	92	20.6	22.7	24.7
21	81	22.1	24.3	26.5
22	52	23.4	25.8	28.1
23	37	24.8	27.2	29.7
24	15	26.0	28.6	31.2
25	16	27.2	30.0	32.7
26	13	28.4	31.2	34.1
27	10	29.5	32.5	35.5
28	20	30.5	33.7	36.8
29	11	31.5	34.8	38.1
30	14	32.5	35.9	39.3
31	18	33.4	37.0	40.6
32	24	34.3	38.0	41.6
33	16	35.2	39.0	42.9
34	18	36.0	40.0	44.0
35	20	36.8	41.0	45.1
36	21	37.6	41.9	46.1
37	18	38.4	42.8	47.2
38	13	39.1	43.7	48.2
39	5	39.8	44.5	49.2
40	8	40.5	45.3	50.1
41	1	41.2	46.1	51.1
42	1	41.9	46.9	52.0

Source

Sonograms on twenty-first century American patients—males and females combined.

Notes

Authors propose that their measurements replace those of Yarkoni et al. (1978) as a result of the resolution improvements in modern ultrasound equipment.

Reference

Sherer, D., Sokolovski, M., Dalloul, M., Khoury-Collado, F., Osho, J., Lamarque, M., and Abulafia, O. (2006). Fetal clavicle length throughout gestation: A nomogram. *Ultrasound in Obstetrics and Gynecology* **27**: 306–310 © Copyright 2006 International Society of Ultrasound in Obstetrics & Gynecology. Reproduced with permission. Permission is granted by John Wiley & Sons Ltd on behalf of ISUOG.

Black and Scheuer

Dry Bone Postnatal Measurements-Clavicle

		Max Length (mm)	
Post-Natal Age	*n*	**Mean**	**Range**
0-6 mths	11	44.4	38.8–54.5
7-12 mths	9	54.1	48.0–60.9
12-18 mths	11	59.5	54.3–66.0
19-24 mths	4	63.0	61.4–64.6
2-3 yrs	13	66.5	58.5–72.6
3-4 yrs	7	73.4	69.1–77.0
4-5 yrs	8	74.4	65.3–82.0
5-6 yrs	2	75.9	74.7–77.0
6-7 yrs	4	86.5	85.4–88.8
7-8 yrs	1	89.5	–
8-9 yrs	3	89.0	78.5–98.7
9-10 yrs	0	–	–
10-11 yrs	2	103.7	103.0–104.4
11-12 yrs	2	105.0	104.5–105.0
12-13 yrs	3	106.4	102.5–111.3
13-14 yrs	2	118.6	117.0–120.1
14-15 yrs	2	118.5	113.5–123.5
15-16 yrs	3	137.7	127.0–154.0

Source

Nineteenth century English (Spitalfields, St. Bride's, and St. Barnabas) and twentieth century Portuguese (Lisbon collection) documented remains—males and females combined.

Reference

Black, S.M. and Scheuer, J.L. (1996). Age changes in the clavicle: From the early neonatal period to skeletal maturity. *International Journal of Osteoarchaeology* **6**: 425–434. Copyright John Wiley & Sons Limited. Reproduced with permission.

Appearance and Union Times

Webb and Suchey

Dry Bone Assessment-Medial Clavicle										
	Males % - Stage of Union					Females % - Stage of Union				
Age	*n*	1	2	3	4	*n*	1	2	3	4
14	6	100	–	–	–	4	100	–	–	–
15	12	100	–	–	–	9	100	–	–	–
16	24	96	4	–	–	5	100	–	–	–
17	21	82	9	9	–	7	58	14	28	–
18	32	56	16	28	–	14	21	29	50	–
19	29	41	18	41	–	11	46	18	36	–
20	12	26	17	57	–	15	7	13	80	–
21	30	10	7	80	3	9	11	–	78	11
22	39	5	–	10	85	14	–	–	86	14
23	29	3	–	83	14	12	8	–	75	17
24	25	4	–	60	36	16	–	–	50	50
25	36	–	–	42	58	5	–	–	20	80
26	17	–	–	47	53	14	–	–	29	71
27	30	–	–	27	73	9	–	–	44	56
28	20	–	–	15	85	18	–	–	6	94
29	20	–	–	5	95	10	–	–	–	100
30	28	–	–	4	96	11	–	–	18	82

Notes

Stage 1: Nonunion without epiphysis
Stage 2: Nonunion with separate epiphysis
Stage 3: Partial union
Stage 4: Complete union

Source

Multiracial American autopsy sample collected between 1977 and 1979.

Reference

Webb, P.A.O. and Suchey, J.M. (1985). Epiphyseal union of the anterior iliac crest and medial clavicle in a modern sample of American males and females. *American Journal of Physical Anthropology* **68**: 457–466.

Schaefer

Dry Bone Assessment-Medial Clavicle				
Male % - Stage of Union				
Age	*n*	0	1	2
14	3	100	–	–
15	6	100	–	–
16	13	100	–	–
17	20	95	5	–
18	22	82	18	–
19	18	55	45	–
20	21	57	43	–
21	22	27	68	5
22	11	18	73	9
23	12	16	67	17
24	16	–	56	44
25	17	–	59	41
26	12	–	50	50
27	11	–	18	82
28	13	–	46	54
29	9	–	11	89
30	7	–	–	100

Notes

Stage 0: Nonunion
Stage 1: Partial Union
Stage 2: Complete union marked by obliteration of the epiphyseal line (scar may be present)

Source

Bosnian war dead from the fall of Srebrenica (1995)—males only. Age reflects those individuals half a year above and half a year below (e.g., age 18 = 17.5–18.5).

Reference

Schaefer, M. (2008). A summary of epiphyseal union timings in Bosnian males. *International Journal of Osteoarchaeology*. DOI: 10.1002/oa.959. Copyright. John Wiley & Sons Limited. Reproduced with permission.

McKern and Stewart

Dry Bone Assessment-Medial Clavicle						
		Male % - Stage of Union				
Age	*n*	**0**	**1**	**2**	**3**	**4**
17	10	–	–	–	–	–
18	45	86	12	2	–	–
19	52	73	21	4	–	–
20	45	56	35	7	2	–
21	37	47	32	13	8	–
22	24	1	33	37	29	–
23	26	–	8	43	40	9
24/25	27	–	3	10	52	37
26/27	25	–	–	–	36	64
28/29	18	–	–	–	31	69
30	11	–	–	–	9	91
31	54	–	–	–	–	100

Notes

Stage 0: Nonunion of epiphysis
Stage 1: ¼ of epiphysis united
Stage 2: ½ of epiphysis united
Stage 3: ¾ of epiphysis united
Stage 4: Complete union of epiphysis

Source

American war dead from Korea (1951–1957)—males only.

Reference

McKern, T.W. and Stewart, T.D. (1957). Skeletal age changes in young American males, analysed from the standpoint of age identification. *Headquarters Quartermaster Research and Development Command, Technical Report.* EP-45. Natick, MA.

Jit and Kulkarni

Radiographic Assessment-Medial Clavicle										
	Male % - Stage of Union					Female % - Stage of Union				
Age	*n*	1	2	3	4	*n*	1	2	3	4
11	0	–	–	–	–	2	50	50	–	–
12	2	100	–	–	–	9	78	22	–	–
13	0	–	–	–	–	19	68	32	–	–
14	10	90	10	–	–	14	86	14	–	–
15	21	77	23	–	–	31	42	58	–	–
16	19	74	26	–	–	16	56	44	–	–
17	40	30	70	–	–	26	23	77	–	–
18	94	32	55	13	–	56	18	64	18	–
19	76	–	67	33	–	23	–	74	26	–
20	30	–	50	50	–	24	–	13	87	–
21	25	–	24	76	–	17	–	6	94	–
22	22	–	–	77	23	12	–	–	100	–
23	10	–	–	30	70	10	–	–	60	40
24	12	–	–	17	83	12	–	–	–	100
25	10	–	–	–	100	10	–	–	–	100
26	20	–	–	–	100	12	–	–	–	100

Notes

Stage 1: Nonunion without epiphysis
Stage 2: Nonunion with separate epiphysis
Stage 3: Partial union
Stage 4: Complete union

Source

Radiographs from mid twentieth century Indian students.

Reference

Jit, I. and Kulkarni, M. (1976). Times of appearance and fusion of epiphyses at the medial end of the clavicle. *Indian Journal of Medical Research* **64**: 773–782. Table 1. Reprinted with permission from the Indian Journal of Medical Research.

Schultz et al.

Computer Tomographic (CT Scan)-Medial Clavicle				
	Males		Females	
Stage	Range	Mean	Range	Mean
2	15.2–23.9	18.9	15.0–21.6	18.2
3	17.5–27.2	20.9	16.6–28.6	20.5
4	21.2–30.4	25.2	21.5–29.9	25.1
5	22.4–30.9	27.6	21.9–30.9	27.4

Notes

Stage 1: Ossification center not ossified
Stage 2: Ossification center ossified, epiphyseal cartilage not ossified
Stage 3: Epiphyseal cartilage partly ossified
Stage 4: Epiphyseal cartilage fully ossified, epiphyseal scar visible
Stage 5: Epiphyseal cartilage fully ossified, epiphyseal scar no longer visible

Source

Clinical CT scans of German patients taken between the years of 1997 to 2003.

Reference

Schultz, R., Mühler, M., Mutze, S., Schmidt, S., Reisinger, W., and Schmeling, A. (2005). Studies on the time frame for ossification of the medial epiphysis of the clavicle as revealed by CT scans. *International Journal of Legal Medicine* **119**: 142–145.

Summary Compilation of Union Times

Summary of Fusing Times-Clavicle					
	Assessment	Study	Open	Fusing	Closed
Male					
	Dry Bone	Schaefer	≤23	17–29	≥21
		McKern & Stewart	≤22	18–30	≥23
		Webb & Suchey	≤21	16–30	≥21
		Coqueugniot & Weaver	≤24	19–29+	≥25
	Radiographic	Jit & Kulkarni	≤21	18–24	≥22
Female					
	Dry Bone	Webb & Suchey	≤20	17–33	≥21
		Coqueugniot & Weaver	≤24	17–29+	≥23
	Radiographic	Jit & Kulkarni	≤21	18–23	≥23

Morphological Summary

Prenatal	
Wks 5–6	Primary ossification centers appear
Wk 7	Two centers fuse to form a single mass
Wks 8–9	Clavicle becomes S-shaped
Wk 11	Clavicle adopts adult morphology
Birth	Clavicle is represented by shaft only and is essentially adult in its morphology
12–14 yrs	Medial epiphyseal flake forms
17–23 yrs	Fusion of flake commences at medial extremity
19–20 yrs	Lateral epiphysis may form and fuse
29+ yrs	Fusion of medial epiphysis will be complete in all individuals

THE SCAPULA

The Body of Scapula

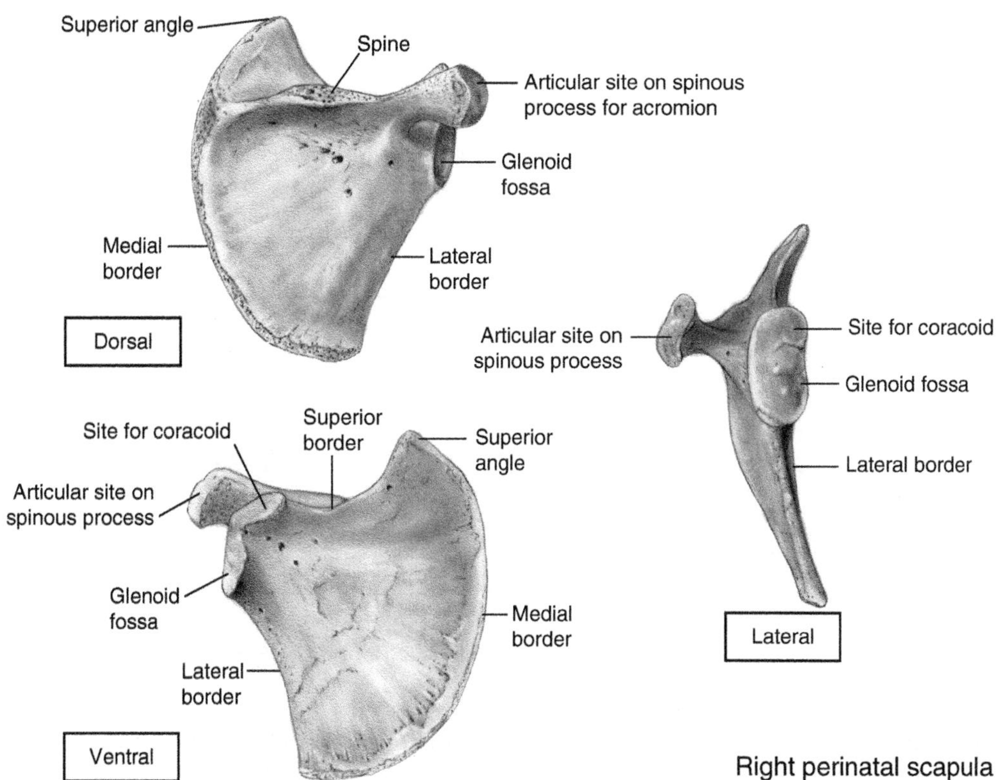

Right perinatal scapula

Identification

- Fragments may be confused with calvarial bones or the blade of the ilium although presence of the spine should prevent this confusion. The perinatal scapula also has a similar morphology to the isolated lateral occipital (page 7).

Siding – The main body of the juvenile scapula is recognizable and close to adult form by 12 to 13 prenatal weeks. Therefore, correct sideing follows the same criteria as applied to the adult.

- Dorsal surface is convex and contains the spine
- Ventral surface is concave
- Medial border is typically rounded and almost hemispherical
- Lateral border is typically concave and contains glenoid fossa

The Coracoid Process

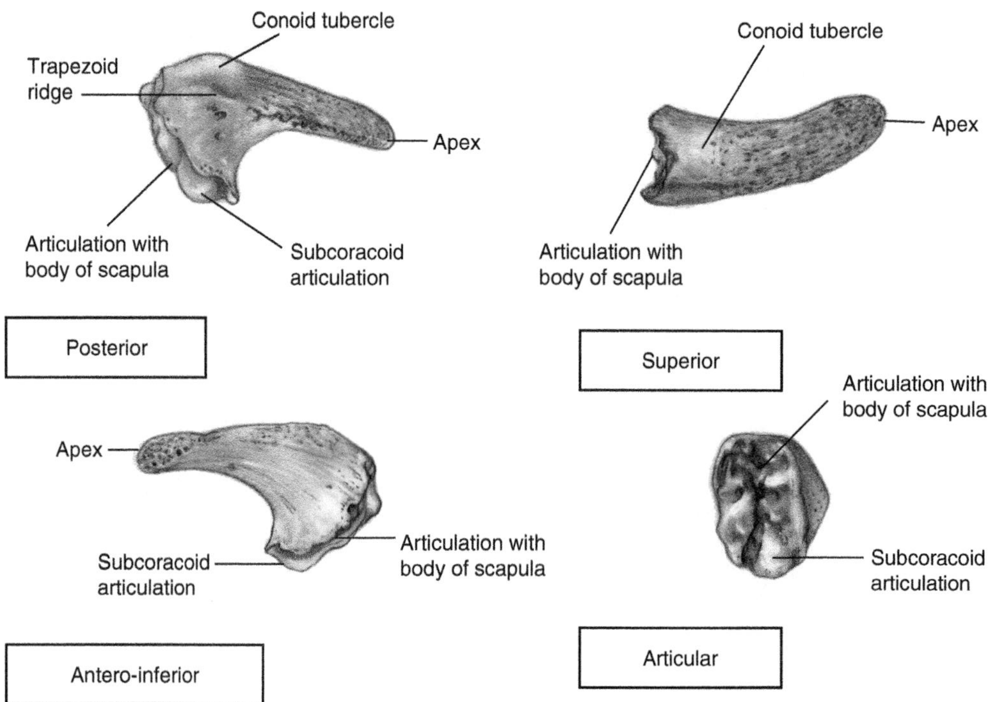

Right unfused coracoid process – female aged 12 years

Identification – The coracoid may be mistaken for rib or vertebral fragments, especially those containing transverse processes.

- The coracoid process lacks the articular facet present on a rib head or transverse process.
- The coracoid process is more hook-shaped.

Siding

- This is difficult and relies on being able to distinguish between the anterio-inferior and the postero-superior surfaces.
- The antero-inferior surface is smooth.
- The postero-superior surface is roughened with the trapezoid ridge.
- The apex of the hook points laterally.
- When positioned with the trapezoid line facing the observer, the apex of the hook points to the side from which the bone originates.

The Subcoracoid Center and Glenoid Epiphyses

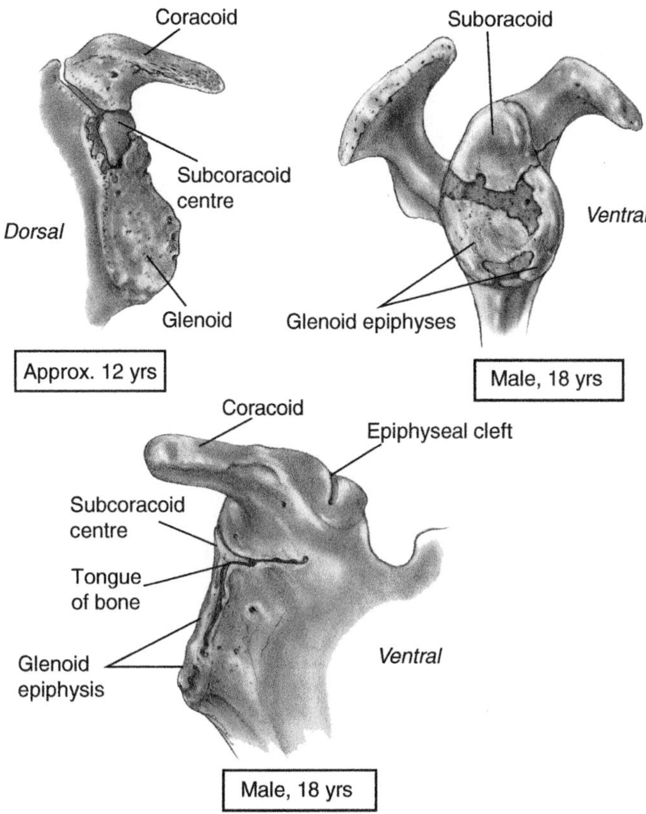

Development of the right subcoracoid and glenoid epiphyses

Identification – Unlikely ever to be recognized as separate centers of ossification.

The Coracoid Epiphyses (angle and apex)

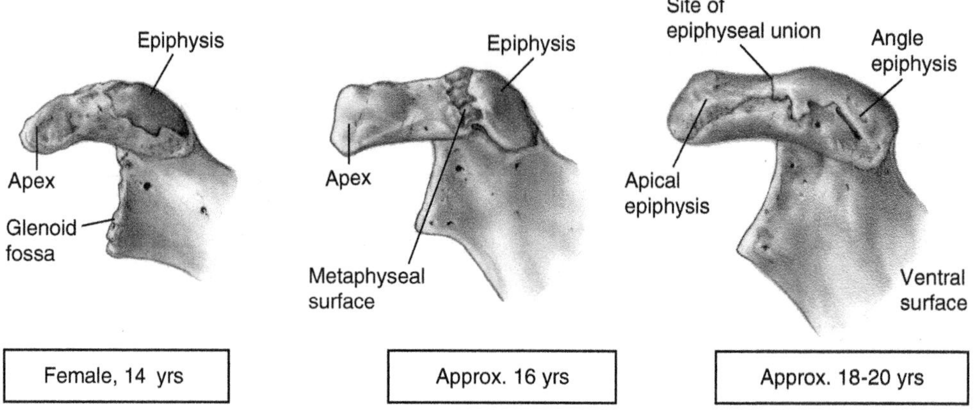

Uniting epiphyses of the apex and angle of the right coracoid process

Identification – Unlikely ever to be recognized as separate centers of ossification.

The Acromial Epiphysis

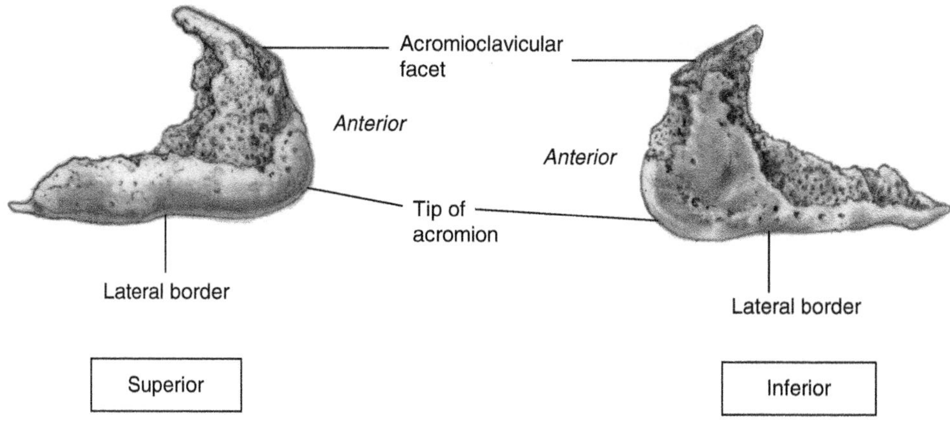

Right unfused acromial epiphysis (female 16-18 yrs)

Identification

- The acromial epiphysis can be identified in isolation from mid to late puberty. It is unlikely that this epiphysis could be confused with any other area of the skeleton.

Siding

- The lateral border is generally longer and thicker than the anterior border and forms a prominence at its lateral extremity.
- The inferior surface is smoother than the superior surface where muscles attach.
- Acromioclavicular facet is located along the medial anterior border.

Metrics

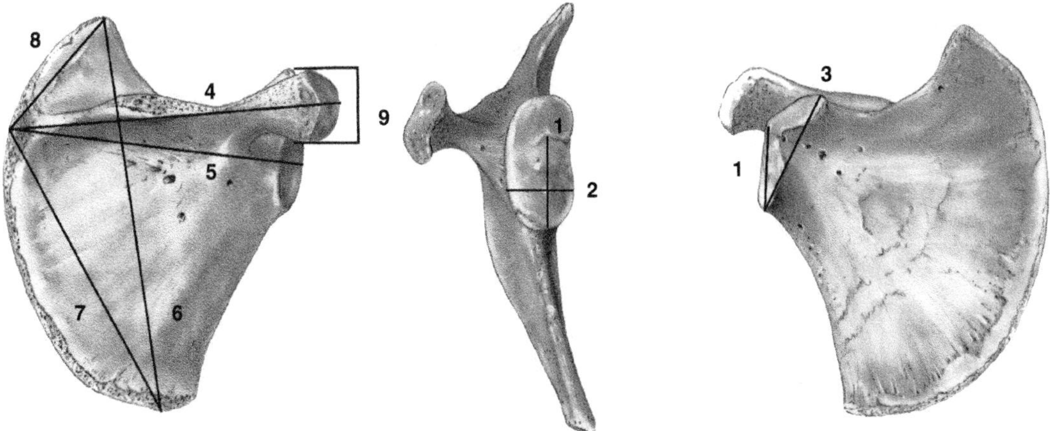

Reference landmarks for scapular measurements

Notes

1. Length of glenoidal surface: Maximum distance between the superior and inferior borders of the glenoid articular surface (does not include the articular surface for the coracoid)
2. Middle diameter of the glenoidal surface: Distance from the middle of the posterior border of the glenoid rim to the anterior border, perpendicular to the length of glenoidal surface
3. Length of glenoidal mass: Distance between the superior border of the articulation site for the coracoid process and the inferior border of the glenoid surface
4. Spine length: Maximum distance between medial end of spine and tip of acromion process
5. Scapular width: Distance between the margin of the glenoid fossa and the medial end of the spine
6. Scapular length: Distance between the superior and inferior angles of the scapula
7. Infra-scapular height: Distance between the point at which the axis of the spine intersects the medial border of the scapula to the inferior angle
8. Supra-scapular height: Distance between the point at which the axis of the spine intersects the medial border of the scapula to the superior angle
9. Acromial width: Maximum distance between the anterior and posterior borders of the acromion process, taken perpendicular to the axis of the spine

Fazekas and Kósa

Dry Bone Fetal Measurements-Scapula							
Prenatal		Scapula Length (mm)		Scapula Width (mm)		Spine Length (mm)	
Age (wks)	*n*	Mean	Range	Mean	Range	Mean	Range
12	2	4.5	3.0–6.0	3.1	2.0–4.0	3.5	2.0–5.0
14	3	7.1	6.5–8.0	5.2	4.5–6.0	5.8	5.5–6.0
16	9	11.6	9.2–14.0	9.0	6.9–11.3	10.2	7.9–12.0
18	15	15.0	12.0–17.0	11.5	11.0–13.0	12.4	11.2–14.0
20	13	17.2	15.0–19.0	13.9	11.0–16.5	15.4	12.0–17.0
22	11	18.8	17.0-20.5	15.4	13.8–16.3	17.0	15.4–18.5
24	12	20.9	19.8–22.7	17.5	15.5–20.0	18.4	16.5–20.0
26	12	22.3	19.6–26.0	18.5	16.5–20.0	19.5	17.0–21.3
28	12	23.1	20.5–25.5	19.4	18.0–21.0	21.2	19.5–23.5
30	12	24.5	22.0–28.0	20.6	19.0–24.0	22.2	20.5–26.0
32	8	26.6	24.5–30.0	22.3	20.0–26.0	23.8	22.5–27.0
34	7	18.1	26.0–30.2	23.3	21.5–27.0	25.3	24.0–27.2
36	5	29.3	28.0–30.0	24.4	23.0–26.0	26.0	25.0–29.0
38	7	33.1	31.0–36.0	26.8	25.0–29.0	29.1	27.0–31.0
40	10	35.5	33.0–39.0	29.5	27.0–32.0	31.6	29.0–35.0

Source

Dry bone measurements on mid twentieth century Hungarian fetal remains from autopsy—males and females combined. Age was estimated based on fetal crown heel length.

Reference

Fazekas, I.Gy. and Kósa, F. (1978). *Forensic Fetal Osteology*. Budapest: Akadémiai Kiadó.

Saunders et al.

Dry Bone Postnatal Measurements-Scapula						
	Scapula Length (mm)			Scapula Width (mm)		
Age	*n*	Mean	S.D.	*n*	Mean	S.D.
Birth-6 mths	10	39.3	4.1	7	31.1	1.9
6 mths-1 yr	15	49.2	4.2	16	37.0	3.4
1-2 yrs	19	60.4	4.9	19	43.3	3.1
2-3 yrs	10	67.8	7.5	8	59.8	27.8
3-4 yrs	5	63.9	33.1	5	56.0	6.2
4-5 yrs	3	81.0	4.6	3	56.8	3.3
5-6 yrs	3	91.7	10.0	3	61.8	7.0
6-7 yrs	6	97.3	5.9	7	66.1	3.2
7-8 yrs	1	94.0	–	2	63.3	2.8
8-9 yrs	1	117.0	–	1	82.5	–
9-10 yrs	2	120.0	6.0	2	77.3	0.3
10-11 yrs	1	121.0	–	2	87.3	2.8
11-12 yrs	1	121.0	–	1	82.0	–

Source

Nineteenth century documented remains from St. Thomas' Church, Ontario—males and females combined.

Reference

Saunders, S., Hoppa, R. and Southern, R. (1993). Diaphyseal growth in a nineteenth-century skeletal sample of subadults from St Thomas' Church, Belleville, Ontario. *International Journal of Osteoarchaeology* 3: 265–281.

Rissech and Black

Dry Bone Postnatal Measurements-Scapula (mm)

Regression equations	R^2
Up to 16 years of age	
age (yrs) = 0.63467 × Length of glenoidal surface – 6.54373	0.88
age (yrs) = 0.855343 × Middle diameter of glenoidal surface – 5.38895	0.78
age (yrs) = 0.440738 × Length of glenoidal mass – 6.300855	0.86
age (yrs) = 0.140472 × Scapular length – 5.059151	0.89
age (yrs) = 0.18983 × Infra-scapular height – 5.751440	0.88
age (yrs) = 0.166100 × Spine length – 5.160903	0.91
Up to 19 years of age	
age (yrs) = 0.262093 × Scapular width – 7.489091	0.91
age (yrs) = 0.528610 × Supra-scapular height – 6.811764	0.84
age (yrs) = −0.012320 × (Acromial width)^2 + 1.06838 × Acromial width – 5.069435	0.92

Source

The Scheuer collection consisting of an accumulation of forensic, anatomical, and archaeological subadult skeletal material housed at the University of Dundee (UK)—males and females were combined (55 individuals). Much of the sample consists of documented remains; however age was estimated in the archaeological specimens.

Reference

Rissech, C. and Black, S. Scapular development from the neonatal period to skeletal maturity: A preliminary study. *International Journal of Osteoarchaeology* **17**(5): 451–464. Copyright John Wiley & Sons Limited. Reproduced with permission.

Union Times

Schaefer

Dry Bone Assessment-Male %								
	Coraco-Glenoid* - Stage of Union				Coracoid Angle - Stage of Union			
Age	*n*	0	1	2	*n*	0	1	2
14	2	100	–	–	2	100	–	–
15	3	33	67	–	2	100	–	–
16	8	12	50	38	9	56	33	11
17	9	–	11	89	7	14	14	72
18	11	–	9	91	11	9	9	82
19	11	–	–	100	11	–	9	81
20	12	–	–	100	12	–	8	92
21+	81	–	–	100	81	–	–	100

*The coracoid process, subcoracoid and glenoid epiphyses are described as one complex.

Dry Bone Assessment-Male %				
		Acromion - Stage of Union		
Age	*n*	0	1	2
15	6	100	–	–
16	13	100	–	–
17	18	50	17	33
18	21	19	38	43
19	19	–	11	89
20	23	4	–	96
21+	130	–	–	100

Dry Bone Assessment-Male %								
	Inferior Angle - Stage of Union				Medial Border - Stage of Union			
Age	*n*	0	1	2	*n*	0	1	2
16	9	100	–	–	8	100	–	–
17	8	74	13	13	6	100	–	–
18	11	64	9	27	8	75	–	25
19	11	27	27	46	11	27	46	27
20	12	8	8	84	8	–	12	88
21	11	9	–	91	11	9	9	82
22	8	–	12	88	8	–	12	88
23+	62	–	–	100	62	–	–	100

Notes

Stage 0: Nonunion
Stage 1: Partial Union
Stage 2: Complete union

Source

Bosnian war dead from fall of Srebrenica (1995)—males only. Age reflects those individuals half a year above and half a year below (e.g., age 18 = 17.5–18.5).

Reference

Schaefer, M. (2008). A summary of epiphyseal union timings in Bosnian males, *International Journal of Osteoarchaeology*, DOI: 10.1002/oa.959. Copyright John Wiley & Sons Limited. Reproduced with permission.

McKern and Stewart

		Dry Bone Assessment-Male %				
		Acromion Process - Stage of Union				
Age	*n*	**0**	**1**	**2**	**3**	**4**
17	10	50	–	–	10	40
18	38	20	4	4	8	64
19	51	10	2	2	4	82
20	43	4	–	2	11	83
21	37	–	–	–	5	95
22	24	4	–	–	–	96
23	26	–	–	–	–	100

		Dry Bone Assessment-Male %									
		Inferior Angle - Stage of Union					Medial Border - Stage of Union				
Age	*n*	**0**	**1**	**2**	**3**	**4**	**0**	**1**	**2**	**3**	**4**
17	10	50	10	–	–	40	60	–	–	10	20*
18	38	38	8	2	12	40	46	10	8	10	26
19	51	21	–	4	11	64	30	–	10	15	46
20	43	9	–	–	4	87	7	5	5	13	70
21	37	5	–	2	2	91	–	6	10	13	71
22	24	–	–	4	–	96	–	4	4	4	88
23	26	–	–	–	–	100	–	–	–	–	100

*Percentages do not add up to 100 – misprinted within the original article.

Notes

Stage 0: Nonunion of epiphysis
Stage 1: ¼ of epiphysis united
Stage 2: ½ of epiphysis united
Stage 3: ¾ of epiphysis united
Stage 4: Complete union of epiphysis

Source

American war dead from Korea (1951–1957)—males only.

Reference

McKern, T.W. and Stewart, T.D. (1957). Skeletal age changes in young American males, analysed from the standpoint of age identification. *Headquarters Quartermaster Research and Development Command, Technical Report* EP-45. Natick, MA.

Coqueugniot and Weaver

Dry Bone Assessment-Scapula						
	Males			Females		
	Open	Partial	Complete	Open	Partial	Complete
Coracoid*	≤16	15–22	≥16	≤12	11–17	≥14
Acromion	≤19	18–21	≥19	≤19	17–21	≥17

*Considers fusion of both the coracoid and the subcoracoid.

Source

Documented Portuguese material born between 1904 and 1938 (Coimbra collection)—including 69 females and 68 males between the ages of 7 and 29 years.

Warning

Many ages are poorly represented.

Reference

Coqueugniot, H. and Weaver, T. (2007). Infracranial maturation in the skeletal collection from Coimbra, Portugal: new aging standards for epiphyseal union. *American Journal of Physical* **134**(3): 424–437.

Summary Compilation of Union Times

Summary of Fusing Times-Coracoid Complex					
	Assessment	Study	Open	Fusing	Closed
Male					
	Dry Bone	Schaefer*	≤16	15–18	≥16
		Coqueugniot & Weaver**	≤16	15–22	≥16
Female					
	Dry Bone	Coqueugniot & Weaver**	≤12	11–17	≥14

*Combined results for union of the coracoid process, subcoracoid and glenoid epiphyses.
**Combined results for union of the coracoid process and subcoracoid epiphysis.

Summary of Fusing Times-Acromial Epiphysis

	Assessment	Study	Open	Fusing	Closed
Male					
	Dry Bone	Schaefer	≤20	17–20	≥17
		McKern & Stewart	≤22	?-22	–
		Coqueugniot & Weaver	≤19	18–21	≥19
Female					
	Dry Bone	Coqueugniot & Weaver	≤19	17–21	≥17

Summary of Fusing Times-Inferior Angle of Scapula

	Assessment	Study	Open	Fusing	Closed
Male					
	Dry Bone	Schaefer	≤21	17–22	≥17
		McKern & Stewart	≤21	?-22	–

Summary of Fusing Times-Medial Border of Scapula

	Assessment	Study	Open	Fusing	Closed
Male					
	Dry Bone	Schaefer	≤21	18–22	≥18
		McKern & Stewart	≤20	?-22	–

Morphological Summary

Prenatal	
Wks 7–8	Primary ossification center appears
Wks 12–14	Main body of the scapula has adopted close to adult morphology
Birth	Majority of main body of scapula ossified but acromion, coracoid, medial border, inferior angle, and glenoidal mass are still cartilaginous
Yr 1	Coracoid commences ossification
Yr 3	The coracoid is recognizable as a separate ossification center
8–10 yrs	Subcoracoid center appears
13–16 yrs	Coracoid and subcoracoid commence fusion to body of the scapula
	Epiphyses appear for glenoid rim
	Epiphyses for angle and apex of coracoid appear
	Acromial epiphysis appears
16–18 yrs	Fusion complete between coracoid, subcoracoid, body of scapula, and glenoid
	Epiphyseal islands appear along medial border
	Epiphysis for inferior angle appears
By 20 yrs	Fusion of acromial epiphyses complete*
By 23 yrs	Fusion complete at both inferior angle and along medial border; therefore, all scapular epiphyses fused and full adult form achieved

*Acromial epiphysis may remain unfused throughout adulthood.

CHAPTER

6

The Upper Limb

THE HUMERUS

Shaft

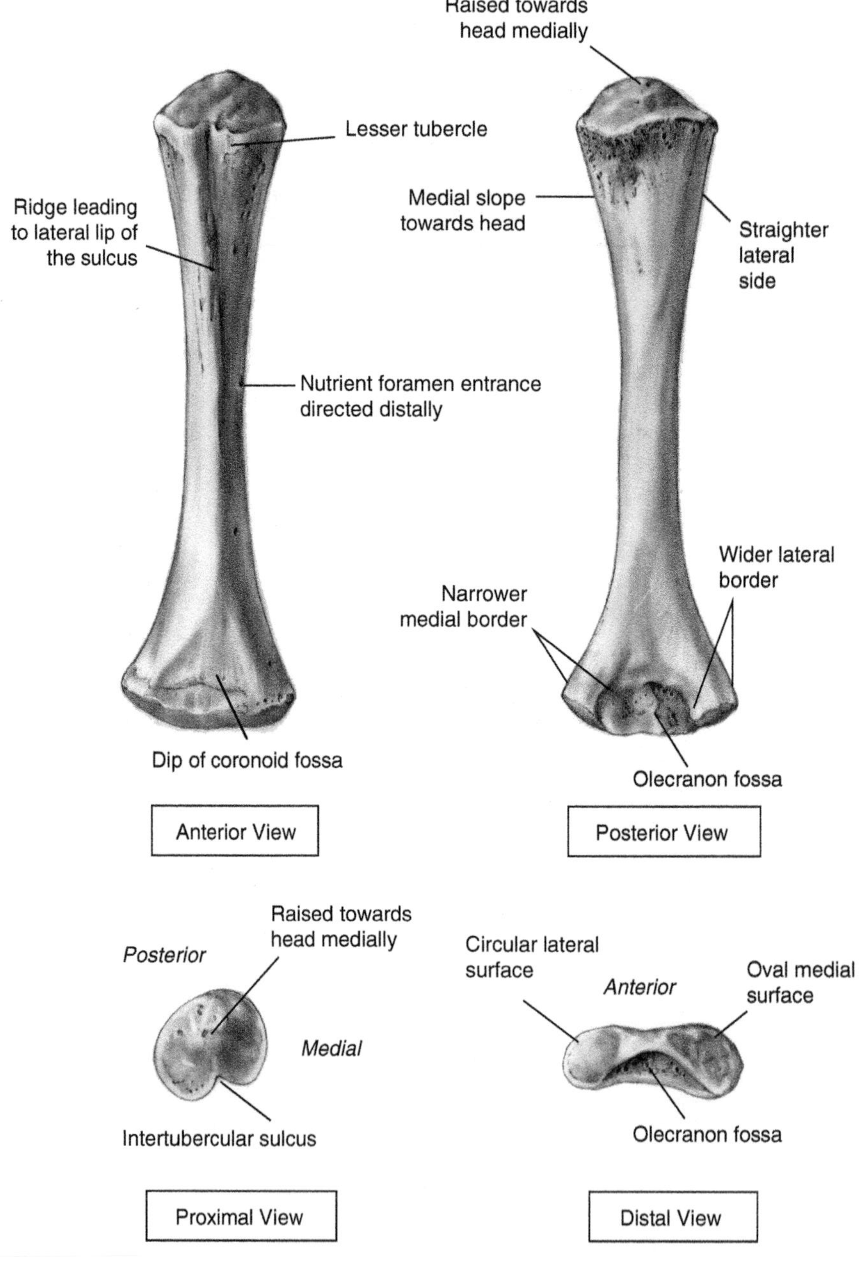
Raised towards head medially
Lesser tubercle
Ridge leading to lateral lip of the sulcus
Medial slope towards head
Straighter lateral side
Nutrient foramen entrance directed distally
Wider lateral border
Narrower medial border
Dip of coronoid fossa
Olecranon fossa
Anterior View
Posterior View
Raised towards head medially
Posterior
Circular lateral surface
Anterior
Oval medial surface
Medial
Intertubercular sulcus
Olecranon fossa
Proximal View
Distal View

Right perinatal humerus

Identification – May be confused with any of the other long bones.

- The perinatal humerus is more robust than the radius, ulna, and fibula.
- Humerus is flattened distally and bears the olecranon fossa posteriorly, unlike the tibia and femur.
- Proximal fragments bare the intertubercular sulcus, unlike the proximal femur or the proximal or distal tibia.

Siding

- Anterior ridge extends to lateral lip of intertubercular sulcus.
- The medial border is more strongly curved than the lateral border.
- Nutrient foramen usually on anteromedial side, with its entrance directed distally.
- The lateral border of olecranon fossa is wider than the medial border.
- When viewed from the proximal end, the metaphyseal surface is raised medially and the intertubercular sulcus lies anteromedially.

Proximal Epiphysis

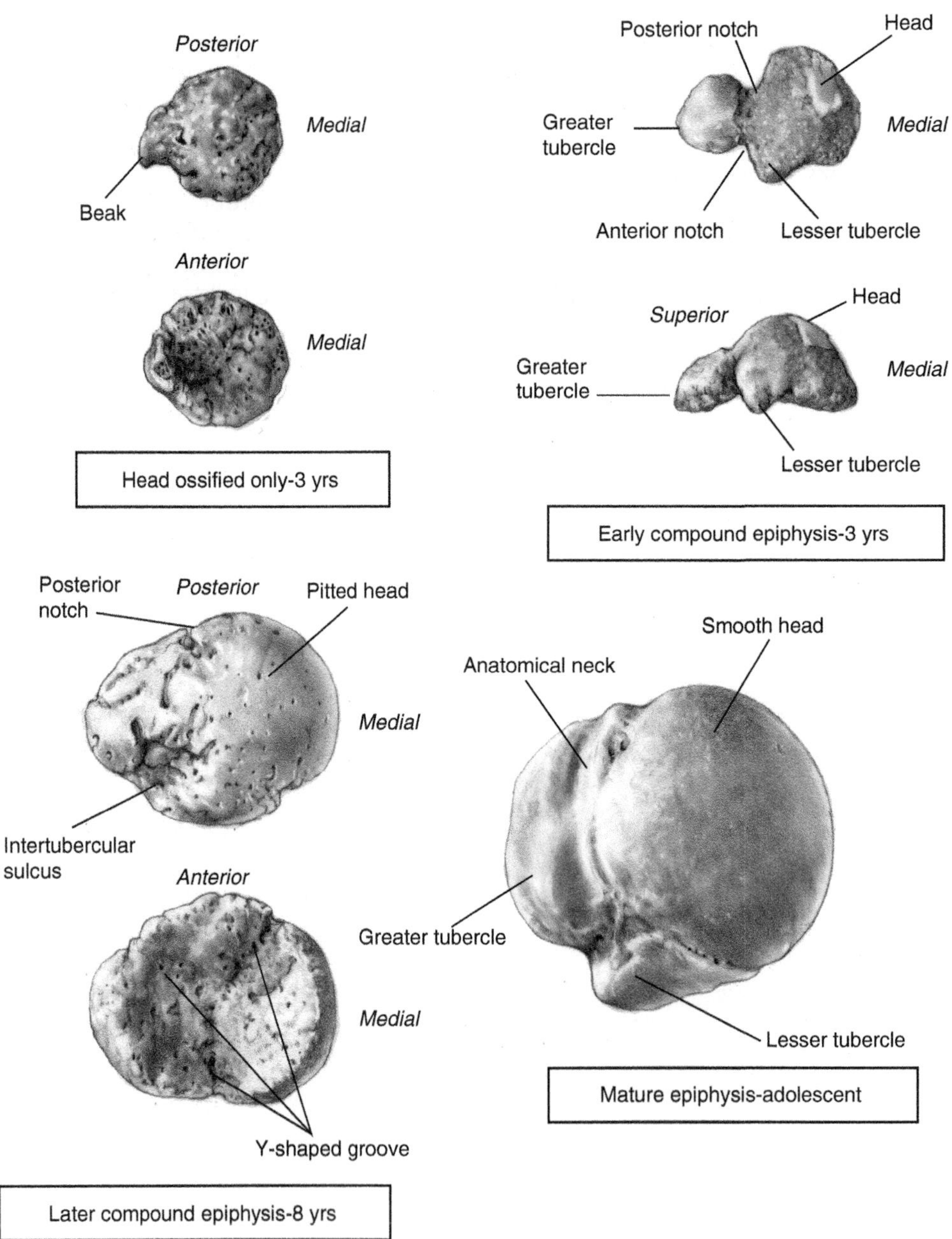

Development of the right proximal humeral epiphysis

Identification – May be confused with the femoral head epiphysis (see page 258).

- The proximal humeral epiphysis is smaller than the femoral head during early development.
- The humeral epiphysis possesses a small laterally pointed beak or a tripartite appearance.
- The metaphyseal surface of the humeral epiphysis displays a Y-shaped groove.

Siding

- The lesser tubercle is positioned along the anterior surface of the head.
- The greater tubercle extends laterally.

Distal Epiphyses

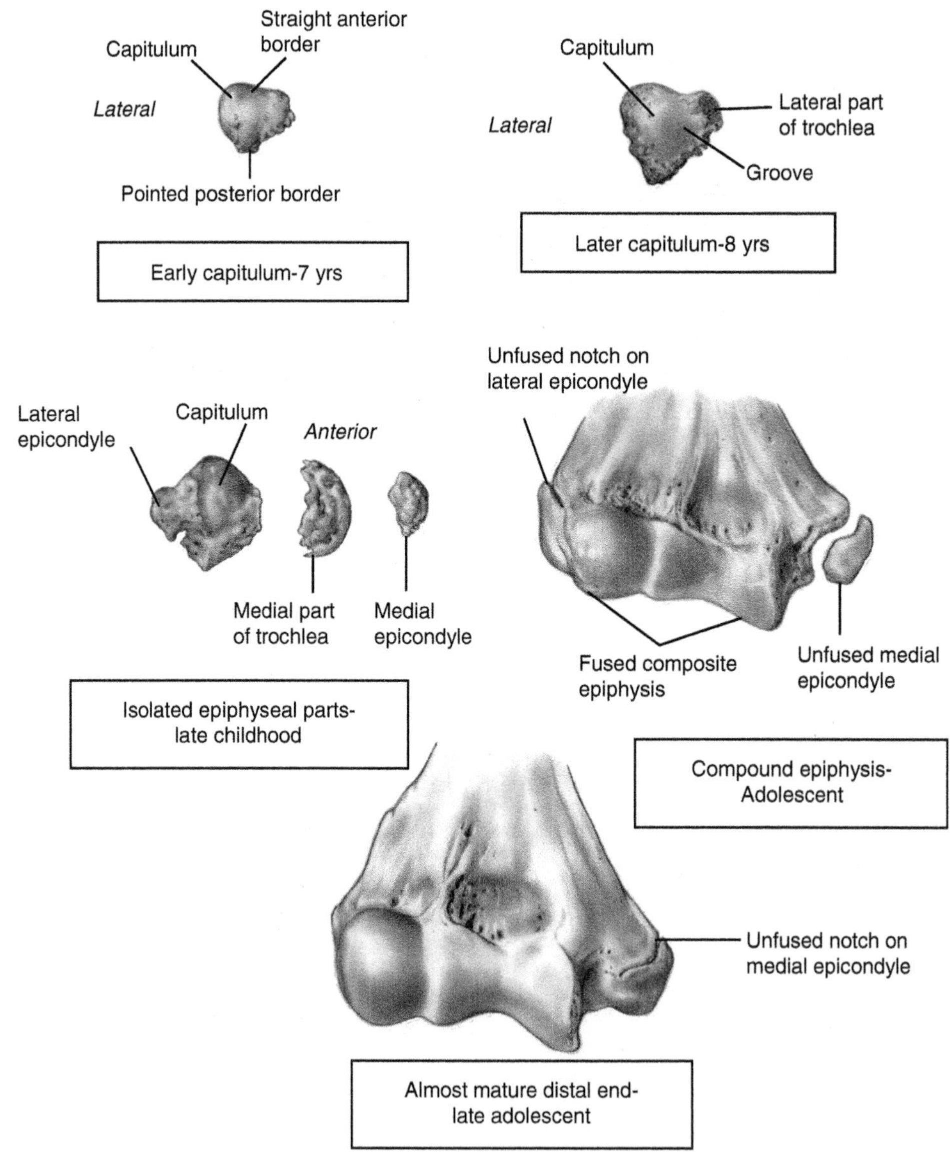

Development of the right distal humeral epiphysis

Identification/Siding – The capitulum is the only distal center that is likely to be recognized in isolation.

- It is wedge-shaped, with a wider lateral end.
- The anterior border is straight; the posterior border is pointed and pitted with nutrient foramina.

Metrics

Fazekas and Kósa

Dry Bone Fetal Measurements-Humerus					
		Max length (mm)		Distal width (mm)	
Prenatal Age (wks)	*n*	Mean	Range	Mean	Range
12	2	8.8	8.5–9.0	1.9	1.9–2.0
14	3	12.4	11.6–14.0	2.2	2.0–2.5
16	9	19.5	18.0–20.5	4.7	3.2–6.0
18	15	25.8	23.0–28.5	6.1	5.5–7.0
20	13	31.8	29.7–35.0	7.8	7.0–9.0
22	11	34.5	32.5–36.9	8.3	7.6–9.0
24	12	37.6	35.0–43.0	9.3	8.4–10.5
26	12	39.9	37.0–45.0	9.9	9.4–10.8
28	12	44.2	40.5–47.0	10.9	9.7–12.0
30	12	45.8	42.0–50.0	11.9	11.0–13.3
32	8	50.4	47.0–53.0	12.5	12.0–13.2
34	7	53.1	51.0–57.1	13.6	13.0–14.0
36	5	55.5	53.6–60.0	14.4	14.0–15.0
38	7	61.3	55.0–62.5	15.7	15.0–17.5
40	10	64.9	61.6–70.0	16.8	15.0–19.0

Notes

Has been shown to be compatible with radiographic measurements taken from American fetuses. (Warren, M.W. (1999). Radiographic determination of developmental age in fetuses and stillborns. *Journal of Forensic Sciences* **44**(4): 708–712.)

Source

Dry bone measurements on mid twentieth century Hungarian fetal remains from autopsy—males and females combined. Age was estimated based on fetal crown heel length.

Reference

Fazekas, I.Gy. and Kósa, F. (1978). *Forensic Fetal Osteology*. Budapest: Akadémiai Kiadó.

Jeanty

Ultrasound Fetal Measurements-Humerus			
	Max Length (mm)-Percentiles		
Prenatal Age (wks)	5	50	95
12	3	9	10
14	5	16	20
16	12	21	25
18	18	27	30
20	23	32	36
22	28	36	40
24	31	41	46
26	36	45	49
28	41	48	52
30	44	52	56
32	47	55	59
34	50	57	62
36	53	60	63
38	55	61	66
40	56	63	69

Source

Sonograms taken from late twentieth century white fetuses in Brussels, Belgium.

Reference

Jeanty, P. (1983). Fetal limb biometry. (Letter). *Radiology* **147**: 601–602.

Scheuer et al.

Radiographic Fetal Measurements-Humerus	
Regression equations of fetal age (weeks) on maximum humeral length (mm)	
Linear	age (weeks) = (0.4585 × humeral length) + 8.6563 ± 2.33
Logarithmic	age (weeks) = (25.069 $\log_e$ × humeral length) − 66.4655 ± 2.26

Source

Radiographic measurements on mid twentieth century premature British fetuses. The sample consisted of 29 male and 36 female fetuses between 24 and 40 weeks. Age was determined using date of last menstrual period.

Reference

Scheuer, J.L, Musgrave, J.H. and Evans, S.P. (1980). The estimation of late fetal and perinatal age from limb bone length by linear and logarithmic regression. *Annals of Human Biology* 7(3): 257–265.

Maresh

Radiographic Postnatal Measurements-Humerus (mm)								
	Males		Percentile		Females		Percentile	
Age	*n*	Mean	10th	90th	*n*	Mean	10th	90th
Diaphyseal length								
1.5 mths	59	72.4	65.7	77.5	69	71.8	67.7	76.2
3 mths	59	80.6	73.1	86.4	65	80.2	75.2	85.1
6 mths	67	88.4	82.6	94.8	78	86.8	79.9	91.6
1 yr	72	105.5	99.3	112.1	81	103.6	97.3	109.1
1.5 yrs	68	118.8	111.6	125.8	84	117.0	110.4	122.7
2 yrs	68	130.0	123.1	138.2	84	127.7	119.7	135.2
2.5 yrs	71	139.0	131.0	146.2	82	136.9	129.8	144.6
3 yrs	71	147.5	138.8	156.2	79	145.3	136.4	153.5
3.5 yrs	73	155.0	146.6	162.9	78	153.4	143.1	162.1
4 yrs	72	162.7	152.8	171.2	80	160.9	151.0	170.7
4.5 yrs	71	169.8	160.6	180.3	78	169.1	158.0	180.7
5 yrs	77	177.4	167.8	189.2	80	176.3	165.4	188.7
6 yrs	71	190.9	181.7	200.6	75	190.0	177.6	204.2
7 yrs	71	203.6	194.1	214.2	86	202.6	190.0	215.5
8 yrs	70	217.3	205.3	230.4	85	216.3	201.8	230.9
9 yrs	76	228.7	217.2	241.5	83	228.0	212.0	244.2
10 yrs	77	241.0	227.9	255.7	84	239.8	222.6	258.1
11 yrs	75	251.7	237.9	265.6	76	251.9	231.7	274.8
12 yrs	73	263.0	247.2	280.4	71	265.6	244.6	286.4
Total length including epiphyses								
10 yrs	76	258.3	244.3	272.1	83	256.1	237.2	276.1
11 yrs	75	270.0	254.8	285.1	76	269.6	248.8	292.5
12 yrs	76	282.0	265.8	298.9	75	287.5	263.8	313.6
13 yrs	69	296.6	277.0	315.6	69	301.0	277.4	324.3
14 yrs	69	313.3	291.1	335.0	64	311.7	290.1	335.3
15 yrs	60	329.0	306.4	349.7	57	315.6	293.9	336.8
16 yrs	60	341.0	322.4	361.7	40	316.5	290.3	342.9
17 yrs	50	347.1	328.6	365.6	18	315.4	292.2	333.7
18 yrs	28	350.6	333.0	372.8	4	–	–	–

Source

American children enrolled in the Child Research Council and born between 1915 and 1967.

Reference

Maresh, M.M. (1970). Measurements from roentgenograms. In: *Human Growth and Development* (R.W. McCammon, Ed.), pp. 157–200. Springfield IL: C.C. Thomas.

Appearance Times

Garn et al.

Radiographic Assessment-Humerus						
	Male Percentiles			Female Percentiles		
Ossification Centre	5th	50th	95th	5th	50th	95th
Head	37g	2w	4m	37g	2w	3m3w
Capitulum	3w	4m	1y1m	3w	3m	9m1w
Greater Tubercle	3m	10m	2y4m	2m2w	6m1w	1y2m
Medial Epicondyle	4y3m	6y3m	8y5m	2y1m	3y5m	5y1m
Lateral Epicondyle	9y3m	11y3m	13y8m	7y2m	9y3m	11y3m

gestational week (g), postnatal week (w), month (m) or year (y).

Source

Participants in the U.S.-based Fels Research Institute Program of Human Development, begun in 1929.

Reference

Garn, S.M., Rohmann, C.G., and Silverman, F.N. (1967). Radiographic standards for postnatal ossification and tooth calcification. *Medical Radiography and Photography* **43**: 45–66.

Elgenmark

Radiographic Assessment-Humerus								
	Males (months)				Female (months)			
Ossification Centre	25%	50%	75%	100%	25%	50%	75%	100%
Head	0.7	2.1	3.6	6.0	0.7	2.1	3.8	6.0
Capitulum	3.7	6.0	8.7	26.0	4.3	5.7	8.0	11.0
Greater Tubercle	9.9	19.5	23.6	–	7.7	9.1	10.7	32.0

Source

Radiographs of children (429 males and 423 females) treated or examined at the Samaritan Children's Hospital, Stockholm, during the years 1942–1945.

Reference

Elgenmark, O. (1946). The normal development of the ossific centres during infancy and childhood. *Acta Paediatrica Scandinavica* **33**(Suppl. 1).

General Development and Union Times

Ogden

2-3 mths
Ossification centre for head appears

By 7 mths
Ossification centre for greater tuberosity appears

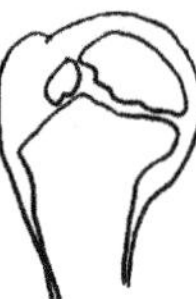

2-3 yrs
Enlarging centres, may exhibit bony bridging or be separate

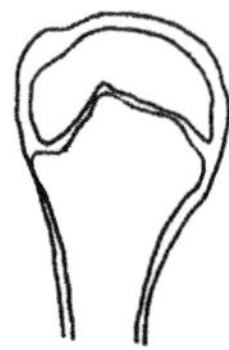

By 5-7 yrs
Complete fusion of two major ossification centres

8-14 yrs
Expanding centre

14 yrs +
Fusion of the compound epiphysis to the diaphysis

Radiographic assessment of proximal humeral development

Source

Radiographic examination of 23 late twentieth century cadaveric proximal humeri obtained by the Human Growth and Development Study Unit in the United States.

Reference

Ogden, J.A., Conlogue, G.J., and Jensen, P. (1978). Radiology of postnatal skeletal development: The proximal humerus. *Skeletal Radiology* **2**: 153–160.

Schaefer

	Dry Bone Assessment-Male %											
	Proximal Humerus - Stage of Union				**Medial Humerus - Stage of Union**				**Distal Humerus - Stage of Union**			
Age	*n*	**0**	**1**	**2**	*n*	**0**	**1**	**2**	*n*	**0**	**1**	**2**
14	3	100	–	–	3	100	–	–	2	100	–	–
15	6	100	–	–	6	100	–	–	3	–	33	67
16	12	92	8	–	11	45	10	45	7	–	14	86
17	19	63	37	–	19	10	16	74	8	–	–	100
18	20	30	55	15	20	5	–	95	10	–	10	90
19	19	–	89	11	19	–	–	100	11	–	–	100
20	22	5	40	55	22	–	–	100	10	–	–	100
21	25	–	16	84	25	–	–	100	12	–	–	100
22	11	–	–	100	11	–	–	100	7	–	–	100
23	12	–	–	100	13	–	–	100	11	–	–	100
24+	83	–	–	100	82	–	–	100	50	–	–	100

Notes

Stage 0: Nonunion
Stage 1: Partial Union
Stage 2: Complete union marked by obliteration of the epiphyseal line (scar may be present)

Source

Bosnian war dead from the fall of Srebrenica (1995)—males only. Age reflects those individuals half a year above and half a year below (e.g., age 18 = 17.5–18.5).

Reference

Schaefer, M. (2008). A summary of epiphyseal union timings in Bosnian males. *International Journal of Osteoarchaeology,* DOI: 10.1002/oa.959. Copyright John Wiley & Sons Limited. Reproduced with permission.

McKern and Stewart

Dry Bone Assessment-Proximal Humerus						
		Male % - Stage of Union				
Age	*n*	**0**	**1**	**2**	**3**	**4**
17-18	55	14	5	25	35	21
19	52	5	2	10	58	25
20	45	2	2	4	40	52
21	37	–	–	2	27	71
22	24	–	–	–	12	88
23	26	–	–	–	4	96
24+	136	–	–	–	–	100

Notes

Stage 0: Nonunion of epiphysis
Stage 1: ¼ of epiphysis united
Stage 2: ½ of epiphysis united
Stage 3: ¾ of epiphysis united
Stage 4: Complete union of epiphysis

Source

American war dead from Korea (1951–1957)—males only.

Reference

McKern, T.W. and Stewart, T.D. (1957). Skeletal age changes in young American males, analysed from the standpoint of age identification. *Headquarters Quartermaster Research and Development Command, Technical Report* EP-45. Natick, MA.

Coqueugniot

Dry Bone Assessment-Humeral Epiphyses

	Males			Females		
	Open	**Partial**	**Complete**	**Open**	**Partial**	**Complete**
Proximal	≤20	19–23	≥20	≤19	17–23	≥20
Medial Epicondyle	≤19	16–20	≥16	≤12	–	≥14
Distal	≤15	–	≥16	≤12	–	≥12

Source

Documented Portuguese material born between 1904 and 1938 (Coimbra collection), including 69 females and 68 males between the ages of 7 and 29 yrs.

Warning

Many ages are poorly represented.

Reference

Coqueugniot, H. and Weaver, T. (2007). Infracranial maturation in the skeletal collection from Coimbra, Portugal: new aging standards for epiphyseal union. *American Journal of Physical Anthropology* **134**(3): 424–437.

Jit and Singh

Radiographic Assessment-Proximal Humerus												
	Male % - Stage of Union						Female % - Stage of Union					
Age	*n*	0	1	2	N	3	*n*	0	1	2	N	3
11	26	100	–	–	–	–	26	100	–	–	–	–
12	25	100	–	–	–	–	25	100	–	–	–	–
13	26	100	–	–	–	–	25	100	–	–	–	–
14	24	96	–	4	–	–	25	76	24	–	–	–
15	26	92	8	–	–	–	33	3	21	34	18	24
16	20	20	50	10	–	20	25	4	24	4	20	48
17	54	0	7	13	30	50	49	2	–	2	22	74
18	133	2	3	9	20	66	83	–	–	–	16	84
19	113	–	1	–	17	82	30	–	–	–	3	97
20	35	–	–	–	–	100	26	–	–	–	–	100
21–25	32	–	–	–	–	100	11	–	–	–	–	100

Notes

Stage 0: Nonunion
Stage 1: Commenced union
Stage 2: Advanced union
Stage N: Remnants of a slight notch along the lateral margin
Stage 3: Complete union

Source

Radiographs from mid twentieth century Indian students.

Reference

Jit, I. and Singh, B. (1971). A radiological study of the time of fusion of certain epiphyses in Punjabees. *Journal of Anatomical Society India* **20**(1): 457–466.

Sahni and Jit

Radiographic Assessment-Medial Humerus						
	Female Frequencies - Stage of Union					
Age	*n*	0	1	2	2.5	3
<12	12	12	–	–	–	–
12	13	10	–	3	–	–
13	22	13	–	1	–	8
14	28	8	–	2	2	16
15	18	3	–	–	–	15
16	20	–	–	–	–	20
17	16	–	–	–	–	16
18	15	–	–	–	–	15
19	5	–	–	–	–	5

Notes

Stage 0: No fusion
Stage 1: Fusion of less than half of the contact area
Stage 2: Fusion of more than half of the contact area
Stage 2.5: Almost complete fusion with retention of a slight unfused notch
Stage 3: Complete fusion

Source

Radiographs of 149 Northwest Indian schoolgirls between the ages of 11 and 19 years, of middle socioeconomic status.

Reference

Sahni, D. and Jit, I. (1995). Time of fusion of epiphyses at the elbow and wrist joints in girls of northwest India. *Forensic Science International* **74**(1–2): 47–55.

Compilation Summary of Union Times

Summary of Fusing Times-Proximal Humerus

	Assessment	Study	Open	Fusing	Closed
Male					
	Dry Bone	Schaefer	≤20	16–21	≥18
		McKern & Stewart	≤20	?–23	–
		Coqueugniot & Weaver	≤20	19–23	≥20
	Radiographic	Jit & Singh	≤18	14–19	≥16
Female					
	Dry Bone	Conqueugniot & Weaver	≤19	17–23	≥20
	Radiographic	Jit & Singh	≤17	14–19	≥15

Summary of Fusing Times-Medial Humerus

	Assessment	Study	Open	Fusing	Closed
Male					
	Dry Bone	Schaefer	≤18	16–18	≥16
		Coqueugniot & Weaver	≤19	16–20	≥16
Female					
	Dry Bone	Conqueugniot & Weaver	≤12	–	≥14
	Radiographic	Sahni & Jit	≤15	12–14	≥13

Summary of Fusing Times-Distal Humerus

	Assessment	Study	Open	Fusing	Closed
Male					
	Dry Bone	Schaefer	≤14	15–18	≥15
		Coqueugniot & Weaver	≤15	–	≥16
Female					
	Dry Bone	Conqueugniot & Weaver	≤12	–	≥12

Morphological Summary

Prenatal	
Wk 7	Primary ossification center appears
Wks 36–40	Secondary ossification center for the head may be visible
Birth	Usually represented by shaft only
2–6 mths	Secondary center for head appears
By yr 1	Secondary center for capitulum usually appears
6 mths–2 yrs	Secondary center for greater tubercle appears
4+ yrs	Secondary center for medial epicondyle appears
	Secondary center for lesser tubercle may appear
2–6 yrs	Centers for head, greater and lesser tubercles fuse to form composite epiphysis
By yr 8	Secondary center for trochlea appears
Yr 10	Secondary center for lateral epicondyle appears
11–15 yrs	Distal composite epiphysis joins shaft in females
14–18 yrs	Distal composite epiphysis joins shaft in males
13–15 yrs	Medial epicondyle fuses to shaft in females
16–18 yrs	Medial epicondyle fuses to shaft in males
14–19 yrs	Proximal epiphysis fuses in females
16–21 yrs	Proximal epiphysis fuses in males

THE RADIUS

Shaft

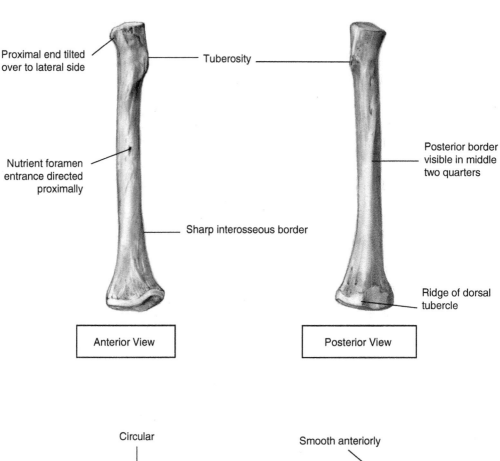

Proximal end tilted over to lateral side

Tuberosity

Nutrient foramen entrance directed proximally

Sharp interosseous border

Posterior border visible in middle two quarters

Ridge of dorsal tubercle

Anterior View

Posterior View

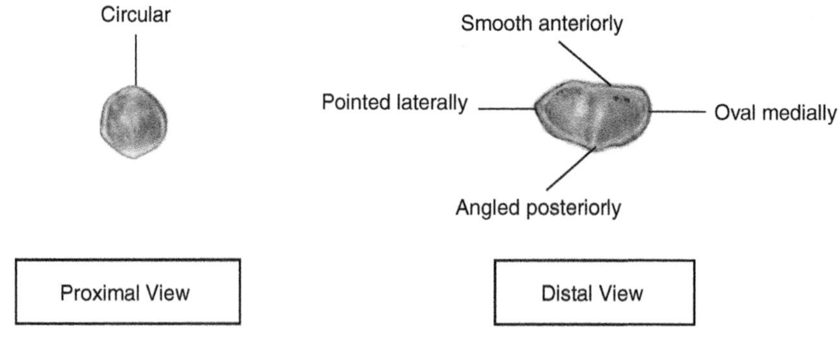

Right perinatal radius

Identification – May be confused with any of the other long bones.

- The perinatal radius is more gracile than the humerus, femur, and tibia, and shorter than the ulna and fibula.
- It is characterized by its tuberosity and flared distal end.
- The proximal metaphyseal surface is tilted to the lateral side, unlike the surfaces of the distal ulna and the two ends of the fibula, which are at right angles to the shaft.
- The distal metaphyseal surface is bigger than that of either the ulna or fibula and has an oval outline, which is usually angled posteriorly.

Siding

- At the proximal end, the bone tilts laterally and the tuberosity is situated medially.
- The anterior surface of the distal end is smooth and slightly concave; the posterior surface is angulated at the dorsal tubercle.
- The sharp interosseous border is medial.
- The nutrient foramen is usually on the anterior surface of the proximal half of the bone with its entrance directed proximally.
- When viewed posteriorly, the proximal end tilts to the side from which the bone comes.

Distal Epiphysis

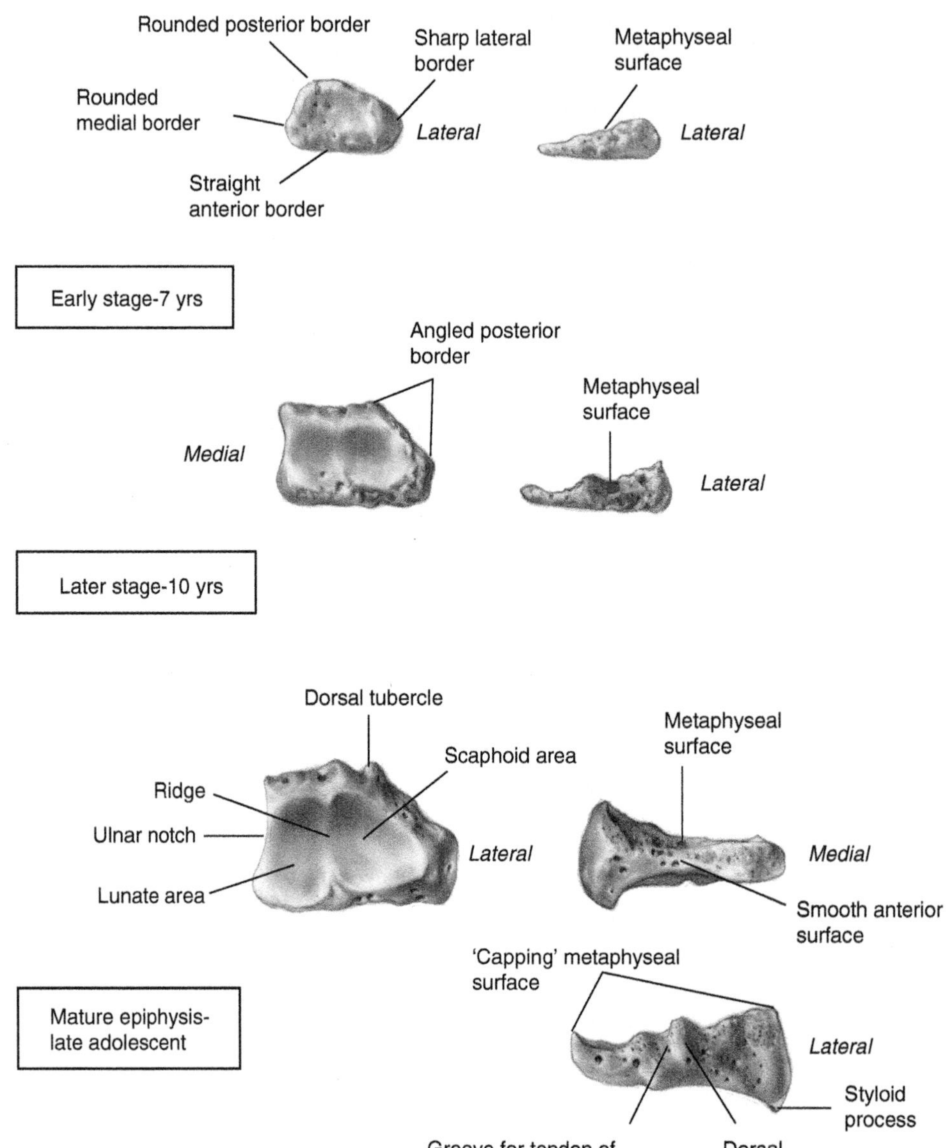

Development of the right distal radial epiphysis

Identification – The distal epiphysis increasingly assumes a triangular wedge shape, although this is less obvious during its early stages of development. Can be confused with the epiphysis of the first metatarsal in early stages.

- The articular surface of the distal radial epiphysis is more concave than that of the first MT, with a transverse ridge that runs anteroposteriorly (becomes present later in development).
- The posterior border of the distal radial epiphysis is more angled; the medial surface of the base of the first MT is more rounded.

Siding

- The lateral side is thicker even prior to development of the styloid process.
- The ulnar notch is located along the medial border.
- The anterior border is straight; the posterior border is rounded or angled.
- The styloid process (lateral) and dorsal tubercle (posterior) can be seen at later stages.

Proximal Epiphysis

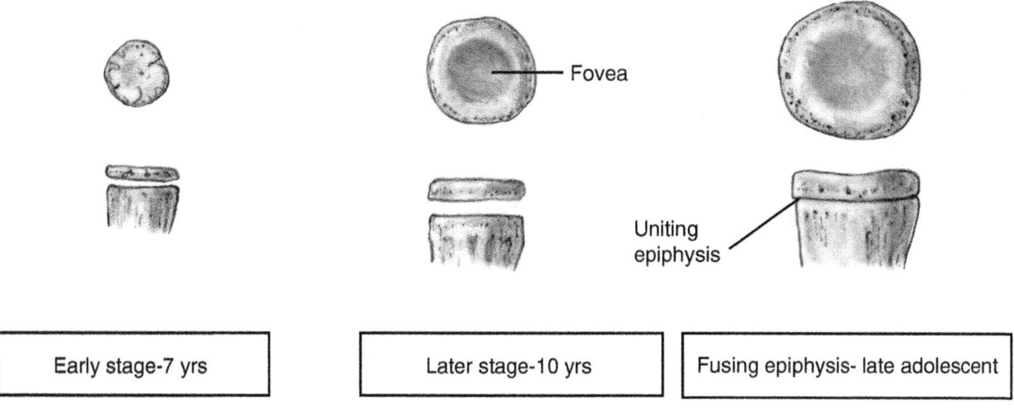

Development of the right proximal radial epiphysis

Identification – May be confused with any flattened, circular-shaped bone, in particular the distal ulna.

- The proximal radial epiphysis will develop a fovea around 10 to 11 years of age.

Siding

- Unable to determine key landmarks useful for sideing isolated proximal radial epiphyses until the epiphysis is sufficiently large to cap the metaphyseal surface of its shaft.

Shaft Metrics

Fazekas and Kósa

Dry Bone Fetal Measurements-Radius			
		Max length (mm)	
Prenatal Age (wks)	*n*	Mean	Range
12	2	6.7	5.5–8.0
14	3	10.1	9.1–11.5
16	9	17.2	15.3–20.5
18	15	21.5	20.0–23.5
20	13	26.2	25.0–29.2
22	11	28.9	26.7–33.0
24	12	31.6	29.0–35.0
26	12	33.4	31.7–38.5
28	12	35.6	33.0–37.1
30	12	38.1	35.5–40.6
32	8	40.8	37.0–43.2
34	7	43.3	41.0–44.6
36	5	45.7	44.0–49.5
38	7	48.8	45.7–51.0
40	10	51.8	47.5–58.0

Source

Dry bone measurements on mid twentieth century Hungarian fetal remains from autopsy—males and females combined. Age was estimated based on fetal crown heel length.

Notes

Has been shown to be compatible with radiographic measurements taken from American fetuses. (Warren, M.W. (1999). Radiographic determination of developmental age in fetuses and stillborns. *Journal of Forensic Sciences* **44**(4): 708–712.)

Reference

Fazekas, I.Gy. and Kósa, F. (1978). *Forensic Fetal Osteology*. Budapest: Akadémiai Kiadó.

Jeanty

Ultrasound Fetal Measurements-Radius (mm)			
	Max Length-Percentiles (mm)		
Prenatal Age (wks)	5	50	95
12	–	7	–
14	8	13	12
16	9	18	21
18	14	22	26
20	21	27	28
22	24	31	34
24	27	34	38
26	30	37	41
28	33	40	45
30	34	43	49
32	37	45	51
34	39	47	53
36	41	48	54
38	45	49	53
40	46	50	54

Source

Sonograms taken from late twentieth century white fetuses in Brussels, Belgium.

Reference

Jeanty, P. (1983). Fetal limb biometry. (Letter). *Radiology* **147**: 601–602.

Scheuer et al.

Radiographic Fetal Measurements-Radius	
Regression equations of fetal age (weeks) on maximum radial length (mm)	
Linear	age (weeks) = (0.5850 × radius length) + 7.7100 ± 2.29
Logarithmic	age (weeks) = (25.695 $\log_e$ × radius length) – 63.6541 ± 2.24

Source

Radiographic measurements on mid twentieth century premature British fetuses. The sample consisted of 29 male and 36 female fetuses between 24 and 40 weeks. Age was determined using date of last menstrual period.

Reference

Scheuer, J.L, Musgrave, J.H., and Evans, S.P. (1980). The estimation of late fetal and perinatal age from limb bone length by linear and logarithmic regression. *Annals of Human Biology* **7**(3): 257–265.

Ghantus

Radiographic Postnatal Measurements-Radial length (mm)

		Male		Female	
Age (mths)	***n***	**Mean**	**Range**	**Mean**	**Range**
3	100	65.90	58.0–73.0	62.85	54.0–70.0
6	100	73.10	66.0–81.0	69.73	60.0–78.0
9	100	80.01	73.0–90.0	76.18	66.5–84.0
12	100	85.72	75.5–95.0	81.73	71.0–91.0
18	100	94.84	84.0–107.0	91.70	82.0–103.0
24	100	102.37	95.0–115.5	99.44	88.0–112.0

Source

Serial radiographic material of the Brush Foundation, Western Reserve University, Cleveland, OH. Only healthy white children were included.

Reference

Ghantus, M. (1951). Growth of the shaft of the human radius and ulna during the first two years of life. *American Journal of Roentgenology* **65**: 784–786.

Maresh

Radiographic Postnatal Measurements-Radius (mm)								
	Males		Percentile		Females		Percentile	
Age	*n*	Mean	10th	90th	*n*	Mean	10th	90th
Diaphyseal length								
1.5 mths	59	59.7	55.3	64.0	69	57.8	54.4	61.3
3 mths	59	66.0	61.7	70.2	65	63.4	59.8	66.8
6 mths	67	70.8	66.1	75.5	78	67.6	63.7	71.5
1 yr	72	82.6	78.0	87.5	81	78.9	74.7	83.0
1.5 yrs	68	91.4	85.8	96.9	83	87.5	81.8	92.1
2 yrs	68	98.6	92.8	104.9	84	95.0	88.9	100.3
2.5 yrs	71	105.2	98.0	110.6	82	101.4	94.9	107.4
3 yrs	71	111.6	104.9	117.6	79	107.7	100.2	114.2
3.5 yrs	73	116.9	109.8	124.7	78	113.8	105.8	121.1
4 yrs	72	123.1	115.7	129.5	80	119.2	111.0	126.1
4.5 yrs	71	128.2	120.4	135.6	78	125.2	115.8	133.6
5 yrs	77	133.8	125.7	141.7	80	130.2	120.2	138.4
6 yrs	71	143.8	135.5	150.5	75	140.0	129.6	149.8
7 yrs	71	153.0	144.4	161.8	86	149.3	138.8	159.8
8 yrs	70	162.9	153.8	172.0	85	158.9	147.6	170.7
9 yrs	76	171.3	162.8	180.5	83	167.6	155.9	180.4
10 yrs	77	180.5	171.4	190.4	84	176.8	163.3	190.3
11 yrs	75	188.7	179.2	200.1	76	186.0	171.3	201.7
12 yrs	74	197.4	186.5	210.8	71	196.9	180.6	213.4
Total length including epiphyses								
10 yrs	76	193.0	183.1	201.5	83	189.3	173.9	204.4
11 yrs	75	202.6	192.6	213.9	76	200.0	182.4	218.4
12 yrs	77	212.3	200.6	226.1	75	213.5	192.3	232.3
13 yrs	73	223.7	209.4	239.5	69	223.6	205.3	239.8
14 yrs	75	236.9	221.0	255.4	64	231.4	215.1	245.7
15 yrs	61	248.7	233.1	267.4	57	234.5	218.8	249.0
16 yrs	61	257.7	243.1	274.4	40	235.0	219.2	249.5
17 yrs	50	261.8	247.8	274.1	18	233.8	219.5	253.3
18 yrs	28	263.2	250.2	278.6	4	–	–	–

Source

American children enrolled in the Child Research Council and born between 1915 and 1967.

Reference

Maresh, M.M. (1970). Measurements from roentgenograms. In: *Human Growth and Development* (R.W. McCammon, Ed.), pp. 157–200. Springfield IL: C.C. Thomas.

Gindhart

Radiographic Postnatal Measurements-Radius (mm)						
	Males			Females		
Age	*n*	Mean	S.D.	*n*	Mean	S.D.
Diaphyseal length						
1 mth	138	55.8	2.9	123	54.0	2.7
3 mths	117	62.4	3.0	102	59.9	3.3
6 mths	200	69.7	3.4	176	66.9	3.7
9 mths	115	75.8	4.1	105	73.5	4.6
1 yr	198	82.3	4.6	169	79.5	4.5
1.5 yrs	117	92.5	6.9	106	89.4	4.9
2 yrs	183	100.2	5.1	162	97.5	5.0
2.5 yrs	110	107.5	5.3	104	104.3	5.7
3 yrs	179	114.4	5.9	166	110.8	5.9
3.5 yrs	101	120.0	5.7	111	117.1	6.5
4 yrs	184	126.0	6.6	175	122.9	6.8
4.5 yrs	99	131.4	6.5	92	128.8	7.6
5 yrs	182	137.5	7.2	165	134.3	7.6
5.5 yrs	86	142.3	7.7	79	140.7	8.0
6 yrs	184	148.9	8.1	165	145.3	8.3
7 yrs	172	159.1	8.7	157	155.3	9.1
8 yrs	163	168.9	8.9	153	165.4	9.8
9 yrs	164	179.5	9.4	145	175.1	10.5
10 yrs	148	188.5	10.3	139	185.4	11.8
11 yrs	140	198.6	10.7	127	196.2	12.9
12 yrs	130	208.6	12.4	116	208.8	13.5
13 yrs	119	220.2	14.3	106	217.7	12.3
14 yrs	118	234.5	15.6	101	223.3	11.2
15 yrs	98	245.2	14.6	91	226.8	11.4
16 yrs	87	253.4	12.0	76	228.3	10.3
17 yrs	73	255.9	12.4	60	228.0	11.3
18 yrs	64	255.7	12.3	45	230.9	11.7

Source

White American children of European descent enrolled in the longitudinal program of the Fels Research Institute by mid 1967.

Reference

Gindhart, P. (1973). Growth standards for the tibia and radius in children aged one month through eighteen years. *American Journal of Physical Anthropology* **39**: 41–48.

Appearance Times

Garn et al.

Radiographic Assessment-Radius						
	Male Percentiles			Female Percentiles		
Ossification Centre	5th	50th	95th	5th	50th	95th
Distal	6m	1y	2y4m	4m	10m	1y8m
Proximal	3y	5y3m	8y	2y3m	3y11m	6y3m

month (m) or year (y).

Source

Participants in the U.S.-based Fels Research Institute Program of Human Development, begun in 1929.

Reference

Garn, S.M., Rohmann, C.G., and Silverman, F.N. (1967). Radiographic standards for postnatal ossification and tooth calcification. *Medical Radiography and Photography* **43**: 45–66.

Elgenmark

Radiographic Assessment-Radius								
	Male (months)				Female (months)			
Ossification Centre	25%	50%	75%	100%	25%	50%	75%	100%
Distal	7.7	10.4	13.1	15.0	7.7	8.0	12.1	20.0
Proximal	47.5	53.3	–	–	34.6	44.2	47.9	–

Source

Radiographs of children (429 males and 423 females) treated or examined at the Samaritan Children's Hospital, Stockholm, during the years 1942–1945.

Reference

Elgenmark, O. (1946). The normal development of the ossific centres during infancy and childhood. *Acta Paediatrica Scandinavica* **33**(Suppl. 1).

Union Times

Schaefer

	Dry Bone Assessement-Male %							
	Proximal Radius - Stage of Union				Distal Radius - Stage of Union			
Age	*n*	0	1	2	*n*	0	1	2
14	2	100	–	–	2	100	–	–
15	6	67	33	–	6	100	–	–
16	8	38	24	38	8	75	25	–
17	17	12	23	65	17	70	18	12
18	20	5	5	90	20	50	20	30
19	19	–	–	100	19	16	42	42
20	21	–	–	100	21	–	33	67
21	24	–	–	100	24	–	–	100
22	10	–	–	100	10	–	–	100
23	13	–	–	100	13	–	–	100
24+	83	–	–	100	83	–	–	100

Notes

Stage 0: Nonunion
Stage 1: Partial Union
Stage 2: Complete union marked by obliteration of the epiphyseal line (scar may be present)

Source

Bosnian war dead from the fall of Srebrenica (1995)—males only. Age reflects those individuals half a year above and half a year below (e.g., age 18 = 17.5–18.5).

Reference

Schaefer, M. (2008). A summary of epiphyseal union timings in Bosnian males. *International Journal of Osteoarchaeology*, DOI: 10.1002/oa.959. Copyright John Wiley & Sons Limited. Reproduced with permission.

McKern and Stewart

Dry Bone Assessment-Distal Radius						
	Male % - Stage of Union					
Age	*n*	**0**	**1**	**2**	**3**	**4**
17–18	55	22	3	14	32	29
19	52	7	–	5	48	40
20	45	4	–	2	24	70
21	37	–	–	–	19	81
22	24	–	–	–	12	88
23	26	–	–	–	–	100
24+	136	–	–	–	–	100

Notes

Stage 0: Nonunion of epiphysis
Stage 1: ¼ of epiphysis united
Stage 2: ½ of epiphysis united
Stage 3: ¾ of epiphysis united
Stage 4: Complete union of epiphysis

Source

American war dead from Korea (1951–1957)—males only.

Reference

McKern, T.W. and Stewart, T.D. (1957). Skeletal age changes in young American males, analysed from the standpoint of age identification. *Headquarters Quartermaster Research and Development Command, Technical Report* EP-45. Natick, MA.

Coqueugniot

Dry Bone Assessment-Radial Epiphyses						
	Males			Females		
	Open	Partial	Complete	Open	Partial	Complete
Proximal	≤16	17–20	≥16	≤12	12–17	≥17
Distal	≤21	19–21	≥20	≤19	17–22	≥20

Source

Documented Portuguese material born between 1904 and 1938 (Coimbra collection), including 69 females and 68 males between the ages of 7 to 29 yrs.

Warning

Many ages are poorly represented.

Reference

Coqueugniot, H. and Weaver, T. (2007). Infracranial maturation in the skeletal collection from Coimbra, Portugal: New aging standards for epiphyseal union. *American Journal of Physical Anthropology* **134**(3): 424–437.

Sahni and Jit

Radiographic Assessment-Female Frequencies											
		Proximal Radius					Distal Radius				
Age	n	0	1	2	2.5	3	0	1	2	2.5	3
<12	12	12	–	–	–	–	12	–	–	–	–
12	13	11	2	–	–	–	13	–	–	–	–
13	22	9	–	4	–	9	22	–	–	–	–
14	28	4	–	1	–	23	16	7	5	–	–
15	18	1	–	1	–	16	8	4	5	1	–
16	20	–	–	–	–	20	2	1	10	3	4
17	16	–	–	–	–	16	–	–	2	7	7
18	15	–	–	–	–	15	–	–	1	3	11
19	5	–	–	–	–	5	–	–	–	–	5

Source

Radiographs of 149 Northwest Indian schoolgirls between the ages of 11 and 19 years, of middle socioeconomic status.

Notes

Stage 0: No fusion
Stage 1: Fusion of less than half of the contact area
Stage 2: Fusion of more than half of the contact area
Stage 2.5: Almost complete fusion with retention of a slight unfused notch
Stage 3: Complete fusion

Reference

Sahni, D. and Jit, I. (1995). Time of fusion of epiphyses at the elbow and wrist joints in girls of northwest India. *Forensic Science International* **74**(1–2): 47–55.

Compilation Summary of Union Times

Summary of Fusing Times-Proximal Radius

	Assessment	Study	Open	Fusing	Closed
Male					
	Dry Bone	Schaefer	≤18	15–18	≥16
		Coqueugniot & Weaver	≤16	17–20	≥16
Female					
	Dry Bone	Coqueugniot & Weaver	≤12	12–17	≥17
	Radiographic	Sahni & Jit	≤15	12–15	≥13

Summary of Fusing Times-Distal Radius

	Assessment	Study	Open	Fusing	Closed
Male					
	Dry Bone	Schaefer	≤19	16–20	≥17
		McKern & Stewart	≤20	?–22	–
		Coqueugniot & Weaver	≤21	19–21	≥20
Female					
	Dry Bone	Coqueugniot & Weaver	≤19	17–22	≥20
	Radiographic	Sahni & Jit	≤16	14–18	≥16

Morphological Summary

Prenatal	
Wk 7	Primary ossification center appears
Birth	Represented by shaft only
1–2 yrs	Secondary center for distal epiphysis appears
Yr 5	Secondary center for head appears
By yr 8	Styloid process forms on distal epiphysis
10–11 yrs	Proximal epiphysis shows foveal indentation
12–16 yrs	Proximal epiphysis fuses in females
14–18 yrs	Proximal epiphysis fuses in males
Puberty	Flake for tuberosity may form as separate center
14–19 yrs	Distal epiphysis fuses in females
16–20 yrs	Distal epiphysis fuses in males

THE ULNA

Shaft

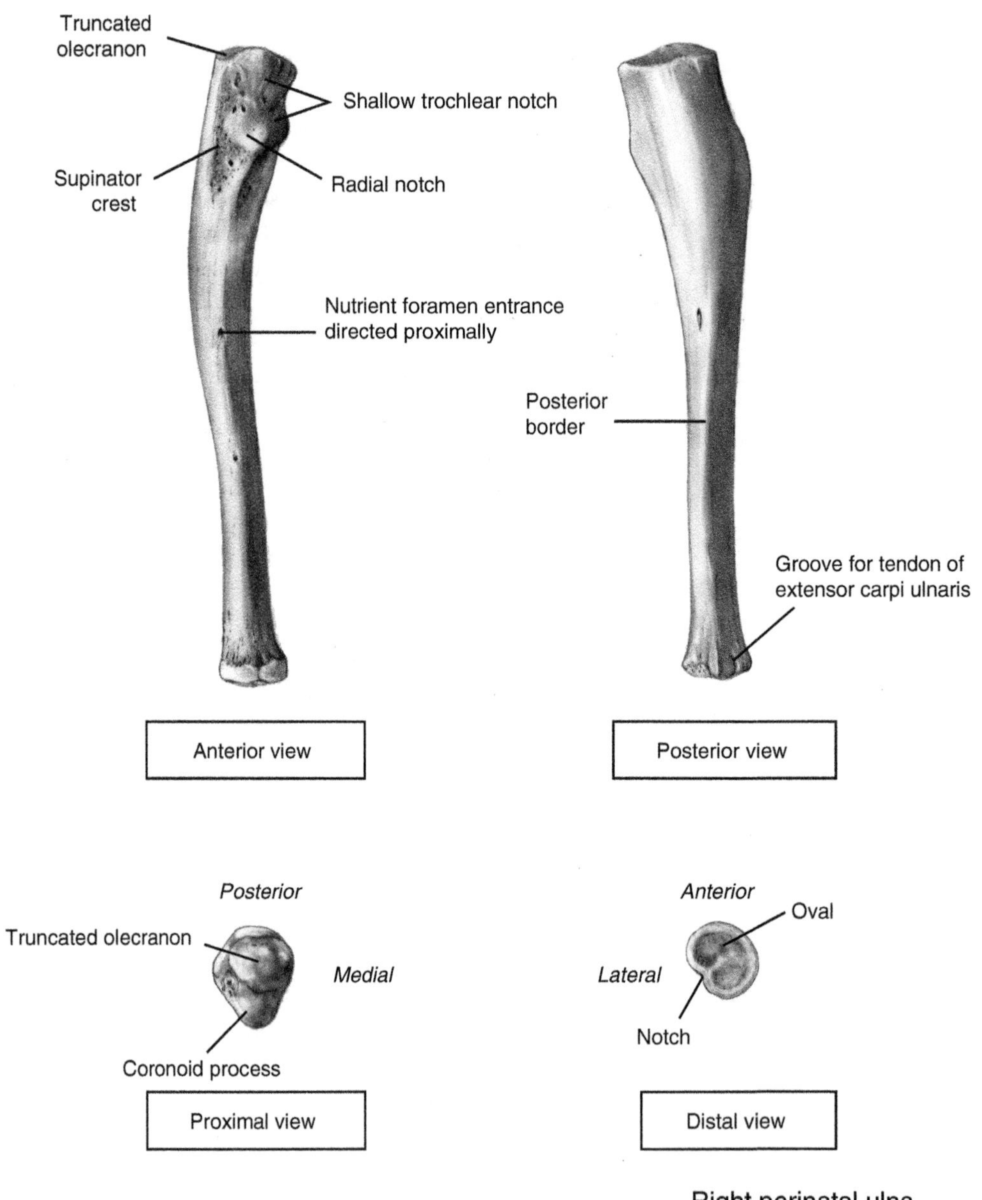
Truncated olecranon
Shallow trochlear notch
Supinator crest
Radial notch
Nutrient foramen entrance directed proximally
Posterior border
Groove for tendon of extensor carpi ulnaris
Anterior view
Posterior view
Posterior
Truncated olecranon
Medial
Coronoid process
Proximal view
Anterior
Oval
Lateral
Notch
Distal view

Right perinatal ulna

Identification – May be confused with any of the other long bones.

- The perinatal ulna is more gracile than the humerus, femur, and tibia; longer than the radius; and similar in length to the fibula (although more robust).
- Proximal fragments contain the trochlear and radial notches.
- Distal metaphyseal surface is more oval than other long bones and may show a notch posterolaterally.

Siding

- Proximally, the radial notch is located on its lateral side.
- The sharp interosseous border is lateral.
- The nutrient foramen is usually located along the anterior upper half of the shaft with its entrance directed proximally.
- Distally, the medial surface is slightly concave.
- The distal metaphyseal surface is oval and contains a notch for the tendon of the extensor carpi ulnaris muscle on its lateral side.
- The proximal end of the bone tilts medially.

Proximal Epiphysis

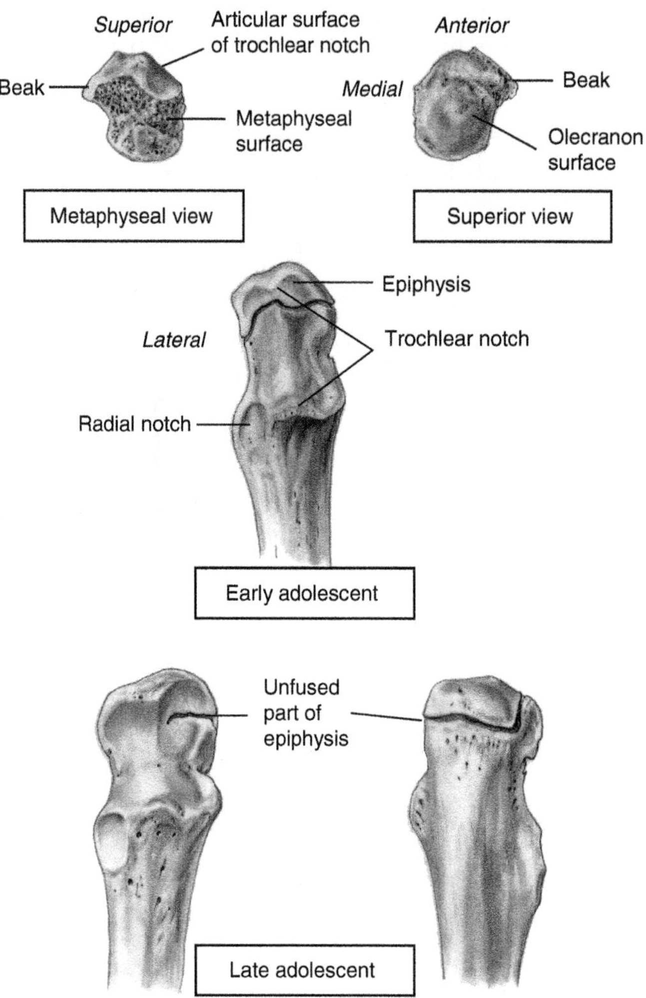

Development of the right proximal ulnar epiphysis

Siding

- Looking at the metaphyseal surface with the trochlear articular surface positioned superiorly, the beak points to the opposite side from which the bone comes (i.e., the beak points laterally).

Distal Epiphysis

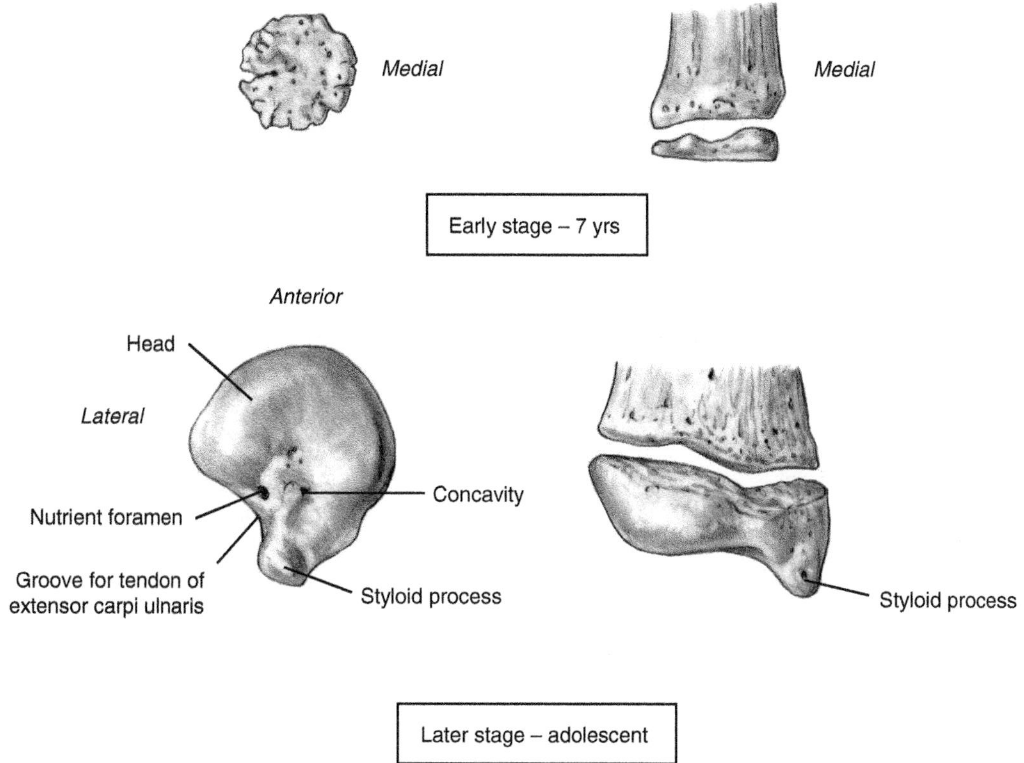

Development of the right distal ulnar epiphysis

Identification – May be confused with any flattened, circular-shaped bone, in particular the proximal radial epiphysis or epiphyses of the phalanges.

- The distal ulnar epiphysis bears a distinct notch; the distal radial epiphysis is round; and the phalangeal epiphyses contain notches that are less obvious.

Siding

- The bone is flattened and circular-shaped with a notch in its posterolateral side.
- As a result of the notch, the right epiphysis is "comma"-shaped when looking at its articular surface.

Shaft Metrics

Fazekas and Kósa

Dry Bone Fetal Measurements-Ulna			
		Max length (mm)	
Prenatal Age (wks)	*n*	Mean	Range
12	2	7.2	5.5–9.0
14	3	11.2	10.2–12.5
16	9	19.0	16.2–22.0
18	15	23.9	21.0–26.6
20	13	29.4	27.0–33.1
22	11	31.6	29.6–33.6
24	12	35.1	31.5–39.0
26	12	37.1	35.0–40.5
28	12	40.2	38.0–43.5
30	12	42.8	40.0–46.6
32	8	46.7	41.2–49.2
34	7	49.1	46.5–51.0
36	5	51.0	49.0–55.4
38	7	55.9	52.7–58.0
40	10	59.3	55.0–66.5

Notes

Has been shown to be compatible with radiographic measurements taken from American fetuses (Warren, M.W. (1999). Radiographic determination of developmental age in fetuses and stillborns. *Journal of Forensic Sciences* **44**(4): 708–712.)

Source

Dry bone measurements on mid twentieth century Hungarian fetal remains from autopsy—males and females combined. Age was estimated based on fetal crown heel length.

Reference

Fazekas, I.Gy. and Kósa, F. (1978). *Forensic Fetal Osteology*. Budapest: Akadémiai Kiadó.

Jeanty

Ultrasound Fetal Measurements-Ulna			
Prental Age (wks)	Max Length (mm)-Percentiles		
	5	50	95
12	–	8	–
14	4	13	17
16	8	19	24
18	13	24	30
20	21	29	32
22	24	33	37
24	29	37	41
26	34	41	44
28	37	44	48
30	38	47	54
32	40	50	58
34	44	53	59
36	47	55	61
38	48	57	63
40	50	58	65

Source

Sonograms taken from late twentieth century white fetuses in Brussels, Belgium.

Reference

Jeanty, P. (1983). Fetal limb biometry. (Letter). *Radiology* **147**: 601–602.

Scheuer et al.

Radiographic Fetal Measurements-Ulna	
Regression equations of fetal age (weeks) on maximum ulnar length (mm)	
Linear	age (weeks) = (0.5072 × Ulna length) + 7.8208 ± 2.20
Logarithmic	age (weeks) = (26.078 $\log_e$ × Ulna length) − 68.7222 ± 2.10

Source

Radiographic measurements on mid twentieth century premature British fetuses. The sample consisted of 29 male and 36 female fetuses between 24 and 40 weeks. Age was determined using date of last menstrual period.

Reference

Scheuer, J.L, Musgrave, J.H., and Evans, S.P. (1980). The estimation of late fetal and perinatal age from limb bone length by linear and logarithmic regression. *Annals of Human Biology* **7**(3): 257–265.

Ghantus

Radiographic Postnatal Measurements-Ulna (mm)

		Male		Female	
Age (mths)	***n***	**Mean**	**Range**	**Mean**	**Range**
3	100	73.55	65.0–82.5	70.58	61.0–80.0
6	100	81.03	73.0–90.5	77.67	69.0–87.0
9	100	88.20	80.0–98.0	84.70	75.0–93.0
12	100	94.84	85.0–104.5	90.73	80.0–102.0
18	100	104.99	93.0–115.0	101.62	90.0–115.0
24	100	112.64	102.0–125.0	109.79	97.0–124.0

Source

Serial radiographic material of the Brush Foundation, Western Reserve University, Cleveland, OH. Only healthy white children were included.

Reference

Ghantus, M. (1951). Growth of the shaft of the human radius and ulna during the first two years of life. *American Journal of Roentgenology* **65**: 784–786.

Maresh

Radiographic Postnatal Measurements-Ulnar Length (mm)								
	Males		Percentile		Females		Percentile	
Age (yrs)	*n*	Mean	10th	90th	*n*	Mean	10th	90th
Diaphyseal length								
1.5 mths	59	67.0	62.8	71.4	69	65.3	61.4	69.0
3 mths	59	73.8	69.4	78.0	65	71.2	67.0	75
6 mths	67	79.1	74.3	83.6	78	75.7	70.2	80.3
1yr	71	92.6	87.4	97.8	81	89.0	84.1	93.8
1.5 yrs	68	102.3	95.9	107.0	83	98.9	93.1	105.0
2 yrs	68	109.7	103.9	115.2	84	107.1	100.6	113.6
2.5 yrs	71	116.6	109.9	121.5	82	113.8	107.2	120.1
3 yrs	71	123.4	116.4	129.6	79	120.6	113.1	127.2
3.5 yrs	73	129.1	120.3	136.4	78	127.2	119.4	134.5
4 yrs	72	135.6	127.9	142.7	80	133.1	124.4	140.4
4.5 yrs	71	141.0	133.4	149.1	78	139.3	130.4	147.2
5 yrs	77	147.0	139.3	155.2	80	144.6	135.4	153.6
6 yrs	71	157.5	149.4	164.9	75	154.9	144.7	164.9
7 yrs	71	167.3	157.9	175.8	86	164.8	154.2	176.3
8 yrs	70	177.3	168.8	185.8	85	174.9	164.2	186.3
9 yrs	76	186.4	176.7	196.0	83	184.3	171.8	198.0
10 yrs	77	196.2	186.6	205.7	84	194.4	180.4	209.4
11 yrs	75	205.1	194.9	217.3	76	204.7	189.8	222.4
12 yrs	73	214.5	202.2	228.0	70	216.4	199.1	233.1
Total length including epiphyses								
10 yrs	76	202.2	191.8	212.8	83	203.8	187.8	221.0
11 yrs	75	213.3	201.5	225.5	76	215.5	198.5	233.6
12 yrs	77	224.9	210.3	239.3	75	229.7	210.3	249.2
13 yrs	73	237.9	221.3	254.8	70	240.0	221.7	257.6
14 yrs	75	252.3	234.7	271.0	65	248.1	232.3	265.0
15 yrs	61	265.1	250.0	284.3	57	251.0	235.8	268.2
16 yrs	61	274.8	260.2	292.6	40	252.3	237.1	269.8
17 yrs	50	279.4	263.9	293.0	17	250.2	232.8	268.4
18 yrs	28	281.6	266.9	300.8	4	–	–	–

Source

American children enrolled in the Child Research Council and born between 1915 and 1967.

Reference

Maresh, M.M. (1970). Measurements from roentgenograms. In: *Human Growth and Development*, (R.W. McCammon Ed.), pp. 157–200. Springfield IL: C.C. Thomas.

Appearance Times

Garn et al.

Radiographic Assessment-Ulna

Ossification Centre	Male Percentiles 5th	Male Percentiles 50th	Male Percentiles 95th	Female Percentiles 5th	Female Percentiles 50th	Female Percentiles 95th
Distal	5y3m	7y1m	9y1m	3y4m	5y5m	7y8m
Proximal	7y9m	9y8m	11y11m	5y8m	8y	9y11m

month (m), or year (y).

Source

Participants in the U.S.-based Fels Research Institute Program of Human Development, begun in 1929.

Reference

Garn, S.M., Rohmann, C.G., and Silverman, F.N. (1967). Radiographic standards for postnatal ossification and tooth calcification. *Medical Radiography and Photography* **43**: 45–66.

Union Times

Schaefer

Dry Bone Assessement-Male %								
	Proximal Ulna - Stage of Union				Distal Ulna - Stage of Union			
Age	*n*	**0**	**1**	**2**	*n*	**0**	**1**	**2**
14	2	100	–	–	2	100	–	–
15	6	–	83	17	6	100	–	–
16	10	–	30	70	10	100	–	–
17	19	–	16	84	19	74	5	21
18	20	–	5	95	20	55	15	30
19	18	–	–	100	18	17	17	66
20	22	–	–	100	22	5	14	81
21	24	–	–	100	24	–	–	100
22	10	–	–	100	10	–	–	100
23	13	–	–	100	13	–	–	100
24+	83	–	–	100	83	–	–	100

Source

Bosnian war dead from the fall of Srebrenica (1995)—males only. Age reflects those individuals half a year above and half a year below (e.g., age 18 = 17.5–18.5).

Notes

Stage 0: Nonunion
Stage 1: Partial Union
Stage 2: Complete union marked by obliteration of the epiphyseal line (scar may be present)

Reference

Schaefer, M. (2008). A summary of epiphyseal union timings in Bosnian males. *International Journal of Osteoarchaeology*, DOI: 10.1002/oa.959. Copyright John Wiley & Sons Limited. Reproduced with permission.

McKern and Stewart

Dry Bone Assessment-Distal Ulna						
		Male % - Stage of Union				
Age	***n***	**0**	**1**	**2**	**3**	**4**
17–18	55	29	1	11	24	35
19	52	7	–	5	32	56
20	45	4	2	–	24	70
21	37	–	–	–	10	90
22	24	–	–	–	8	92
23	26	–	–	–	–	100
24+	136	–	–	–	–	100

Notes

Stage 0: Nonunion of epiphysis
Stage 1: ¼ of epiphysis united
Stage 2: ½ of epiphysis united
Stage 3: ¾ of epiphysis united
Stage 4: Complete union of epiphysis

Source

American war dead from Korea (1951–1957)—males only.

Reference

McKern, T.W., and Stewart, T.D. (1957). Skeletal age changes in young American males, analysed from the standpoint of age identification. *Headquarters Quartermaster Research and Development Command, Technical Report* EP-45. Natick, MA.

Coqueugniot

Dry Bone Assessment-Ulnar Epiphyses						
	Males			Females		
	Open	Partial	Complete	Open	Partial	Complete
Proximal	≤16	16–20	≥16	≤12	–	≥14
Distal	≤21	19–21	≥20	≤19	17–21	≥20

Source

Documented Portuguese material born between 1904 and 1938 (Coimbra collection), including 69 females and 68 males between the ages of 7 to 29 years.

Warning

Many ages are poorly represented.

Reference

Coqueugniot, H. and Weaver, T. (2007). Infracranial maturation in the skeletal collection from Coimbra, Portugal: New aging standards for epiphyseal union. *American Journal of Physical Anthropology* **134**(3): 424–437.

Sahni and Jit

Radiographic Assessment-Proximal Ulna						
	Female Frequencies - Stage of Union					
Age	*n*	0	1	2	2.5	3
< 12	12	12	–	–	–	–
12	13	13	–	–	–	–
13	22	22	–	–	–	–
14	28	14	4	10	–	–
15	18	7	2	6	3	–
16	20	1	–	6	8	5
17	16	–	–	1	3	12
18	15	–	–	–	3	12
19	5	–	–	–	–	5

Notes

Stage 0: No fusion
Stage 1: Fusion of less than half of the contact area
Stage 2: Fusion of more than half of the contact area
Stage 2.5: Almost complete fusion with retention of a slight unfused notch
Stage 3: Complete fusion

Source

Radiographs of 149 Northwest Indian schoolgirls between the ages of 11 and 19 years, of middle socioeconomic status.

Reference

Sahni, D. and Jit, I. (1995). Time of fusion of epiphyses at the elbow and wrist joints in girls of northwest India. *Forensic Science International* **74**(1–2): 47–55.

Compilation Summary of Union Times

Summary of Fusing Times-Proximal Ulna

	Assessment	Study	Open	Fusing	Closed
Male					
	Dry Bone	Schaefer	≤14	15–18	≥15
		Coqueugniot & Weaver	≤16	16–20	≥16
Female					
	Dry Bone	Coqueugniot & Weaver	≤12	–	≥14
	Radiographic	Sahni & Jit	≤16	14–18	≥16

Summary of Fusing Times-Distal Ulna

	Assessment	Study	Open	Fusing	Closed
Male					
	Dry Bone	Schaefer	≤20	17–20	≥17
		McKern & Stewart	≤20	?–22	–
		Coqueugniot & Weaver	≤21	19–21	≥20
Female					
	Dry Bone	Coqueugniot & Weaver	≤19	17–21	≥20

Morphological Summary

Prenatal	
Wk 7	Primary ossification center appears
Birth	Represented by shaft only
5–7 yrs	Secondary center for distal end appears
≈ 8–10 yrs	Styloid process forms on distal epiphysis
	Secondary center(s) for olecranon appear(s)
12–15 yrs	Proximal epiphysis fuses in females
14–18 yrs	Proximal epiphysis fuses in males
15–19 yrs	Distal epiphysis fuses in females
17–20 yrs	Distal epiphysis fuses in males

THE HAND

Primary Centers

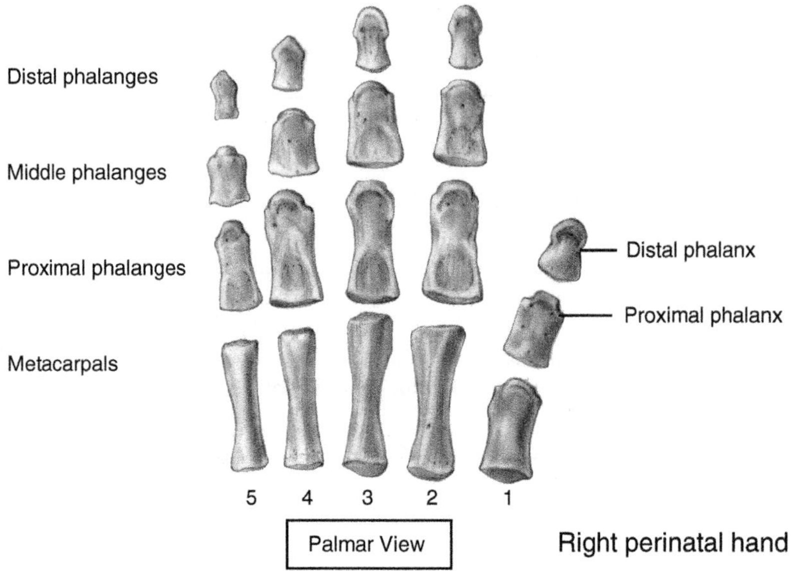

Right perinatal hand

Identification – Easily confused with bones of the foot.

- Carpals are much smaller than tarsal bones.
- Metacarpals are generally shorter and more robust than metatarsals, which are longer, more slender, and slightly compressed in the mediolateral plane.
- The pedal phalanges are considerably shorter, less defined, and more irregular than the phalanges of the hand (with the exception of the phalanges of the big toe).
- Phalanges of the hand are flattened on their palmar surface and rounded dorsally, giving them a D-shaped appearance in cross-section of the shaft; pedal phalanges are more rounded in cross-section.

Identification/Siding – Metacarpals become more recognizable as ossification spreads into the bases and are sided as done so in the adult.

MC1

- Palmar surface: Nutrient foramen generally is located on the medial side of the shaft and is directed distally.
- Palmar surface: Tubercle for the attachment of the abductor pollicis longus muscle is located distally on the lateral side.
- Dorsal surface: Proximal border is angled toward the lateral side.

MC2

- The saddle-shaped proximal base is larger on its medial side (side that is adjacent to MC3).
- Distal metaphyseal surface is wider in the diagonal from its mediodorsal to lateropalmar side and is narrower in the diagonal from laterodorsal to mediopalmar.

MC3

- Proximal base bears the styloid process on its lateral side (side that is adjacent to MC2).
- Distal metaphyseal surface is wider in the diagonal from anteromedial to posterolateral and narrower in the diagonal from anterolateral to posteromedial.

MC4

- Proximal base bears a smaller articular facet on its lateral side (for articulation with MC3) and a larger facet on its medial side (for articulation with MC5).
- Nutrient foramen is generally located on the lateral aspect.

MC5

- Proximal base bears an articular facet on its later surface; there is no facet on its medial surface on its medial end.
- Nutrient foramen is generally on its lateral aspect.

Capitate

- Identifiable by approximately three to four years; however, it cannot be sided until approximately 12 years.
- Adopts the shape of a reversed D, with a flattened medial surface (for articulation with the hamate) and a slightly wider distal transverse diameter.

Hamate

- Identifiable by approximately four to five years; however, it cannot be sided until approximately nine years.
- The hamulus is located on the palmar surface in a somewhat mediodistal location.

Other Carpals

- Most become identifiable between 8.5 to 11 years; however, sideing is not generally possible until around the time of puberty (approximately 12 years in girls and 14–15 years in boys).

The Base of the First Metacarpal

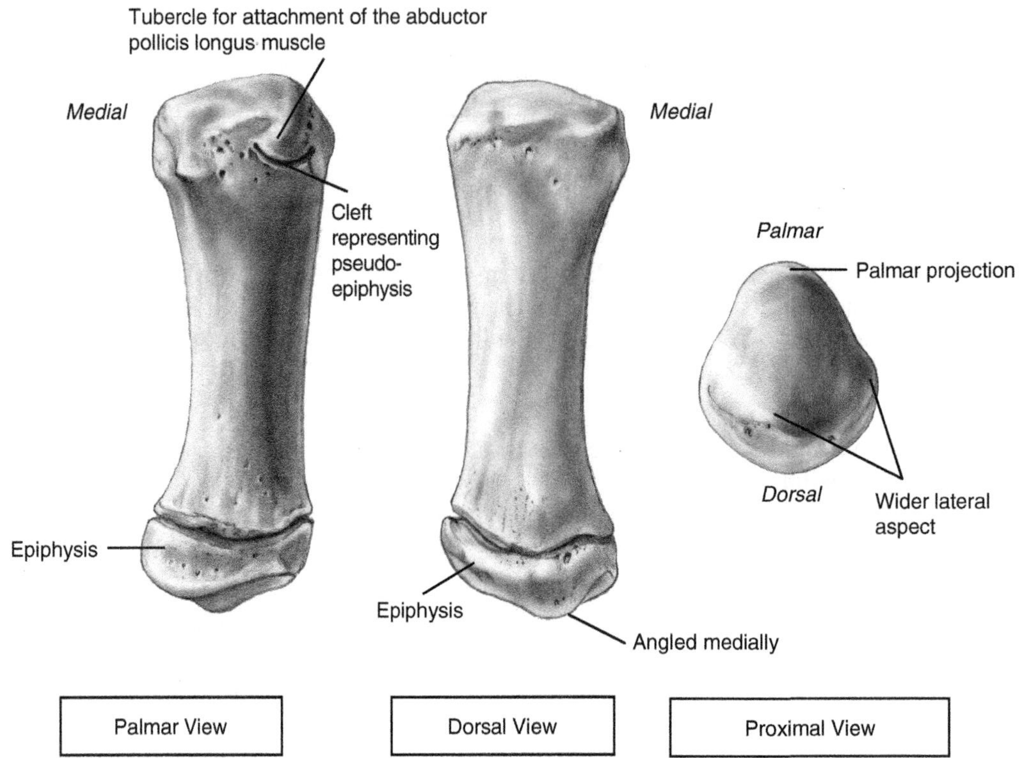

The right first metacarpal epiphysis (male 14-16 yrs)

Identification – Probably not identifiable until around nine to 10 years of age.

- The articular surface is gently saddle-shaped, being convex in the mediolateral plane and slightly concave in its ventrodorsal plane.
- When viewing the dorsal surface, the saddle angles to the side from which the bone originates.
- The lateral surface of the saddle is larger than the medial surface.
- The palmar projection (styloid process) that is instrumental in creating the saddle shape is larger than the dorsal projection.

The Metacarpal Heads 2–5

MC2 MC3 MC4 MC5

Dorsal

Distal Articular Surface

Lateral

Palmar

Diagonal from mediodorsal to lateropalmar is longer on MCs 2 & 3

Palmar

Proximal Metaphyseal Surface

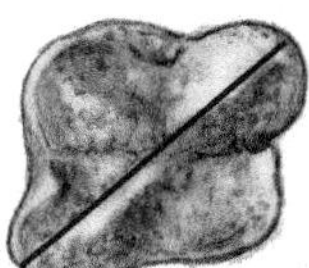
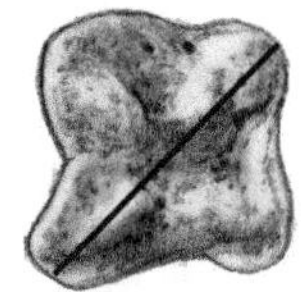
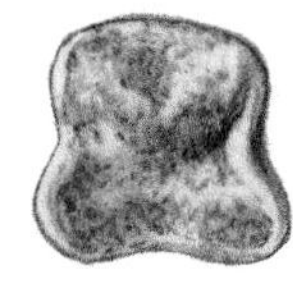
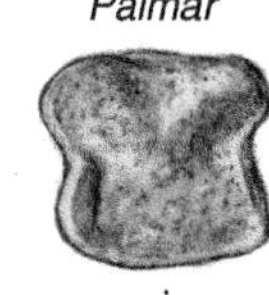

Lateral

Dorsal

Diagonal from mediodorsal to lateropalmar is longer on MCs 2 & 3

The right metacarpal heads 2-5 (female 12-14 yrs)

Identification/Siding – Identification of individual metacarpal heads is difficult and generally relies on the presence of a single individual so that an appropriate head can be fitted to a shaft.

MC Heads of 2&3

- More petaloid (floral) type appearance than MC heads of 4&5
- The mediodorsal to lateropalmar diagonal is longer than the laterodorsal to mediopalmar diagonal

MC Heads of 4&5

- More square in shape with less distinct petaloid silhouettes

The Bases of the Proximal Phalanges

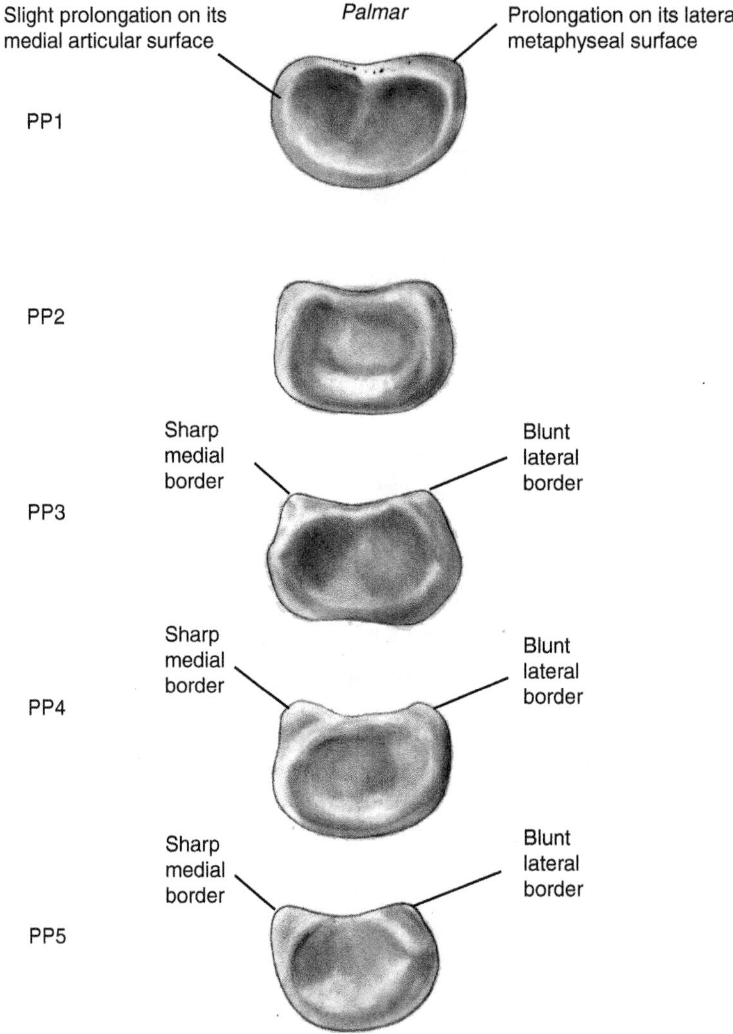

The epiphyses of the right proximal phalanges (female 12-14 yrs)

Regional Identification

- Display single concave articular surfaces with gently convex metaphyseal surfaces
- Wider in their transverse than in their ventrodorsal plane
- Thicker on their lateral border, although becomes less obvious by PP5

Intraregional Identification/Siding

PP1

- Palmar view displays a faint S-shape, formed by a thickened medial prolongation on its articular surface and a lateral prolongation on its metaphyseal surface
- Almost oval in outline, although the palmar surface is gently concave

PP2

- More square-shaped than PP1, although displays soft corners and a slightly concave palmar surface
- Palmar view displays a wedge-shape with a thicker lateral side and a thinner medial side

PP3

- More rectangular in shape than PP2. This is a result of its thinner ventrodorsal plane
- Palmar view also displays a wedge-shape
- The medial border on the palmar surface ends in a sharp projection

PP4

- Semicircular outline with a concave palmar border
- The medial border on the palmar surface ends in a projection that is sharper than that found on PP3

PP5

- Displays an oval outline with a slightly concave palmar border, although is much smaller than PP1
- Lateral aspect of the palmar border is blunt, whereas medial aspect is more pointed

The Bases of the Middle Phalanges

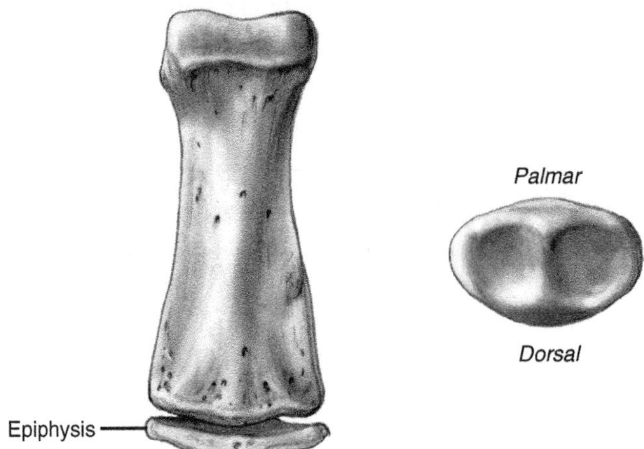

Example of a right middle phalangeal epiphysis (female 12-14 yrs)

Regional Identification

- Biconcave articular surfaces
- Essentially oval in outline, although palmar borders are more gently convex and dorsal borders are more obviously rounded
- Metaphyseal surfaces are slightly convex from palmar to dorsal, with steeper slopes toward the dorsal borders

Intraregional Identification/Siding

- Extremely difficult and unlikely to be achieved with any degree of confidence.

The Bases of the Distal Phalanges

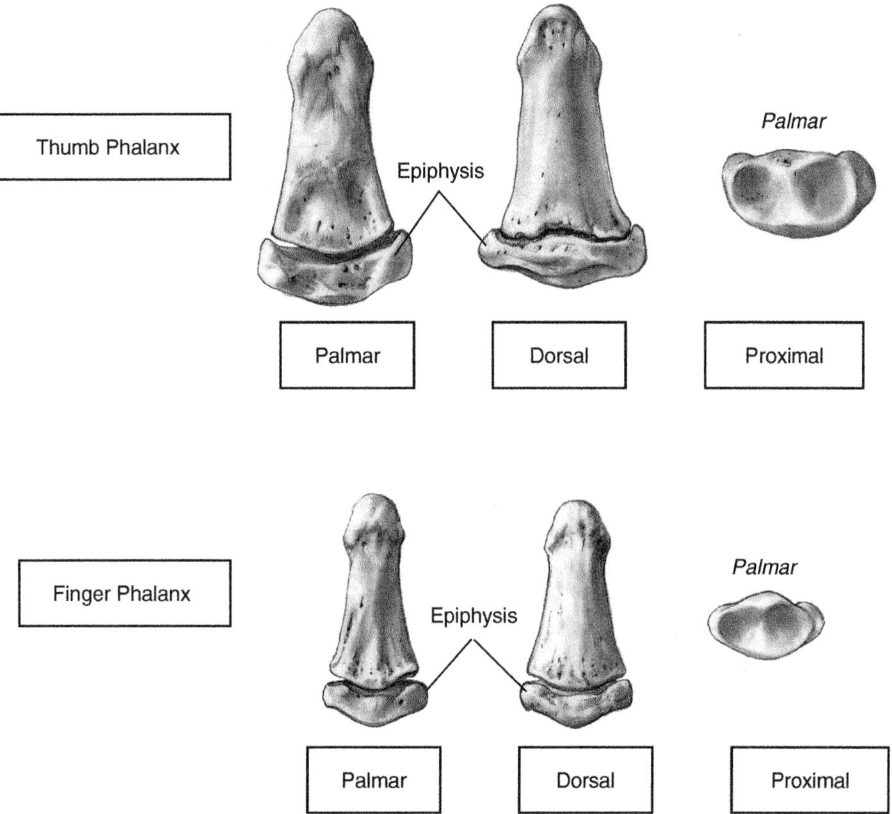

Examples of right distal phalangeal epiphyses (female 12-14 yrs)

Regional Identification

- Biconcave discs, although their delimiting ridge is not as clearly defined as those encountered in the epiphyses of the middle phalanges
- Similar in size, although slightly wider than the bases of the diaphyses to which they attach

Intraregional Identification/Siding

- Extremely difficult and unlikely to be achieved with any degree of confidence, with exception of that for the thumb, which is much larger and more distinctly biconcave

Shaft Metrics

Fazekas and Kósa

Dry Bone Fetal Measurements-First Metacarpal			
		Max length (mm)	
Prenatal Age (wks)	*n*	Mean	Range
16	9	1.8	1.7–1.9
18	15	2.3	2.0–2.9
20	13	3.1	2.8–3.5
22	11	3.7	3.0–4.5
24	12	4.3	3.5–5.0
26	12	4.6	4.0–5.1
28	12	5.1	4.5–5.9
30	12	5.9	5.0–6.5
32	8	6.3	5.8–7.0
34	7	7.2	7.0–7.5
36	5	8.1	7.0–8.5
38	7	8.9	8.1–9.0
40	10	9.3	8.5–10.5

Source

Dry bone measurements on mid twentieth century Hungarian fetal remains from autopsy—males and females combined. Age was estimated based on fetal crown heel length.

Reference

Fazekas, I.Gy. and Kósa, F. (1978). *Forensic Fetal Osteology*. Budapest: Akadémiai Kiadó.

Garn et al.

Fetal Measurements-Mean bone to bone ratios relative to metacarpal 2					
Bone	**1**	**2**	**3**	**4**	**5**
Metacarpal	0.65	–	0.96	0.88	0.82
Proximal phalanx	0.46	0.57	0.61	0.57	0.47
Middle phalanx	–	0.34	0.38	0.36	0.29
Distal phalanx	0.43	0.31	0.32	0.31	0.27

Note

Fetal ratios are very similar to those attained for adults.

Source

Micrometric measurements of optically projected histological hand sections of 56 embryos and fetuses between 15 and 104 mm crown-rump length.

Reference

Garn, S.M., Burdi, A.R., Babler, W.J., and Stinson, S. (1975). Early prenatal attainment of adult metacarpal-phalangeal rankings and proportions. *American Journal of Physical Anthropology* **43**: 327–332.

Kimura

	Radiographic Postnatal Measurements-Second Metacarpal (mm)									
	Males					Females				
Age (yrs)	*n*	Diaphyseal length mean	S^2	Midshaft width mean	S^2	*n*	Diaphyseal length mean	S^2	Midshaft width mean	S^2
1	11	21.9	3.1	4.3	0.1	11	22.9	1.3	4.0	0.12
2	13	29.2	7.7	5.0	0.2	11	30.0	5.6	4.7	0.0
3	14	32.6	11.6	5.2	0.2	16	33.3	4.2	5.0	0.27
4	14	35.8	4.2	5.4	0.3	9	35.6	5.6	5.2	0.15
5	12	37.4	3.9	5.5	0.2	17	38.5	5.9	5.4	0.15
6	20	39.8	6.6	5.8	0.3	12	40.9	7.1	5.4	0.27
7	54	43.9	5.8	5.9	0.3	40	45.2	8.7	5.7	0.28
8	33	48.1	5.1	6.1	0.3	43	46.9	6.9	5.8	0.24
9	38	49.3	9.6	6.3	0.3	36	49.6	8.5	6.2	0.18
10	56	51.3	9.6	6.5	0.4	32	50.8	10.8	6.3	0.36
11	35	53.3	8.8	6.8	0.3	41	54.4	10.4	6.8	0.30
12	76	55.2	13.2	7.2	0.4	39	57.0	7.5	7.1	0.20
13	16	57.4	9.7	7.8	0.6	16	57.9	5.0	7.2	0.32
14	27	59.9	10.2	8.1	0.7	24	58.4	6.9	7.4	0.34
15	27	62.2	7.9	8.5	0.6	24	58.9	7.1	7.3	0.43
16	26	63.7	6.2	8.7	0.6	24	59.4	7.2	7.4	0.36
17	20	64.6	6.1	8.8	0.5	20	59.5	7.1	7.6	0.35
18	7	65.0	6.2	8.9	0.3	9	59.4	10.0	7.6	0.40

Source

Radiographs taken from mid twentieth century Japanese children. Ages represent half a year below and half a year above the given age (i.e., age 5 = 4.5–5.5 yrs).

Reference

Kimura, K. (1976). Growth of the second metacarpal according to chronological age and skeletal maturation. *The Anatomical Record* **184**: 147–158.

Plato et al.

Radiographic Postnatal Measurements-Second Left Metacarpal (mm)										
	Males					Females				
		Maximum length*		Midshaft width			Maximum length*		Midshaft width	
Age (yrs)	*n*	mean	S.E	mean	S.E	*n*	mean	S.E	mean	S.E
5	6	37.8	1.7	4.5	0.2	5	38.7	0.6	4.5	0.2
6	9	42.6	2.2	5.1	0.1	1	40.4	–	5.3	–
7	18	42.6	0.7	5.3	0.1	10	43.9	1.0	5.4	0.2
8	18	46.0	0.5	5.5	0.1	15	46.3	0.4	5.4	0.1
9	18	45.9	0.7	5.8	0.2	15	47.6	0.7	5.6	0.1
10	14	49.3	0.1	6.1	0.2	17	50.7	1.1	5.9	0.2
11	22	51.4	0.7	6.2	0.1	17	52.5	0.9	6.2	0.1
12	15	53.1	1.4	6.2	0.2	14	55.4	1.3	6.6	0.1
13	21	54.6	0.6	6.6	0.1	20	57.9	1.0	6.6	0.2
14	18	57.7	0.9	7.2	0.2	12	61.5	0.9	7.0	0.2
15	13	59.2	1.4	7.3	0.2	11	62.2	0.8	6.9	0.2
16	16	63.7	1.4	7.4	0.2	7	61.6	1.2	6.7	0.2
17	–	–	–	–	–	2	64.9	0.7	7.2	0.2

*Includes the shaft and epiphysis.

Source

Radiographs from Guamanian Chamorro children between the ages of 5 and 17 years.

Warning

Guamanian children exhibited smaller dimensions (length and width) than their black, white, or Mexican-American counterparts (Plato et al., 1984).

Reference

Plato, C.C., Greulich, W.W., Garruto, R.M., and Yanagihara, R. (1984). Cortical bone loss and measurements of the second metacarpal bone: II. Hypodense bone in postwar Guamanian children. *American Journal of Physical Anthropology* **63**: 57–63.

Appearance Times

Garn et al.

Radiographic Assessment-Hand

Ossification Center	Male Percentiles 5th	50th	95th	Female Percentiles 5th	50th	95th
Capitate	–	3m	7m	–	2m	7m
Hamate	2w	4m	10m	2w	2m	7m
Epiphysis of proximal phalanx of 3rd finger	9m	1y4m	2y1m	5m	10m	1y7m
Epiphysis of proximal phalanx of 2nd finger	9m	1y5m	2y2m	5m	10m	1y8m
Epiphysis of proximal phalanx of 4th finger	10m	1y6m	2y5m	5m	11m	1y8m
Epiphysis of distal phalanx of 1st finger	9m	1y5m	2y8m	5m	12m	1y9m
Epiphysis of 2nd metacarpal	11m	1y7m	2y10m	8m	1y1m	1y8m
Epiphysis of 3rd metacarpal	11m	1y9m	3y	8m	1y2m	1y11m
Epiphysis of proximal phalanx of 5th finger	12m	1y10m	2y10m	8m	1y2m	2y1m
Epiphysis of middle phalanx of 3rd finger	12m	2y	3y4m	8m	1y3m	2y4m
Epiphysis of 4th metacarpal	1y1m	2y	3y7m	9m	1y3m	2y2m
Epiphysis of middle phalanx of 4th finger	12m	2y1m	3y3m	8m	1y3m	2y5m
Epiphysis of 5th metacarpal	1y3m	2y2m	3y10m	10m	1y4m	2y4m
Epiphysis of middle phalanx of 2nd finger	1y4m	2y2m	3y4m	8m	1y5m	2y7m
Epiphysis of distal phalanx of 3rd finger	1y4m	2y5m	3y9m	9m	1y5m	2y8m
Triquetral	6m	2y5m	5y6m	3m	1y8m	3y9m
Epiphysis of distal phalanx of 4th finger	1y4m	2y5m	3y9m	9m	1y6m	2y10m
Epiphysis of 1st metacarpal	1y5m	2y7m	4y4m	11m	1y7m	2y8m
Epiphysis of proximal phalanx of 1st finger	1y10m	3y	4y7m	11m	1y8m	2y10m
Epiphysis of distal phalanx of 2nd finger	1y10m	3y2m	5y	1y1m	2y6m	3y4m
Epiphysis of distal phalanx of 5th finger	2y1m	3y4m	5y	1y	2y	3y6m
Epiphysis of middle phalanx of 5th finger	1y11m	3y5m	5y10m	11m	2y	3y7m
Lunate	1y6m	4y1m	6y9m	1y1m	2y8m	5y8m
Scaphoid	3y7m	5y8m	7y10m	2y4m	4y1m	6y
Trapezium	3y7m	5y4m	9y	1y11m	4y1m	6y4m
Trapezoid	3y1m	6y3m	8y6m	2y5m	4y2m	6y

Postnatal week (w), month (m) or year (y).

Source

Participants in the United States based Fels Research Institute Program of Human Development, begun in 1929.

Reference

Garn, S.M., Rohmann, C.G., and Silverman, F.N. (1967). Radiographic standards for postnatal ossification and tooth calcification. *Medical Radiography and Photography* **43**: 45–66.

Birkner

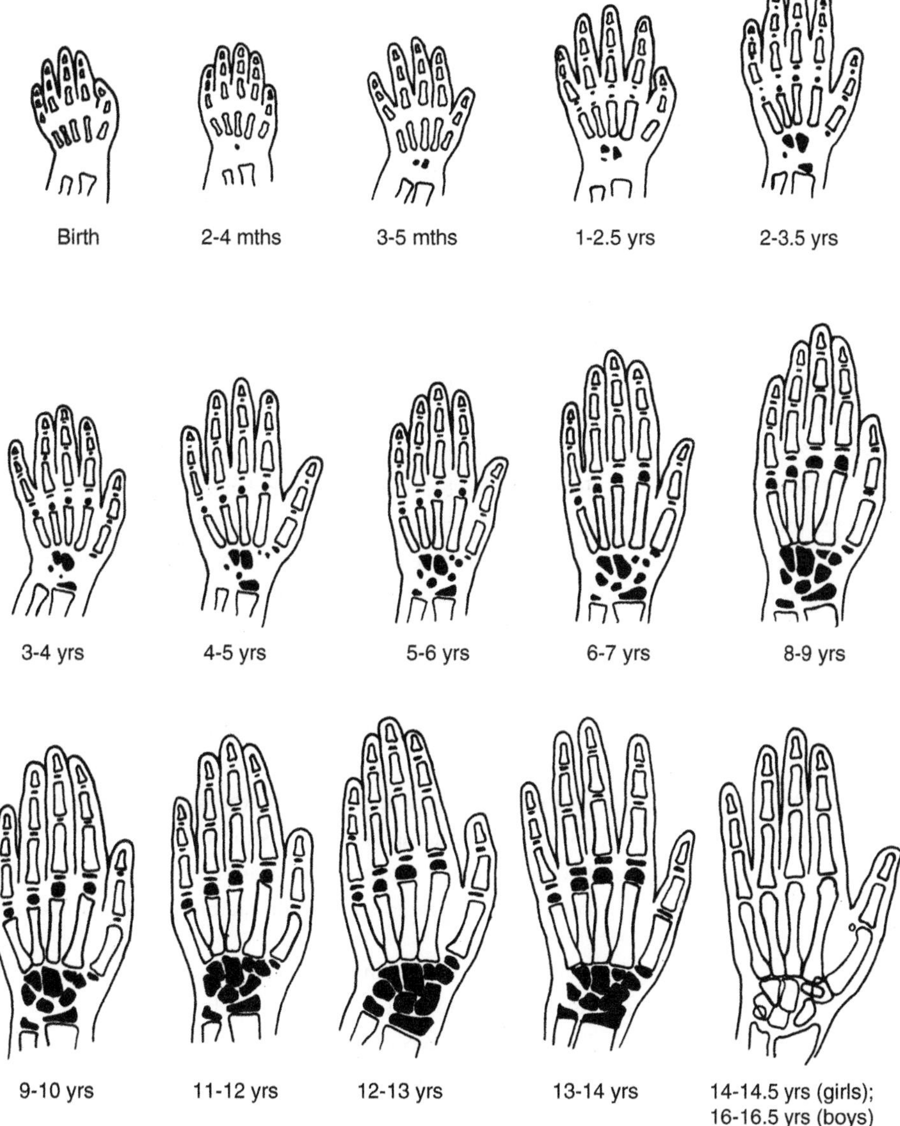

Osseous development of the hand and wrist

Reference

Birkner, R. (1978). *Normal Radiographic Patterns and Variances of the Human Skeleton – An X-ray Atlas of Adults and Children.* Baltimore (Munich): Urban and Schwarzenberg.

Overall Summary

Prenatal	
7–9 wks	Primary ossification centers appear for distal phalanges
8–10 wks	Primary ossification centers appear for metacarpals
9–11 wks	Primary ossification centers appear for proximal phalanges
10–12 wks	Primary ossification centers appear for middle phalanges
Birth	All 19 primary centers for the long bones of the hand are present (ossification centers for capitate and hamate can be present)
2–3 mths (f); 3–4 mths (m)	Ossification center appears for capitate
3–4 mths (f); 4–5 mths (m)	Ossification center appears for hamate
1–2 yrs	Ossification center appears for triquetral
10–17 mths (f); 14 mths–2 yrs (m)	Epiphyses for bases of proximal phalanges 2–5 appear
17 mths (f); 22 mths (m)	Epiphyses for base of distal phalanx 1 appears
16–19 mths (f); 22 mths–2.5 yrs (m)	Epiphyses for heads of metacarpals 2–5 appear
19 mths (f); 2.5 yrs (m)	Epiphyses for bases of middle phalanges 2–4 appear
2 yrs (f); 2–3 yrs (m)	Epiphyses for bases of distal phalanges 3–4 appear
	Epiphyses for base of metacarpal 1 and proximal phalanx 1 appear
2.5 yrs (f); 3.5 yrs (m)	Epiphyses for bases of distal and middle phalanges of finger 5 appear
3 yrs (f); 4 yrs (m)	Ossification center appears for lunate
	The capitate can be recognized in a dry bone state
4 yrs (f); 5 yrs (m)	Ossification center appears for trapezium
	The hamate can be recognized in a dry bone state
5 yrs (f); 6 yrs (m)	Ossification centers appear for trapezoid and scaphoid
8 yrs (f); 10 yrs (m)	Ossification center appears for pisiform
	Triquetral can be recognized in a dry bone state
9–10 yrs	Trapezium, trapezoid, and lunate can be recognized in a dry bone state
9.5–11 yrs	Scaphoid can be recognized in a dry bone state
10–12 yrs	Hook of hamate appears and fuses to body
12 yrs	Pisiform can be recognized in a dry bone state
11–15 yrs (f); 13–18 yrs (m)	Sesamoid bones commence ossification
13.5 yrs (f); 16 yrs (m)	Distal phalangeal epiphyses fuse
14–14.5 (f); 16.5 yrs (m)	Base of metacarpal 1 fuses
	Proximal and middle phalangeal epiphyses fuse
14.5–15 yrs (f); 16.5 yrs (m)	Heads of metacarpals 2–5 fuse

(f) indicates female, while (m) indicates male.

CHAPTER

7

The Pelvic Girdle

PRIMARY CENTERS

Ilium

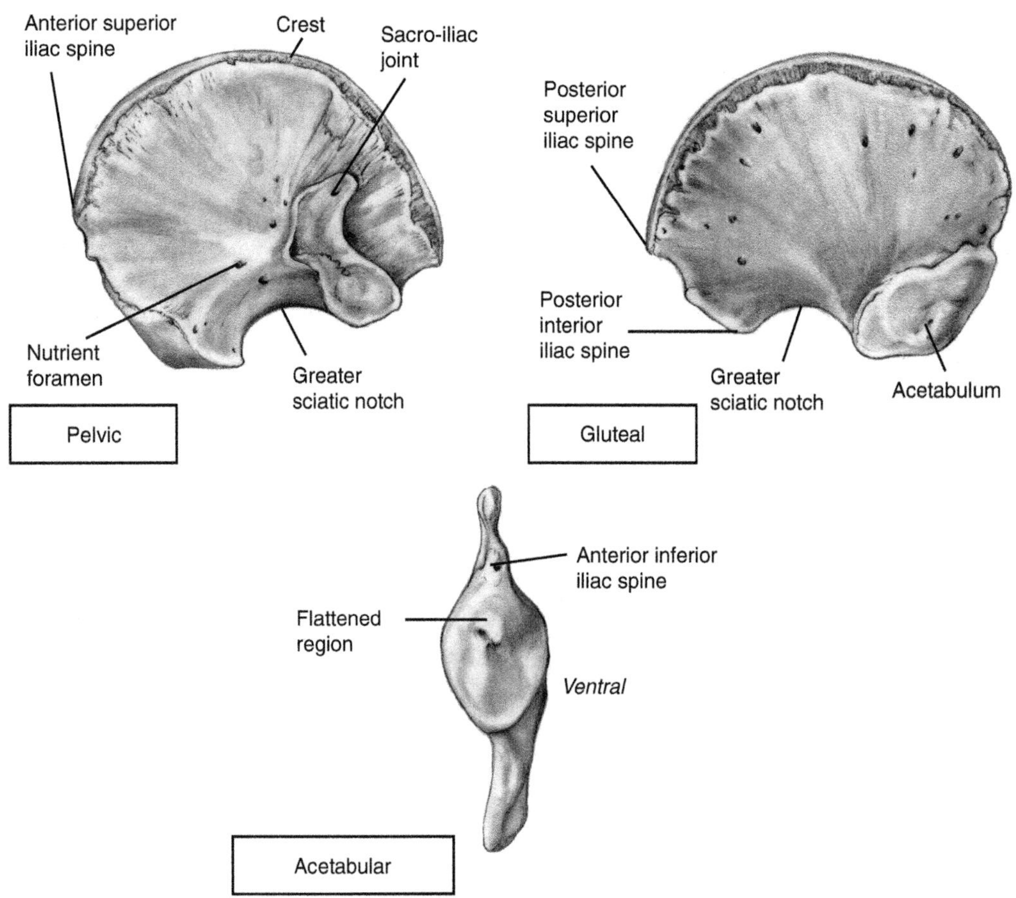

Right perinatal ilium

Identification – The ilium may be confused with fragments of other flat bones such as the skull or scapula.

- The ilium is uniquely composed of two discrete compact shells surrounding a core of coarse trabeculae.
- Nutrient foramina are clearly defined on the ilium.
- Borders of the ilium are rounded, unlike the serrated borders of cranial bones.

Siding
- Most easily achieved through identification of the greater sciatic notch and the auricular surface of the sacro iliac joint.
- Hold ilium with greater sciatic notch facing inferiorly and the auricular surface facing you; the auricular surface will be on the side of the body from which the bone originates.

Ischium

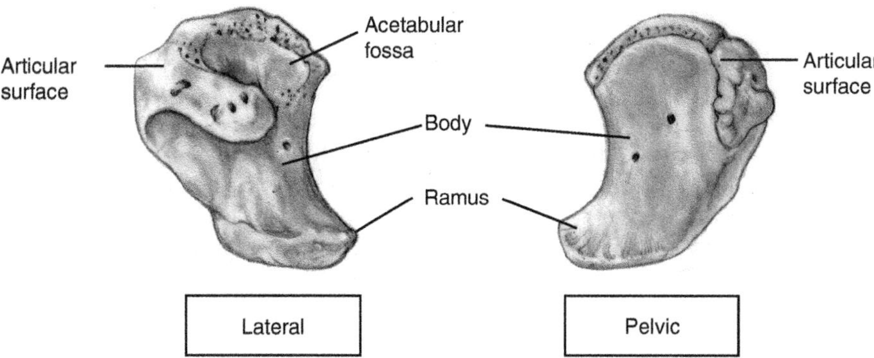

Right perinatal ischium

Identification
- Unlikely to be confused with any other element.

Siding
- Relies on identifying the smooth pelvic surface (internally), the acetabular surface on the lateral aspect, and the thinner arm of the ischial ramus inferiorly.
- Hold specimen with the outer (acetabular) surface facing you and the ramal surface inferiorly; the ramus will point to the side from which the bone belongs.

Pubis

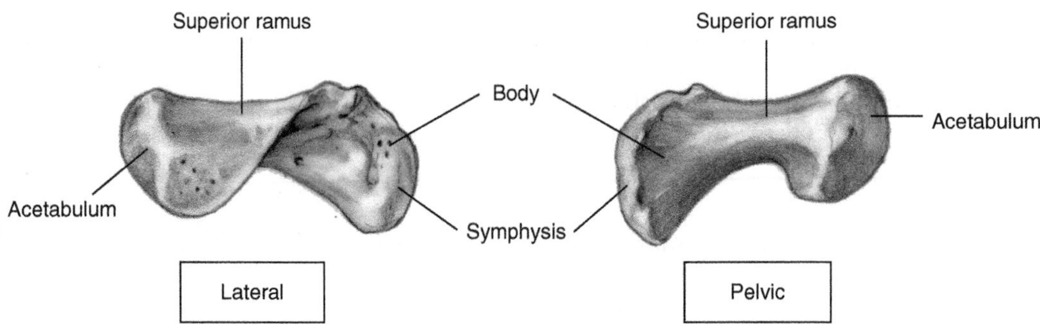

Right perinatal pubis

Identification – Unlikely to be confused with any other element.

Siding – Most easily achieved through identification of the symphyseal, pelvic, and lateral surfaces.

- Symphyseal surface is longer and thinner; acetabular extremity is thicker and more club-shaped.
- Pelvic surface is smooth and relatively featureless.
- Lateral surface is twisted in the region of the obturator notch.
- Superior border of ramus is more linear whereas the inferior border is hooked.
- Hold specimen so that the upper border of the ramus is superior and the lateral surface is facing you. The symphysis will point to the side of the body from which the bone originated.

Acetabular Changes with Age

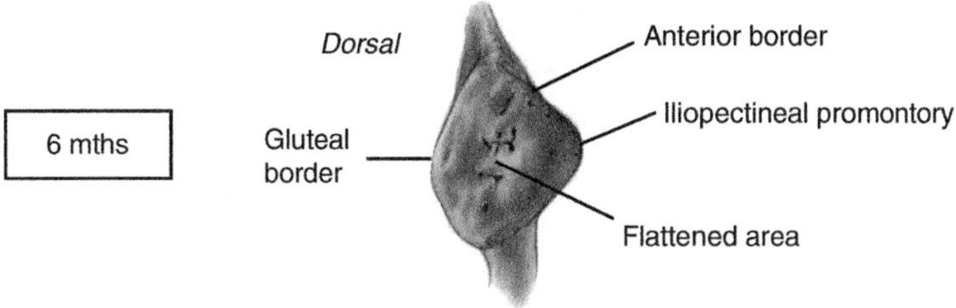

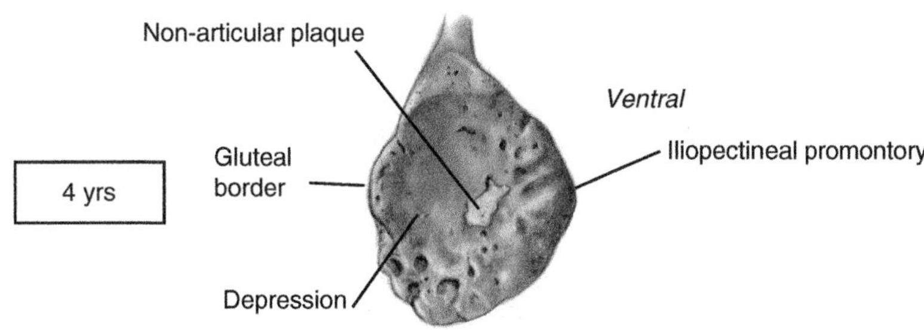

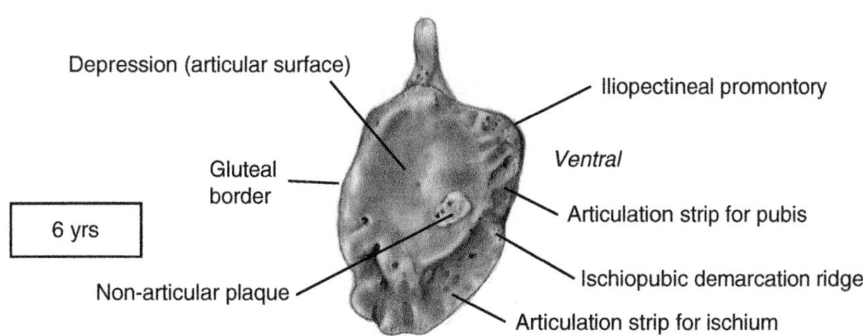

Development of the right iliac acetabular surface

Ilium

- The iliopectineal promontory is evident by six months.
- By four or five years, a well-defined plaque of bone is present, representing the future nonarticular region of the iliac acetabular fossa.
- By six years there is a well-defined demarcation between the articulation for the pubis and the ischium.

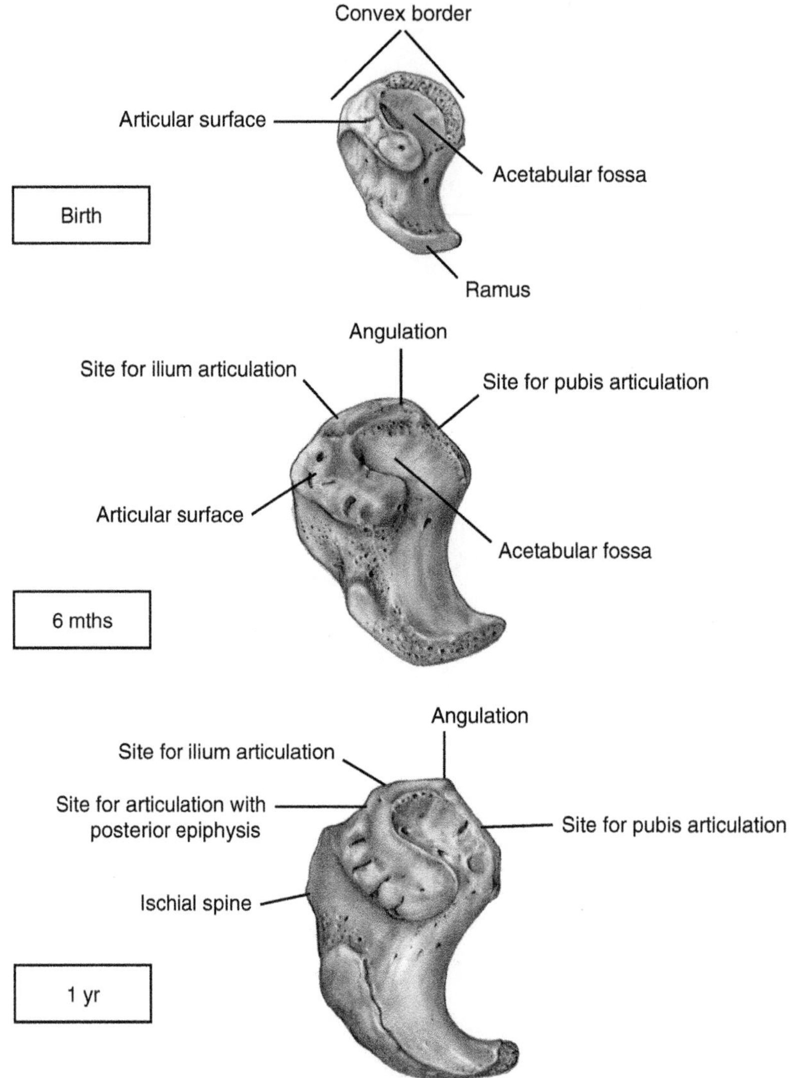

Development of the right ischial acetabular surface

Ischium

- By six months the superior border develops an angulation for articulation with the pubis anteriorly and the ilium posteriorly.
- By one year, the border is no longer convex but highly angulated.
- The ischial spine is well developed by one year of age.

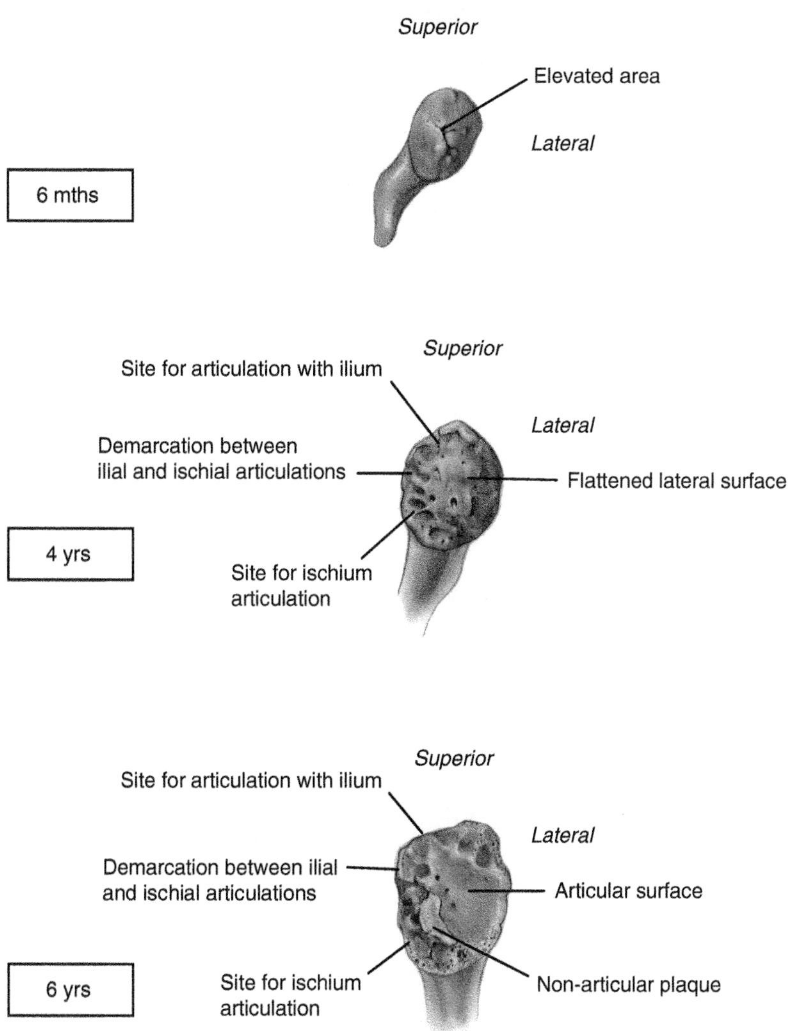

Development of the right pubic acetabular surface

Pubis

- Around six months the articular surface becomes somewhat elevated from the remainder of the surface.
- Demarcation between the articular surfaces for the ilium and the ischium becomes apparent around three to four years of age (becomes more clearly defined as ischio-pubic fusion approaches).
- By five to six years, a nonarticular plaque becomes evident in the acetabular depression on the posterior margin adjacent to the region of articulation with the ischium.

The Tri-radiate and Acetabular Epiphyses

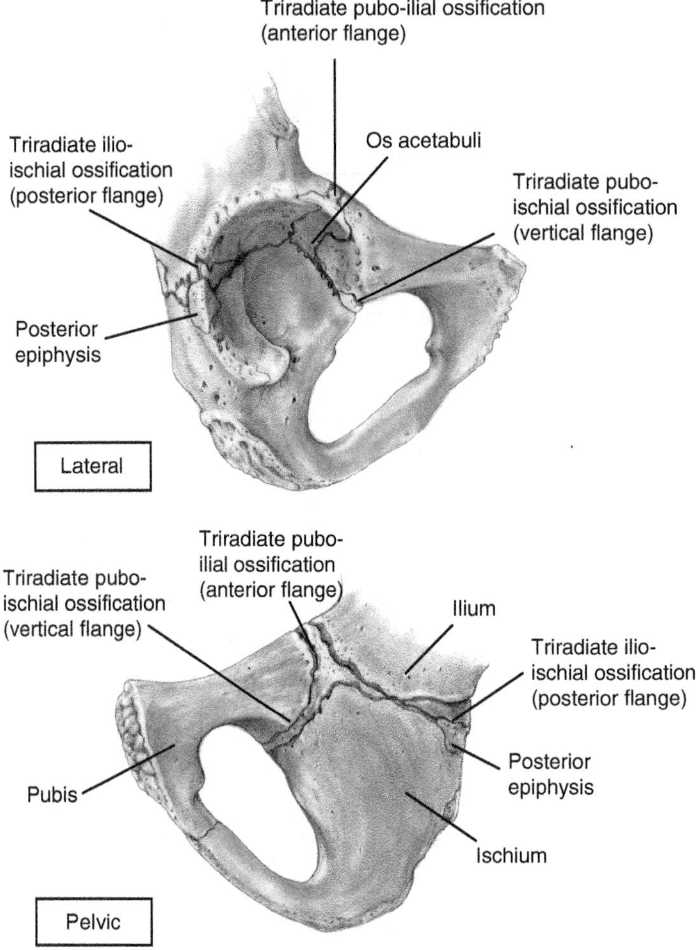

Ossification of the right tri-radiate and acetabular epiphyses (approx.15 yrs)

Identification – Unlikely to be found isolated from the primary bones; however, if separated, the acetabular epiphyses are identifiable by their smooth, concave articular surface opposite a rough convex, internal surface.

The Anterior Inferior Iliac Spine

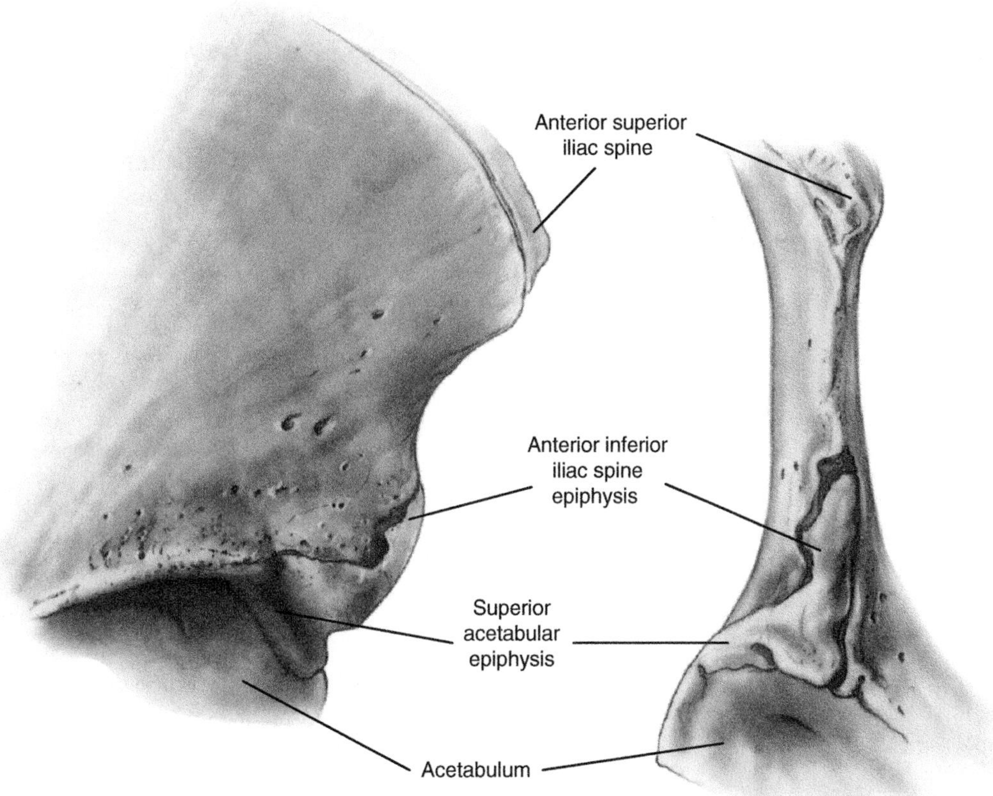

A right fusing anterior inferior iliac spine epiphysis (female, 14 years)

Identification – Unlikely to be found in isolation.

The Iliac Crest Epiphyses

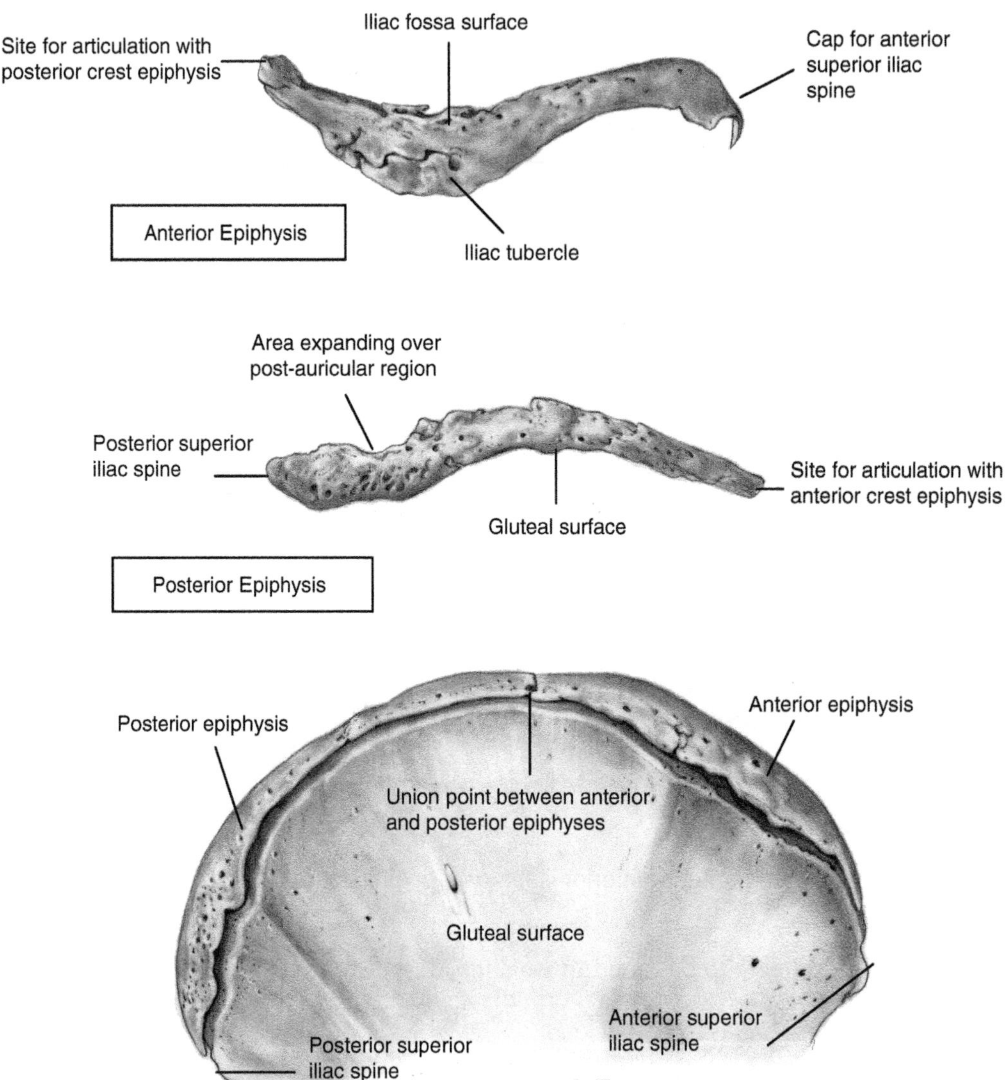

Isolated right iliac crest epiphyses and their position on the iliac crest (approx. 17 years)

Identification

- The epiphyses of the iliac crest are identifiable by their S-shaped curvature.
- They are long thin strips of bone.

The Ischial Epiphyses for the Tuberosity and Ramus

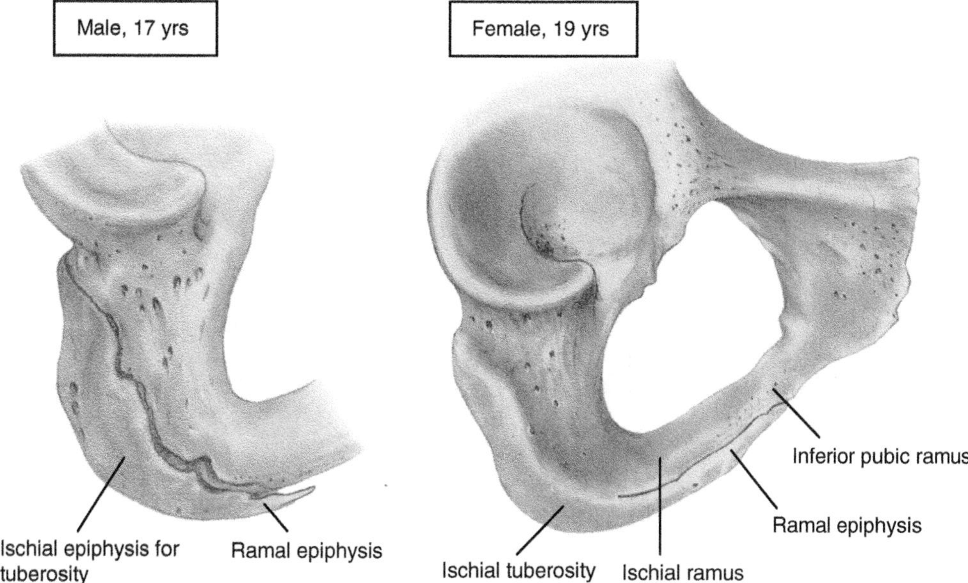

The right ischial tuberosity and ramal epiphysis

Identification

Ischial Epiphysis

- Can be easily confused with the epiphysis for the calcaneal tuberosity.
- Ischial epiphysis is slightly flatter than the calcaneal epiphysis.
- Inferior border of ischial epiphysis narrows centrally; inferior border of calcaneal epiphysis angles to one side.
- Calcaneal epiphysis displays microporosity at the attachment site of the tendocalcaneus attachment.

Ramal Epiphysis

- Unlikely to be found in isolation as it grows as an extension from the ischial epiphysis, however, broken fragments may be found.

Siding

Ischial Epiphysis

- The superior aspect is thicker than the narrowing inferior border.
- The superior border slants toward the acetabular surface, thus the side from which the epiphysis comes.

Metrics

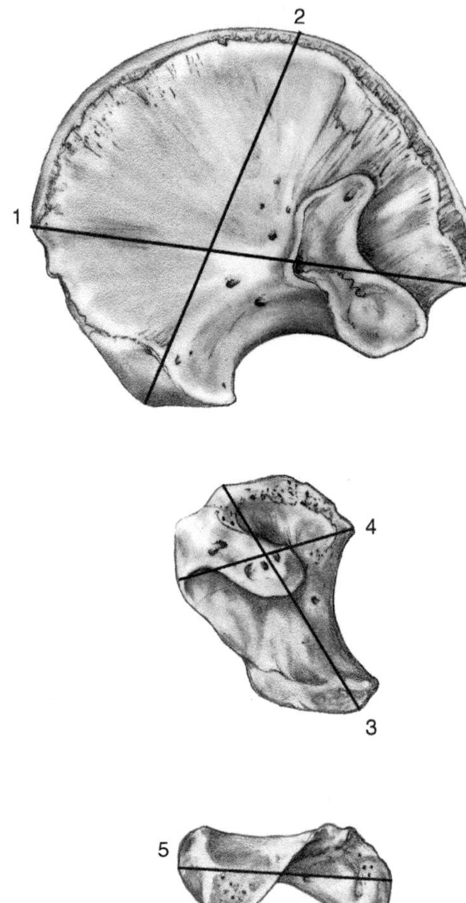

Notes

1. Maximum iliac length: Greatest distance between the anterior and posterior superior iliac spines
2. Maximum iliac width: Greatest distance between the mid point of the iliac crest and the convexity of the acetabular extremity
3. Maximum ischium length: Greatest distance between the convexity of the acetabular extremity and the tip of the ischial ramus
4. Maximum ischium width: Greatest distance across the broad superior extremity
5. Maximum pubic length: Greatest distance between the symphysis and the iliac articulation

Fazekas and Kósa

Dry Bone Fetal Measurements-Ilium (mm)					
Prenatal Age (wks)	*n*	Max Length		Max Width	
		Mean	Range	Mean	Range
12	2	4.8	4.5–5.1	3.2	3.0–3.5
14	3	5.7	5.2–6.0	3.8	3.1–4.5
16	9	9.7	8.0–12.3	7.8	6.0–9.8
18	15	12.0	9.5–16.6	9.8	8.0–11.5
20	13	15.6	13.5–18.1	12.6	11.0–15.0
22	11	16.5	14.2–18.2	14.2	12.5–15.4
24	12	18.3	15.5–21.5	15.6	14.5–17.5
26	12	19.6	17.0–22.2	17.1	15.0–18.5
28	12	21.3	20.0–23.5	19.1	17.3–21.7
30	12	22.1	20.0–25.0	20.1	18.8–22.0
32	8	25.1	23.0–27.0	22.2	20.0–24.0
34	7	26.8	26.0–28.0	24.6	23.0–26.0
36	5	28.7	27.7–31.1	26.0	25.0–27.5
38	7	32.1	28.5–34.7	28.5	25.5–31.8
40	10	34.5	32.0–38.0	30.4	27.0–34.0

Dry Bone Fetal Measurements-Ischium (mm)					
Prenatal Age (wks)	*n*	Max Length		Max Width	
		Mean	Range	Mean	Range
16	9	3.1	1.9–4.0	2.2	2.1–2.5
18	15	3.8	3.0–4.2	2.9	2.3–3.1
20	13	5.5	4.5–7.0	3.5	3.1–4.0
22	11	6.4	5.4–8.7	4.3	3.8–5.0
24	12	7.5	6.5–8.8	5.6	5.4–6.1
26	12	8.7	7.1–10.0	6.0	5.5–6.5
28	12	9.7	8.7–11.0	6.6	6.0–7.2
30	12	10.3	9.0–12.0	7.6	7.0–8.3
32	8	12.1	11.0–13.5	8.1	7.5–9.0
34	7	13.6	11.5–14.4	9.3	8.9–9.8
36	5	16.2	14.5–17.0	10.4	10.0–10.5
38	7	17.2	16.0–18.2	11.6	11.0–12.4
40	10	18.5	17.0–20.5	12.4	11.5–13.5

Dry Bone Fetal Measurements-Pubis (mm)			
		Max Length	
Prenatal Age (wks)	*n*	Mean	Range
20	13	3.6	3.0–4.0
22	11	4.5	3.0–5.0
24	12	5.5	5.0–6.3
26	12	6.0	5.1–7.0
28	12	6.6	5.5–7.5
30	12	8.0	6.5–10.0
32	8	9.9	8.5–11.0
34	7	12.4	12.0–13.0
36	5	14.1	13.0–15.0
38	7	15.0	13.2–16.1
40	10	16.6	15.0–18.0

Source

Dry bone measurements on mid twentieth century Hungarian fetal remains from autopsy—males and females combined. Age was estimated based on fetal crown heel length.

Reference

Fazekas, I.Gy. and Kósa, F. (1978). *Forensic Fetal Osteology*. Budapest: Akadémiai Kiadó.

Molleson and Cox

Dry Bone Postnatal Measurements-Ilium (mm)					
		Max Length		Max Width	
Age	*n*	Mean	Range	Mean	Range
0–3 mths	10	30.9	27.8–36.2	33.3	30.5–37.3
4–6 mths	2	35.4	30.6–40.1	37.3	34.1–40.41
7–9 mths	2	42.3	38.5–46.1	47.3	42.9–51.6
10–12 mths	2	47.4	46.5–48.2	53.8	53.1–54.5
13–18 mths	6	47.7	43.5–51.2	54.0	50.0–58.7
19–24 mths	3	54.4	51.5–57.6	57.3	56.3–58.3
2–3 yrs	11	59.2	49.2–64.9	63.7	50.5–71.5

Source

Dry bone inspection of early eighteenth to mid nineteenth century documented remains from Spitalfields, London.

Reference

Molleson, T. and Cox, M. (1993). *The Spitalfields Project Volume 2 – The Anthropology – The Middling Sort,* Research Report 86. London: Council for British Archaeology.

Appearance and Union Times

Webb and Suchey

Dry Bone Assessment-Anterior Iliac Crest										
	Male % - Stage of Union					Female % - Stage of Union				
Age	*n*	**1**	**2**	**3**	**4**	*n*	**1**	**2**	**3**	**4**
11	2	100	–	–	–	1	100	–	–	–
12	–	–	–	–	–	–	–	–	–	–
13	3	67	33	–	–	–	–	–	–	–
14	4	50	50	–	–	3	–	67	33	–
15	9	11	78	11	–	4	–	75	25	–
16	17	6	29	65	–	5	–	–	100	–
17	10	–	20	70	10	3	–	–	100	–
18	11	–	9	55	36	8	–	–	63	37
19	17	–	12	29	59	5	–	–	40	60
20	14	–	–	21	79	4	–	–	25	75
21	13	–	–	15	85	4	–	–	–	100
22	20	–	–	–	100	6	–	–	–	100
23	14	–	–	7	93	5	–	–	20	80
24–40	185	–	–	–	100	68	–	–	–	100

Source

Multiracial American autopsy sample (1977–1979).

Notes

Stage 1: Nonunion without epiphysis
Stage 2: Nonunion with separate epiphysis
Stage 3: Partial union
Stage 4: Complete union

Reference

Webb, P.A.O. and Suchey, J.M. (1985). Epiphyseal union of the anterior iliac crest and medial clavicle in a modern sample of American males and females. *American Journal of Physical Anthropology* **68**: 457–466.

Schaefer

	Dry Bone Assessment-Male %							
	Tri-radiate Complex* - Stage of Union				Ant Inf Iliac - Spine Stage of Union			
Age	*n*	0	1	2	*n*	0	1	2
14	2	–	100	–	2	100	–	–
15	3	–	100	–	3	100	–	–
16	11	–	64	36	11	37	18	45
17	7	–	29	71	6	17	–	83
18	12	–	17	83	12	17	–	83
19+	137	–	–	100	105	–	–	100

*Tri-radiate complex includes both the acetabular and the tri-radiate epiphyses.

	Dry Bone Assessment-Male %							
	Ischial Tuberosity - Stage of Union				Iliac Crest - Stage of Union			
Age	*n*	0	1	2	*n*	0	1	2
15	6	100	–	–	6	100	–	–
16	15	53	47		14	100	–	–
17	15	33	60	7	17	53	47	–
18	24	13	74	13	24	42	54	4
19	18	–	67	33	19	–	89	11
20	25	–	32	68	25	4	48	48
21	25	–	–	100	25	–	24	76
22	12	–	–	100	12	–	–	100
23+	95	–	–	100	95	–	–	100

Source

Bosnian war dead from the fall of Srebrenica (1995)—males only.

Notes

Stage 0: Nonunion
Stage 1: Partial Union
Stage 2: Complete union marked by obliteration of the epiphyseal line (scar may be present)

Reference

Schaefer, M. (2008). A summary of epiphyseal union timings in Bosnian males. *International Journal of Osteoarchaeology*, DOI: 10.1002/0a.959. Copyright John Wiley & Sons Limited. Reproduced with permission.

McKern and Stewart

		Dry Bone Assessment-Male %									
		Ischial Tuberosity - Stage of Union					Iliac Crest - Stage of Union				
Age	*n*	**0**	**1**	**2**	**3**	**4**	**0**	**1**	**2**	**3**	**4**
17	10	50	10	20	10	10	40	10	10	40	–
18	45	52	13	12	12	11	18	16	26	20	20
19	52	14	24	13	17	32	5	4	27	28	36
20	45	11	13	9	23	44	2	6	4	24	64
21	37	10	6	3	25	56	–	5	8	13	74
22	24	4	–	–	4	92	–	–	4	4	92
23	26	–	–	4	4	92	–	–	–	–	100
24–25	27	–	–	–	–	100	–	–	–	–	100

Source

American war dead from Korea (1951–1957)—males only.

Notes

Stage 0: Nonunion of epiphysis
Stage 1: ¼ of epiphysis united
Stage 2: ½ of epiphysis united
Stage 3: ¾ of epiphysis united
Stage 4: Complete union of epiphysis

Reference

McKern, T.W. and Stewart, T.D. (1957). Skeletal age changes in young American males, analysed from the standpoint of age identification. *Headquarters Quartermaster Research and Development Command, Technical Report* EP-45. Natick, MA.

Coqueugniot and Weaver

Dry Bone Assessment-Innominate Bone						
	Males			Females		
	Open	Partial	Complete	Open	Partial	Complete
Tri-radiate Complex*	≤16	15–20	≥17	≤19	9–17	≥14
Anterior Inferior Iliac Spine	≤16	16–20	≥16	≤12	14–19	≥17
Ischial Tuberosity	≤20	16–24	≥23	≤12	14–26	≥20
Iliac Crest	≤20	16–24	≥20	≤19	17–26	≥22

*Reflects combination data for union of the three primary elements.

Source

Documented Portuguese material born between 1904 and 1938 (Coimbra collection), including 69 females and 68 males between the ages of 7 and 29 years.

Warning

Many ages are poorly represented.

Reference

Coqueugniot, H. and Weaver, T. (2007). Infracranial maturation in the skeletal collection from Coimbra, Portugal: New aging standards for epiphyseal union. *American Journal of Physical Anthropology* **134**(3): 424–437.

Cardoso

Dry Bone Assessment-Tri-radiate Complex*								
	Males % - Stage of Union				Females % - Stage of Union			
Age	*n*	1	2	3	*n*	1	2	3
9	2	100	–	–	2	100	–	–
10	2	100	–	–	4	100	–	–
11	5	80	20	–	4	75	25	–
12	2	100	–	–	2	100	–	–
13	1	100	–	–	2	–	100	–
14	3	66	33	–	2	50	–	50
15	3	–	66	33	4	–	–	100
16	4	–	25	75	3	–	33	66
17	4	–	25	75	3	–	–	100
18	2	–	50	50	5	–	–	100
19	3	–	–	100	4	–	–	100

*Tri-radiate complex-considers both the acetabular and tri-radiate epiphyses as a whole.

Dry Bone Assessment-Ischial Tuberosity								
	Males % - Stage of Union				Females % - Stage of Union			
Age	*n*	1	2	3	*n*	1	2	3
13	1	100	–	–	3	100	–	–
14	3	100	–	–	2	50	50	–
15	3	66	33	–	5	20	80	–
16	3	66	33	–	3	–	66	33
17	4	–	50	50	3	–	66	33
18	1	–	100	–	5	–	20	80
19	4	–	25	75	3	–	66	33
20	5	–	–	100	4	–	–	100
21	4	–	25	75	5	–	–	100
22–23	7	–	–	100	6	–	–	100

Dry Bone Assessment-Iliac Crest

	Males % - Stage of Union				Females % - Stage of Union			
Age	*n*	**1**	**2**	**3**	*n*	**1**	**2**	**3**
14	3	100	–	–	2	100	–	–
15	3	100	–	–	5	80	20	–
16	3	66	33	–	3	100	–	–
17	4	25	75	–	3	–	100	–
18	2	50	50	–	4	–	40	60
19	4	–	50	50	3	–	100	–
20	5	–	40	60	4	–	75	25
21	4	–	25	75	5	–	100	–
22–23	4	–	–	100	6	–	–	100

Dry Bone Assessment-Ramal Epiphysis

	Males % - Stage of Union				Females % - Stage of Union			
Age	*n*	**1**	**2**	**3**	*n*	**1**	**2**	**3**
16	3	100	–	–	3	100	–	–
17	4	50	50	–	3	100	–	–
18	2	50	–	50	5	60	20	20
19	3	33	66	–	3	33	33	33
20	5	20	20	60	4	75	–	25
21	4	25	25	50	4	–	100	–
22	–	–	–	–	3	–	33	66
23–24	4	–	–	100	6	–	–	100

Source

Portuguese individuals buried between 1903 and 1975 (Lisbon collection).

Notes

Stage 1: No union
Stage 2: Partial union
Stage 3: Complete union—no visible gaps, however an epiphyseal scar may be retained

Reference

Cardoso, H. (2008). Epiphyseal union at the innominate and lower limb in a modern Portuguese skeletal sample, and age estimation in adolescent and young adult male and female skeletons. *American Journal of Physical Anthropology*, **135**(2): 161–170.

Jit and Singh

Radiographic Assessment-Ischial Tuberosity												
	Male % - Stages of Union						Female % - Stages of Union					
Age	*n*	NA	0	1	2	3	*n*	NA	0	1	2	3
11	12	100	–	–	–	–	27	100	–	–	–	–
12	27	100	–	–	–	–	27	100	–	–	–	–
13	25	96	4	–	–	–	27	85	15	–	–	–
14	24	88	12	–	–	–	24	54	46	–	–	–
15	24	92	8	–	–	–	34	18	73	6	3	–
16	20	50	50	–	–	–	23	9	65	17	9	–
17	41	2	47	22	12	17	54	4	24	46	22	4
18	118	–	23	23	20	34	85	–	11	36	38	15
19	99	–	4	12	24	60	31	–	–	13	39	48
20	34	–	–	6	12	82	25	–	4	8	32	56
21	19	–	–	–	–	100	12	–	–	–	33	67
22–25	13	–	–	–	–	100	8	–	–	–	–	100

Radiographic Assessment-Iliac Crest

	Male % - Stages of Union						Female % - Stages of Union					
Age	*n*	**NA**	**0**	**1**	**2**	**3**	*n*	**NA**	**0**	**1**	**2**	**3**
11	27	100	–	–	–	–	27	100	–	–	–	–
12	27	100	–	–	–	–	27	93	7	–	–	–
13	23	100	–	–	–	–	27	37	63	–	–	–
14	25	88	12	–	–	–	25	36	64	–	–	–
15	25	52	48	–	–	–	35	3	83	6	8	–
16	22	9	86	57	–	–	26	–	58	27	15	–
17	51	–	57	12	12	19	56	2	19	36	25	18
18	136	–	32	14	20	34	90	–	13	21	20	46
19	112	–	4	7	18	71	34	–	–	–	9	90
20	37	–	–	8	5	87	25	–	4	4	12	80
21	19	–	–	–	–	100	12	–	–	–	–	100
22–25	13	–	–	–	–	100	8	–	–	–	–	100

Source

Radiographs from mid twentieth century Indian students.

Notes

Stage NA: Center not appeared
Stage 0: Nonunion with separate epiphysis
Stage 1: Commenced union
Stage 2: Advanced union
Stage 3: Complete union

Reference

Jit, I. and Singh, B. (1971). A radiological study of the time of fusion of certain epiphyses in Punjabees. *Journal of Anatomical Society India* **20**(1): 1–27.

Compilation Summary of Union Times

Summary of Fusing Times-Tri-radiate Complex*

Assessment	Study	Open	Fusing	Closed
Male				
Dry Bone	Schaefer	–	?–18	≥16
	Cardoso	≤14	11–18	≥15
	Coqueugniot & Weaver	≤16	15–20	≥17
Female				
Dry Bone	Cardoso	≤14	11–16	≥14
	Coqueugniot & Weaver	≤19	9–17	≥14

*Combined results for union of the triradiate and acetabular epiphyses.

Summary of Fusing Times-Anterior Inferior Iliac Spine

Assessment	Study	Open	Fusing	Closed
Male				
Dry Bone	Schaefer	≤18	16–18	≥16
	Coqueugniot & Weaver	≤16	16–20	≥16
Female				
Dry Bone	Coqueugniot & Weaver	≤12	14–19	≥17

Summary of Fusing Times-Ischial Tuberosity				
Assessment	**Study**	**Open**	**Fusing**	**Closed**
Male				
Dry Bone	Schaefer	≤18	16–20	≥17
	McKern & Stewart	≤22	?–23	–
	Cardoso	≤16	15–21	≥17
	Coqueugniot & Weaver	≤20	16–24	≥23
Radiographic	Jit & Singh	≤19	17–20	≥17
Female				
Dry Bone	Cardoso	≤15	14–19	≥16
	Coqueugniot & Weaver	≤12	14–26	≥20
Radiographic	Jit & Singh	≤20	15–21	≥17

Summary of Fusing Times-Iliac Crest				
Assessment	**Study**	**Open**	**Fusing**	**Closed**
Male				
Dry Bone	Schaefer	≤20	17–21	≥18
	McKern & Stewart	≤20	?–22	–
	Webb & Suchey	≤19	15–23	≥17
	Cardoso	≤18	16–21	≥19
	Coqueugniot & Weaver	≤20	16–24	≥20
Radiographic	Jit & Singh	≤19	16–20	≥17
Female				
Dry Bone	Webb & Suchey	≤15	14–23	≥18
	Cardoso	≤16	14–21	≥18
	Coqueugniot & Weaver	≤19	17–26	≥22
Radiographic	Jit & Singh	≤20	15–20	≥17

Morphological Summary

Prenatal	
Mths 2–3	Ilium commences ossification
Mths 4–5	Ischium commences ossification and ilium is recognizable
Mths 5–6	Pubis commences ossification
Mths 6–8	Ischium is recognizable in isolation
Birth	All three primary bony components are represented
By 6 mths	The ilium displays a prominence on its acetabular extremity formed by the development of the iliopectineal line
	Angulation of the superior border of the ischium has occurred
By yr 1	The superior border of the ischium is square and the ischial spine, pubic tubercle, and crest have developed
By yr 2	The anterior border of the ilium has bent forward in the vertical plane
By yrs 3–4	The demarcation of the iliac and ischial articulation sites are clearly defined on the pubis
By yrs 4–5	The nonarticular acetabular area is well defined on the ilium
By yrs 5–6	The nonarticular acetabular area is well defined on the pubis
5–16 yrs	Fusion of the ischiopubic ramus occurs
9–10 yrs	The anterior acetabular epiphysis or "os acetabuli" appears and ossific islands appear in triradiate cartilage
10–11 yrs	The posterior acetabular epiphysis commences ossification
10–13 yrs	Center appears for the anterior inferior iliac spine
11–16 yrs	The acetabulum commences and completes fusion in females
12–15 yrs	The superior acetabular epiphysis appears and the iliac crest commences ossification in the female
13–16 yrs	The ischial epiphysis commences ossification
14–18 yrs	The acetabulum commences and completes fusion in males
	The iliac crest commences ossification in the male
	The iliac crest commences fusion in the female
By 18 yrs	The anterior inferior iliac spine has fused
16–20 yrs	The ischial tuberosity is complete
17–20 yrs	The iliac crest epiphyses commence fusion in the male
19–20 yrs	The ischial epiphysis extends halfway along the ramus
20–23 yrs	The iliac crest completes union

CHAPTER

8

The Lower Limb

THE FEMUR

Shaft

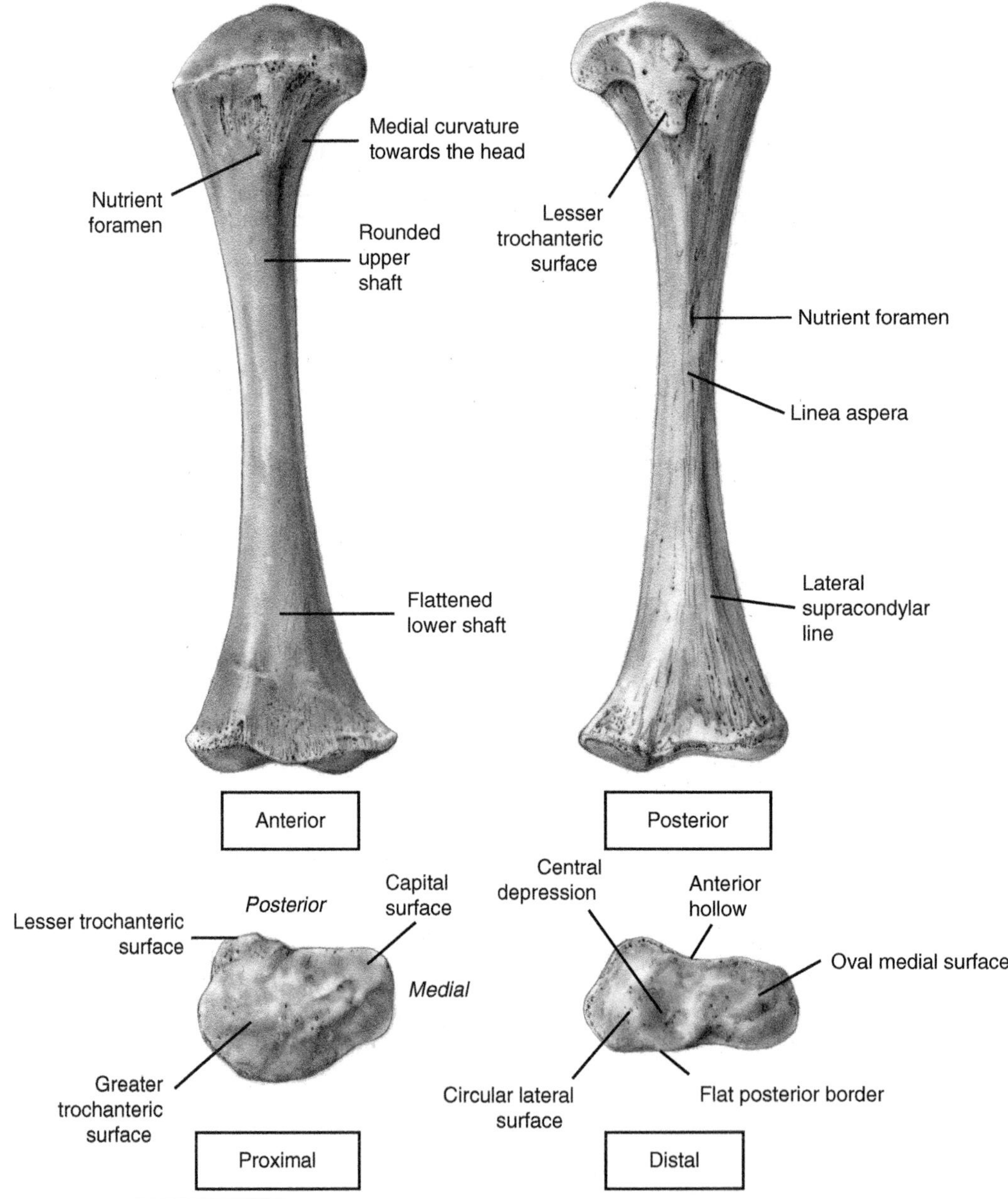
Medial curvature towards the head
Nutrient foramen
Rounded upper shaft
Flattened lower shaft
Anterior
Lesser trochanteric surface
Nutrient foramen
Linea aspera
Lateral supracondylar line
Posterior
Lesser trochanteric surface
Posterior
Capital surface
Medial
Greater trochanteric surface
Proximal
Central depression
Anterior hollow
Oval medial surface
Circular lateral surface
Flat posterior border
Distal

Identification – May be confused with any of the other long bones.

- The femur is the largest of the long bones.
- The proximal metaphyseal surface is roughly oval and angulated (each side corresponding to the cartilaginous head and greater trochanter) that continues posteriorly into the lesser trochanter surface.
- The shaft flattens distally like the humerus, however, lacks its recognizable olecranon fossa.
- The distal metaphyseal surface is oval like the proximal tibia, however lacks its recognizable tuberosity.

Siding

- The posterior surface of the perinatal shaft has an anterior curvature, whereas the anterior surface is flat.
- The shaft widens toward the proximal end, curving medially toward the head.
- The lesser trochanter lies on the posterior surface.
- There are usually two nutrient foramina in the upper and middle thirds of the linea aspera.
- The distal metaphyseal surface is wider laterally than medially (in the anteroposterior plane).

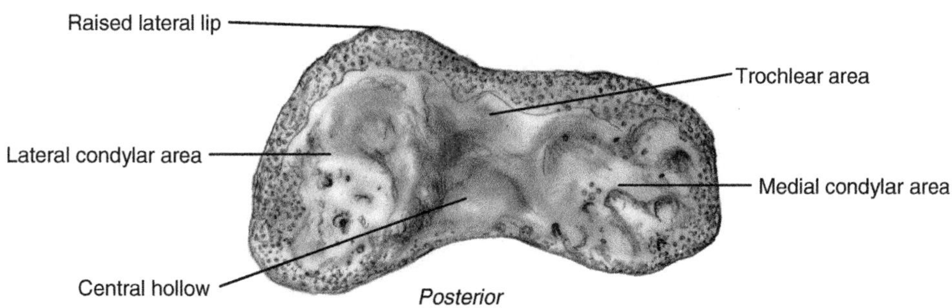

Right distal metaphyseal surface – female, 4 years

The Femoral Head

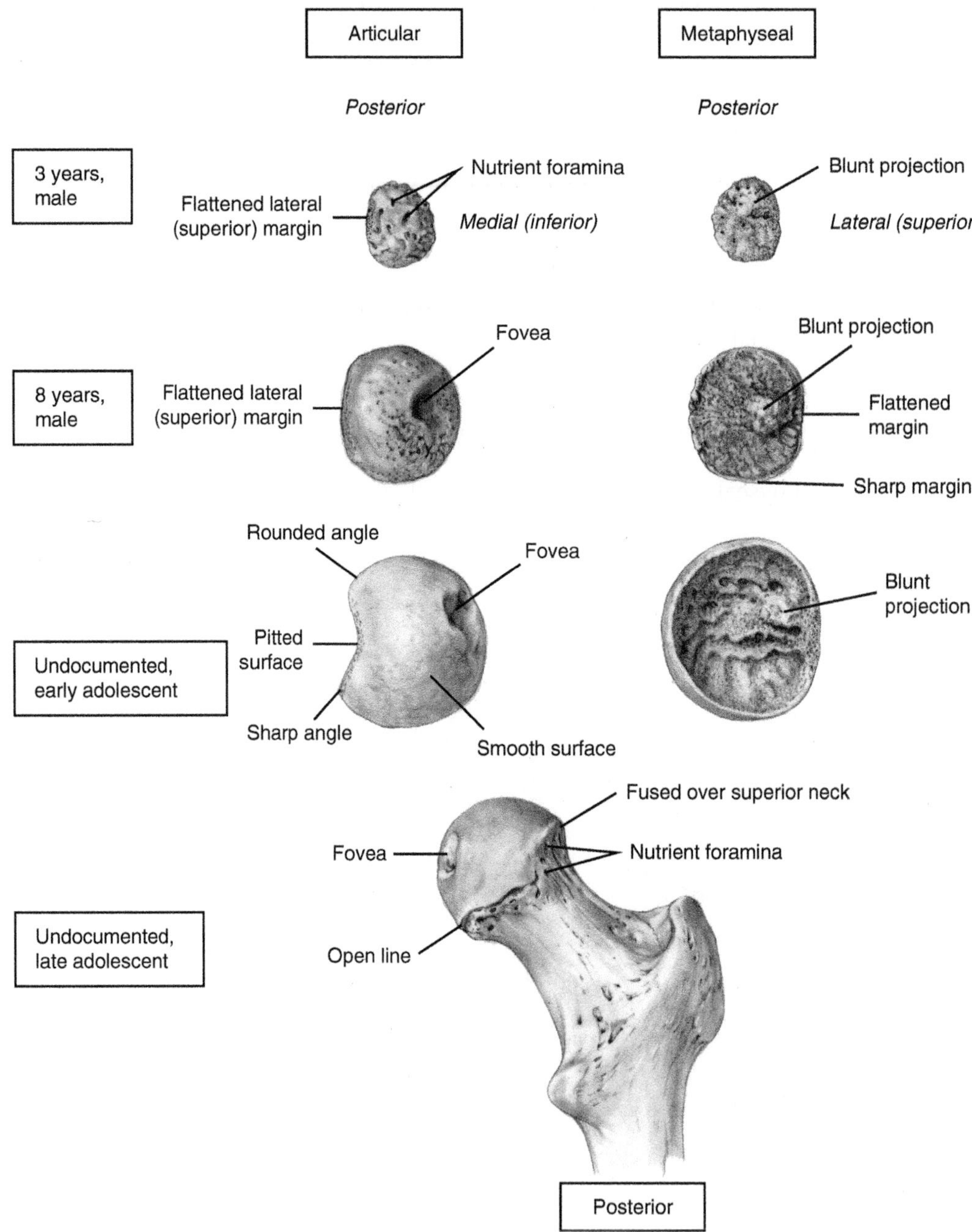

Development of the right capital femoral epiphysis

Identification – May be confused with the humeral head epiphysis (see p. 168).

- Femoral head epiphysis is more circular with a flattened lateral (superior) border.
- Femoral epiphysis has a blunt projection on its metaphyseal surface; proximal humeral epiphysis has a Y-shaped groove.
- Fovea capitis is present on the femoral epiphysis from six to eight years onward.

Siding

- Is possible from about the age of three to four years onward.
- Flattened along its lateral (superior) border.
- Fovea is positioned slightly inferiorly.
- Looking at the metaphyseal surface when in correct superior/inferior orientation, the blunt projection will be positioned slightly to the opposite side from which the bone comes; in other words, the blunt metaphyseal projection is positioned slightly posteriorly when in correct anatomical position.
- In more developed epiphyses, the sharp angle along the lateral (superior) border is positioned anteriorly.

The Greater Trochanter

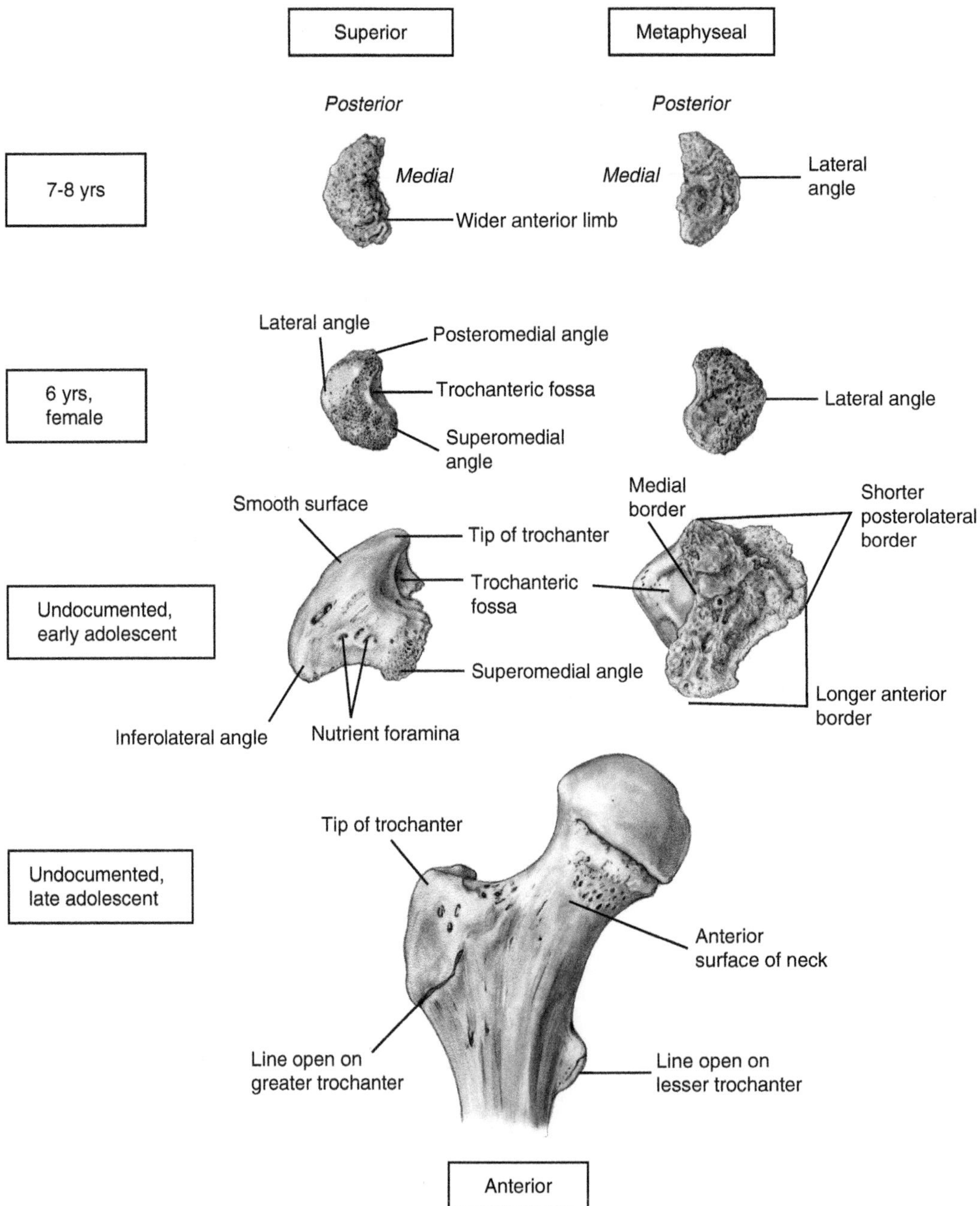

Development of the right greater trochanteric epiphysis

Identification/Siding

- Assumes a boomerang-shaped appearance by five to six years, with the angle on its lateral side.
- Anterior limb is slightly wider than the posterior limb in early development; anterior border becomes longer than posterolateral border later in development.
- Once the trochanteric fossa becomes obvious, it is situated posteriorly along the medial surface.

Distal Epiphysis

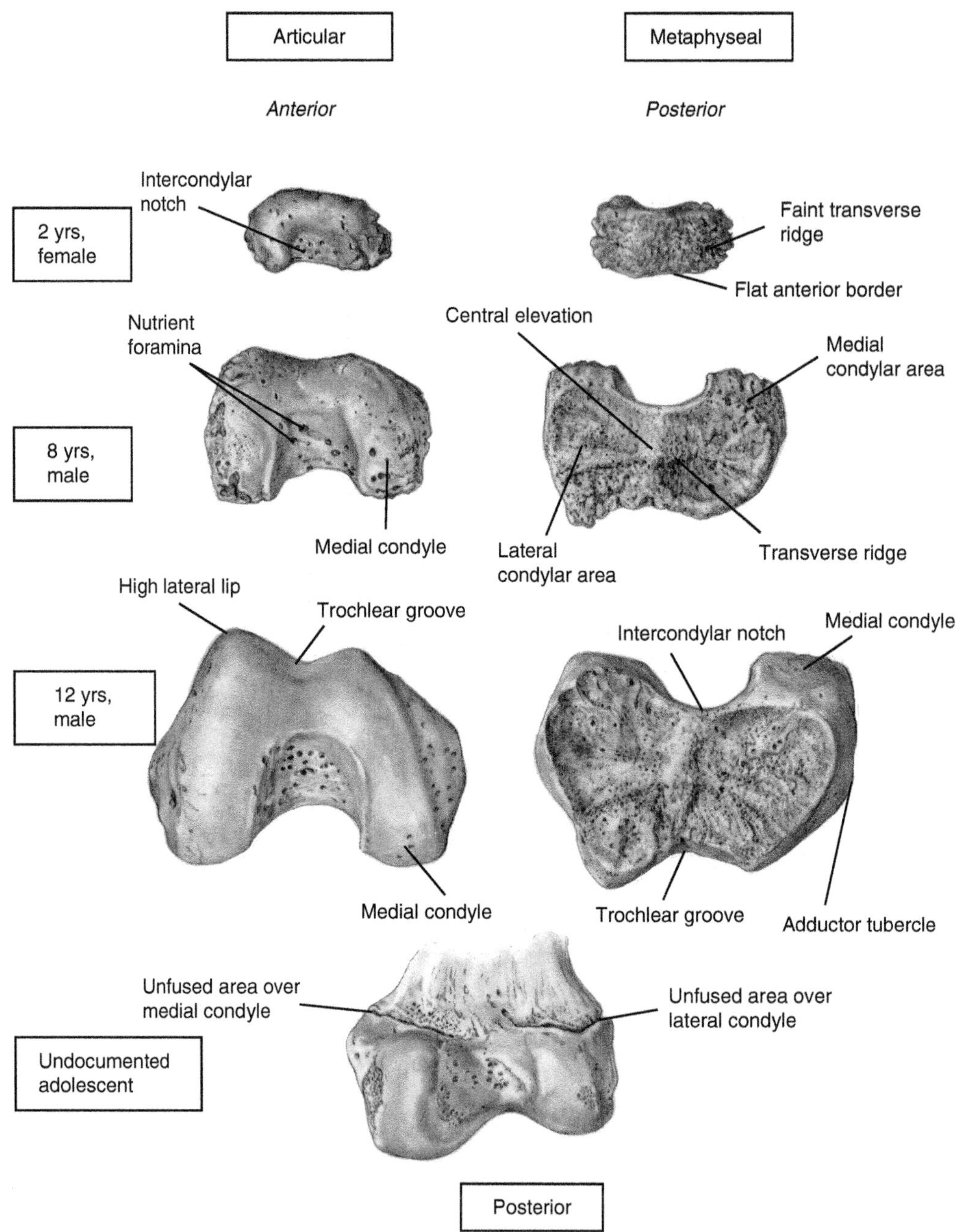

Development of the right distal femoral epiphysis

Identification – Identification is possible from about two years of age. May be confused with the proximal tibial epiphysis early in development.

- The distal femoral epiphysis is larger than the proximal tibial epiphysis.
- The epiphysis of the distal femur displays a central elevation on its metaphyseal surface; the epiphysis of the proximal tibia displays a central elevation (intercondylar eminence) on it articular surface.
- The epiphysis of the distal femur displays raised condyles on its articular surface; the proximal tibial epiphysis displays slightly concaved condyles in association with its articular surface.

Siding – Siding is possible from about two years of age.

- Is roughly kidney shaped early in development with a flat anterior border and an indented posterior border that forms the shallow intercondylar notch.
- The lateral condyle is longer in an anteroposterior direction with a higher lateral lip than the medial condyle.

Shaft Metrics

Fazekas and Kósa

Dry Bone Fetal Measurements-Femur					
		Max length (mm)		Distal width (mm)	
Prenatal Age (wks)	*n*	Mean	Range	Mean	Range
12	2	8.5	7.0–10.0	1.9	1.8–2.0
14	3	12.4	11.5–13.8	2.2	2.0–2.5
16	9	20.7	18.0–24.0	4.7	3.4–6.2
18	15	26.4	24.0–29.0	6.2	5.6–7.0
20	13	32.6	29.0–36.2	8.0	6.2–9.2
22	11	35.7	32.6–39.7	8.8	8.3–10.0
24	12	40.3	37.2–45.0	9.8	9.0–11.1
26	12	41.9	38.5–46.2	10.6	9.2–12.1
28	12	47.0	44.5–49.0	11.8	10.5–13.0
30	12	48.7	45.0–54.0	12.3	11.0–14.0
32	8	55.5	52.5–59.0	14.3	13.0–15.6
34	7	59.8	57.0–66.0	15.3	14.0–19.0
36	5	62.5	60.0–67.5	16.4	15.0–18.0
38	7	68.9	64.0–73.5	18.7	17.0–20.5
40	10	74.3	69.0–79.0	19.9	18.0–22.0

Source

Dry bone measurements on mid twentieth century Hungarian fetal remains from autopsy—males and females combined. Age was estimated based on fetal crown heel length.

Notes

Has been shown to be compatible with radiographic measurements taken from American fetuses (Warren, M.W. (1999). Radiographic determination of developmental age in fetuses and stillborns. *Journal of Forensic Sciences* **44**(4): 708–712.)

Reference

Fazekas, I.Gy. and Kósa, F. (1978). *Forensic Fetal Osteology*. Budapest: Akadémiai Kiadó.

Jeanty

Ultrasound Fetal Measurements-Femur			
	Max Length (mm)-Percentiles		
Prenatal Age (wks)	5	50	95
12	–	9	–
14	5	15	19
16	13	22	24
18	19	28	31
20	22	33	39
22	29	39	44
24	34	44	49
26	39	49	53
28	45	53	57
30	49	58	62
32	53	62	67
34	57	65	70
36	61	69	74
38	62	72	79
40	66	75	81

Source

Sonograms taken from late twentieth century white fetuses in Brussels, Belgium.

Reference

Jeanty, P. (1983). Fetal limb biometry. (Letter). *Radiology* **147**: 601–602.

Scheuer et al.

Radiographic Measurements-Femur	
Regression equations of fetal age (weeks) on maximum femoral length (mm)	
Linear	age (weeks) = (0.3303 × femoral length) + 13.5583 ± 2.08
Logarithmic	age (weeks) = (19.727 $\log_e$ × femoral length) – 47.1909 ± 2.04

Source

Radiographic measurements on mid twentieth century premature British fetuses. The sample consisted of 29 male and 36 female fetuses between 24 and 40 weeks. Age was determined using date of last menstrual period.

Reference

Scheuer, J.L, Musgrave, J.H., and Evans, S.P. (1980). The estimation of late fetal and perinatal age from limb bone length by linear and logarithmic regression. *Annals of Human Biology* 7(3): 257–265.

Maresh

Radiographic Postnatal Measurements-Femoral Length (mm)								
	Males		Percentile		Females		Percentile	
Age (yrs)	*n*	Mean	10th	90th	*n*	Mean	10th	90th
Diaphyseal length								
1.5 mths	59	86.0	79.4	92.7	68	87.2	81.3	91.8
3 mths	59	100.7	94.1	107.4	65	100.8	95.6	105.8
6 mths	67	112.2	104.5	118.2	78	111.1	105.2	116.6
1 yr	72	136.6	129.4	143.0	81	134.6	128.0	139.6
1.5 yrs	68	155.4	146.6	163.3	84	153.9	145.2	163.6
2 yrs	68	172.4	164.3	181.1	84	170.8	161.9	180.8
2.5 yrs	72	187.2	178.0	196.5	82	185.2	175.3	196.9
3 yrs	71	200.3	190.9	211.6	79	198.4	187.5	211.4
3.5 yrs	73	212.1	200.2	226.0	78	211.1	198.8	225.3
4 yrs	72	224.1	213.8	237.2	80	223.2	209.7	238.4
4.5 yrs	71	235.7	225.0	250.3	78	235.5	218.9	250.7
5 yrs	77	247.5	236.0	263.4	80	247.0	233.4	261.6
6 yrs	71	269.7	256.5	288.2	75	268.9	252.1	287.8
7 yrs	71	291.1	274.8	308.2	86	288.8	273.0	308.0
8 yrs	70	312.1	293.7	331.2	85	309.8	289.5	331.0
9 yrs	76	330.4	312.8	349.2	83	328.7	305.1	351.8
10 yrs	77	349.3	330.6	371.6	84	347.9	324.2	373.6
11 yrs	75	367.0	348.9	389.8	76	367.0	338.6	402.0
12 yrs	74	386.1	364.1	409.8	71	387.6	359.2	416.2
Tolal length including epiphyses								
10 yrs	76	385.1	364.9	407.1	83	382.8	355.1	412.3
11 yrs	75	405.2	383.5	430.0	76	403.5	374.2	438.6
12 yrs	77	425.6	400.1	451.3	74	427.9	393.1	461.8
13 yrs	73	447.4	418.0	475.0	69	447.2	415.1	479.3
14 yrs	75	470.8	437.4	499.1	64	459.9	426.5	487.4
15 yrs	61	489.0	456.0	522.0	57	464.4	434.6	493.2
16 yrs	60	502.8	475.4	536.7	40	466.7	435.8	500.2
17 yrs	50	508.9	483.0	541.0	18	462.9	432.0	504.6
18 yrs	28	511.7	485.7	548.3	4	–	–	–

Source

American children enrolled in the Child Research Council and born between 1915 and 1967.

Reference

Maresh, M.M. (1970). Measurements from roentgenograms. In: *Human Growth and Development* (R.W. McCammon, Ed.), pp. 157–200. Springfield IL: C.C. Thomas.

Appearance Times

Garn et al.

Radiographic Assessment-Femur						
	Male Percentiles			Female Percentiles		
Ossification Center	5th	50th	95th	5th	50th	95th
Head	3w	4m1w	7m3w	2w	4m	7m2w
Greater Trochanter	1y11m	3y	4y4m	11m2w	1y10m	3y

Postnatal week (w), month (m) or year (y).

Source

Participants in the U.S.-based Fels Research Institute Program of Human Development, begun in 1929.

Reference

Garn, S.M., Rohmann, C.G., and Silverman, F.N. (1967). Radiographic standards for postnatal ossification and tooth calcification. *Medical Radiography and Photography* **43**: 45–66.

Elgenmark

Radiographic Assessment-Femur								
	Males (months)				Female (months)			
Ossification Center	25%	50%	75%	100%	25%	50%	75%	100%
Head	3.9	5.6	6.7	10.0	3.6	4.9	6.2	8.0
Greater Trochanter	43.2	46.1	51.5	–	27.2	30.2	34.0	51.5
Distal	0.3	0.5	0.8	3.0	0.3	0.6	0.9	5.0

Source

Radiographs of children (429 males and 423 females) treated or examined at the Samariten Children's Hospital, Stockholm, during the years 1942–1945.

Reference

Elgenmark, O. (1946). The normal development of the ossific centres during infancy and childhood. *Acta Paediatrica Scandinavica* **33**(Suppl. 1).

Union Times

Schaefer

Dry Bone Assessment-Male %								
	Proximal Femur - Stage of Union				Greater & Lesser Troch* - Stage of Union			
Age	*n*	0	1	2	*n*	0	1	2
14–15	9	100	–	–	9	100	–	–
16	15	33	60	7	14	57	36	7
17	17	18	35	47	18	22	28	50
18	24	8	17	75	24	8	29	63
19	20	–	5	95	20	–	5	95
20	24	–	4	96	25	–	4	96
21+	133	–	–	100	133	–	–	100

*Results were combined as both reflect nearly identical fusing times.

Dry Bone Assessment-Male %				
		Distal Femur - Stage of Union		
Age	*n*	0	1	2
14–15	9	100	–	–
16	14	93	7	–
17	18	61	22	17
18	24	21	50	29
19	20	5	25	70
20	25	–	8	92
21+	132	–	–	100

Source

Bosnian war dead from the fall of Srebrenica (1995)—males only.

Notes

Stage 0: Nonunion
Stage 1: Partial union
Stage 2: Complete union marked by obliteration of the epiphyseal line (scar may be present)

Reference

Schaefer, M. (2008). A summary of epiphyseal union timings in Bosnian males. *International Journal of Osteoarchaeology,* DOI: 10.1002/oa.959. Copyright John Wiley & Sons Limited. Reproduced with permission.

McKern and Stewart

Dry Bone Assessment-Distal Femur						
		Male % - Union Stage				
Age	*n*	**0**	**1**	**2**	**3**	**4**
17–18	55	16	2	3	18	61
19	52	4	–	1	9	86
20	45	–	–	2	9	89
21	37	–	–	–	8	92
22	24	–	–	–	–	100
23	26	–	–	–	–	100
24+	136	–	–	–	–	100

Source

American war dead from Korea (1951–1957)—males only.

Notes

Stage 0: Nonunion of epiphysis
Stage 1: ¼ of epiphysis united
Stage 2: ½ of epiphysis united
Stage 3: ¾ of epiphysis united
Stage 4: Complete union of epiphysis

Reference

McKern, T.W. and Stewart, T.D. (1957). Skeletal age changes in young American males, analysed from the standpoint of age identification. *Headquarters Quartermaster Research and Development Command, Technical Report* EP-45. Natick, MA.

Coqueugniot

Dry Bone Assessment-Femur						
	Males			Females		
	Open	Partial	Complete	Open	Partial	Complete
Head	≤20	16–24	≥19	≤17	12–22	≥17
Greater Trochanter	≤20	16–20	≥16	≤12	17–19	≥14
Lesser Trochanter	≤20	16–21	≥19	≤12	14–19	≥17
Distal Femur	≤20	16–21	≥19	≤19	17–19	≥17

Source

Documented Portuguese material born between 1904 and 1938 (Coimbra collection), including 69 females and 68 males between the ages of 7 and 29 years.

Warning

Many ages are poorly represented.

Reference

Coqueugniot, H. and Weaver, T. (2007). Infracranial maturation in the skeletal collection from Coimbra, Portugal: New aging standards for epiphyseal union. *American Journal of Physical Anthropology,* **134**(3): 424–437.

Cardoso

Dry Bone Assessment-Proximal Femur								
	Males % - Stage of Union				Female % - Stage of Union			
Age	*n*	1	2	3	*n*	1	2	3
12	2	100	–	–	2	100	–	–
13	1	100	–	–	3	100	–	–
14	3	100	–	–	2	50	50	–
15	3	66	33	–	5	20	60	20
16	4	50	25	25	3	–	66	33
17	4	–	25	75	3	–	–	100
18	2	–	50	50	5	–	–	100
19	4	–	–	100	4	–	–	100
20	6	–	–	100	4	–	–	100

Dry Bone Assessment-Greater and Lesser Trochanter*								
	Males % - Stage of Union				Female % - Stage of Union			
Age	*n*	1	2	3	*n*	1	2	3
11	5	100	–	–	4	100	–	–
12	2	100	–	–	2	100	–	–
13	1	100	–	–	3	66	33	–
14	3	100	–	–	2	50	–	50
15	3	66	33	–	5	20	40	40
16	4	50	25	25	3	–	66	33
17	4	–	25	75	3	–	–	100
18	2	–	50	50	5	–	–	100
19	4	–	–	100	4	–	–	100
20	6	–	–	100	4	–	–	100

*Results were combined as both reflect nearly identical fusing times.

Dry Bone Assessment-Distal Femur								
	Males % - Stage of Union				Females % - Stage of Union			
Age	*n*	**1**	**2**	**3**	*n*	**1**	**2**	**3**
12	2	100	–	–	2	100	–	–
13	1	100	–	–	3	100	–	–
14	3	100	–	–	2	50	50	–
15	3	100	–	–	5	60	40	–
16	4	75	–	25	3	33	66	–
17	4	25	25	50	3	–	33	66
18	2	50	–	50	5	–	20	80
19	4	–	–	100	4	–	25	75
20	6	–	–	100	4	–	–	100
21	5	–	–	100	5	–	–	100

Source

Portuguese individuals buried between 1903 and 1975 (Lisbon collection).

Notes

Stage 1: No union
Stage 2: Partial union
Stage 3: Complete union—no visible gaps, however an epiphyseal scar may be retained

Reference

Cardoso, H. (2008). Epiphyseal union at the innominate and lower limb in a modern Portuguese skeletal sample, and age estimation in adolescent and young adult male and female skeletons. *American Journal of Physical Anthropology*, **135**(2): 161–170.

Jit and Singh

Radiographic Assesment-Femoral Head										
	Male % - Stage of Union					Female % - Stage of Union				
Age	*n*	0	1	2	3	*n*	0	1	2	3
11	28	100	–	–	–	25	100	–	–	–
12	28	100	–	–	–	27	66	15	15	4
13	26	76	12	12	–	28	–	18	21	61
14	25	64	8	16	12	24	8	–	17	75
15	25	68	8	12	12	35	–	–	3	97
16	21	–	10	19	71	26	–	–	4	96
17	55	–	–	2	98	55	–	–	–	100
18	134	–	–	–	100	90	–	–	–	100
19	114	–	–	–	100	33	–	–	–	100
20–25	72	–	–	–	100	45	–	–	–	100

Source

Radiographs from mid twentieth century Indian students.

Notes

Stage 0: Nonunion
Stage 1: Commenced union
Stage 2: Advanced union
Stage 3: Complete union

Reference

Jit, I. and Singh, B. (1971). A radiological study of the time of fusion of certain epiphyses in Punjabees. *Journal of Anatomical Society India* **20**(1): 1–27.

Compilation Summary of Union Times

Summary of Fusing Times-Proximal Femur					
	Assessment	Study	Open	Fusing	Closed
Male					
	Dry Bone	Schaefer	≤18	16–20	≥16
		Coqueugniot & Weaver	≤20	16–24	≥19
		Cardoso	≤16	15–18	≥16
	Radiographic	Jit & Singh	≤15	13–17	≥14
Female					
	Dry Bone	Coqueugniot & Weaver	≤17	12–22	≥17
		Cardoso	≤15	14–16	≥15
	Radiographic	Jit & Singh	≤14	12–16	≥12

Summary of Fusing Times-Greater and Lesser Trochanter					
	Assessment	Study	Open	Fusing	Closed
Male					
	Dry Bone	Schaefer	≤18	16–20	≥16
		Coqueugniot & Weaver	≤20	16–21	≥16
		Cardoso	≤16	15–18	≥16
Female					
	Dry Bone	Coqueugniot & Weaver	≤12	17–19	≥14
		Cardoso	≤15	13–16	≥14

Summary of Fusing Times-Distal Femur					
	Assessment	Study	Open	Fusing	Closed
Male					
	Dry Bone	Schaefer	≤19	16–20	≥17
		McKern & Stewart	≤19	?–21	–
		Coqueugniot & Weaver	≤20	16–21	≥19
		Cardoso	≤18	16–18	≥16
Female					
	Dry Bone	Coqueugniot & Weaver	≤19	17–19	≥17
		Cardoso	≤16	14–19	≥17

Morphological Summary

Prenatal	
Wk 7–8	Primary ossification center appears in shaft
Wks 36–40	Secondary ossification center for distal epiphysis appears
Birth	Represented by shaft and distal epiphysis
By yr 1	Secondary center for head appears
2–5 yrs	Secondary center for greater trochanter appears
By yrs 3–4	Epiphysis of head hemispherical and recognizable
By yrs 3–5	Distal epiphysis recognizable by characteristic shape
3–6 yrs	Ossification appears in the patella
6–8 yrs	Greater trochanter becomes recognizable
7–12 yrs	Secondary center for lesser trochanter appears
14–17 yrs	Head, greater trochanter, and lesser trochanter fuse in females
16–19 yrs	Head, greater trochanter, and lesser trochanter fuse in males
14–19 yrs	Distal epiphysis fuses in females
16–20 yrs	Distal epiphysis fuses in males

THE PATELLA

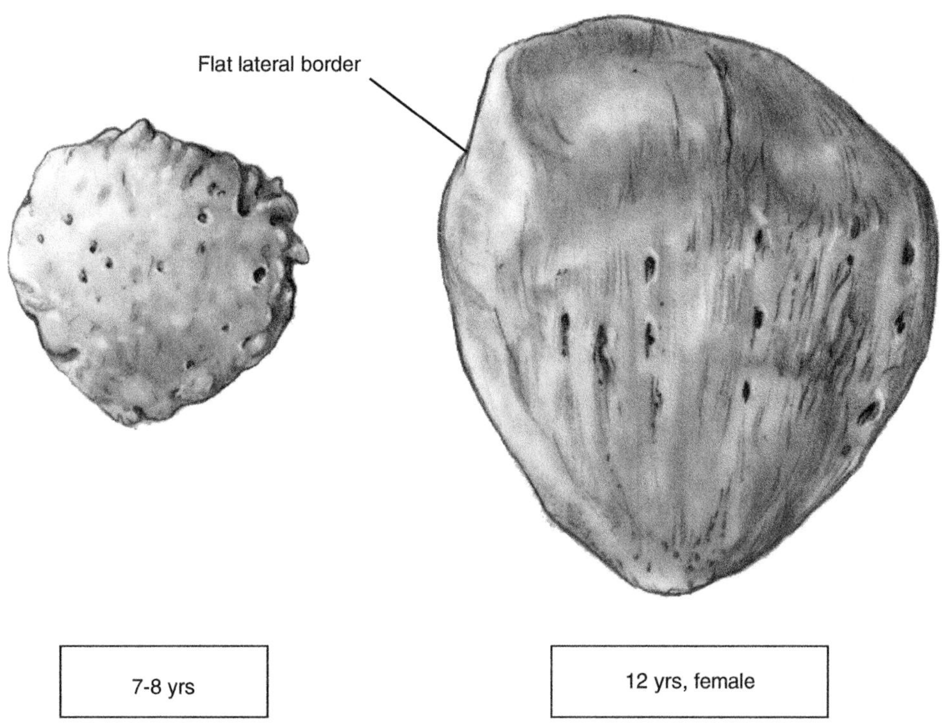

Development of the right patella

Identification/Siding – Difficult to side until ossification has spread well into the articular surface, which is not until late childhood. Once this occurs, side as if an adult patella.

- In early development, the patella is a biconvex disc with a slightly pointed apex and two surfaces composed of porous bone.
- In early adolescence, the superior part of the lateral border is often flat.

THE TIBIA

Shaft

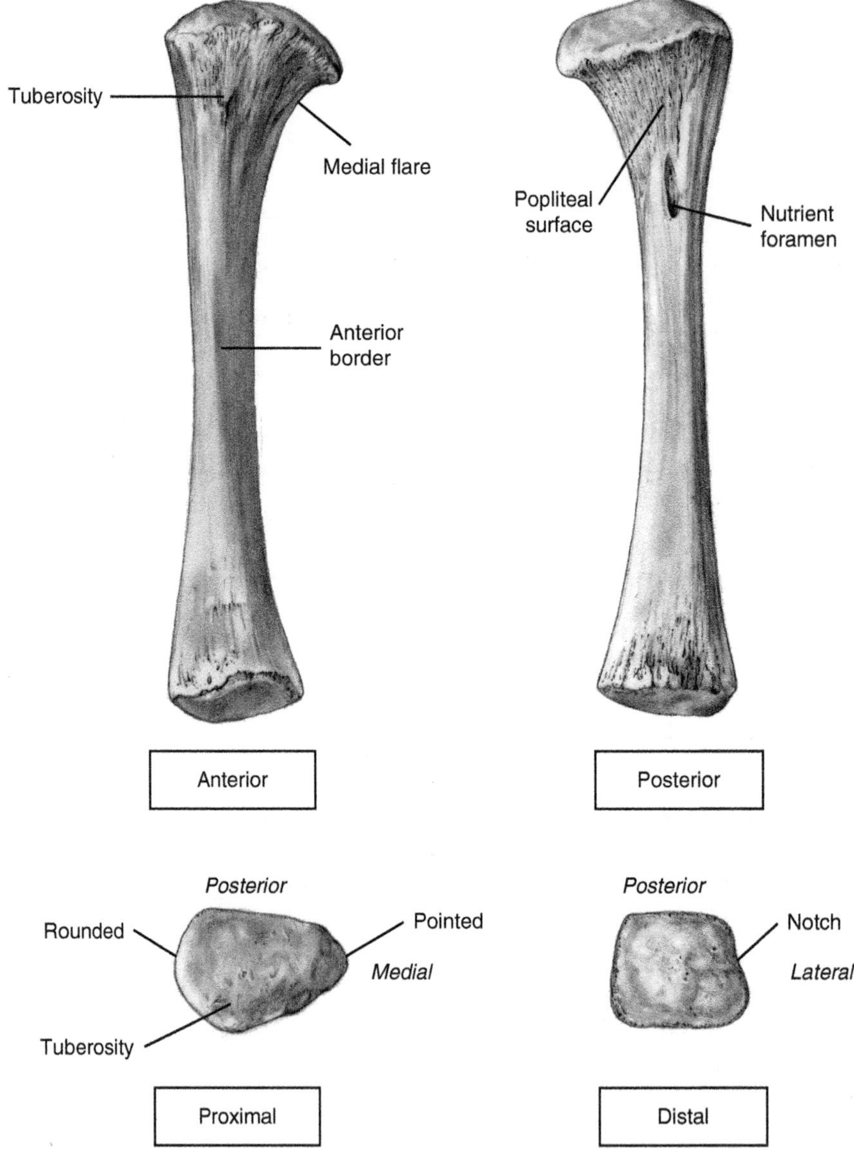

Right perinatal tibia

Identification – May be confused with any of the other long bones.

- The perinatal tibia is more robust than the radius, ulna, and fibula, shorter than the femur and similar in length to the humerus.
- The tibial shaft is triangular and flares out both proximally and distally, unlike the humerus, which is flattened distally and displays the obvious olecranon fossa.
- The proximal tibia is oval like the distal femur but is smaller and distinguished by the presence of the tuberosity anteriorly.
- A distal tibial fragment is about the same size as the proximal humerus but is flat, with a D-shaped outline and a straight lateral border, unlike the proximal humerus, which has a rounded surface and evidence of the intertubercular sulcus.

Siding

- The proximal end is rounded and more flared; the distal end is flatter and flared to a much lesser degree.
- The anterior surface is marked by a sharp border that curves medially at its distal end.
- The posterior surface has a very large nutrient foramen that is situated inferolateral to the popliteal area.
- On the posterior surface, the obliquity of the popliteal line extends from a superolateral position to an inferomedial position.
- The medial border of the proximal end is more concave than the lateral border.
- At the distal metaphyseal surface the lateral side is flat and often marked by a small notch.

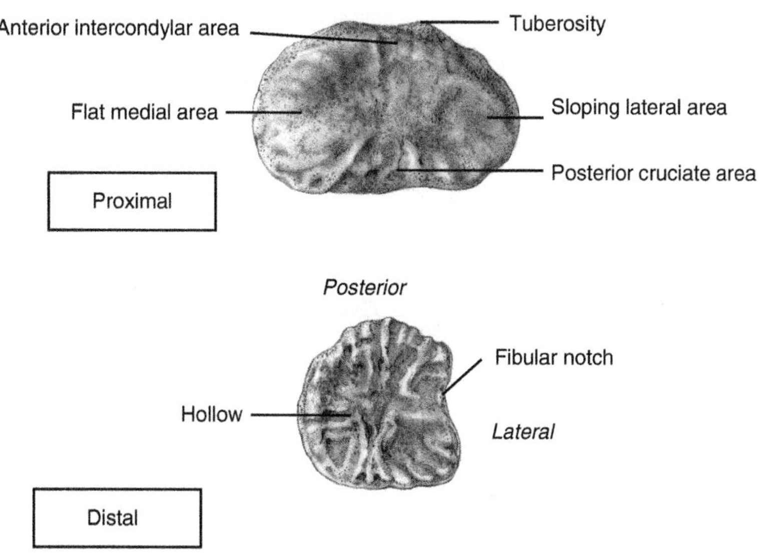

Right tibial metaphyseal surfaces – 8 yrs, male

Proximal Epiphysis

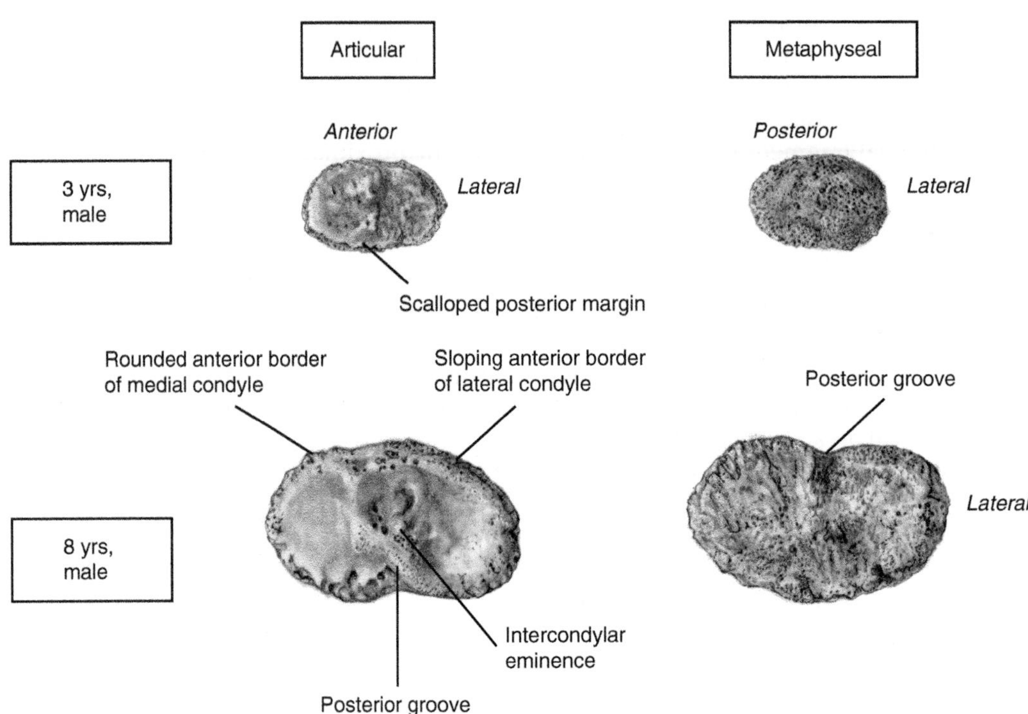

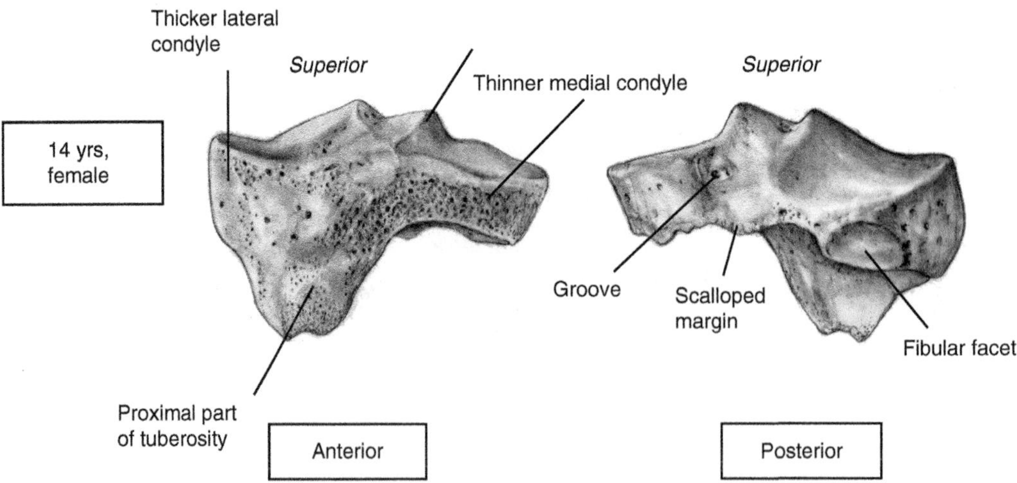

Development of the right proximal tibial epiphysis

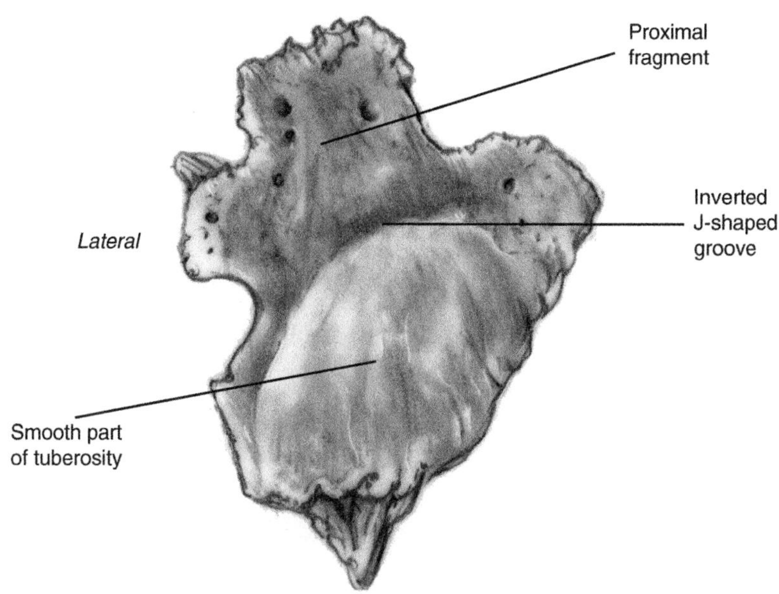

Fragment of tibial tuberosity

Identification – The proximal tibia is identifiable during the second year but may be confused with the distal femoral epiphysis (see page 262). The tibial tuberosity develops as part of, yet distinct from, the main part of the epiphysis.

Siding – Unlikely to achieve confident siding until three to four years of age.

- The proximal tibial epiphysis is roughly oval in outline with a groove on its posterior surface where the posterior cruciate ligament lies.
- In early development the medial condyle projects further anteriorly than the lateral condyle, although becomes more variable once adult morphology is attained.
- The anterior border of the lateral condyle is more sloping, whereas the anterior border of the medial condyle is more rounded.
- The tibial tuberosity projects inferolaterally.
- An inverted J-shaped groove extends inferolaterally on the tibial tuberosity.
- Once the proximal tibial epiphysis attains adult morphology, the anterior aspect of the lateral condyle is thicker than the medial condyle.

Distal Epiphysis

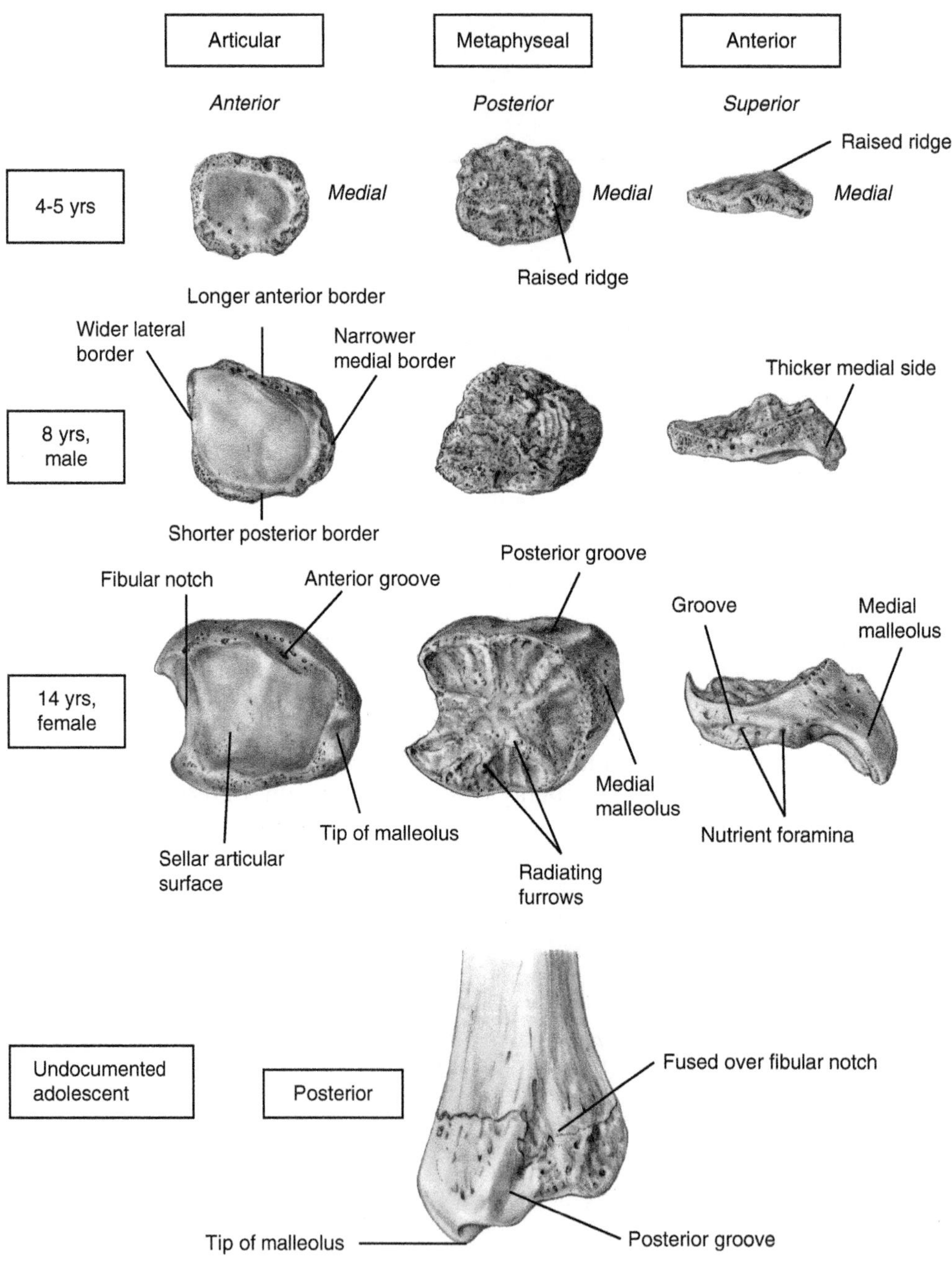

Development of the right distal tibial epiphysis

Identification

Once it becomes distinct (around three to four years of age) it is unlikely to be confused with any other bone.

Siding

- The medial (malleolar) border is thicker, however, less wide in an anteroposterior direction, than the lateral border.
- Displays a distinct raised ridge on its medial side along the metaphyseal surface.
- The anterior border is longer than the posterior border.
- The lateral border will eventually become notched.
- The anterior surface displays a horizontal groove.
- From about 11 to 12 years onward, the posterior surface displays an oblique groove for passage of the tendon of the tibialis posterior muscle.

Shaft Metrics

Fazekas and Kósa

Dry Bone Fetal Measurements-Tibia			
		Max length (mm)	
Prenatal Age (wks)	*n*	Mean	Range
12	2	6.0	5.1–7.0
14	3	10.2	9.1–12.0
16	9	17.4	15.0–21.0
18	15	23.4	21.0–28.0
20	13	28.5	24.0–32.0
22	11	32.6	28.8–37.7
24	12	35.8	32.0–41.0
26	12	37.9	35.0–41.6
28	12	42.0	39.0–44.2
30	12	43.9	41.0–48.0
32	8	48.2	43.7–52.0
34	7	52.7	51.0–57.6
36	5	54.8	50.7–59.0
38	7	59.9	56.0–64.0
40	10	65.1	60.0–71.5

Source

Dry bone measurements on mid twentieth century Hungarian fetal remains from autopsy—males and females combined. Age was estimated based on fetal crown heel length.

Notes

Has been shown to be compatible with radiographic measurements taken from American fetuses (Warren, M.W. (1999). Radiographic determination of developmental age in fetuses and stillborns. *Journal of Forensic Sciences* **44**(4): 708–712.)

Reference

Fazekas, I.Gy. and Kósa, F. (1978). *Forensic Fetal Osteology*. Budapest: Akadémiai Kiadó.

Jeanty

Ultrasound Fetal Measurements-Tibia			
Prenatal Age (wks)	Max Length (mm)-Percentiles		
	5	50	95
12	–	7	–
14	2	13	19
16	7	19	25
18	14	24	29
20	19	29	35
22	25	34	39
24	28	39	45
26	33	43	49
28	38	47	52
30	41	51	56
32	46	54	59
34	47	57	64
36	49	60	68
38	54	62	69
40	58	65	69

Source

Sonograms taken from late twentieth century white fetuses in Brussels, Belgium.

Reference

Jeanty, P. (1983). Fetal limb biometry. (Letter). *Radiology* **147**: 601–602.

Scheuer et al.

Radiographic Fetal Measurements-Tibia	
Regression equations of fetal age (weeks) on maximum tibial length (mm)	
Linear	age (weeks) = (0.4207 × tibial length) + 11.4724 ± 2.12
Logarithmic	age (weeks) = (21.207 $\log_e$ × tibial length) – 50.2331 ± 2.11

Source

Radiographic measurements on mid twentieth century premature British fetuses. The sample consisted of 29 male and 36 female fetuses between 24 and 40 weeks. Age was determined using date of last menstrual period.

Reference

Scheuer, J.L, Musgrave, J.H., and Evans, S.P. (1980). The estimation of late fetal and perinatal age from limb bone length by linear and logarithmic regression. *Annals of Human Biology* **7**(3): 257–265.

Maresh

Radiographic Postnatal Measurements-Tibal Length (mm)								
	Males		Percentile		Females		Percentile	
Age (yrs)	*n*	Mean	10th	90th	*n*	Mean	10th	90th
Diaphyseal length								
1.5 mths	59	70.8	63.1	77.9	69	70.3	64.7	76.2
3 mths	58	81.9	75.8	88.7	65	80.8	74.6	87.2
6 mths	67	91.0	84.4	98.1	78	88.9	81.6	95.6
1 yr	72	110.3	104.0	117.4	81	108.5	102.6	115.8
1.5 yrs	68	126.1	118.9	133.2	84	124.0	116.8	131.6
2 yrs	68	140.1	132.1	148.5	84	138.2	129.8	146.6
2.5 yrs	72	152.5	144.0	161.2	82	150.1	141.0	160.8
3 yrs	72	163.5	154.6	173.1	79	161.1	151.3	172.1
3.5 yrs	73	172.8	161.7	184.8	78	171.2	159.5	182.9
4 yrs	72	182.8	172.2	194.4	80	180.8	168.5	193.6
4.5 yrs	71	191.8	180.9	204.6	78	190.9	177.3	205.3
5 yrs	77	201.4	189.2	214.2	80	199.9	183.9	215.8
6 yrs	71	218.9	207.3	232.3	75	217.4	200.7	235.0
7 yrs	71	236.2	222.3	250.7	86	234.1	215.8	253.8
8 yrs	70	253.3	236.2	268.2	85	281.7	251.7	275.2
9 yrs	76	268.7	252.4	285.6	83	265.5	267.5	292.2
10 yrs	77	284.9	267.3	303.9	84	284.3	258.2	312.5
11 yrs	75	299.8	281.1	319.7	76	300.8	273.0	331.8
12 yrs	73	315.9	292.9	337.8	71	318.2	289.6	348.7
Total length including epiphyses								
10 yrs	76	320.0	300.0	337.7	83	321.1	292.5	351.1
11 yrs	75	338.6	316.5	360.2	76	340.1	310.6	374.1
12 yrs	76	357.3	332.2	381.8	75	360.9	329.5	394.5
13 yrs	69	376.7	349.6	403.4	69	374.5	344.4	406.2
14 yrs	69	397.4	369.2	425.6	64	384.3	354.2	410.1
15 yrs	60	412.2	385.1	441.4	57	385.7	358.1	412.4
16 yrs	60	422.6	396.8	447.2	40	386.8	356.9	415.4
17 yrs	50	426.5	400.6	451.4	18	380.7	353.6	413.8
18 yrs	28	429.5	398.0	454.9	4	–	–	–

Source

American children enrolled in the Child Research Council and born between 1915 and 1967.

Reference

Maresh, M.M. (1970). Measurements from roentgenograms. In: *Human Growth and Development* (R.W. McCammon, Ed.), pp. 157–200. Springfield IL: C.C. Thomas.

Gindhart

Radiographic Postnatal Measurements-Tibia (mm)						
	Males			Females		
Age	*n*	Mean	S.D.	*n*	Mean	S.D.
Diaphyseal length						
1 mth	156	72.1	4.9	108	71.3	4.5
3 mths	118	84.8	4.2	98	85.0	18.1
6 mths	176	99.3	5.3	132	97.1	5.0
9 mths	116	110.1	5.0	101	109.5	17.3
1 yr	155	119.6	5.8	122	117.1	5.8
1.5 yrs	110	135.5	6.9	90	134.2	7.0
2 yrs	133	150.1	7.4	108	149.1	7.5
2.5 yrs	92	162.7	7.5	84	163.0	19.0
3 yrs	130	174.2	9.3	107	173.1	9.9
3.5 yrs	84	184.0	9.1	85	183.7	10.5
4 yrs	132	194.0	10.7	115	193.7	11.3
4.5 yrs	85	203.6	10.3	77	203.6	12.0
5 yrs	125	212.4	11.7	109	213.2	12.5
6 yrs	157	233.0	13.1	118	231.2	15.2
7 yrs	150	250.4	14.3	113	250.3	16.9
8 yrs	147	268.4	15.9	109	270.5	20.2
9 yrs	144	288.0	17.4	100	290.7	21.5
10 yrs	127	305.6	18.4	98	308.0	20.1
11 yrs	98	322.2	19.2	82	323.9	19.2
12 yrs	73	337.0	19.3	55	336.2	20.3
13 yrs	53	358.1	27.6	42	346.5	20.2
14 yrs	31	372.4	27.7	33	352.7	19.9
15 yrs	21	386.9	45.6	20	357.8	19.6
16 yrs	19	402.1	29.0	23	366.6	20.7
17 yrs	18	411.7	27.3	15	374.2	24.5
18 yrs	18	404.2	23.9	11	367.1	31.5

Source

White American children of European descent enrolled in the longitudinal program of the Fels Research Institute by mid 1967.

Reference

Gindhart, P. (1973). Growth standards for the tibia and radius in children aged one month through eighteen years. *American Journal of Physical Anthropology* **39**: 41–48.

Appearance Times

Garn et al.

Radiographic Assessment-Tibia						
	Male Percentiles			Female Percentiles		
Ossification Centre	5th	50th	95th	5th	50th	95th
Proximal	34g	2w	5w	34g	1w	2w
Tuberosity	9y11m	11y10m	13y5m	7y11m	10y3m	11y10m

gestational week (g), postnatal week (w), month (m) or year (y).

Source

Participants in the U.S.-based Fels Research Institute Program of Human Development, begun in 1929.

Reference

Garn, S.M., Rohmann, C.G., and Silverman, F.N. (1967). Radiographic standards for postnatal ossification and tooth calcification. *Medical Radiography and Photography* **43**: 45–66.

Elgenmark

Radiographic Assessment-Tibia								
	Males (months)				Female (months)			
Ossification Centre	25%	50%	75%	100%	25%	50%	75%	100%
Proximal	0.4	0.7	1.8	4.0	0.4	0.8	2.3	5.0
Distal	3.9	5.7	6.7	10.0	4.7	5.6	6.6	7.0

Source

Radiographs of children (429 males and 423 females) treated or examined at the Samariten Children's Hospital, Stockholm, during the years 1942–1945.

Reference

Elgenmark, O. (1946). The normal development of the ossific centres during infancy and childhood. *Acta Paediatrica Scandinavica* **33**(Suppl. 1).

Union Times

Schaefer

Dry Bone Assessment-Male %								
	Proximal Tibia - Stage of Union				**Distal Tibia - Stage of Union**			
Age	***n***	**0**	**1**	**2**	***n***	**0**	**1**	**2**
14	3	100	–	–	3	100	–	–
15	6	100	–	–	6	100	–	–
16	13	69	31	–	10	40	40	20
17	17	35	30	35	17	18	24	58
18	21	10	48	42	20	5	5	90
19	19	–	21	79	19	–	–	100
20	23	–	9	91	23	–	–	100
21	24	–	–	100	24	–	–	100
22+	107	–	–	100	107	–	–	100

Notes

Stage 0: Nonunion
Stage 1: Partial union
Stage 2: Complete union marked by obliteration of the epiphyseal line (scar may be present)

Source

Bosnian war dead from the fall of Srebrenica (1995)—males only. Age reflects those individuals half a year above and half a year below (e.g., age 18 = 17.5–18.5).

Reference

Schaefer, M. (2008). A summary of epiphyseal union timings in Bosnian males. *International Journal of Osteoarchaeology,* DOI: 10.1002/oa.959. Copyright John Wiley & Sons Limited. Reproduced with permission.

McKern and Stewart

Dry Bone Assessment-Proximal Tibia						
		Male % - Stage of Union				
Age	*n*	**0**	**1**	**2**	**3**	**4**
17–18	55	2	2	7	23	66
19	52	1	–	1	17	81
20	45	–	–	–	13	87
21	37	–	–	–	5	95
22	24	–	–	–	4	96
23	26	–	–	–	–	100
24+	136	–	–	–	–	100

Source

American war dead from Korea (1951–1957)—males only.

Notes

Stage 0: Nonunion of epiphysis
Stage 1: ¼ of epiphysis united
Stage 2: ½ of epiphysis united
Stage 3: ¾ of epiphysis united
Stage 4: Complete union of epiphysis

Reference

McKern, T.W. and Stewart, T.D. (1957). Skeletal age changes in young American males, analysed from the standpoint of age identification. *Headquarters Quartermaster Research and Development Command, Technical Report* EP-45. Natick, MA.

Coqueugniot

Dry Bone Assessment-Tibia						
	Males			Females		
	Open	Partial	Complete	Open	Partial	Complete
Proximal	≤20	16–21	≥19	≤17	12–22	≥19
Distal	≤19	16–20	≥16	≤17	14–19	≥17

Source

Documented Portuguese material born between 1904 and 1938 (Coimbra collection), including 69 females and 68 males between the ages of 7 and 29 years.

Warning

Many ages are poorly represented.

Reference

Coqueugniot, H., and Weaver, T. (2007). Infracranial maturation in the skeletal collection from Coimbra, Portugal: New aging standards for epiphyseal union. *American Journal of Physical Anthropology*, **134**(3): 424–437.

Cardoso

Dry Bone Assessment-Proximal Tibia								
	Male % - Stage of Union				Female % - Stage of Union			
Age	*n*	1	2	3	*n*	1	2	3
12–13	3	100	–	–	5	100	–	–
14	3	100	–	–	2	50	50	–
15	3	100	–	–	5	20	80	–
16	4	75	25	–	3	33	66	–
17	4	–	75	25	3	–	100	–
18	2	50	–	50	5	–	20	80
19	4	–	75	25	4	–	50	50
20	6	–	–	100	4	–	–	100

Dry Bone Assessment-Distal Tibia								
	Male % - Stage of Union				Female % - Stage of Union			
Age	*n*	1	2	3	*n*	1	2	3
12–13	3	100	–	–	5	100	–	–
14	3	100	–	–	2	50	50	–
15	3	33	66	–	5	20	60	20
16	4	50	25	25	3	33	33	33
17	4	–	25	75	3	–	–	100
18	2	50	–	50	5	–	–	100
19	4	–	–	100	4	–	–	100
20	6	–	–	100	4	–	–	100

Source

Portuguese individuals buried between 1903 and 1975 (Lisbon collection).

Notes

Stage 1: No union
Stage 2: Partial union
Stage 3: Complete union—no visible gaps, however an epiphyseal scar may be retained

Reference

Cardoso, H. (2008). Epiphyseal union at the innominate and lower limb in a modern Portuguese skeletal sample, and age estimation in adolescent and young adult male and female skeletons. *American Journal of Physical Anthropology*, **135**(2): 161–170.

Crowder and Austin

Radiographic Assessment-Distal Tibia					
	Group	Stage 1	Stage 2	Stage 3	Stage 4
Male					
	European American	≤15	12–16	13–17	≥15
	African American	≤15	13–15	13–18	≥13
	Mexican American	≤15	13–15	12–17	≥13
Female					
	European American	≤13	10–13	11–15	≥11
	African American	≤13	10–13	11–15	≥12
	Mexican American	≤13	10–13	11–15	≥11

Source

Radiographs of children born between 1969 and 1991, obtained from the Cook Children's Medical Center, Ft. Worth, Texas. Each age group, sex and ethnicity was represented by 10 radiographs for a total of 270 females (ages 9–17) and 300 males (ages 11–20).

Notes

Stage 1: No fusion: Absence of bony bridging between the diaphysis and the epiphysis
Stage 2: Unclear: Relationship of the epiphysis and the diaphysis is not discernable from stage 1 and early stage 3
Stage 3: Partial fusion: Partial to nearly complete fusion of the diaphyseo-epiphyseal junction
Stage 4: Complete fusion: Epiphysis is completely fused to the diaphysis

Reference

Crowder, C., and Austin, D. (2005). Age ranges of epiphyseal fusion in the distal tibia and fibula of contemporary males and females. *Journal of Forensic Sciences* **50**(5): 1000–1007. Wiley-Blackwell.

Compilation Summary of Union Times

Summary of Fusing Times-Proximal Tibia					
	Assessment	Study	Open	Fusing	Closed
Male					
	Dry Bone	Schaefer	≤18	16–20	≥17
		McKern & Stewart	≤19	?–22	–
		Coqueugniot & Weaver	≤20	16–21	≥19
		Cardoso	≤18	16–19	≥17
Female					
	Dry Bone	Coqueugniot & Weaver	≤17	12–22	≥19
		Cardoso	≤16	14–19	≥18

Summary of Fusing Times-Distal Tibia					
	Assessment	Study	Open	Fusing	Closed
Male					
	Dry Bone	Schaefer	≤18	16–18	≥16
		Coqueugniot & Weaver	≤19	16–20	≥16
		Cardoso	≤18	15–18	≥16
	Radiographic	Crowder (pooled sample)	≤16	12–18	≥14
Female					
	Dry Bone	Coqueugniot & Weaver	≤17	14–19	≥17
		Cardoso	≤16	14–16	≥15
	Radiographic	Crowder (pooled sample)	≤12	11–15	≥12

Morphological Summary

Prenatal	
Wk 7–8	Primary ossification center appears in the shaft
Wks 36–40	Secondary ossification center for proximal epiphysis appears
Birth	Represented by shaft and usually proximal epiphysis
By 6 wks	Proximal secondary center appears
3–10 mths	Distal secondary center appears
3–5 yrs	Medial malleolus starts to ossify
8–13 yrs	Distal part of tuberosity starts to ossify from one or more centers
12–14 yrs	Proximal and distal parts of tuberosity unite
14–17 yrs	Distal epiphysis fuses in females
16–18 yrs	Distal epiphysis fuses in males
14–18 yrs	Proximal epiphysis fuses in females
16–20 yrs	Proximal epiphysis fuses in males

THE FIBULA

Shaft

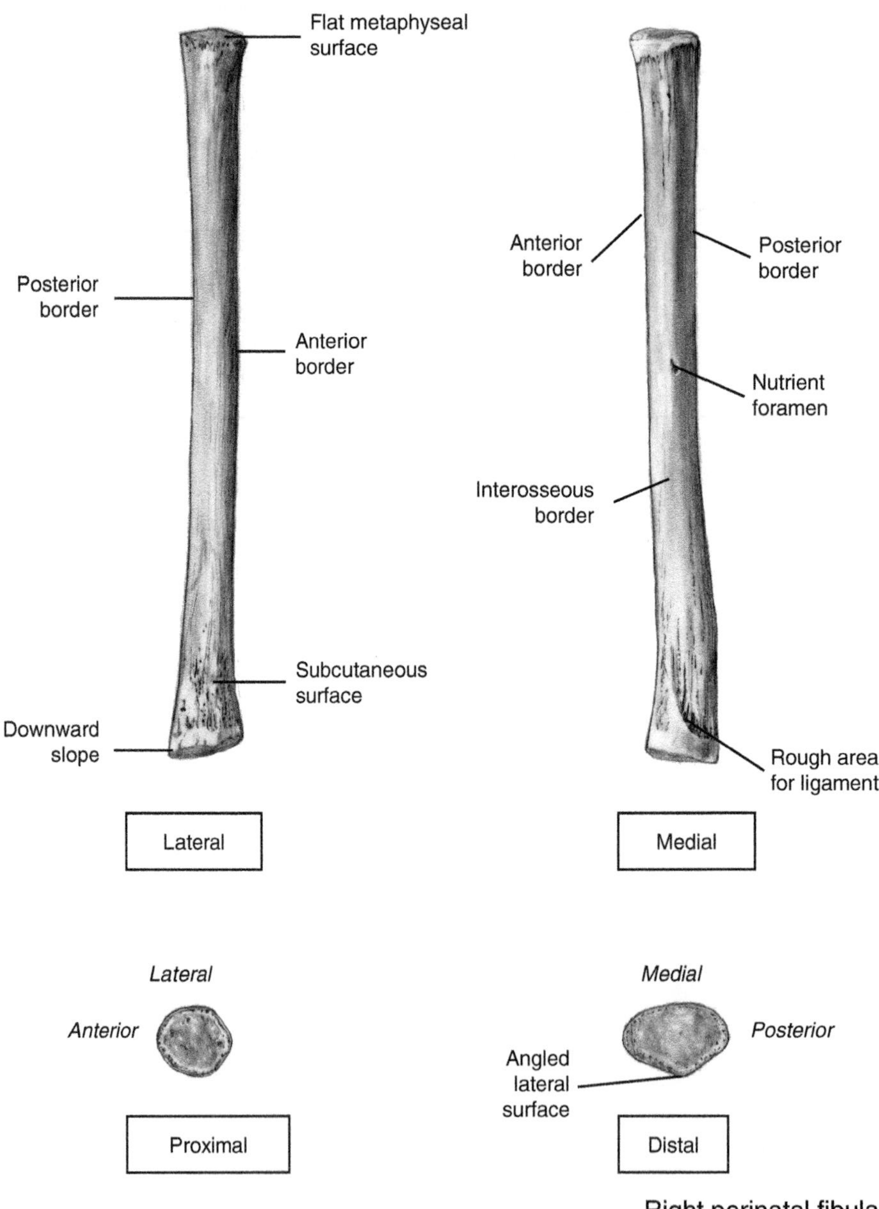

Right perinatal fibula

Identification – May be confused with any of the other long bones.

- The perinatal fibula is shorter and less robust than the humerus, femur, and tibia.
- The perinatal fibula is similar in length to the ulna, however, the ulna is more bulky and displays its characteristic proximal end.
- The fibula is straight, narrow, and relatively featureless.
- A proximal fibular fragment will display a rounded shaft and a circular metaphyseal surface. This is unlike the distal ulna, which is slightly curved anteriorly and has a notch posteriorly, and unlike the distal radius, which is flared, curved anteriorly and has a larger metaphyseal surface.
- The distal fibular shaft is flattened mediolaterally and the metaphyseal surface is triangulated.

Siding

- Very difficult to side as the fibula is relatively featureless.
- The proximal metaphyseal surface is more rounded; the distal metaphyseal surface is more oval or triangular.
- Nutrient foramina are nearly always found on the medial side.
- The interosseous border may be present along the middle third of the medial border.
- The inferior aspect of the medial side bears a roughened triangle for the inferior part of the posterior tibio-fibular ligament that runs distally from anterior to posterior.
- The division of the sharp anterior border at the distal end to form the subcutaneous triangle may be seen on the lateral side.
- The distal metaphyseal surface slopes down posteriorly.

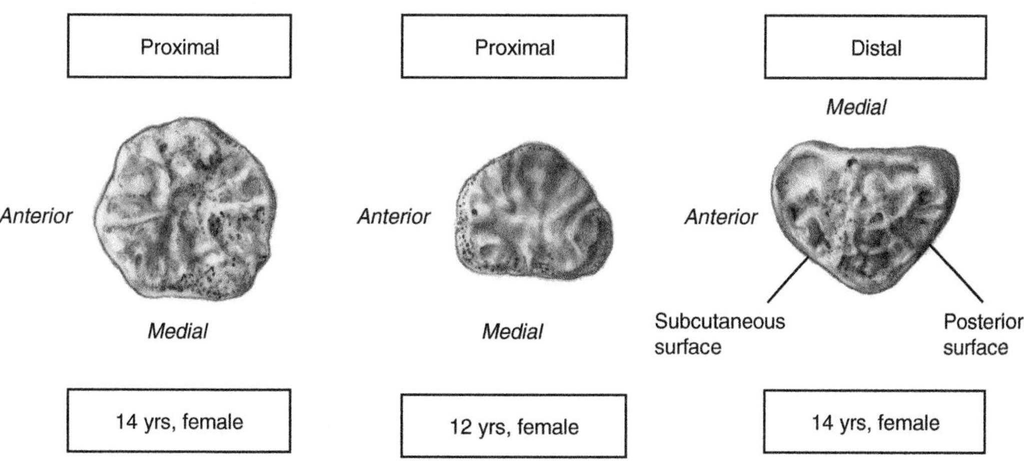

Right fibular metaphyseal surfaces

Distal Epiphysis

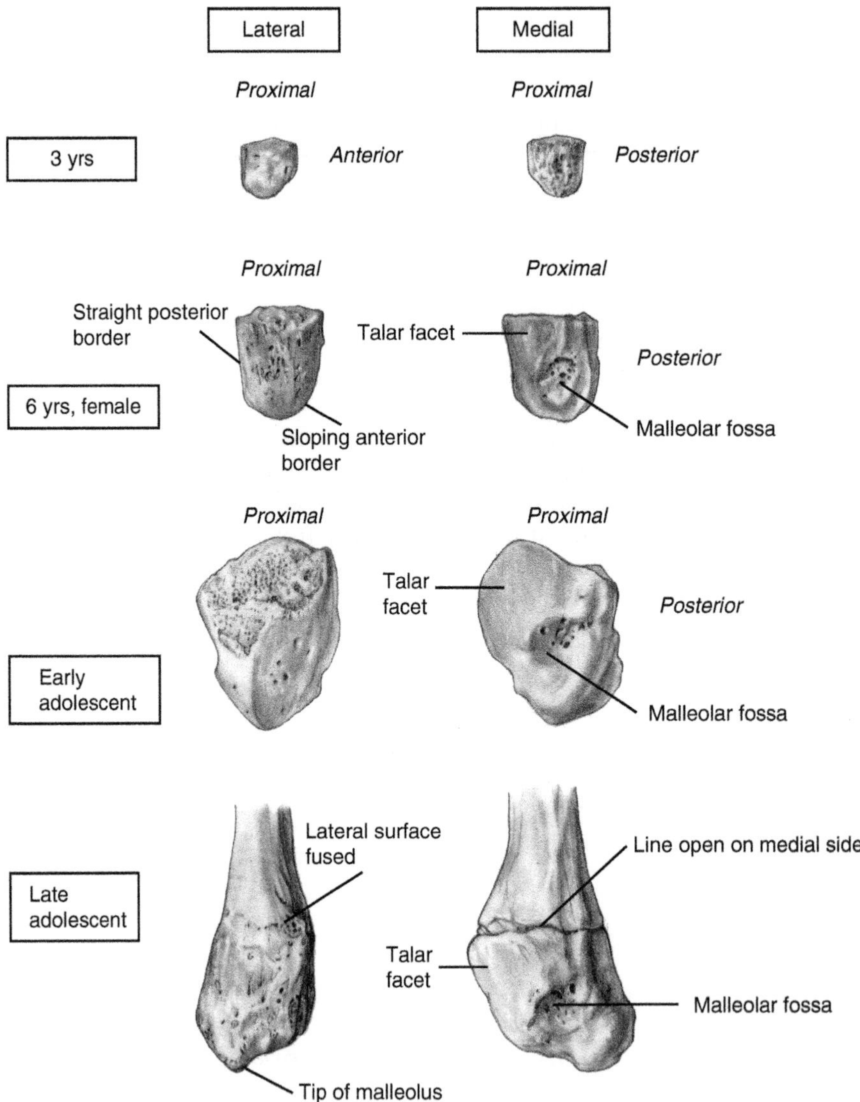

Development of the right distal fibular epiphysis

Identification/Siding – Recognition and sideing is generally possible once ossification has spread into the region of the malleolar fossa, around three to four years of age.

- The flat articular surface is medial and the malleolar fossa is posterior.

Proximal Epiphysis

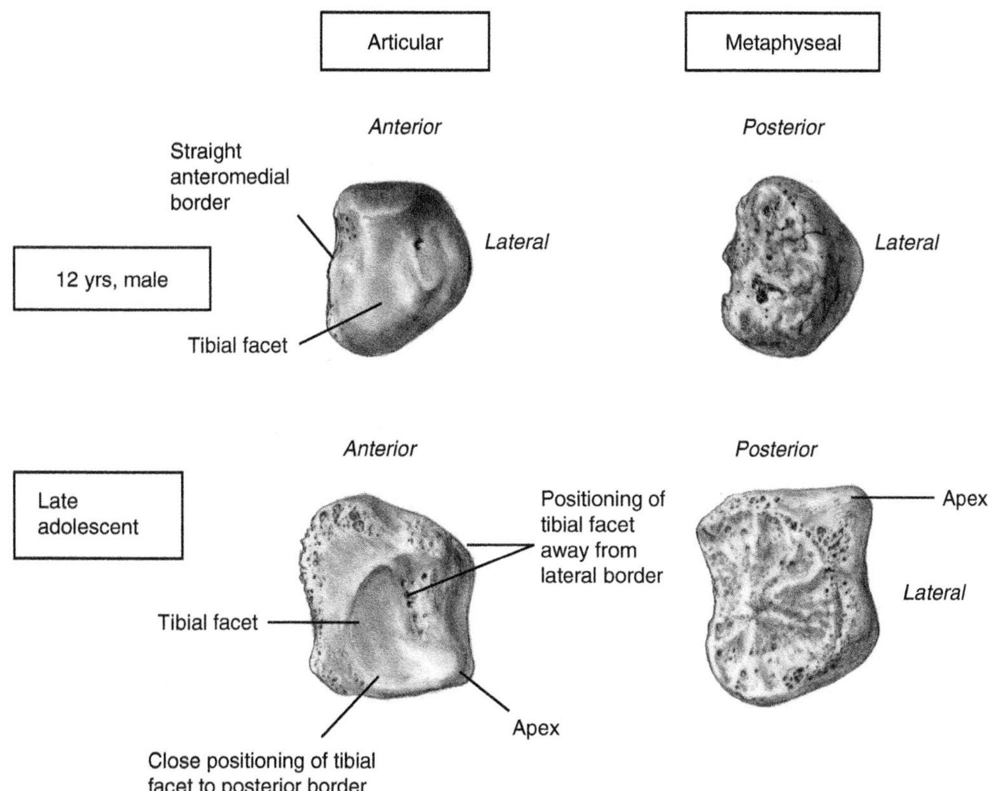

Development of the right proximal fibular epiphysis

Identification/Siding – Probably not recognizable until mid-childhood when its distinctive features have developed.

- The tibial facet and the straight border face anteromedially.
- The apex, or styloid process, projects from the posterolateral corner.
- The tibial facet is positioned closer to the posterior border than the lateral border.

Shaft Metrics

Fazekas and Kósa

Dry Bone Fetal Measurements-Fibula			
		Max length (mm)	
Prenatal Age (wks)	*n*	Mean	Range
12	2	6.0	5.0–7.0
14	3	9.9	8.5–12.0
16	9	16.7	14.0–20.5
18	15	22.6	19.5–27.0
20	13	27.8	24.0–32.0
22	11	31.1	28.5–36.0
24	12	34.3	30.0–39.5
26	12	36.5	34.9–40.5
28	12	40.0	37.0–43.3
30	12	42.8	39.5–47.0
32	8	46.8	41.0–50.2
34	7	50.5	48.0–54.2
36	5	51.6	48.5–56.0
38	7	57.6	53.6–60.0
40	10	62.3	58.0–68.5

Source

Dry bone measurements on mid twentieth century Hungarian fetal remains from autopsy—males and females combined.

Notes

Has been shown to be compatible with radiographic measurements taken from American fetuses (Warren, M.W. (1999). Radiographic determination of developmental age in fetuses and stillborns. *Journal of Forensic Sciences* **44**(4): 708–712.)

Reference

Fazekas, I.Gy. and Kósa, F. (1978). *Forensic Fetal Osteology*. Budapest: Akadémiai Kiadó.

Jeanty

Ultrasound Fetal Measurements-Fibula			
Prenatal Age (wks)	Max Length (mm)-Percentiles		
	5	50	95
12	–	5	–
14	6	11	10*
16	6	17	22
18	10	22	28
20	18	27	30
22	21	31	37
24	26	35	41
26	32	39	43
28	36	43	47
30	38	47	52
32	40	50	56
34	46	52	56
36	51	55	56
38	54	57	59
40	54	59	62

*Misprinted within original text.

Source

Sonograms taken from late twentieth century white fetuses in Brussels, Belgium.

Reference

Jeanty, P. (1983). Fetal limb biometry. (Letter). *Radiology* **147**: 601–602.

Maresh

Radiographic Postnatal Measurements-Fibular Length (mm)								
	Males		Percentile		Females		Percentile	
Age (yrs)	*n*	Mean	10th	90th	*n*	Mean	10th	90th
Diaphyseal length								
1.5 mths	59	68.1	61.2	75.4	69	66.8	61.0	72.6
3 mths	58	78.6	72.9	85.7	65	77.1	71.6	82.6
6 mths	67	87.2	80.8	94.1	78	84.9	77.4	91.2
1 yr	72	107.1	100.0	114.9	81	105.0	98.0	111.7
1.5 yrs	68	123.9	116.1	130.9	84	121.3	113.1	128.2
2 yrs	68	138.1	130.7	146.3	84	136.0	127.1	145.2
2.5 yrs	72	150.7	142.0	160.1	82	147.9	138.3	157.5
3 yrs	72	162.1	152.3	171.9	79	159.4	149.4	169.8
3.5 yrs	73	171.6	160.7	181.6	78	169.6	158.7	181.2
4 yrs	72	181.8	171.3	192.8	80	179.5	166.8	191.5
4.5 yrs	71	190.8	179.8	201.7	78	189.4	175.6	203.6
5 yrs	77	200.4	189.2	211.4	80	198.6	184.4	213.4
6 yrs	71	217.5	205.6	229.2	75	216.0	199.4	233.3
7 yrs	71	234.2	220.6	249.6	86	232.1	214.7	250.5
8 yrs	70	251.0	234.9	267.3	85	248.8	229.3	270.2
9 yrs	76	265.6	249.9	283.4	83	263.7	242.6	287.2
10 yrs	77	281.3	263.3	299.4	84	279.4	257.1	306.3
11 yrs	75	294.9	277.3	313.8	76	294.4	270.5	324.5
12 yrs	73	310.1	289.0	332.0	71	311.1	282.6	342.1
Total length including epiphyses								
10 yrs	76	310.4	292.0	330.4	83	307.9	282.8	335.9
11 yrs	75	326.2	306.9	345.4	76	324.7	297.2	354.8
12 yrs	76	342.8	319.0	366.9	75	344.6	313.6	376.1
13 yrs	69	360.2	333.2	385.5	69	358.5	329.2	388.4
14 yrs	69	380.3	352.4	410.5	64	367.9	339.2	395.4
15 yrs	60	395.3	370.1	422.4	57	370.2	343.4	398.6
16 yrs	60	406.3	382.0	435.6	40	372.4	344.3	400.8
17 yrs	50	410.4	382.4	440.2	18	366.8	337.6	400.6
18 yrs	28	412.8	384.4	411.4	4	–	–	–

Source

American children enrolled in the Child Research Council and born between 1915 and 1967.

Reference

Maresh, M.M. (1970). Measurements from roentgenograms. In: *Human Growth and Development* (R.W. McCammon, Ed.), pp. 157–200. Springfield IL: C.C. Thomas.

Appearance Times

Garn et al.

Radiographic Assessment-Fibula						
	Male Percentiles			Female Percentiles		
Ossification Centre	**5th**	**50th**	**95th**	**5th**	**50th**	**95th**
Proximal	1y10m	3y6m	5y3m	1y4m	2y7m	3y11m

Postnatal week (w), month (m) or year (y).

Source

Participants in the U.S.-based Fels Research Institute Program of Human Development, begun in 1929.

Reference

Garn, S.M., Rohmann, C.G., and Silverman, F.N. (1967). Radiographic standards for postnatal ossification and tooth calcification. *Medical Radiography and Photography* **43**: 45–66.

Elgenmark

Radiographic Assessment-Fibula								
	Males (months)				Female (months)			
Ossification Center	**25%**	**50%**	**75%**	**100%**	**25%**	**50%**	**75%**	**100%**
Distal	9.7	10.8	22.5	35.0	7.3	8.8	10.7	20.0
Proximal	40.8	51.3	56.4	–	30.1	34.5	43.5	57.5

Source

Radiographs of children (429 males and 423 females) treated or examined at the Samariten Children's Hospital, Stockholm, during the years 1942–1945.

Reference

Elgenmark, O. (1946). The normal development of the ossific centres during infancy and childhood. *Acta Paediatrica Scandinavica* **33**(Suppl. 1).

Union Times

Schaefer

Dry Bone Assessment-Male %								
	Proximal Fibula - Stage of Union				Distal Fibula - Stage of Union			
Age	*n*	0	1	2	*n*	0	1	2
14	3	100	–	–	2	100	–	–
15	6	100	–	–	6	100	–	–
16	10	90	10	–	10	60	40	–
17	16	50	19	31	18	28	33	39
18	21	38	24	38	19	5	37	58
19	17	–	6	94	19	–	–	100
20	21	5	10	85	22	–	9	91
21	23	–	–	100	23	–	–	100
22	11	–	–	100	11	–	–	100
23	12	–	–	100	12	–	–	100
24+	82	–	–	100	82	–	–	100

Source

Bosnian war dead from the fall of Srebrenica (1995)—males only. Age reflects those individuals half a year above and half a year below (e.g., age 18 = 17.5–18.5).

Notes

Stage 0: Nonunion
Stage 1: Partial Union
Stage 2: Complete union marked by obliteration of the epiphyseal line (scar may be present)

Reference

Schaefer, M. (2008). A summary of epiphyseal union timings in Bosnian males. *International Journal of Osteoarchaeology*. DOI: 10.1002/oa.959. Copyright John Wiley & Sons Limited. Reproduced with permission.

McKern and Stewart

Dry Bone Assessment-Proximal Fibula						
		Male % - Stage of Union				
Age	*n*	**0**	**1**	**2**	**3**	**4**
17–18	55	14	–	3	12	71
19	52	4	–	6	4	86
20	45	–	–	2	–	98
21	37	–	–	–	5	95
22+	186	–	–	–	–	100

Source

American war dead from Korea (1951–1957)—males only.

Notes

Stage 0: Nonunion of epiphysis
Stage 1: ¼ of epiphysis united
Stage 2: ½ of epiphysis united
Stage 3: ¾ of epiphysis united
Stage 4: Complete union of epiphysis

Reference

McKern, T.W. and Stewart, T.D. (1957). Skeletal age changes in young American males, analysed from the standpoint of age identification. *Headquarters Quartermaster Research and Development Command, Technical Report* EP-45. Natick, MA.

Coqueugniot and Weaver

Dry Bone Assessment-Fibula						
	Males			Females		
	Open	Partial	Complete	Open	Partial	Complete
Proximal	≤20	16–21	≥19	≤19	17–19	≥20
Distal	≤20	16–21	≥16	≤17	17–21	≥19

Source

Documented Portuguese material born between 1904 and 1938 (Coimbra collection), including 69 females and 68 males between the ages of 7 and 29 years.

Reference

Coqueugniot, H. and Weaver, T. (2007). Infracranial maturation in the skeletal collection from Coimbra, Portugal: New aging standards for epiphyseal union. *American Journal of Physical Anthropology* **134**(3): 424–437.

Cardoso

Dry Bone Assessment-Proximal Fibula								
	Male % - Stage of Union				Female % - Stage of Union			
Age	*n*	1	2	3	*n*	1	2	3
12–13	3	100	–	–	5	100	–	–
14	3	100	–	–	2	50	50	–
15	3	100	–	–	4	50	50	–
16	4	75	–	25	3	66	33	–
17	4	25	25	50	3	–	33	66
18	2	50	–	50	4	–	–	100
19–20	8	–	–	100	8	–	–	100

Dry Bone Assessment-Distal Fibula								
	Male % - Stage of Union				Female % - Stage of Union			
Age	*n*	1	2	3	*n*	1	2	3
12–13	3	100	–	–	5	100	–	–
14	3	100	–	–	2	50	50	–
15	3	33	66	–	5	60	20	20
16	4	50	50	–	3	33	33	33
17	4	–	25	75	3	–	–	100
18	2	–	50	50	5	–	–	100
19–20	10	–	–	100	8	–	–	100

Source

Portuguese individuals buried between 1903 and 1975 (Lisbon collection).

Notes

Stage 1: No union
Stage 2: Partial union
Stage 3: Complete union—no visible gaps, however an epiphyseal scar may be retained

Reference

Cardoso, H. (2008). Epiphyseal union at the innominate and lower limb in a modern Portuguese skeletal sample, and age estimation in adolescent and young adult male and female skeletons. *American Journal of Physical Anthropology*, **135**(2): 161–170.

Crowder and Austin

Radiographic Assessment-Distal Fibula					
	Group	Stage 1	Stage 2	Stage 3	Stage 4
Males					
	European American	<17	13–16	14–17	>15
	African American	<16	13–15	14–18	>13
	Mexican American	<15	13–15	12–17	>13
Female					
	European American	<14	11–14	12–15	>11
	African American	<13	11–13	11–15	>12
	Mexican American	<13	11–13	12–15	>11

Source

Radiographs of children born between 1969 and 1991, obtained from the Cook Children's Medical Center, Ft. Worth, Texas. Each age group, sex, and ethnicity was represented by 10 radiographs for a total of 270 females (ages 9–17) and 300 males (ages 11–20).

Notes

Stage 1: No fusion: Absence of bony bridging between the diaphysis and the epiphysis
Stage 2: Unclear: Relationship of the epiphysis and the diaphysis is not discernable from stage 1 and early stage 3
Stage 3: Partial fusion: Partial to nearly complete fusion of the diaphyseo-epiphyseal junction
Stage 4: Complete fusion: Epiphysis is completely fused to the diaphysis

Reference

Crowder, C. and Austin, D. (2005). Age ranges of epiphyseal fusion in the distal tibia and fibula of contemporary males and females. *Journal of Forensic Sciences* **50**(5): 1000–1007. Wiley-Blackwell.

Compilation Summary of Union Times

Summary of Fusing Times-Proximal Fibula					
	Assessment	Study	Open	Fusing	Closed
Male					
	Dry Bone	Schaefer	≤20	16–20	≥17
		McKern & Stewart	≤19	?–21	-
		Coqueugniot & Weaver	≤20	16–21	≥19
		Cardoso	≤18	16–18	≥16
Female					
	Dry Bone	Coqueugniot & Weaver	≤19	17–19	≥20
		Cardoso	≤16	14–17	≥17

Summary of Fusing Times-Distal Fibula					
	Assessment	Study	Open	Fusing	Closed
Male					
	Dry Bone	Schaefer	≤18	16–20	≥17
		Coqueugniot & Weaver	≤20	16–21	≥16
		Cardoso	≤16	15–18	≥17
	Radiographic	Crowder (pooled sample)	≤17	12–18	≥14
Female					
	Dry Bone	Coqueugniot & Weaver	≤17	17–21	≥19
		Cardoso	≤16	14–16	≥15
	Radiographic	Crowder (pooled sample)	≤15	11–15	≥12

Morphological Summary

Prenatal	
Wk 8	Primary ossification center appears in the shaft
Birth	Represented by shaft only
9–22 mths	Distal secondary center appears
During 4th yr	Proximal secondary center appears in girls
During 5th yr	Proximal secondary center appears in boys
During 8th yr	Styloid process ossifies in girls
During 11th yr	Styloid process ossifies in boys
14–17 yrs	Proximal and distal epiphysis fuses in females
15–20 yrs	Proximal and distal epiphysis fuses in males

THE FOOT

Primary Centers

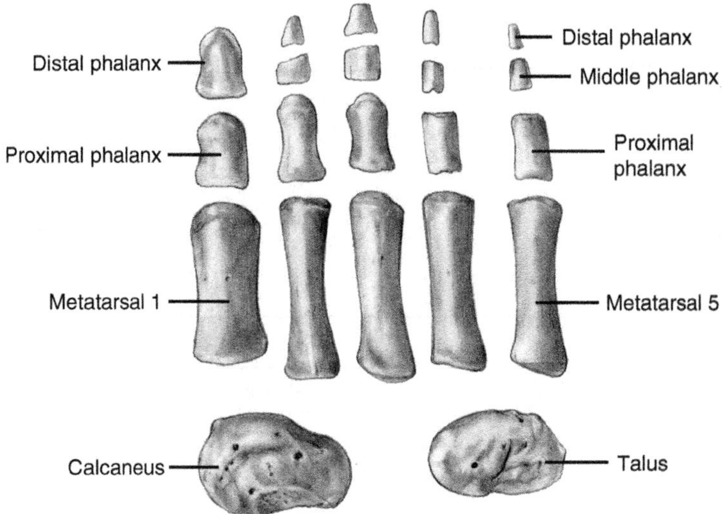

Right perinatal foot

Regional Identification

Metatarsals – Easily confused with metacarpals.

- Metatarsals are longer and more slender than metacarpals, with straighter shafts that are compressed in the mediolateral direction.
- Arrangement of articular facets on the base will differ from those found in the hand bones.

Phalanges – Easily confused with phalanges of the hand.

- Pedal phalanges are consistently shorter and more irregular in appearance than hand phalanges.
- The proximal pedal phalanges have relatively large bases and heads, but slender, mediolaterally compressed shafts; those in the hand tend to be longer, more robust, and flattened on the palmar surface.
- The middle and distal pedal phalanges are very short and have shafts that are concave on both the dorsal and the plantar surfaces; those of the hand are longer and convex on the dorsal surface.
- The distal pedal phalanges tend to have more pronounced ungual tuberosities than the distal phalanges of the hand.

Intraregional Identification/Siding

Become more recognizable once ossification has spread into the articular surface of the bases.

MT1

- Considerably more robust but shorter than the other four metatarsals.
- Toward the base, the dorsal aspect of the shaft angles downward toward its medial side.
- The base of the shaft is convex along its medial border and concave or straight along its lateral border.
- A tuberosity is present along the lateral border of the proximal plantar surface for attachment of the peroneus longus muscle.

MT2

- Is the longest metatarsal.
- Triangulated base that is obliquely oriented with its lateral side more proximal than its medial side.
- Displays one facet for articulation with MT1 on its medial surface and two facets for articulation with MT3 on its lateral surface.

MT3

- Base is roughly triangular, however is more narrow with a less pointed apex than the base of MT2; also slopes proximally toward the lateral side.
- Displays two facets for articulation with MT2 medially (although the more plantar of the two facets is frequently absent) and one facet for articulation with MT4 laterally.
- The lateral border of the shaft thickens toward the proximal end.

MT4

- Is smaller than MT3.
- The lateral border of the shaft thickens toward the proximal end.
- Displays one facet on each side for articulation with MT3 and MT4.

MT5

- The base has a well-defined tubercle (styloid process) on its lateral aspect.
- The distal end displays a slight flare along the plantar-lateral surface, whereas the dorsal medial surface is straighter.
- Displays one facet on its medial side for articulation with MT4.

Phalanges

- With exception to the first digit, it is virtually impossible to assign a phalanx to a specific digital ray let alone side the bone.
- The proximal phalanx of the big toe has a longer medial border than lateral border.
- The same is true for the distal phalanx of the big toe.

The Calcaneus

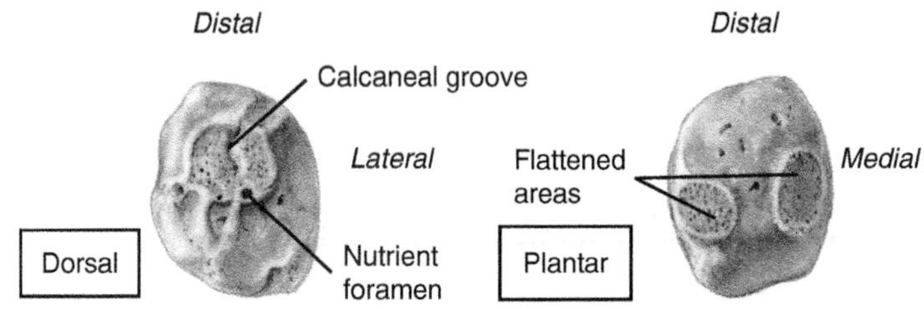

Right perinatal calcaneus

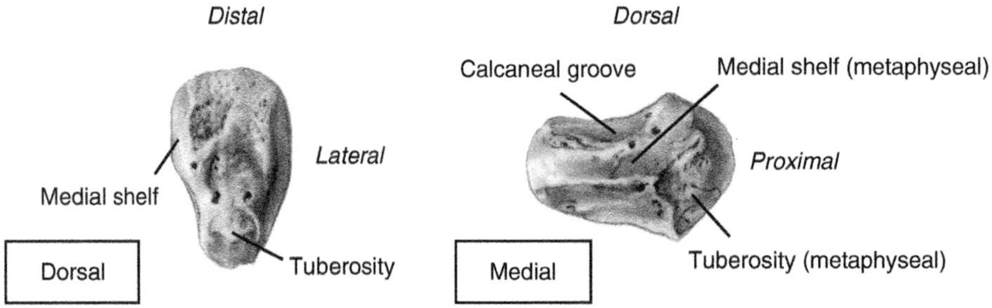

Right calcaneus from a child of approximately 3 months

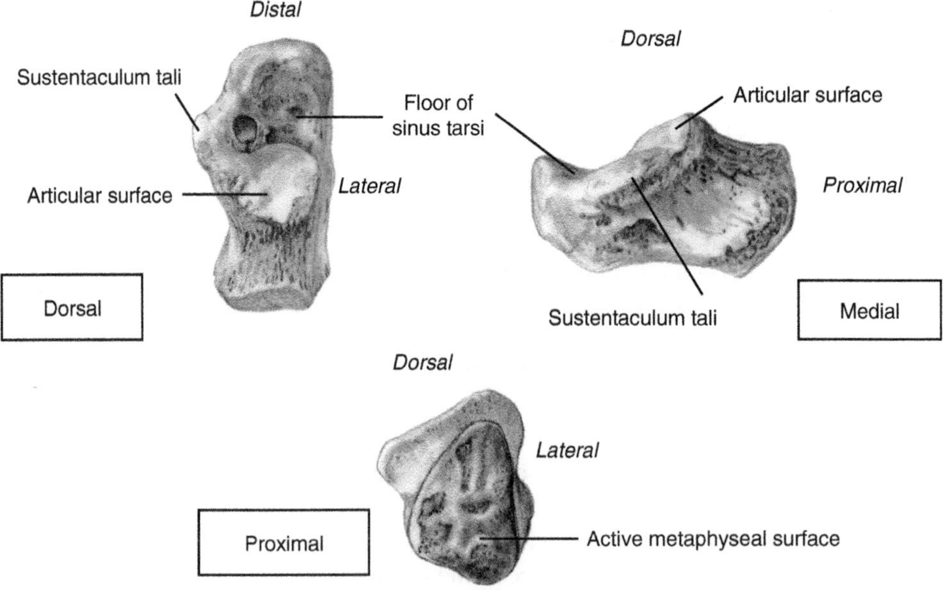

Right calcaneus from a child of approximately 3-4 years of age

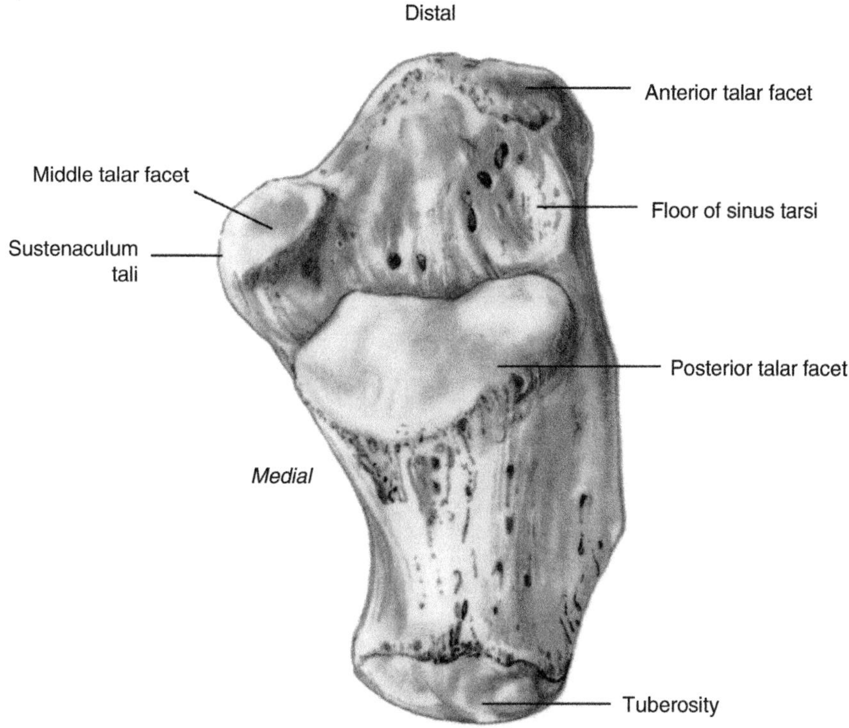

Right calcaneus from a female aged 6 years

Identification/Siding – It is possible to correctly side the neonatal calcaneus, although it is much easier to do so by the end of the first year.

- At birth, the indentation that will form the calcaneal groove (floor of the sinus tarsi) is located on the distal aspect of the dorsal (superior) surface.
- The larger of the two flattened regions is located on the medial aspect of the plantar surface.
- Within the first few months after birth, the medial projection of the sustentaculum tali begins to form.

The Talus

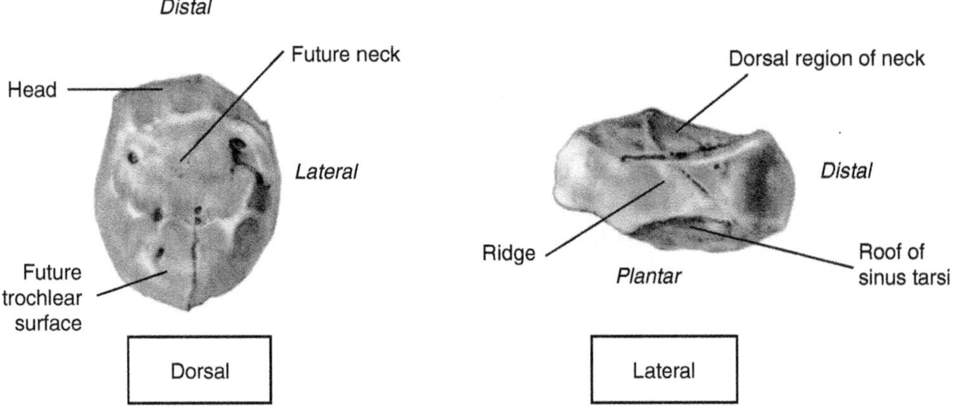

Right perinatal talus

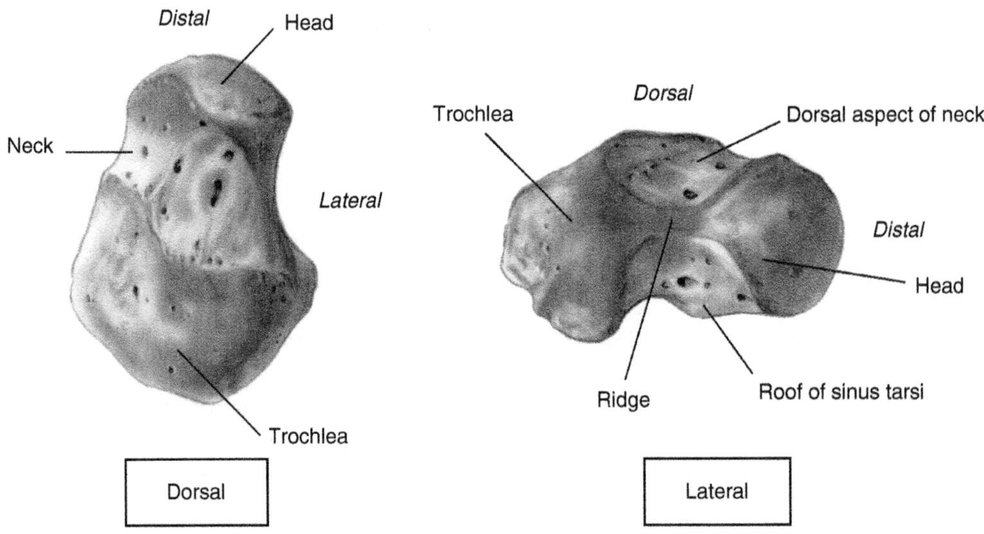

Right talus from a female aged 2 years

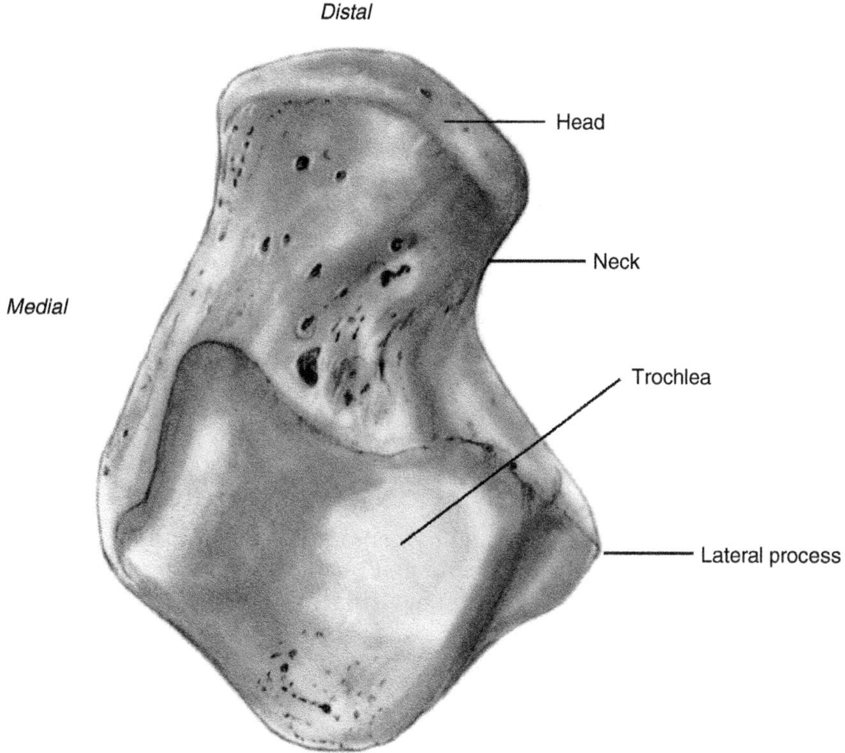

Right talus from a female aged 6 years

Identification/Siding – Siding of the talus can be achieved by full term.

- Both the dorsal and plantar surfaces display depressions that are situated toward the distal extremity (in the position of the future talar neck).
- The two depressions are separated on the lateral aspect by a clearly defined ridge of bone, and on the medial aspect, by a considerable expanse of bone with no distinguishing characteristics.

The Medial Cuneiform

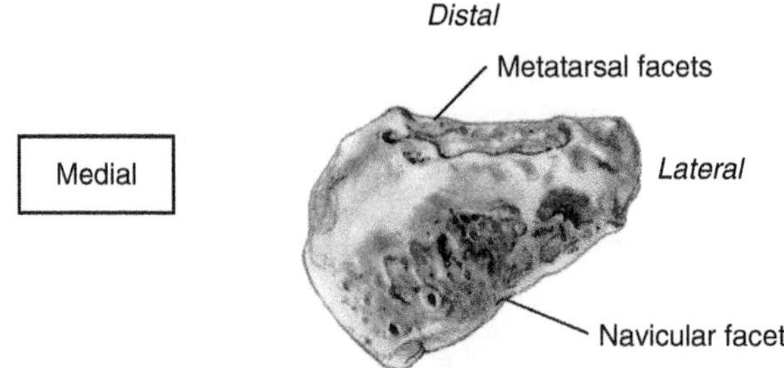

Right medial cuneiform from a child of approximately 3-4 years

Identification/Siding

- Can be identified and sided by around three to four years of age.
- The plantar area is thick and rounded, whereas the dorsal aspect narrows to form a projection that is positioned more distally.
- Relatively flat medial surface and a slightly concave lateral surface.
- The distal surface that articulates with the first metatarsal is larger than that of the proximal surface that articulates with the navicular.

The Intermediate Cuneiform

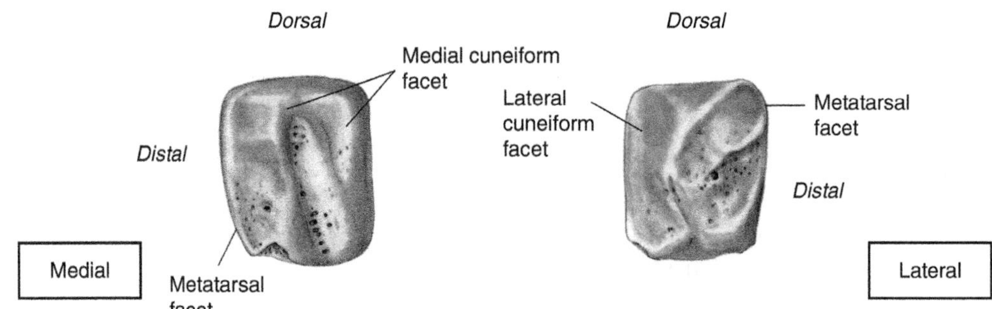

Right intermediate cuneiform from a female aged 6 years

Identification/Siding – Can be readily identified and sided by around six years of age.

- The dorsal surface is flat whereas the plantar surface displays a blunt ridge.
- Both lateral and medial aspects display facets for articulation with the appropriate cuneiforms, however they are very irregular in their positioning.
- The distal surface slopes slightly downward in a lateral direction.

The Lateral Cuneiform

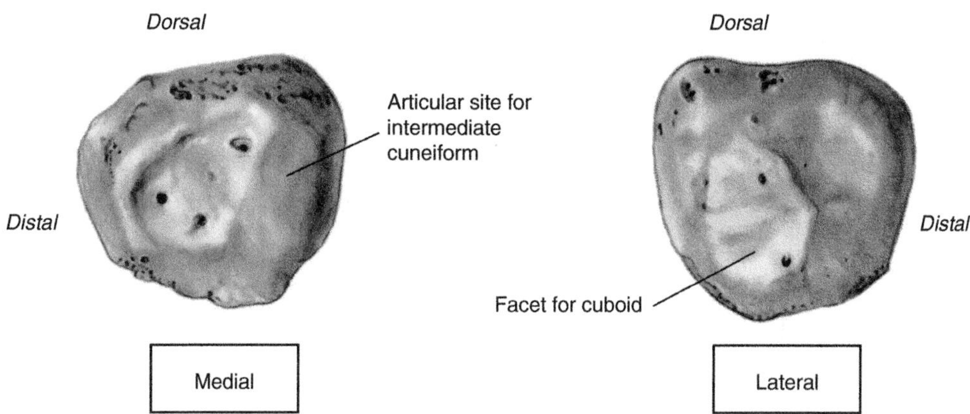

Right lateral cuneiform from a female aged 4 years

Identification/Siding – Can be readily identified and sided by around four years of age.

- The dorsal surface is flat whereas the plantar surface ends in a blunt ridge.
- The medial surface displays a facet along its proximal border for articulation with the intermediate cuneiform.
- The lateral surface bears a rounded articular facet for the cuboid, which is located on the proximal margin.
- When viewing the dorsal surface, the distal half of the bone angles medially (toward the intermediate cuneiform).

The Navicular

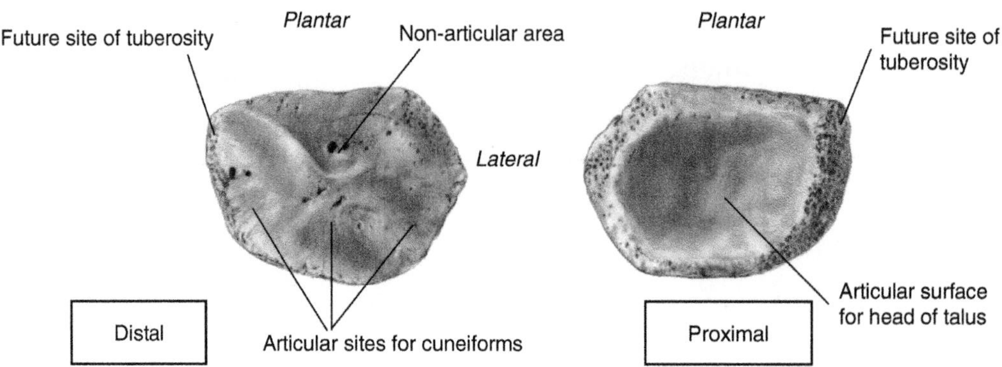

Right navicular from a male aged 8 years

Identification/Siding – Can probably be recognized by around five years of age, however, it cannot be sided with confidence until the site of the tuberosity is established, around seven or eight years of age.

- The proximal talar surface is concave, whereas the distal cuneiform surface is convex.
- The tuberosity develops on the plantomedial aspect of the bone.

The Cuboid

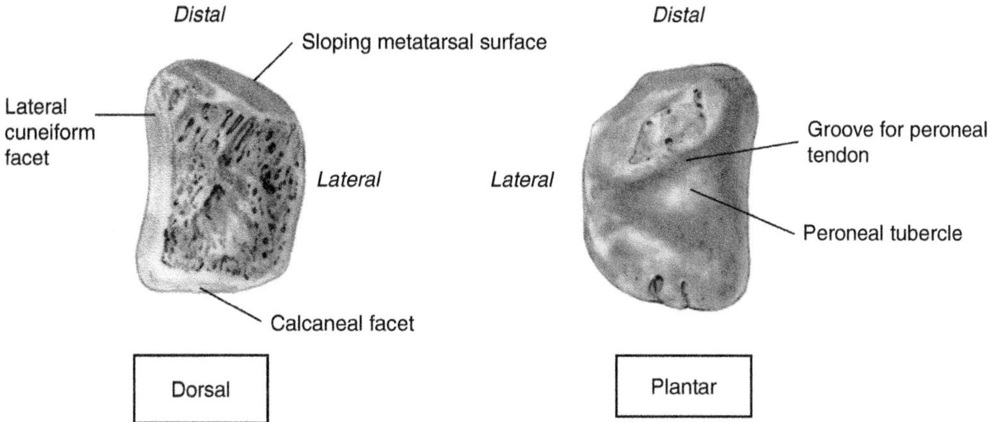

Right cuboid from a child of approximately 3-4 years

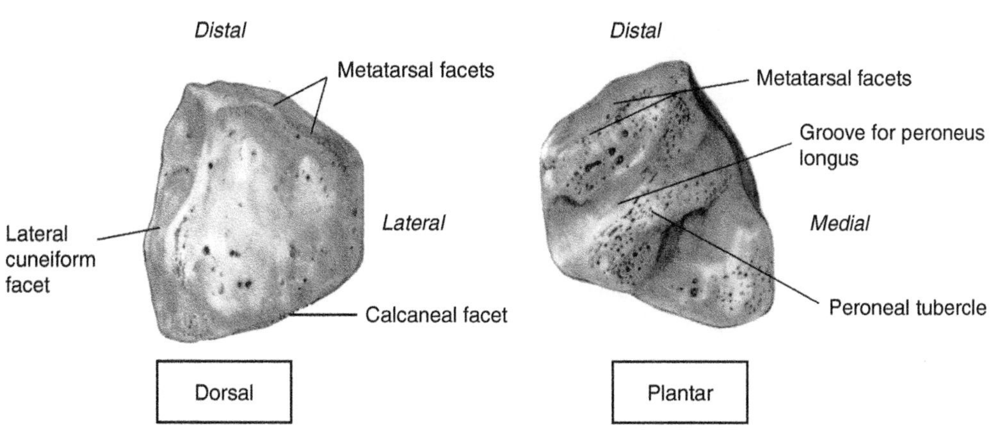

Right cuboid from a male aged 8 years

Identification/Siding – Can be readily identified and sided by around three to four years of age.

- The plantar surface bears a groove caused by the tendon of the peroneus longus muscle, whereas the dorsal aspect is flattened and clearly nonarticular.
- The distal surface is flat and relatively short compared to the longer and more concave proximal aspect.
- The lateral border is short with no distinguishing characteristics, whereas the medial border is longer and bears a well-defined articular facet for the lateral cuneiform.

The Metatarsal Heads 2–5

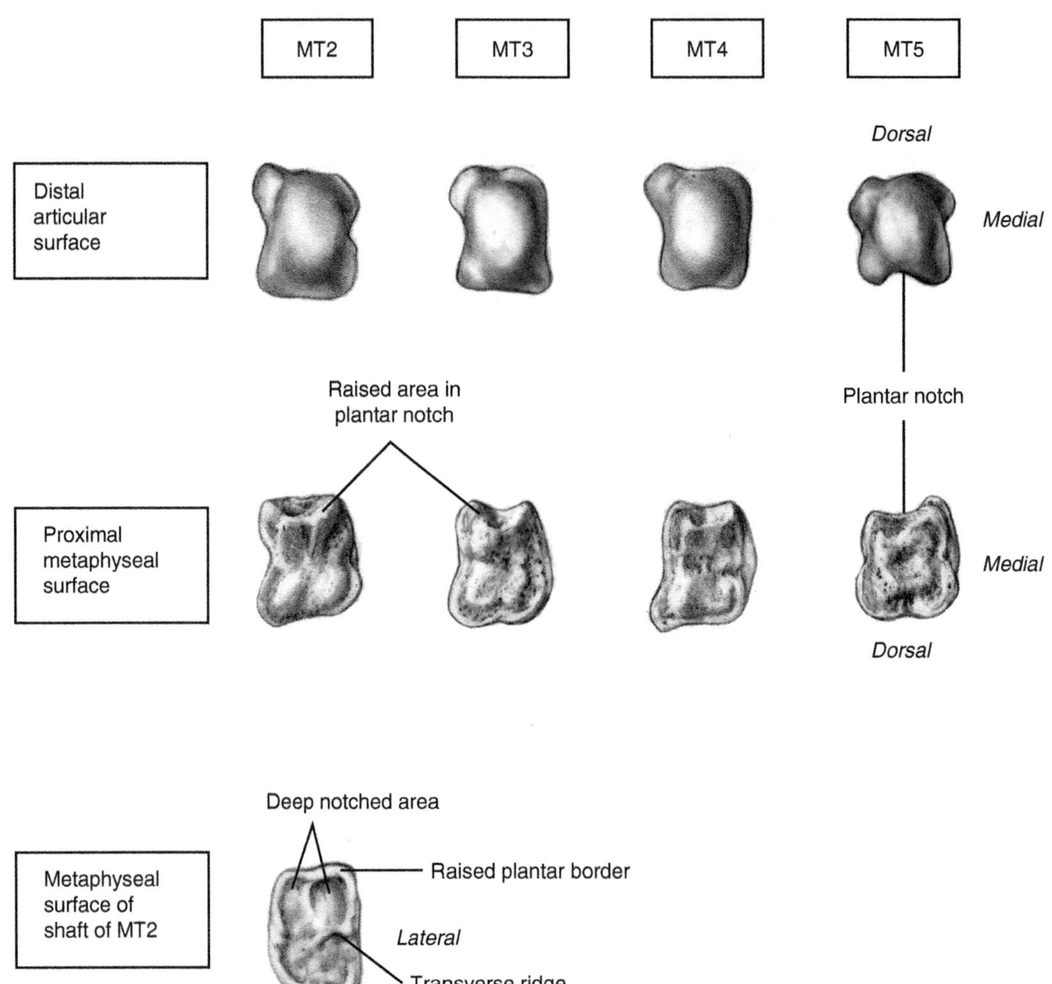

Right metatarsal head epiphyses (approx. 12 years)

Identification – Identification of individual metatarsal heads is difficult and generally relies on the presence of a single individual that is close to puberty so that an appropriate head can be fitted to its appropriate shaft. Metatarsal heads as a whole can be easily confused with metacarpal heads.

- The metaphyseal surfaces of the metatarsal heads are flatter and have a more elongated oval outline.
- The metaphyseal surfaces of the metatarsal heads also bear a gently raised central region that is traversed from medial to lateral by a depression, which corresponds with a ridge on the metaphyseal surface of the metatarsal shaft.

Siding

- All metatarsal heads display a plantar notch for passage of the long flexor tendon.
- The head of MT2 is larger than those of the other metatarsals.
- The head of MT5 is distinct in that the medial surface of the head is almost vertical, whereas the lateral surface has a distinct shallow slope.

The Base of the First Proximal Phalanx

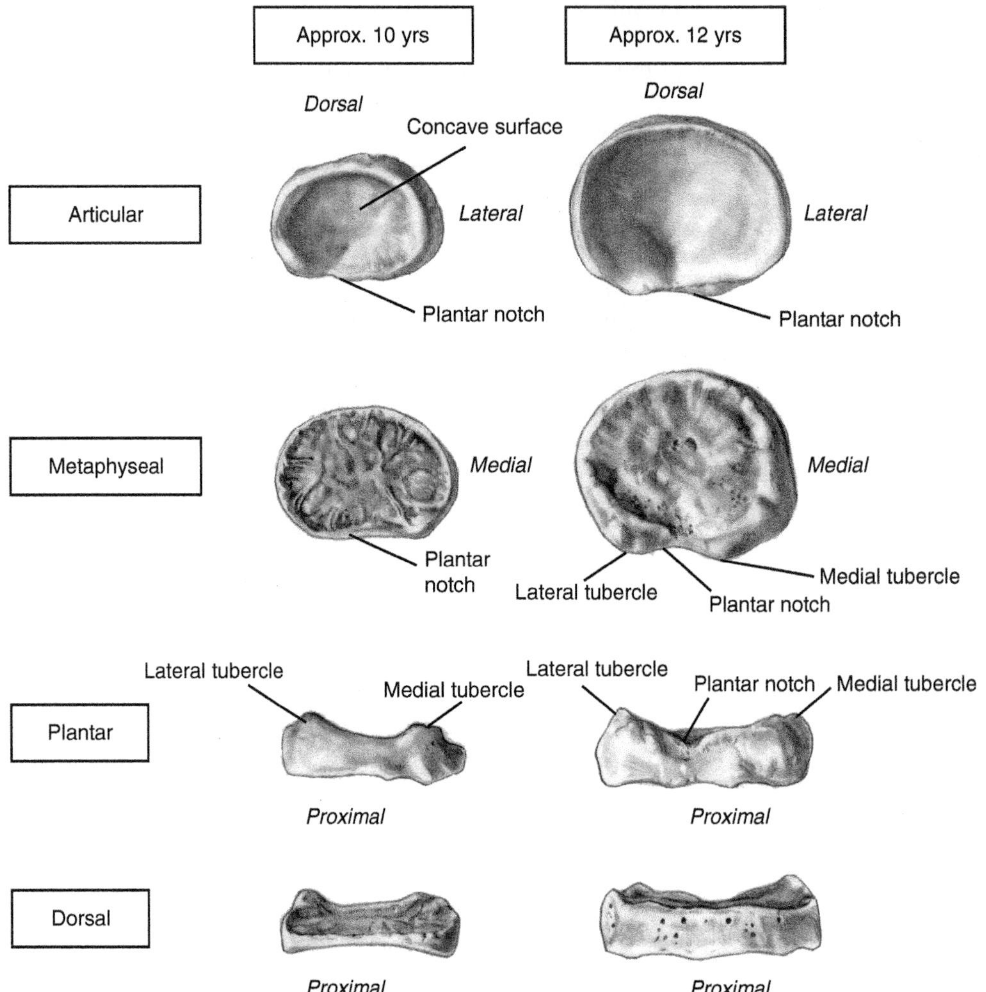

The epiphysis at the base of the right hallucial proximal phalanx

Identification/Siding

- Recognizable by seven to 10 years of age when its contours become more characteristic.
- Larger and more robust than the bases of proximal phalanges 2–5.
- The articular surface is deeply concave and wider in the transverse than in the dorsoplantar plane.
- The dorsal, medial, and lateral borders are circular in shape, whereas the plantar border is straighter.
- The plantar border is raised into medial and lateral tubercles with an intervening notch for passage of the flexor hallucis longus tendon.

The Bases of Proximal Phalanges 2–5

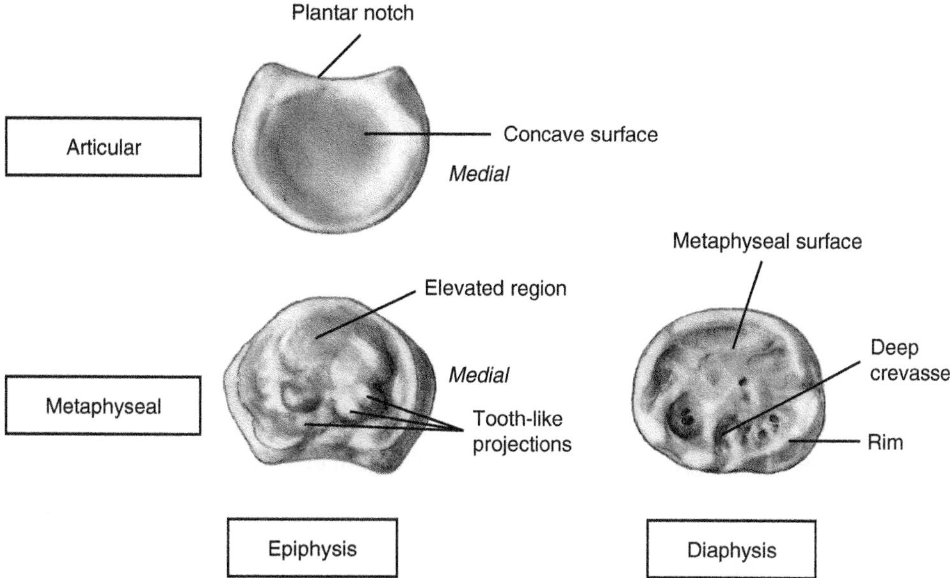

Right proximal phalangeal epiphysis from a child of approximately 7 years

Regional Identification

- The proximal articular surface is smooth and concave and slightly wider in the transverse than in the dorsoplantar plane.
- They are vaguely heart-shaped.
- The plantar margin is straight or slightly concave; the dorsal margin is gently rounded.
- The distal (metaphyseal) surface is roughened with a central elevated region that displays at least one, and often two, tooth-like structures close to the region of the plantar notch.
- The shafts of the proximal phalanges display a deep recess on their plantar borders to accommodate the epiphyseal projections.

Intraregional Identification – Assigning a particular epiphysis to a specific proximal phalanx can be achieved with any degree of accuracy only when one individual is represented and the epiphyses have formed a true cap over the diaphysis to allow a best-fit scenario.

The Bases of Middle and Distal Phalanges 2–5

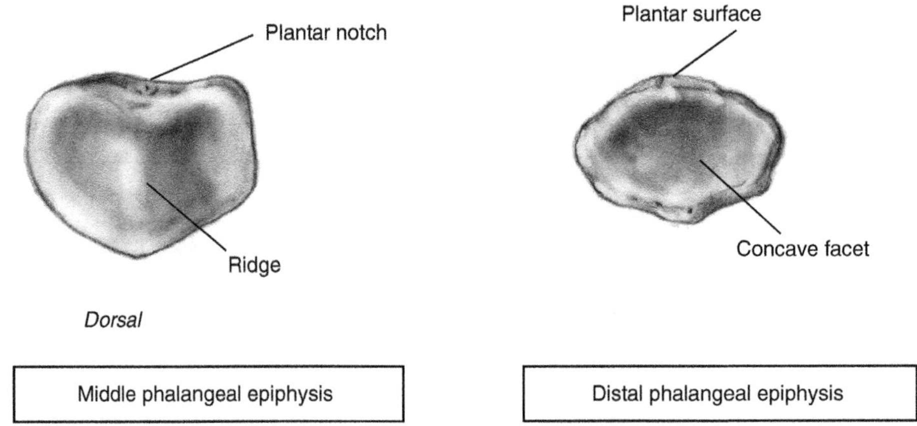

Comparison of the right middle and distal phalangeal epiphyses (approx. 10 yrs)

Regional Identification

Middle Phalanges

- Disc-like structures with a biconcave facet located proximally for articulation with the head of the proximal phalanx.
- The two facets are separated by a weak ridge that runs from the plantar to the dorsal rim of the surface.
- The plantar border is indented and the dorsal border is gently rounded.

Distal Phalanges

- Small oval discs.
- Articular surfaces are concave both from plantar to dorsal and medial to lateral.

Intraregional Identification

Both middle and distal phalanges are very difficult to identify and assign to a specific digit, with the exception of the distal hallucial phalanx.

The Base of the First Distal Phalanx

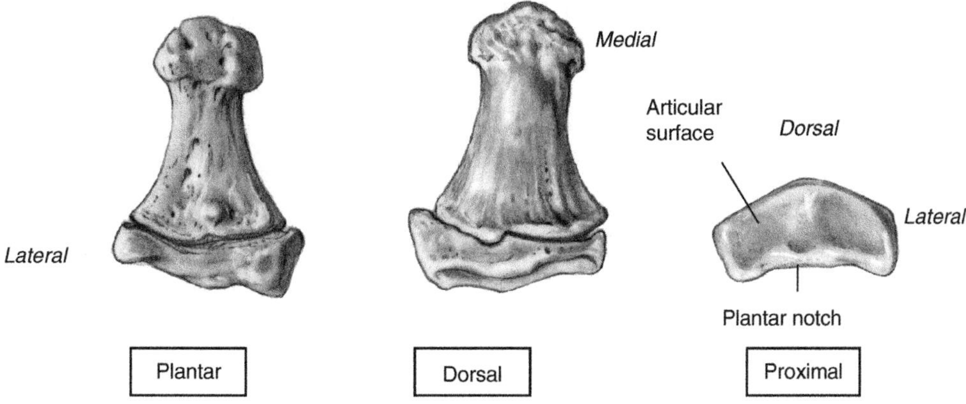

Right distal hallucial phalanx from a child of approximately 10 years

Identification/Siding

- The epiphysis of the hallucial distal phalanx is larger and more robust than distal phalanges 2–5.
- It displays a wide plantar notch and gently rounded dorsal border.
- The medial aspect of the epiphysis is considerably thicker than the lateral aspect.

The Base of the First Metatarsal

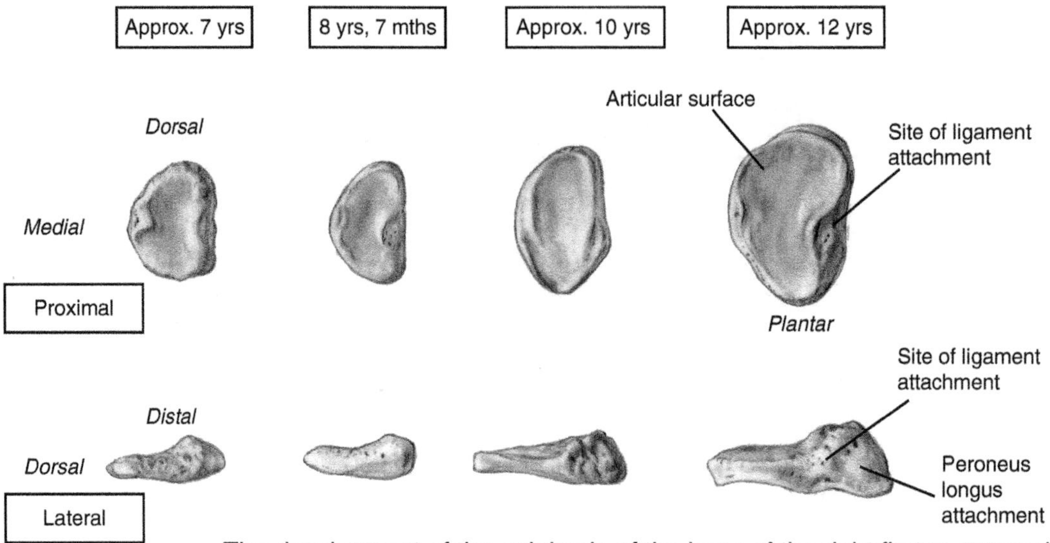

The development of the epiphysis of the base of the right first metatarsal

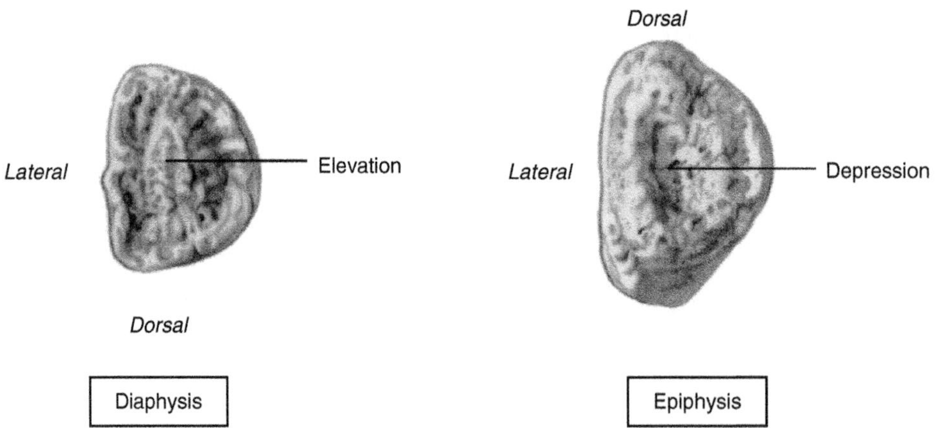

The metaphyseal surfaces of the diaphysis and epiphysis of the right first metatarsal from a child of approximately 12 years

Identification – Recognizable by six or seven years of age. May by confused with the epiphysis of the distal radius (see page 186).

- The epiphysis of the first metatarsal is larger than that of the distal radius.
- Early in development, the mediolateral diameter of the first metatarsal epiphysis is much wider than the anteroposterior diameter of the distal radius.
- Later in development, the first metatarsal epiphysis is more rounded than the angular posterior surface of the distal radius.

Siding

- D-shaped appearance with a rounded medial border and a straightened lateral border.
- The plantar margin is slightly thicker than the dorsal margin; the lateral side of both plantar and dorsal margins is thicker than the medial side.
- A particularly thickened area occurs along the plantolateral border for attachment of the peroneus longus muscle.
- A central depression is located on the metaphyseal surface that corresponds to a raised mound on the metaphyseal surface of the diaphysis.

The Calcaneal Epiphysis

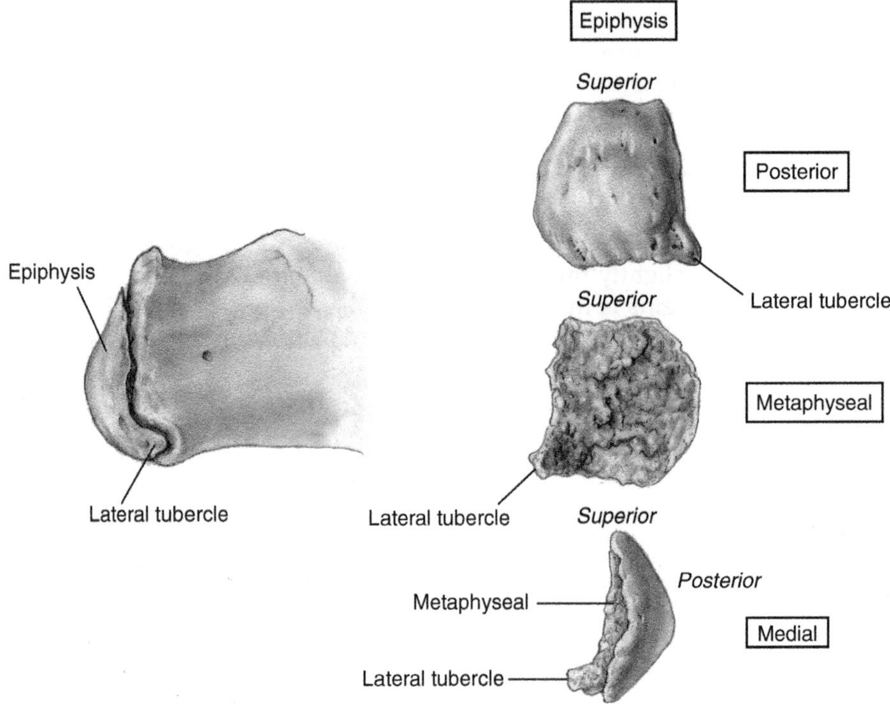

Right calcaneal epiphysis from a child of approximately 10 years

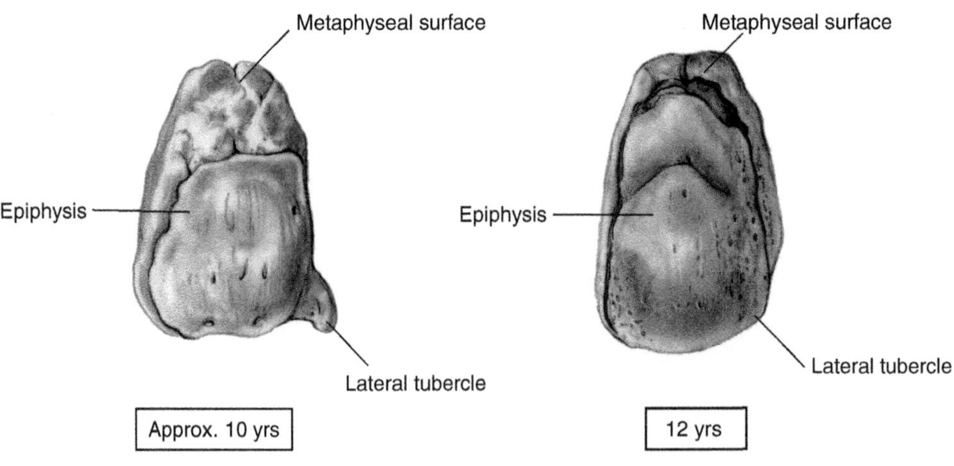

Fusion of the right calcaneal epiphysis

Identification

Unlikely to be identified in isolation prior to eight years in girls and 10 years in boys. May be confused with the epiphysis of the ischial tuberosity (see page 240).

Siding

- The epiphysis is convex on its posterior aspect and concave on its metaphyseal surface.
- The lower plantar region is thicker, whereas the upper extension is more scale-like.
- The lower border angles to the lateral side where a tubercle may be present.

Shaft Metrics

Fazekas and Kósa

Dry Bone Fetal Measurements-First Metatarsal

Prenatal Age (wks)	*n*	Max Length (mm) Mean	Max Length (mm) Range
16	9	2.4	2.2–2.9
18	15	3.2	3.0–3.5
20	13	4.0	3.2–4.3
22	11	5.0	4.2–6.8
24	12	5.8	4.9–6.5
26	12	6.3	5.8–7.0
28	12	7.3	6.1–8.0
30	12	8.2	7.0–8.7
32	8	9.1	8.5–10.0
34	7	10.7	10.0–11.2
36	5	11.5	11.2–12.0
38	7	12.3	12.0–12.5
40	10	13.2	12.5–14.5

Source

Dry bone measurements on mid twentieth century Hungarian fetal remains from autopsy—males and females combined. Age was estimated based on fetal crown heel length.

Reference

Fazekas, I.Gy. and Kósa, F. (1978). *Forensic Fetal Osteology.* Budapest: Akadémiai Kiadó.

de Vasconcellos et al.

Dry Bone Fetal Measurements-Metatarsals											
		Maximum diaphyseal length (mm)									
		MT1		MT2		MT3		MT4		MT5	
Prenatal Age (wks)	*n*	Mean	S.D	Mean	S.D	Mean	S.D	Mean	S.D	Mean	S.D
14	5	2.04	0.37	2.80	0.44	2.34	0.46	2.34	0.45	2.02	0.46
15	10	2.88	0.54	3.87	0.84	3.61	0.87	3.57	0.90	3.33	0.73
16	4	3.35	0.30	4.45	0.43	4.43	0.54	4.18	0.28	–	–
17	8	4.00	0.41	5.40	0.53	4.94	0.61	4.55	0.50	4.30	0.42
18	8	4.29	0.38	5.68	0.71	5.56	0.50	5.20	0.47	4.88	0.61
19	12	4.45	0.56	6.02	0.77	5.73	0.66	5.35	0.68	5.06	0.56
20	9	5.26	0.41	7.24	0.60	6.87	0.74	6.30	0.79	5.96	0.59
21	7	5.20	0.62	7.27	0.95	6.84	0.48	6.43	0.52	5.97	0.81
22	8	6.06	0.86	7.96	1.19	7.70	1.02	7.38	1.00	–	–
23	7	6.20	0.30	8.23	0.24	7.86	0.59	7.39	0.50	6.87	0.45

Source

Dry bone measurements taken from late twentieth century spontaneously aborted Brazilian fetuses.

Reference

de Vasconcellos, H.A. and Ferreira, E. (1998). Metatarsal growth during the second trimester: A predictor of gestational age? *Journal of Anatomy* **193**: 145–149. Wiley-Blackwell.

Appearance Times

Garn et al.

Radiographic Assessment-Foot

Ossification centre	**Male Percentiles**			**Female Percentiles**		
	5th	**50th**	**95th**	**5th**	**50th**	**95th**
Cuboid	37g	3w	3m3w	37g	3w	2m
Lateral cuneiform	3w	5m	1y7m	–	3m	1y2m
Middle phalanx of 5th toe	–	12m	3y10m	–	9m	2y1w
Epiphysis of distal phalanx of 1st toe	8m	1y1m	2y1m	5m	9m	1y8m
Epiphysis of middle phalanx of 4th toe	5m	1y2m	2y11m	5m	11m	3y
Epiphysis of middle phalanx of 3rd toe	5m	1y5m	4y3m	3m	12m	2y6m
Epiphysis of proximal phalanx of 3rd toe	11m	1y7m	2y6m	6m	1y1m	1y10m
Epiphysis of proximal phalanx of 4th toe	11m	1y7m	2y8m	7m	1y3m	2y1m
Epiphysis of proximal phalanx of 2nd toe	12m	1y9m	2y8m	8m	1y2m	2y1m
Epiphysis of middle phalanx of 2nd toe	11m	2y1m	4y1m	6m	1y2m	2y3m
Medical cuneiform	11m	2y2m	3y9m	6m	1y5m	2y10m
Epiphysis of 1st metatarsal	1y4m	2y2m	3y1m	12m	1y7m	2y3m
Epiphysis of proximal phalanx of 1st toe	1y5m	2y4m	3y4m	11m	1y6m	2y5m
Epiphysis of proximal phalanx of 5th toe	1y6m	2y6m	3y8m	12m	1y8m	2y8m
Intermediate cuneiform	1y2m	2y8m	4y3m	10m	1y9m	3y
Epiphysis of 2nd metatarsal	1y11m	2y10m	4y4m	1y2m	2y2m	3y5m
Navicular	1y1m	3y	5y5m	9m	1y11m	3y7m
Epiphysis of 3rd metatarsal	2y4m	3y6m	5y	1y5m	2y6m	3y8m
Epiphysis of distal phalanx of 5th toe	2y4m	3y11m	6y4m	1y2m	2y4m	4y1m
Epiphysis of 4th metatarsal	2y11m	4y	5y9m	1y9m	2y10m	4y1m
Epiphysis of distal phalanx of 3rd toe	3y	4y4m	6y2m	1y4m	2y9m	4y1m
Epiphysis of 5th metatarsal	3y1m	4y5m	6y4m	2y1m	3y3m	4y11m
Epiphysis of distal phalanx of 4th toe	2y11m	4y5m	6y5m	1y4m	2y7m	4y1m
Epiphysis of distal phalanx of 2nd toe	3y3m	4y8m	6y9m	1y6m	2y11m	4y6m
Calcaneal epiphysis	5y2m	7y7m	9y7m	3y7m	5y5m	7y4m

gestational week (g), postnatal week (w), month (m), or year (y).

Source

Participants in the U.S.-based Fels Research Institute Program of Human Development, begun in 1929.

Reference

Garn, S.M., Rohmann, C.G., and Silverman, F.N. (1967). Radiographic standards for postnatal ossification and tooth calcification. *Medical Radiography and Photography* **43**: 45–66.

The Birkner

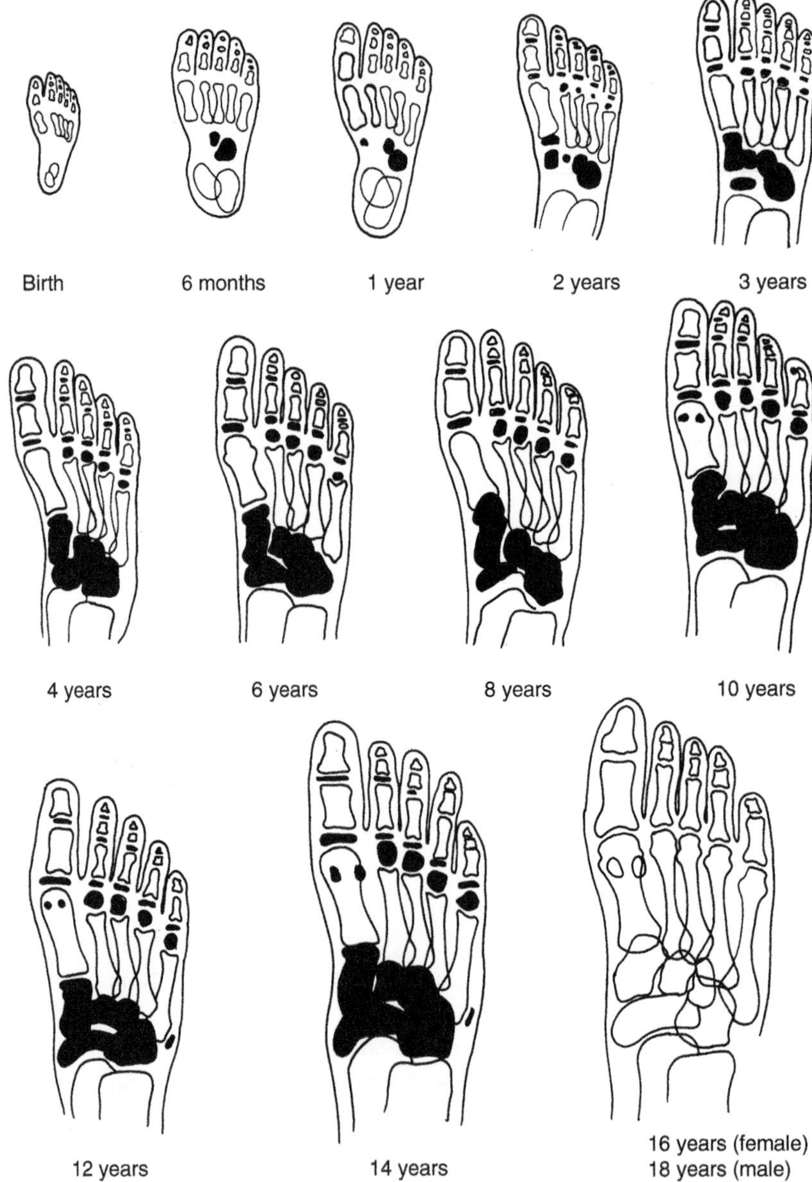

Osseous development of the foot and ankle

Reference

Birkner, R. (1978). *Normal Radiographic Patterns and Variances of the Human Skeleton – An X-ray Atlas of Adults and Children*. Baltimore (Munich): Urban and Schwarzenberg.

Union Times

Coqueugniot and Weaver

Dry Bone Assessment-Calcaneus						
	Males			Females		
	Open	Partial	Complete	Open	Partial	Complete
Posterior	≤16	16–20	≥16	≤12	10–17	≥14

Source

Documented Portuguese material born between 1904 and 1938 (Coimbra collection), including 69 females and 68 males between the ages of 7 and 29 years.

Warning

Many ages are poorly represented.

Reference

Coqueugniot, H. and Weaver, T. (2007). Infracranial maturation in the skeletal collection from Coimbra, Portugal: New aging standards for epiphyseal union. *American Journal of Physical Anthropology,* **134**(3): 424–437.

Morphological Summary

Prenatal	
8–10 wks	Primary ossification centers appear for metatarsals 2–5
9–12 wks	Primary ossification centers appear for distal phalanges
12 wks	Primary ossification center appears for base of metatarsal 1
14–16 wks	Primary ossification centers appear for proximal phalanges
16–20 wks	Primary ossification centers appear for middle phalanges
5–6 mths	Ossification center appears for calcaneus
6–7 mths	Ossification center appears for talus
Birth	At least 16 of the primary centers of ossification for the long bones of the foot are present (middle phalanges of the lateral toes may appear after birth). Both the calcaneus and talus are present and can be identified in isolation (cuboid center of ossification may be present).
1–3 mths	Ossification center appears for cuboid
3–6 mths	Ossification center appears for lateral cuneiform
9 mths (f) 14 mths (m)	Epiphysis for base of distal phalanx 1 appears
11–14 mths (f) 14–24 mths (m)	Epiphyses for middle phalanges 2–4 appear
11–20 mths (f) 18–28 mths (m)	Epiphyses for the proximal phalanges appear
12–24 mths (f) 24–36 mths (m)	Ossification center appears for medial cuneiform
18–20 mths (f) 26–31 mths (m)	Epiphysis for base of metatarsal 1 appears
19–24 mths (f) 27–34 mths (m)	Epiphysis for head of metatarsal 2 appears
24–36 mths (f) 36–48 mths (m)	Ossification center appears for intermediate cuneiform
2.5 yrs (f) 3.5 yrs (m)	Epiphysis for head of metatarsal 3 appears
2.5 yrs (f) 4 yrs (m)	Epiphysis for head of metatarsal 4 appears
2–3 yrs (f) 4–5 yrs (m)	Ossification center appears for navicular and epiphyses of the distal phalanges 2–4 and epiphysis for head of metatarsal 5

3–5 yrs (f) 5–7 yrs (m)	The cuboid, navicular, cuneiforms, and metatarsal heads are all identifiable in isolation
5–6 yrs (f) 7–8 yrs (m)	Epiphysis for calcaneus appears
8 yrs (f) 11 yrs (m)	Epiphysis for talus appears
10–12 yrs (f) 11–14 yrs (m)	Calcaneal epiphysis commences fusion
11–13 yrs (f) 14–16 yrs (m)	Epiphyseal fusion in distal phalanges, middle phalanges, and metatarsal heads 2–5
13–15 yrs (f) 16–18 yrs (m)	Epiphyseal fusion in proximal phalanges and base of metatarsal 1
15–16 yrs (f) 18–20 yrs (m)	Completion of fusion at the calcaneal epiphysis

(f) indicates female, while (m) indicates male.

CHAPTER

9

Summaries, Recording Forms, and Practical Sequencing Information

SUMMARY ILLUSTRATIONS

Summary illustrations originally developed within *Developmental Juvenile Osteology* (with additional ones added in *The Juvenile Skeletons*) are once again provided to serve as a quick source for obtaining useful ageing information on each bone. It must be emphasized, however, that some of the ranges have been updated from the original text in response to the additional research on epiphyseal union timing that recently has become available since publication of the first two books.

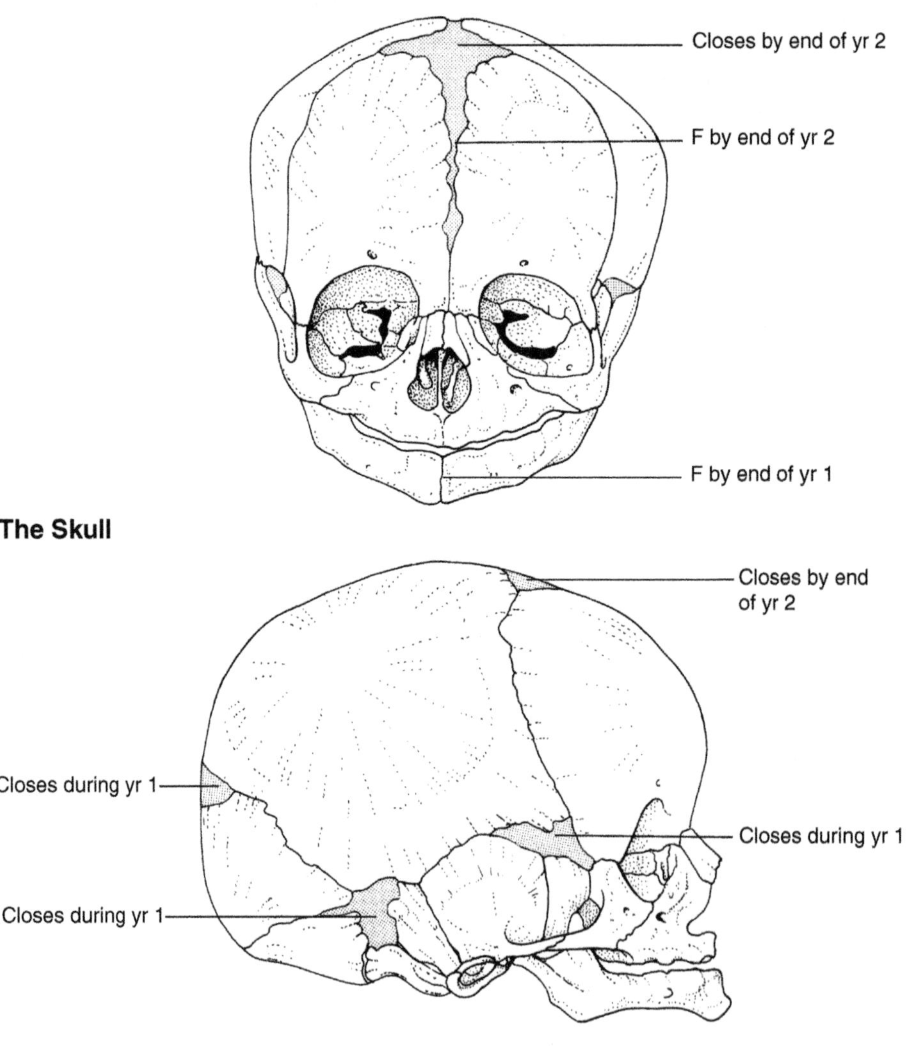

A = appearance; F = fusion

The Base of the Skull

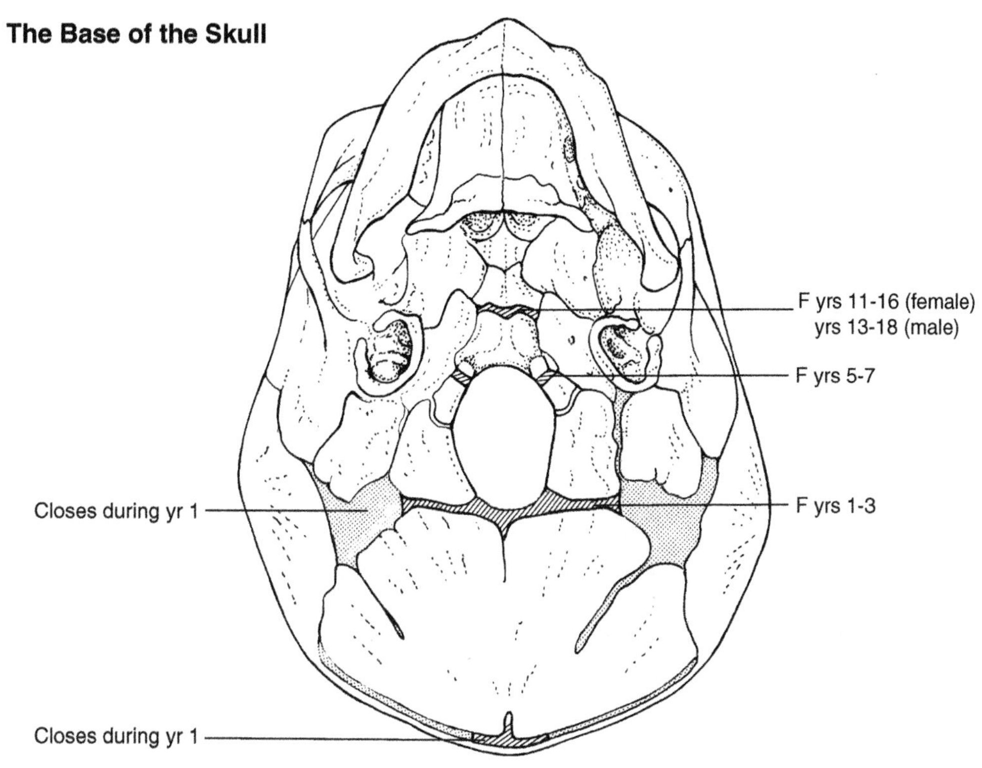

The Temporal

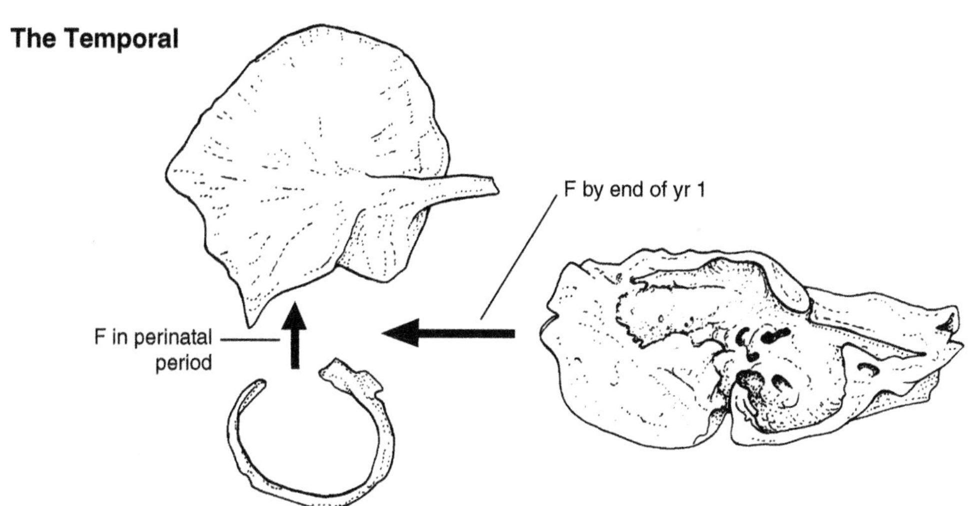

The Sphenoid

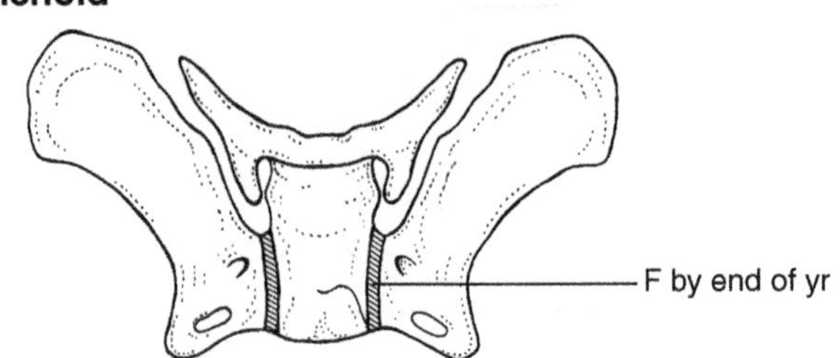
F by end of yr 1

C 1

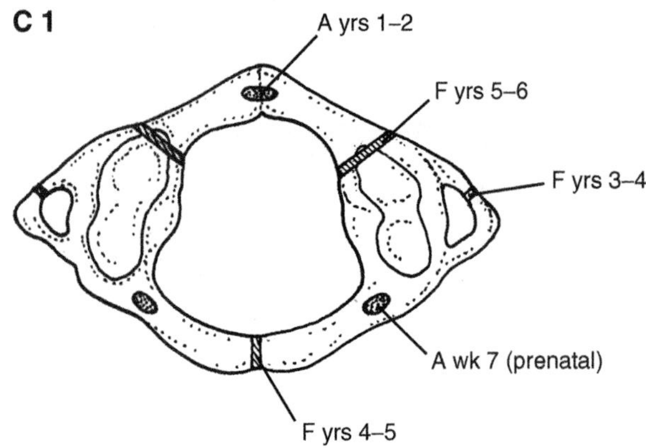
A yrs 1–2
F yrs 5–6
F yrs 3–4
A wk 7 (prenatal)
F yrs 4–5

C 2

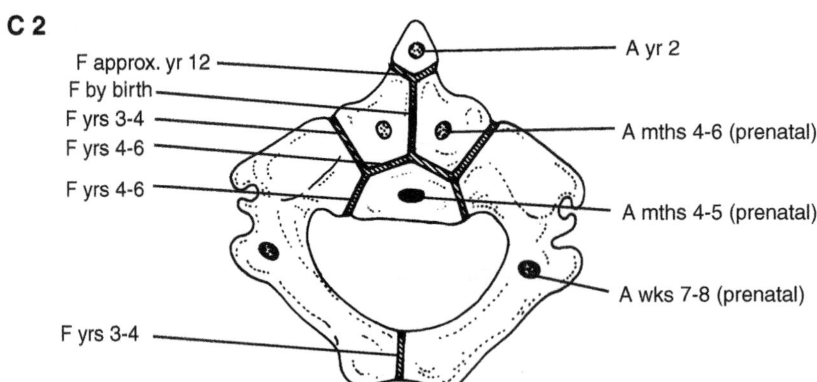
F approx. yr 12
F by birth
F yrs 3-4
F yrs 4-6
F yrs 4-6
F yrs 3-4
A yr 2
A mths 4-6 (prenatal)
A mths 4-5 (prenatal)
A wks 7-8 (prenatal)

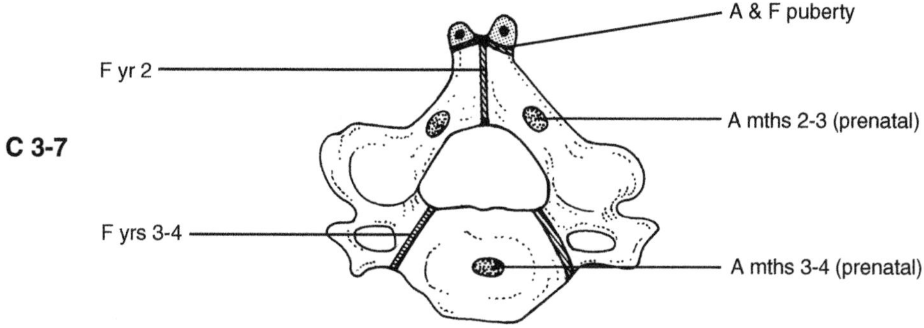

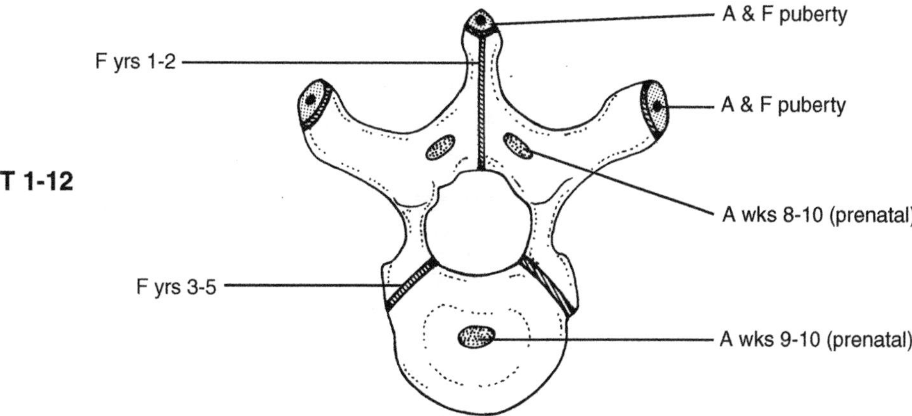

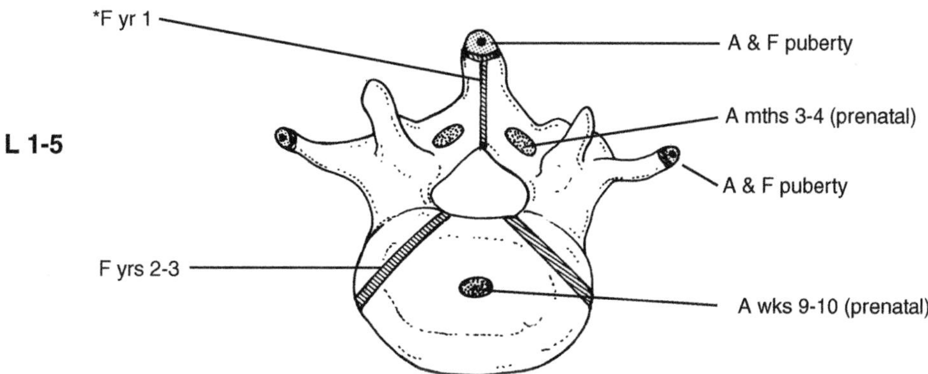

* Does not always fuse in L5

The Sacrum

F yrs 18-25
F yrs 2-6
F yrs 25+
F yrs 12-14
F yrs 2-6
F yrs 12-14
F puberty
F yrs 2-6
F yrs 12
A yrs 15-16
A mth 6-8 (prenatal)
A mth 3 (prenatal)
A mths 6-8 (prenatal)
A mth 4 (prenatal)
A mth 5 (prenatal)
A mth 5 (prenatal)
A yr 1
A yrs 3-6
A approx. yr 10
A puberty

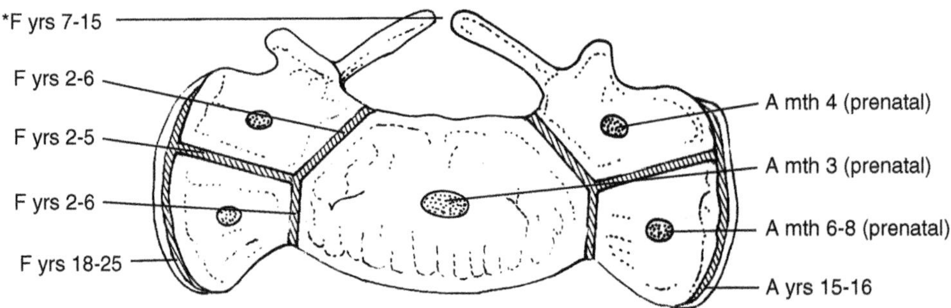

*Does not always fuse

The Sternum

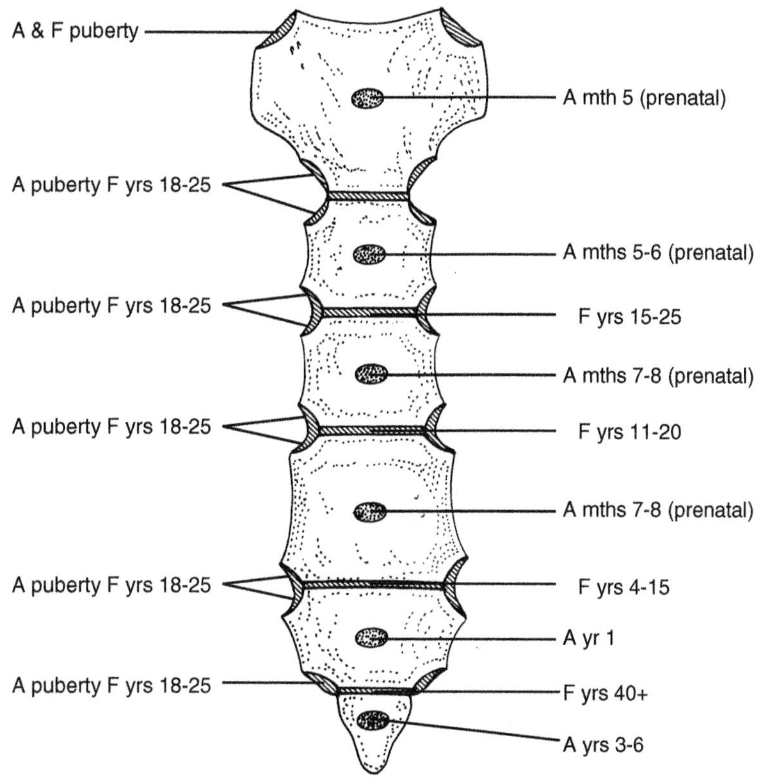
A & F puberty
A mth 5 (prenatal)
A puberty F yrs 18-25
A mths 5-6 (prenatal)
A puberty F yrs 18-25
F yrs 15-25
A mths 7-8 (prenatal)
A puberty F yrs 18-25
F yrs 11-20
A mths 7-8 (prenatal)
A puberty F yrs 18-25
F yrs 4-15
A yr 1
A puberty F yrs 18-25
F yrs 40+
A yrs 3-6

The Ribs

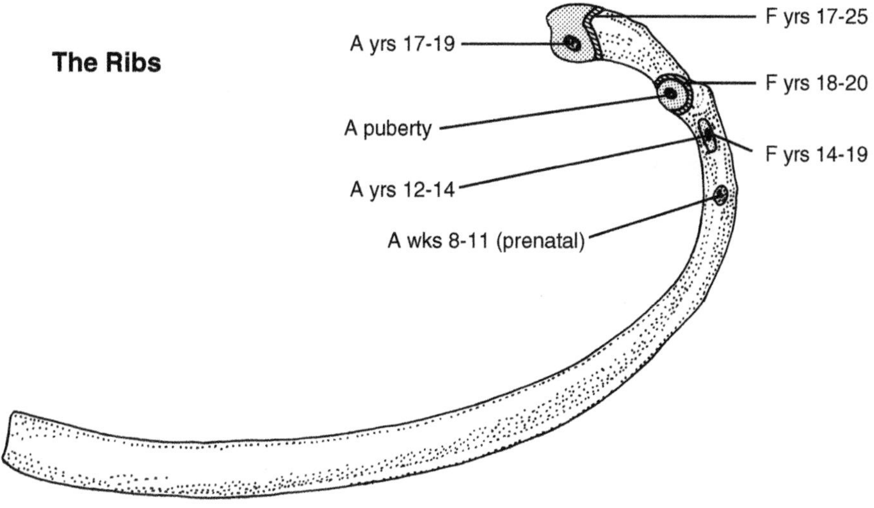
F yrs 17-25
A yrs 17-19
F yrs 18-20
A puberty
F yrs 14-19
A yrs 12-14
A wks 8-11 (prenatal)

The Clavicle

Lateral epiphysis
F wk 7 (prenatal)
Medial epiphysis
A yrs 18-20
F yrs 18-20
A yrs 13-14
F yrs 17-30
A wks 5-6 (prenatal)

The Scapula

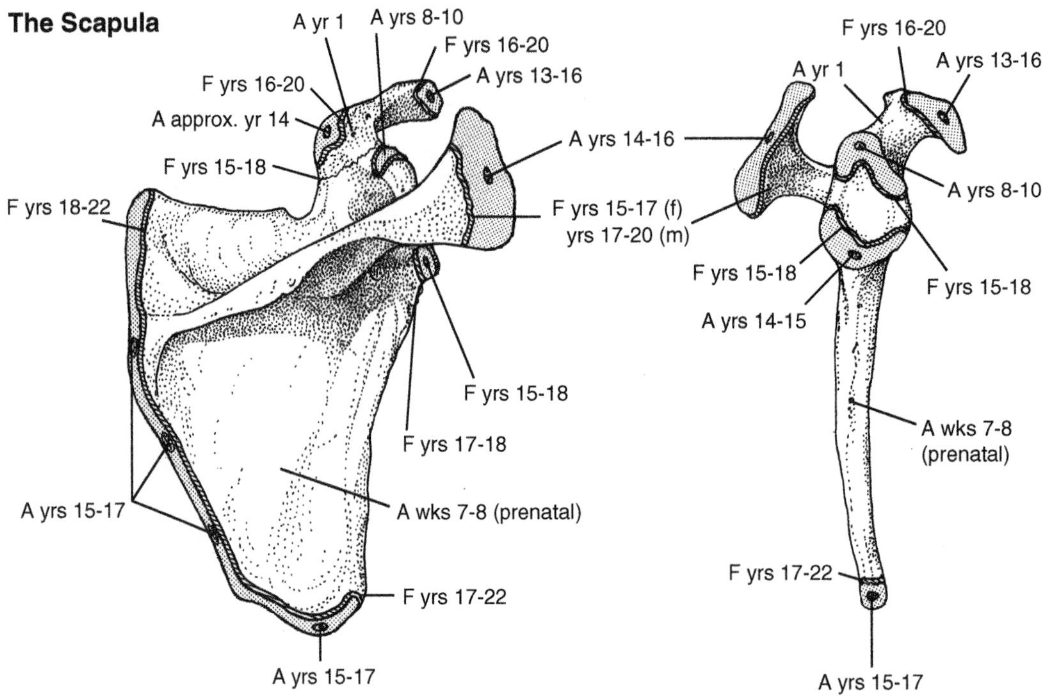

The Humerus

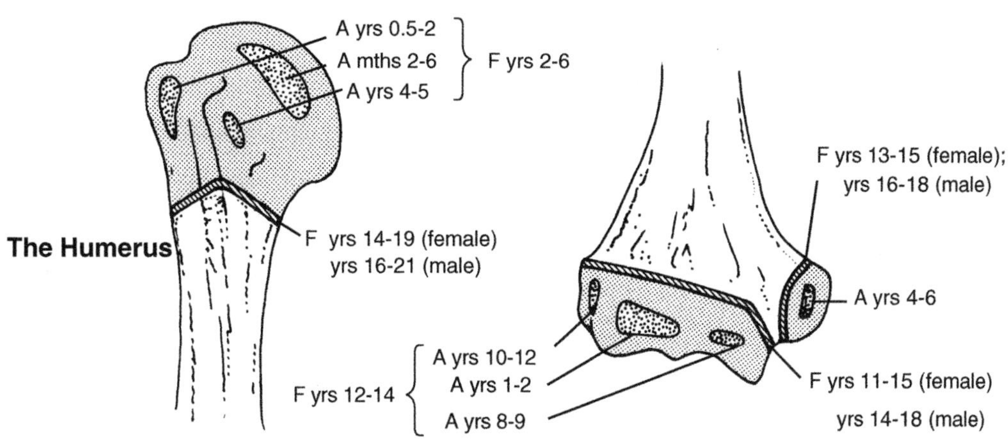
A yrs 0.5-2
A mths 2-6
A yrs 4-5
F yrs 2-6
F yrs 14-19 (female)
yrs 16-21 (male)
F yrs 13-15 (female);
yrs 16-18 (male)
A yrs 4-6
A yrs 10-12
A yrs 1-2
A yrs 8-9
F yrs 12-14
F yrs 11-15 (female)
yrs 14-18 (male)

The Radius

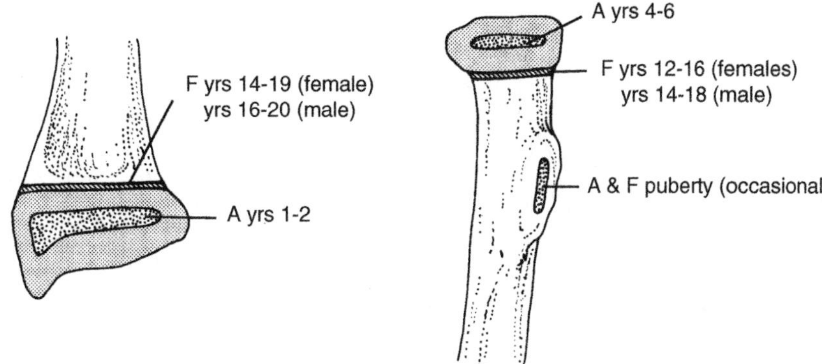
F yrs 14-19 (female)
yrs 16-20 (male)
A yrs 1-2
A yrs 4-6
F yrs 12-16 (females)
yrs 14-18 (male)
A & F puberty (occasional)

The Ulna

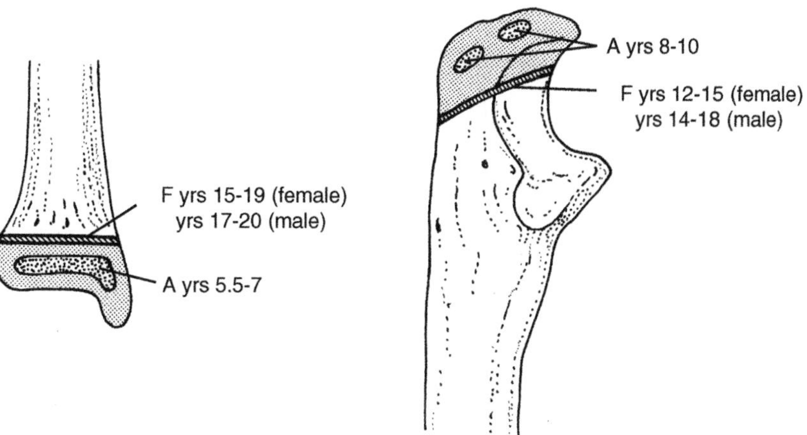
F yrs 15-19 (female)
yrs 17-20 (male)
A yrs 5.5-7
A yrs 8-10
F yrs 12-15 (female)
yrs 14-18 (male)

The Hand

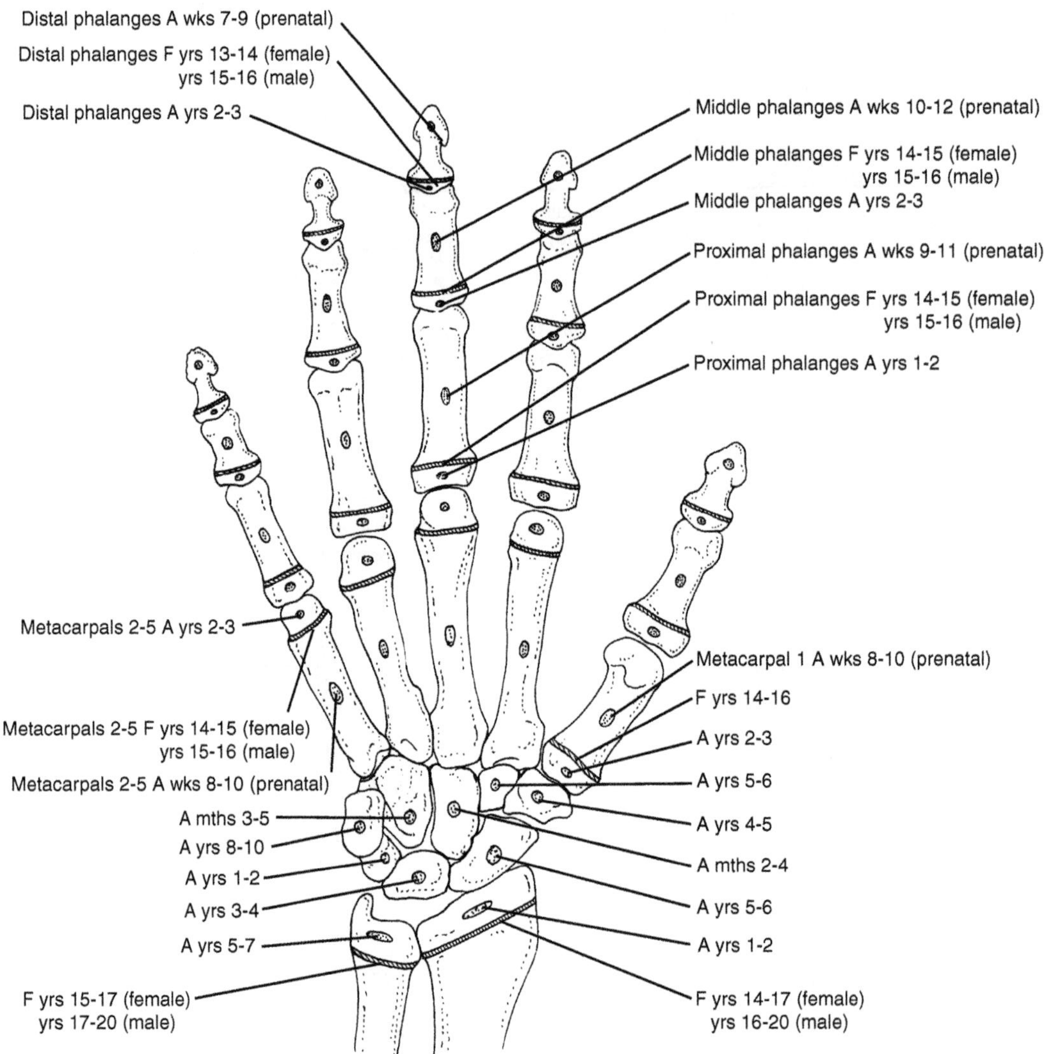
Distal phalanges A wks 7-9 (prenatal)
Distal phalanges F yrs 13-14 (female)
yrs 15-16 (male)
Distal phalanges A yrs 2-3
Middle phalanges A wks 10-12 (prenatal)
Middle phalanges F yrs 14-15 (female)
yrs 15-16 (male)
Middle phalanges A yrs 2-3
Proximal phalanges A wks 9-11 (prenatal)
Proximal phalanges F yrs 14-15 (female)
yrs 15-16 (male)
Proximal phalanges A yrs 1-2
Metacarpals 2-5 A yrs 2-3
Metacarpals 2-5 F yrs 14-15 (female)
yrs 15-16 (male)
Metacarpals 2-5 A wks 8-10 (prenatal)
A mths 3-5
A yrs 8-10
A yrs 1-2
A yrs 3-4
A yrs 5-7
F yrs 15-17 (female)
yrs 17-20 (male)
Metacarpal 1 A wks 8-10 (prenatal)
F yrs 14-16
A yrs 2-3
A yrs 5-6
A yrs 4-5
A mths 2-4
A yrs 5-6
A yrs 1-2
F yrs 14-17 (female)
yrs 16-20 (male)

The Innominate

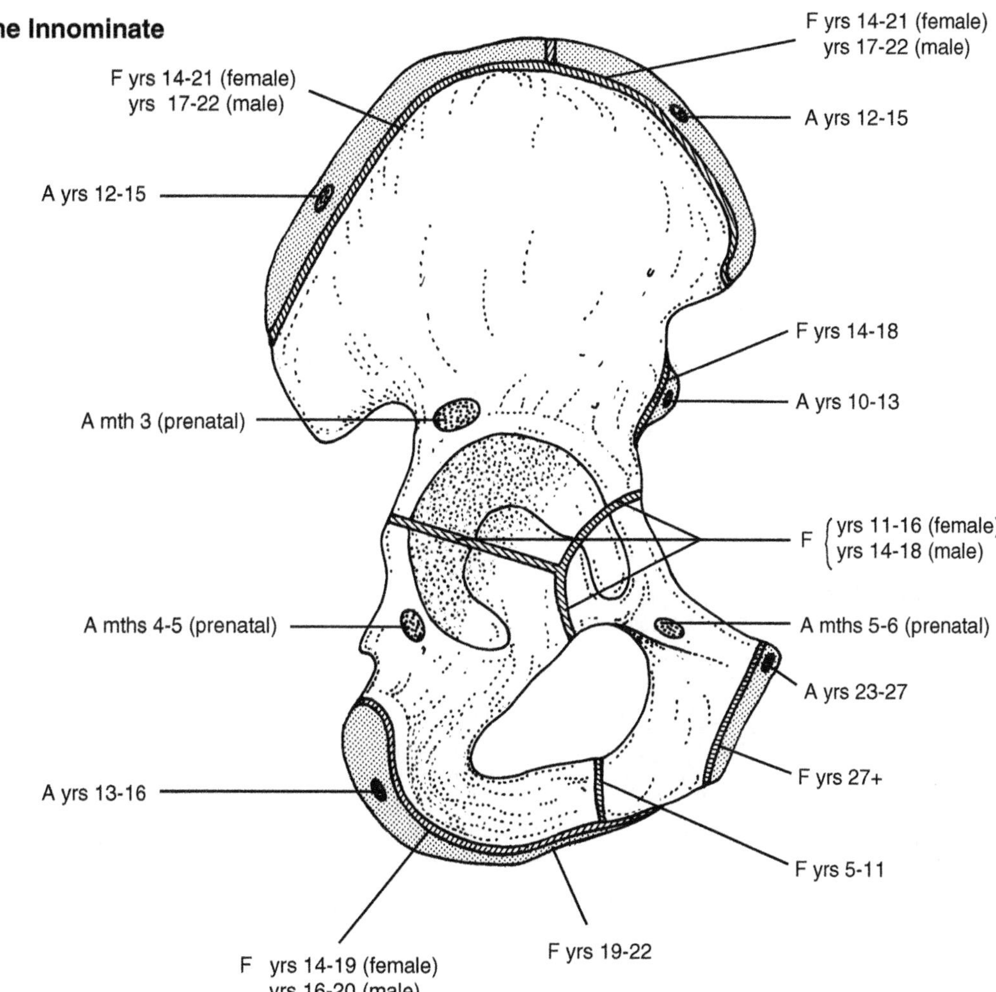
F yrs 14-21 (female)
yrs 17-22 (male)
F yrs 14-21 (female)
yrs 17-22 (male)
A yrs 12-15
A yrs 12-15
F yrs 14-18
A yrs 10-13
A mth 3 (prenatal)
F yrs 11-16 (female)
yrs 14-18 (male)
A mths 4-5 (prenatal)
A mths 5-6 (prenatal)
A yrs 23-27
F yrs 27+
A yrs 13-16
F yrs 5-11
F yrs 19-22
F yrs 14-19 (female)
yrs 16-20 (male)

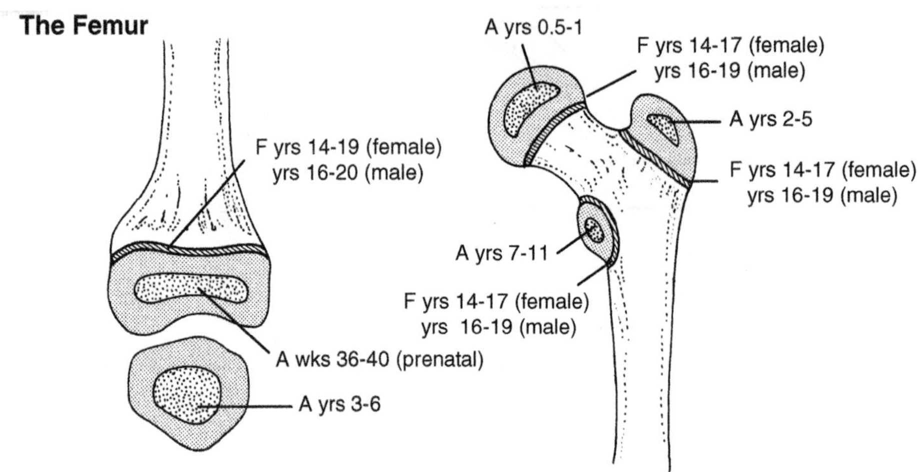
The Femur
A yrs 0.5-1
F yrs 14-17 (female)
yrs 16-19 (male)
A yrs 2-5
F yrs 14-19 (female)
yrs 16-20 (male)
F yrs 14-17 (female)
yrs 16-19 (male)
A yrs 7-11
F yrs 14-17 (female)
yrs 16-19 (male)
A wks 36-40 (prenatal)
A yrs 3-6

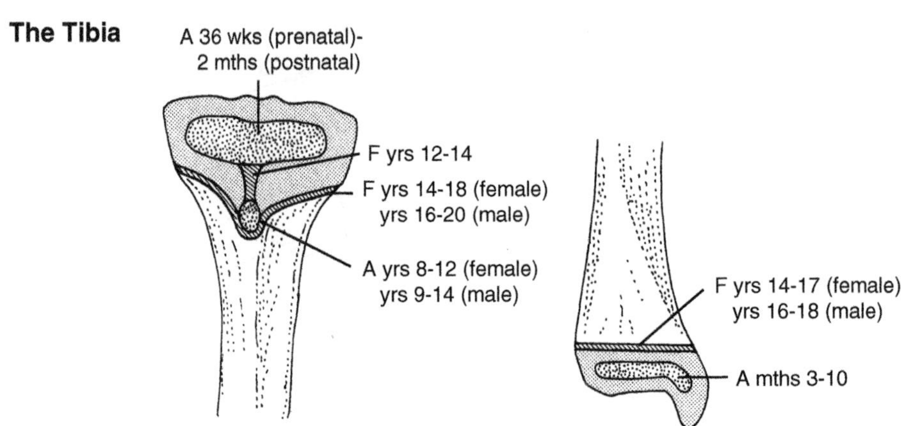
The Tibia
A 36 wks (prenatal)-
2 mths (postnatal)
F yrs 12-14
F yrs 14-18 (female)
yrs 16-20 (male)
A yrs 8-12 (female)
yrs 9-14 (male)
F yrs 14-17 (female)
yrs 16-18 (male)
A mths 3-10

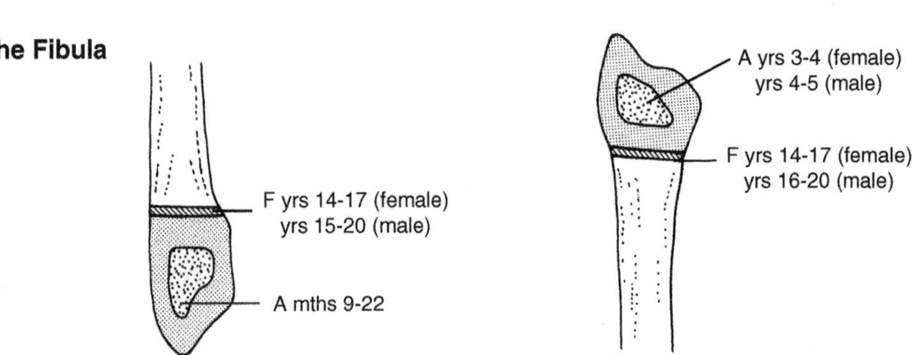
The Fibula
A yrs 3-4 (female)
yrs 4-5 (male)
F yrs 14-17 (female)
yrs 16-20 (male)
F yrs 14-17 (female)
yrs 15-20 (male)
A mths 9-22

The Foot

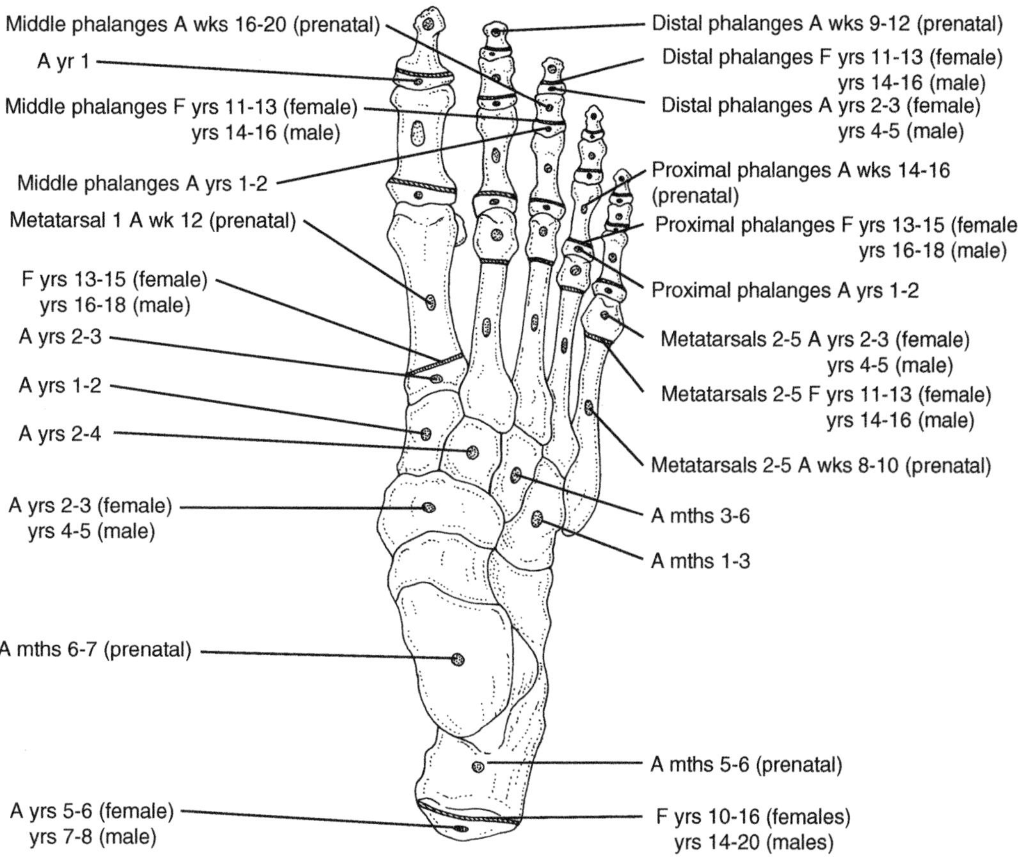
Middle phalanges A wks 16-20 (prenatal)
A yr 1
Middle phalanges F yrs 11-13 (female)
yrs 14-16 (male)
Middle phalanges A yrs 1-2
Metatarsal 1 A wk 12 (prenatal)
F yrs 13-15 (female)
yrs 16-18 (male)
A yrs 2-3
A yrs 1-2
A yrs 2-4
A yrs 2-3 (female)
yrs 4-5 (male)
A mths 6-7 (prenatal)
A yrs 5-6 (female)
yrs 7-8 (male)
Distal phalanges A wks 9-12 (prenatal)
Distal phalanges F yrs 11-13 (female)
yrs 14-16 (male)
Distal phalanges A yrs 2-3 (female)
yrs 4-5 (male)
Proximal phalanges A wks 14-16
(prenatal)
Proximal phalanges F yrs 13-15 (female)
yrs 16-18 (male)
Proximal phalanges A yrs 1-2
Metatarsals 2-5 A yrs 2-3 (female)
yrs 4-5 (male)
Metatarsals 2-5 F yrs 11-13 (female)
yrs 14-16 (male)
Metatarsals 2-5 A wks 8-10 (prenatal)
A mths 3-6
A mths 1-3
A mths 5-6 (prenatal)
F yrs 10-16 (females)
yrs 14-20 (males)

AGING FORMS

These forms have been designed to provide practical parameters for estimating age based on the observed status of various osseous material. Two general techniques for age estimation have been considered, both the appearance and union of primary and secondary ossification centers. When estimating age based on appearance times, it is generally recommended that the technique is restricted to radiographic analysis (or analysis in which the practitioner is certain that the entire skeleton is present), as the absence of material in a dry bone state may simply be the result of poor recovery or lost material rather than lack of appearance. Age estimation based on union times can be used with both radiographic and dry bone assessment of material; however, the practitioner must be vigilant that these forms provide only general age parameters. For specific and more accurate information regarding ageing, it is advised that standards derived from a representative population, with comparable means of assessment (as provided within the individual chapters) be consulted.

PRENATAL RADIOGRAPHIC AGING FORM

Appearance of Ossification Centers		Absent	Present
1st Trimester	Clavicle	≤6 f wks	≥5 f wks
	Humerus, Radius & Ulna	≤7 f wks	≥7 f wks
	Axis & Atlas Neural Arch	≤8 f wks	≥7 f wks
	Scapula	≤8 f wks	≥7 f wks
	Femur & Tibia	≤8 f wks	≥7 f wks
	Distal Phalanges- Manual	≤9 f wks	≥7 f wks
	Fibula	≤9 f wks	≥8 f wks
	MT 2-5	≤10 f wks	≥8 f wks
	Thoracic Neural Arches	≤10 f wks	≥8 f wks
	Metacarpals 1-5	≤10 f wks	≥8 f wks
	Thoracic & Lumbar Centra	≤10 f wks	≥9 f wks
	Ribs	≤11 f wks	≥8 f wks
	Proximal Phalanges- Manual	≤11 f wks	≥9 f wks
	Cervical Neural Arches	≤12 f wks	≥8 f wks
	Distal Phalanges- Pedal	≤12 f wks	≥9 f wks
	Middle Phalanges- Manual	≤12 f wks	≥10 f wks
	Metatarsal 1	≤12 f wks	≥12 f wks
	Ilium	≤12 f wks	≥12 f wks
	Sacral Centrum	≤12 f wks	≥12 f wks
2nd Trimester	Cervical Centra	≤4 f mths	≥3 f mths
	Proximal Phalanges- Pedal	≤4 f mths	≥3 f mths
	Lumbar Neural Arches	≤4 f mths	≥3 f mths
	Sacral Neural Arch	≤4 f mths	≥4 f mths
	Axis Centrum	≤5 f mths	≥4 f mths
	Ischium	≤5 f mths	≥4 f mths
	Axis Dens	≤6 f mths	≥4 f mths
	Middle Phalanges-Pedal	≤5 f mths	≥5 f mths
	Pubis	≤6 f mths	≥5 f mths
	Calcaneus	≤6 f mths	≥5 f mths
3rd Trimester	Manubrium & Sternebra 1	≤8 f mths	≥5 f mths
	Talus	≤7 f mths	≥6 f mths
	Sacral Lateral Element	≤8 f mths	≥6 f mths
	Sternebrae 2 & 3	≤9 f mths	≥7 f mths
	Distal Femur	≤1 mth	≥9 f mths
	Proximal Tibia	≤2 mths	≥9 f mths

f = fetal weeks or months; all other ages are postnatal.

POSTNATAL RADIOGRAPHIC AGING FORM

Appearance of Ossification Centers		Absent	Present
Shoulder	Coracoid Process	≤12 mths	≥37 f wks
	Humeral Head	≤6 mths	≥37 f wks
	Greater Tubercle	≤2.5 yrs	≥2 mths
	Acromion Process	≤16 yrs	≥10 yrs
Elbow	Capitulum	≤2 yrs	≥1 mth
	Proximal Radius	≤8 yrs	≥2 yrs
	Medial Epicondyle Humerus	≤8.5 yrs	≥2 yrs
	Proximal Ulna	≤12 yrs	≥6 yrs
	Lateral Epicondyle Humerus	≤14 yrs	≥7 yrs
Hand & Wrist	Capitate	≤7 mths	≥37 f wks
	Hamate	≤10 mths	≥38 f wks
	Distal Radius	≤2.5 yrs	≥4 mths
	Triquetral	≤5.5 yrs	≥3 mths
	Bases of Proximal Phalanges	≤3 yrs	≥5 mths
	MC Heads 2-5; Base of MC1	≤4 yrs	≥8 mths
	Bases of Middle & Dist. Phalanges	≤5 yrs	≥8 mths
	Lunate	≤7 yrs	≥1 yr
	Scaphoid	≤8 yrs	≥2.5 yrs
	Greater Multangular/Trapezium	≤9 yrs	≥2 yrs
	Lesser Multangular/Trapezoid	≤8.5 yrs	≥2.5 yrs
	Distal Ulna	≤9 yrs	≥3 yrs
Hip	Proximal Femur	≤10 mths	≥2 wks
	Greater Trochanter	≤4.5 yrs	≥1 yr
Knee	Distal Femur	≤1 mth	≥34 f wks
	Proximal Tibia	≤2 mths	≥34 f wks
	Proximal Fibula	≤5.5 yrs	≥1.5 yrs
Foot & Ankle	Cuboid	≤4 mths	≥37 f wks
	Lateral Cuneiform	≤1.5 yrs	≥1 mth
	Distal Tibia	≤10 mths	≥4 mths
	Bases of Prox & Middle Phalanges	≤4 yrs	≥5 mths
	Bases of Distal Phalanges	≤7 yrs	≥4 mths
	Distal Fibula	≤2.5 yrs	≥7 mths
	Medial Cuneiform	≤4 yrs	≥6 mths
	Base of 1st Metatarsal	≤3 yrs	≥1 yr
	Middle Cuneiform	≤4.5 yrs	≥10 mths
	Navicular	≤5.5 yrs	≥9 mths
	Metatarsal Heads 2-5	≤6.5 yrs	≥1 yr
	Calcaneal Epiphysis	≤9.5 yrs	≥3.5 yrs

f = fetal weeks; all other ages are postnatal.

PERINATAL TO ADOLESCENT AGING

	Fusion of Primary Elements	Open	Fused (Not Obliterated)
Sphenoid	Lesser Wings to Sphenoid Body	≤1 mths	≥5 f mths
	Pre Sphenoid to Post Sphenoid	≤2 mths	≥8 f mths
	Greater Wings to Sphenoid Body	≤12 mths	≥1 mth
	Foramen Ovale (Greater Wing)	≤6 mths	≥1 mth
Temporal	Tympanic Ring to Temporal Squamous	≤1 mths	≥9 f mths
	Petromastoid to Squamotympanic	≤12 mths	≥9 f mths
Occipital	Supra-Occipital to Interparietal Squama	≤5 f mths	≥5 f mths
	Superior Median Fissure	≤11 mths	≥5 mths
	Sutura Mendosa	≤1.5 yrs	≥5 mths
	Partes Laterales to Squama	≤4 yrs	≥1 yr
	Hypoglossal Canal (Pars Laterales)	≤4 yrs	≥1.5 yrs
	Partes Laterales to Pars Basilaris	≤7 yrs	≥3 yrs
Mandible	Mandibular Symphysis	≤8 mths	≥3 mths
Frontal	Fusion of 2 halves of Frontal Bone	≤2 yrs	≥9 mths
	Obliteration of Metopic Suture (generally)	≤4 yrs	≥2 yrs
Vertebrae	Intradental union (C2)	≤full term	≥full term
	Neural Arches of C3-L5	≤2 yrs	≥6 mths
	Neural Arches of C2	≤4 yrs	≥3 yrs
	Neural Arches of C1	≤5 yrs	≥4 yrs
	Neural Arches to Centrum (C3-L5)	≤5 yrs	≥2 yrs
	Dens to Neural Arch (C2)	≤4 yrs	≥3 yrs
	Centrum to Neural Arch (C2)	≤6 yrs	≥4 yrs
	Neural Arch to Anterior Bar (C1)	≤5 yrs	≥4 yrs
	Ossiculum Terminale of dens	≤13 yrs	≥11 yrs
Sacrum	Lateral Element to Neural Arch	≤5 yrs	≥2 yrs
	Wing (Lat Element & NA) to Centra	≤6 yrs	≥2 yrs
Pelvis	Ischiopubic ramus	≤11 yrs	≥5 yrs
Humerus	Greater and Lesser Tubercles to Head	≤6 yrs	≥2 yrs

f = fetal; all other ages are postnatal.

ADOLESCENT AND POSTADOLESCENT AGING (YEARS)

Epiphyseal Union in Males		Open	Partial	Complete
Humerus	Proximal	≤20	16–21	≥18
	Medial	≤18	16–18	≥16
	Distal	≤15	14–18	≥15
Radius	Proximal	≤18	14–18	≥16
	Distal	≤19	16–20	≥17
Ulna	Proximal	≤16	14–18	≥15
	Distal	≤20	17–20	≥17
Hand	MCs & Phalanges	≤17	14–18	≥15
Femur	Head	≤18	16–19	≥16
	Greater Trochanter	≤18	16–19	≥16
	Lesser Trochanter	≤18	16–19	≥16
	Distal	≤19	16–20	≥17
Tibia	Proximal	≤18	16–20	≥17
	Distal	≤18	16–18	≥16
Fibula	Proximal	≤19	16–20	≥17
	Distal	≤18	15–20	≥17
Foot	Calcaneus	≤16	14–20	≥16
	MTs & Phalanges	≤17	14–16	≥15
Scapula	Coraco-Glenoid*	≤16	15–18	≥16
	Acromion	≤20	17–20	≥17
	Inferior Angle	≤21	17–22	≥17
	Medial Border	≤21	18–22	≥18
Pelvis	Tri-radiate Complex**	≤16	14–18	≥15
	Ant Inf Iliac Spine	≤18	16–18	≥16
	Ischial Tuberosity	≤18	16–20	≥17
	Iliac Crest	≤20	17–22	≥18
Sacrum	Auricular Surface	≤21	17–21	≥18
	S1-S2 Bodies	≤27	19–30+	≥25
	S1-S2 Alae	≤20	16–27	≥19
	S2-5 Bodies	≤20	16–28	≥20
	S2-5 Alae	≤16	16–21	≥16
Vertebrae***	Annular Rings	≤21	14–23	≥18
Ribs***	Heads	≤21	17–22	≥19
Clavicle	Medial	≤23	17–30	≥21
Manubrium	1st Costal Notch	≤23	18–25	≥21

*Includes union of the coracoid process, and the subcoracoid and glenoid epiphyses.

**Includes union of primary elements on both pelvic and acetabular surfaces and the acetabular epiphyses.

***At least one vertebra or one rib displays this type of activity.

ADOLESCENT AND POSTADOLESCENT AGING

Epiphyseal Union in Females		Open	Partial	Complete
Humerus	Proximal	≤17	14–19	≥16
	Medial	≤15	13–15	≥13
	Distal	≤15	11–15	≥12
Radius	Proximal	≤15	12–16	≥13
	Distal	≤18	14–19	≥15
Ulna	Proximal	≤15	12–15	≥12
	Distal	≤18	15–19	≥15
Hand	MCs & Phalanges	≤15	11–16	≥12
Femur	Head	≤15	14–17	≥14
	Greater Trochanter	≤15	14–17	≥14
	Lesser Trochanter	≤15	14–17	≥14
	Distal	≤16	14–19	≥17
Tibia	Proximal	≤17	14–18	≥18
	Distal	≤17	14–17	≥15
Fibula	Proximal	≤17	14–17	≥15
	Distal	≤17	14–17	≥15
Foot	Calcaneus	≤12	10–17	≥14
	MTs and Phalanges	≤13	11–13	≥11
Scapula	Coracoid-Glenoid Complex*	≤16	14–18	≥16
	Acromion	≤18	15–17	≥15
	Inferior Angle	≤21	17–22	≥17
	Medial Border	≤21	18–22	≥18
Pelvis	Tri-radiate Complex**	≤14	11–16	≥14
	Ant Inf Iliac Spine	≤14	14–18	≥15
	Ischial Tuberosity	≤15	14–19	≥16
	Iliac Crest	≤16	14–21	≥18
Sacrum	Auricular Surface	≤20	15–21	≥17
	S1-S2 Bodies	≤27	14–30+	≥21
	S1-S2 Alae	≤19	11–26	≥14
	S2-5 Bodies	≤20	12–26	≥19
	S2-5 Alae	≤14	10–19	≥13
Vertebrae***	Bodies	≤21	14–23	≥18
Ribs***	Heads	≤21	17–22	≥19
Clavicle	Medial	≤23	17–30	≥21
Manubrium	1st Costal Notch	≤23	18–25	≥21

*Includes union of the coracoid process, and the subcoracoid and glenoid epiphyses.

**Includes union of the primary elements on both pelvic and acetabular surfaces and the acetabular epiphyses.

***At least one vertebra within the column displays this type of activity.

SKELETAL RECORDING FORMS

A series of three recording forms, representing three life stages (perinatal remains, early childhood, and late childhood/adolescence) have been provided to permit a more realistic template of the skeletal development that we might expect to encounter during those time periods. This offers the practitioner a general idea of the ossification centers and the union that we might expect to be present based on the broad life stage of the individual.

Tables have been constructed within each of the forms for recording the total count of intraregional osseous material. This was done to eradicate the need to assign specific identity to material that is difficult to seriate or side (i.e., specific vertebral or rib level). The skeletal material listed within each table varies from form to form, as the practitioner's ability to identify such material should change with increasing age.

SKULL RECORDING FORMS

A series of two skull recording forms were developed, representing perinatal and early childhood development. A form was not provided for late childhood/adolescent remains as, with the exception to union of the basi-occipital synchondrosis and perhaps some minor proportional differences, an adult form should provide sufficient representation.

Illustrations of the skeletal and skull recording forms were kindly provided by Caroline Needham (University of Dundee).

PERINATAL SKELETAL RECORDING FORM

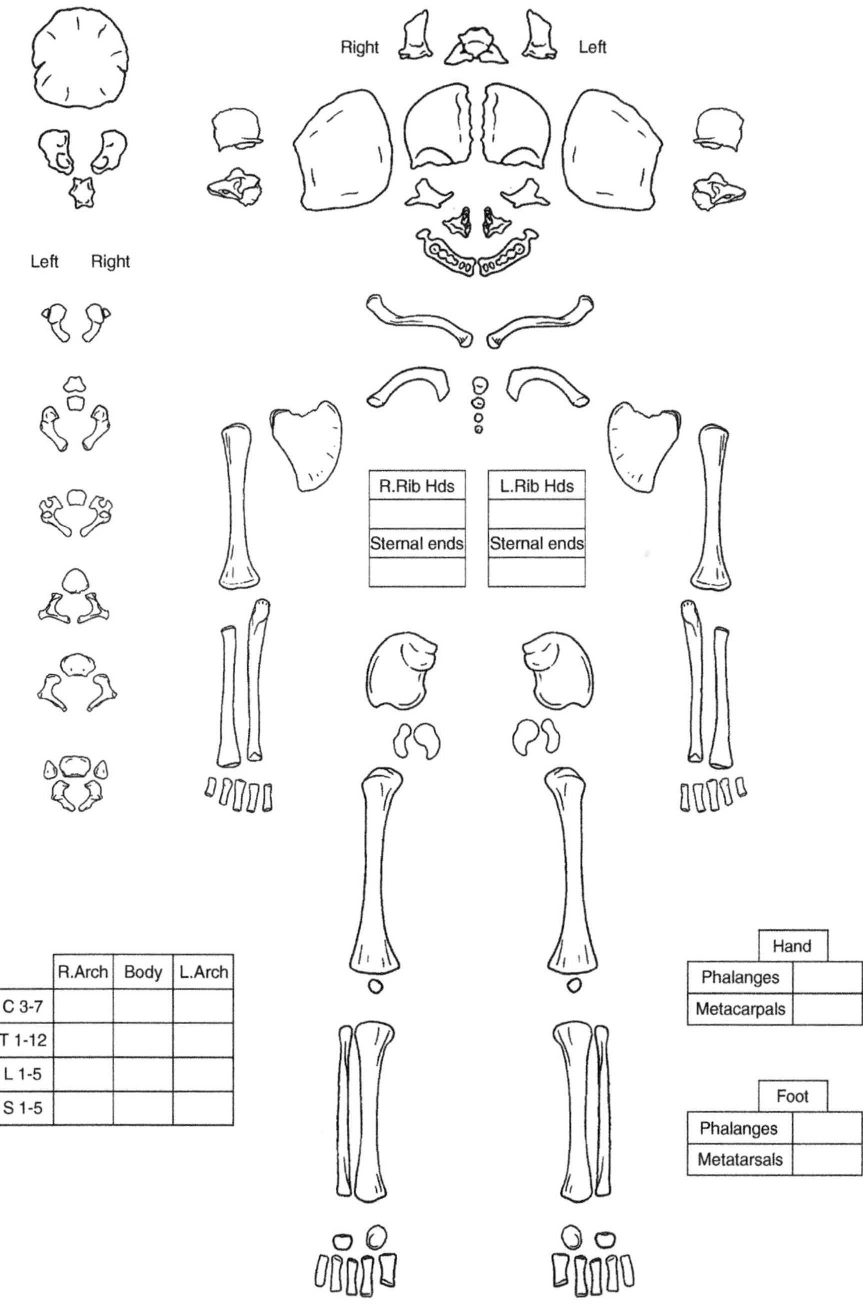

R.Rib Hds
Sternal ends

L.Rib Hds
Sternal ends

	R.Arch	Body	L.Arch
C 3-7			
T 1-12			
L 1-5			
S 1-5			

	Hand
Phalanges	
Metacarpals	

	Foot
Phalanges	
Metatarsals	

EARLY CHILDHOOD SKELETAL RECORDING FORM

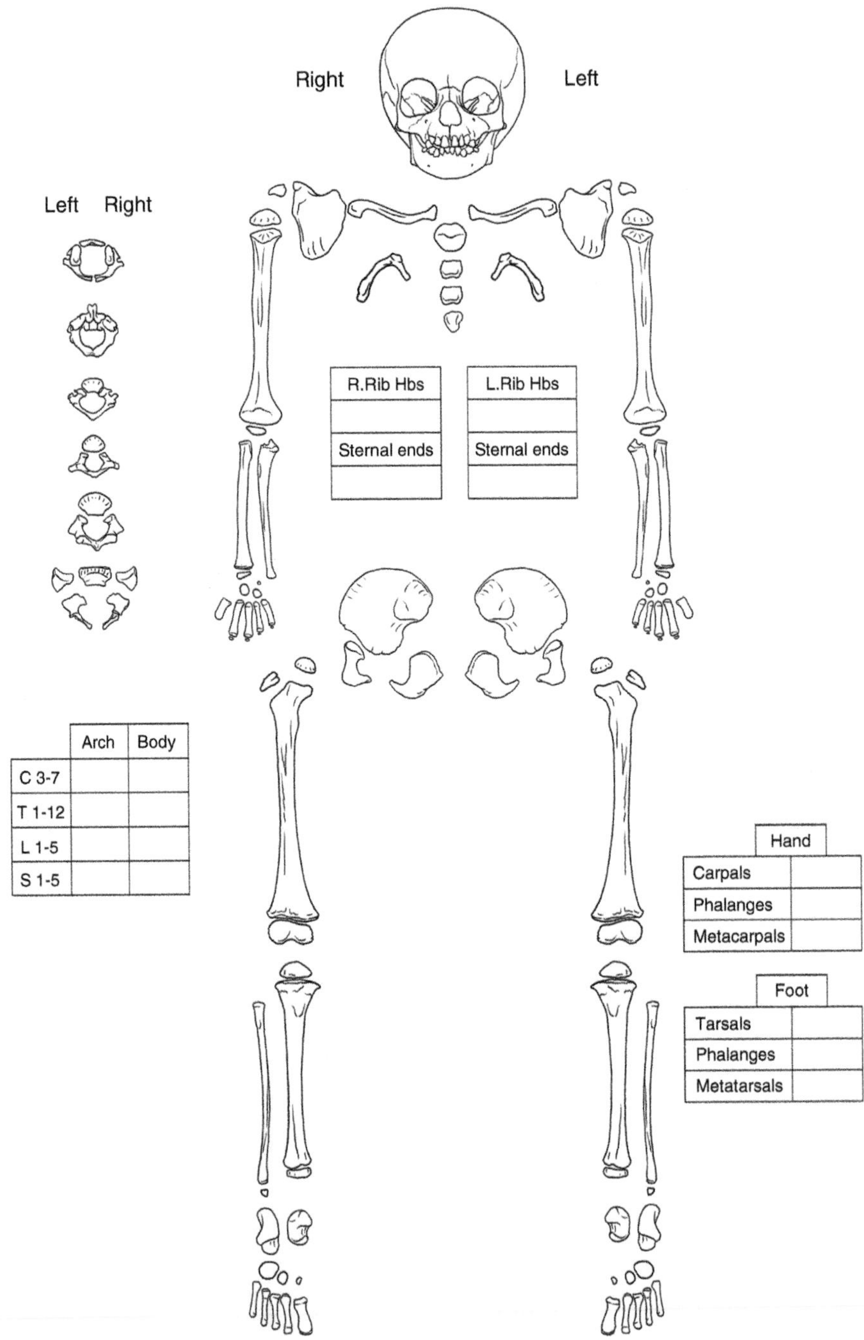

R.Rib Hbs
Sternal ends

L.Rib Hbs
Sternal ends

	Arch	Body
C 3-7		
T 1-12		
L 1-5		
S 1-5		

	Hand
Carpals	
Phalanges	
Metacarpals	

	Foot
Tarsals	
Phalanges	
Metatarsals	

LATE CHILDHOOD SKELETAL RECORDING FORM

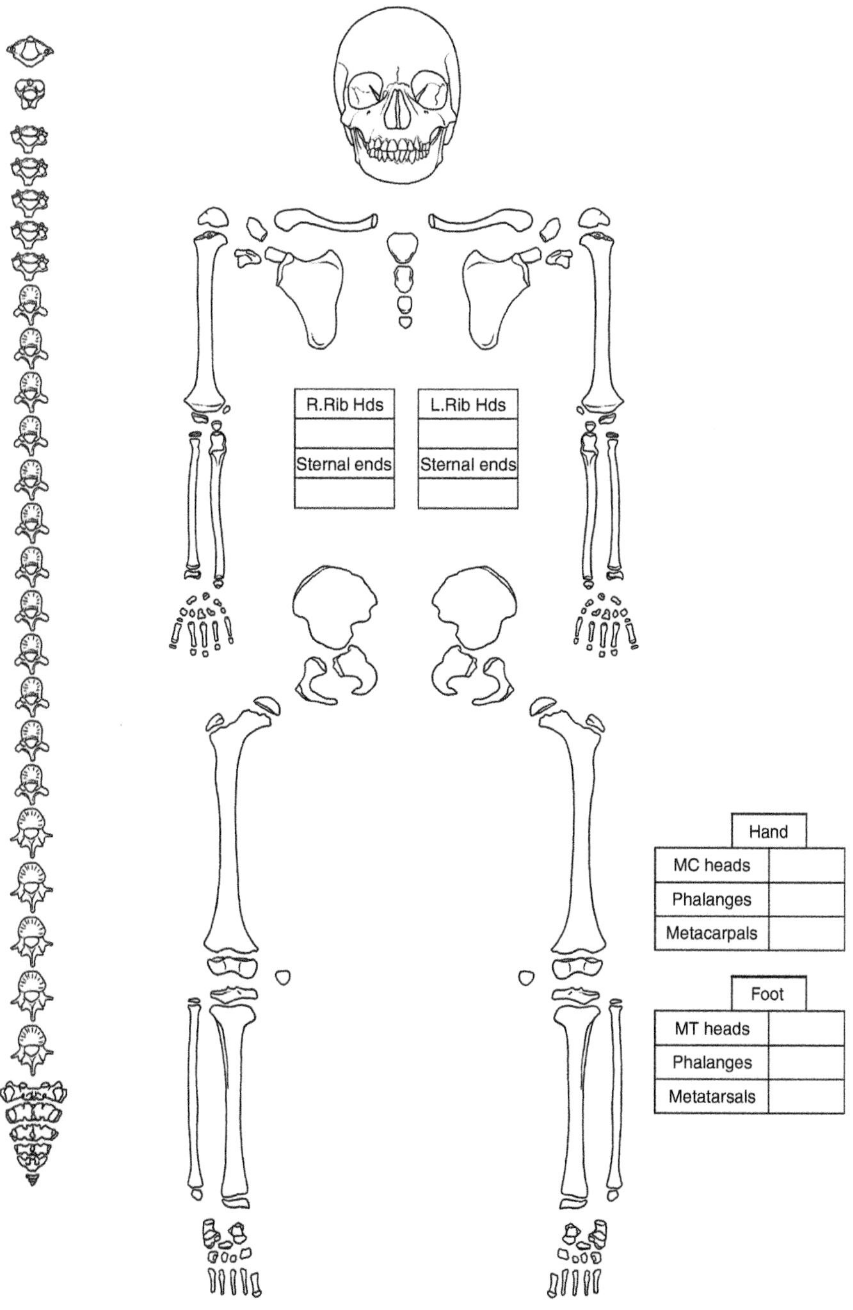

Hand	
MC heads	
Phalanges	
Metacarpals	

Foot	
MT heads	
Phalanges	
Metatarsals	

PERINATAL SKULL RECORDING FORM

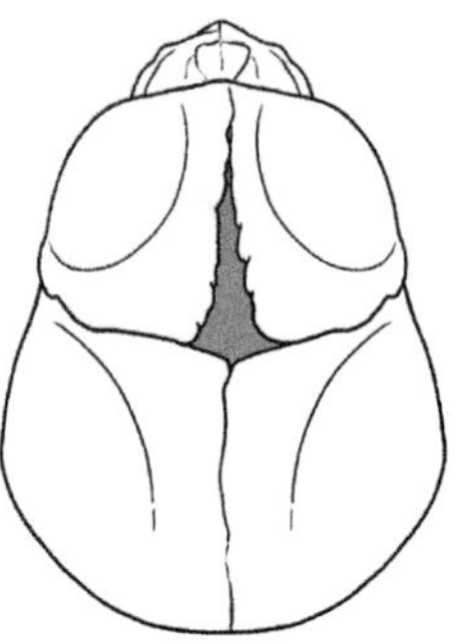

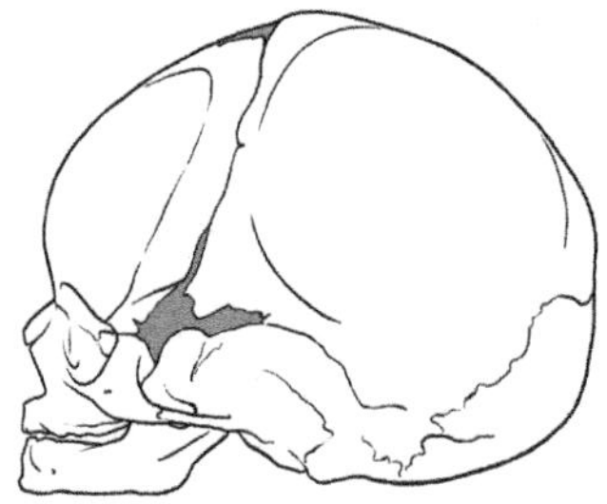

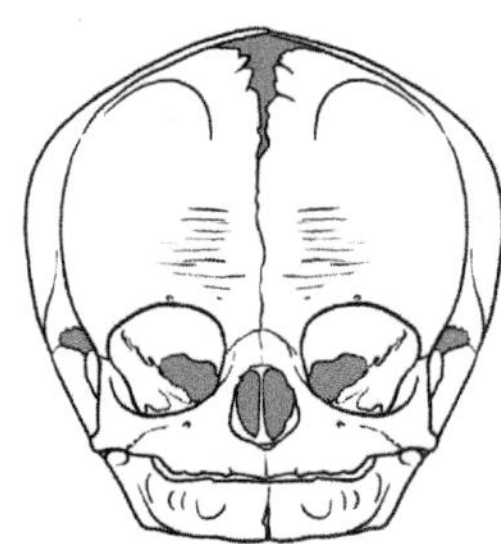

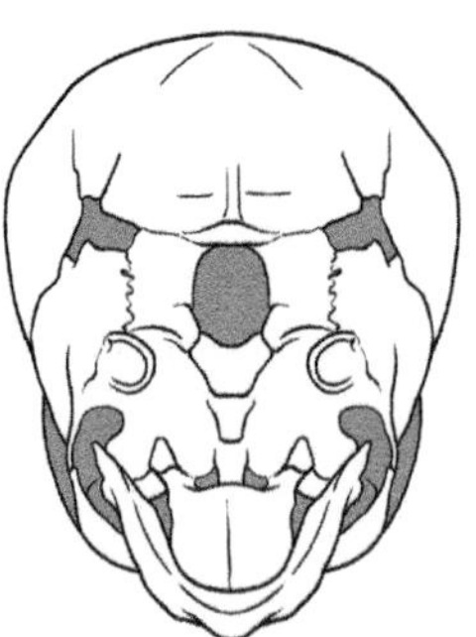

EARLY CHILDHOOD SKULL RECORDING FORM

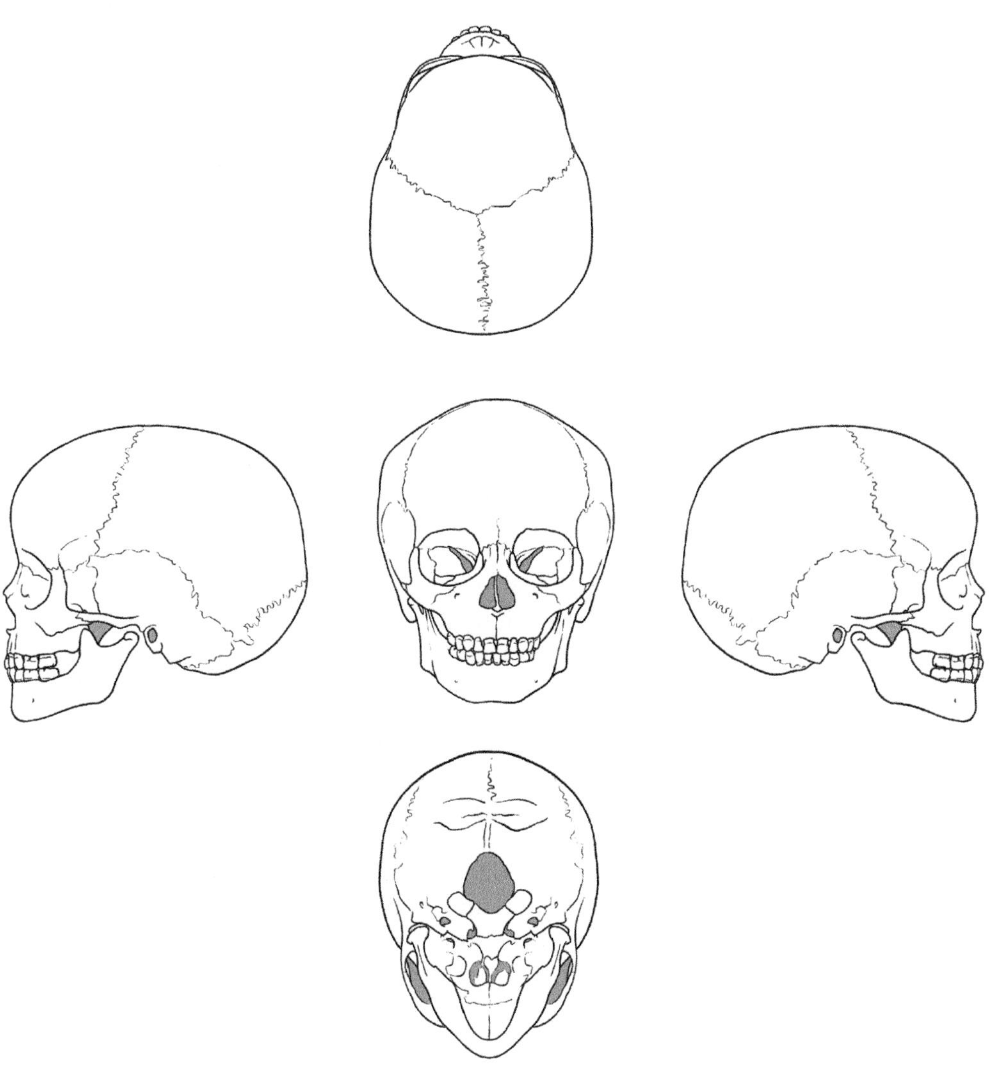

EPIPHYSEAL SEQUENCING: AN AID TO RECOGNIZING COMMINGLED REMAINS

Background Information

Understanding the sequence in which epiphyses begin and complete union can be used as an important tool in the detection and separation of commingled remains. Osseous material that has been recognized as developmentally incompatible may provide sufficient evidence to indicate the presence of two or more individuals. Thus, documentation of union sequence among the epiphyses may help to identify outlying elements whose union status does not adhere to expected sequencing patterns, thereby suggesting the presence of commingled remains.

How to Use the Sequence Trees

Sequence tree diagrams demonstrate the overall sequence in which epiphyses begin and complete union. Each figure displays a modal sequence pattern, as demonstrated by a majority of individuals in the sample, in addition to all observed variations to that pattern. The modal sequence pattern is represented by the central "tree trunk" and demonstrates progressive maturity from top to bottom. Variations to the modal pattern are demonstrated through the use of "tree branches." Each branch signifies the extent of variation that occurs in relation to the reference trunk epiphysis. The "twig" projections extending from the branches identify those epiphyses that exhibit the minority pattern; those positioned to the left of the trunk occasionally were observed to commence/complete union *before* the referenced trunk epiphysis, and those located to the right sometimes were observed to commence/complete union *after* the referenced trunk epiphysis. Also listed in association with each twig epiphysis represents the frequency with which that pattern was observed to occur; that is, the number of individuals that displayed the alternative pattern in relation to the total number of cases utilized for defining the sequence. This provides an indication as to the confidence that we can assign to that pattern. Epiphyses that have no branches extending from their trunk were not seen to exhibit any variation in sequence order to that of the modal pattern in this sample. Likewise, any epiphysis not listed within a branch did not vary in its union sequence with the reference trunk epiphysis.

Source

Bosnian war dead from the fall of Srebrenica (1995)—males only.

Reference

Schaefer, M. and Black, S. (2007). Epiphyseal Union Sequencing: Aiding in the Recognition and Sorting of Commingled Remains. *Journal of Forensic Sciences* **52**(2): 277–285. Wiley-Blackwell.

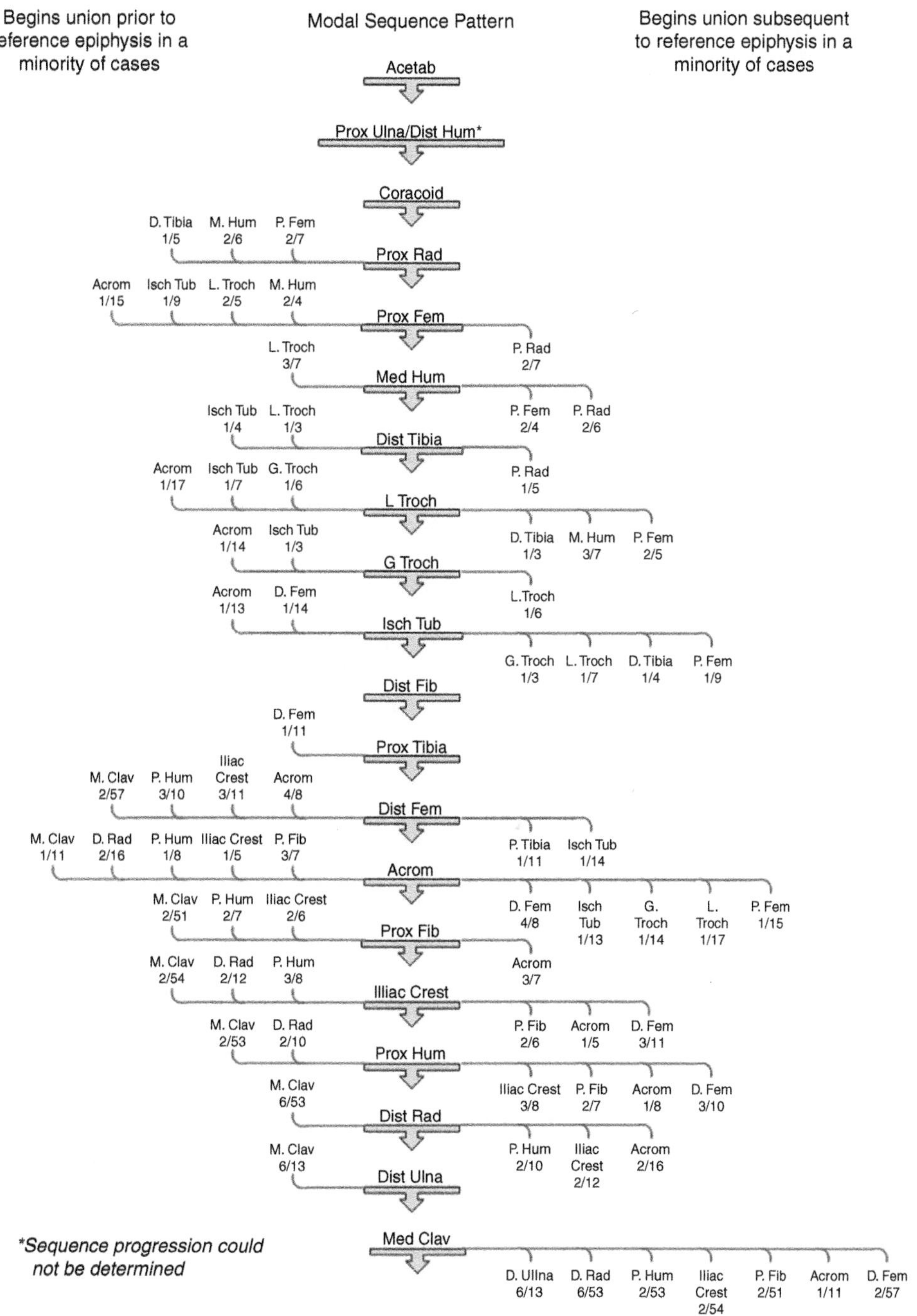
"Beginning" Union
Begins union prior to reference epiphysis in a minority of cases
Modal Sequence Pattern
Begins union subsequent to reference epiphysis in a minority of cases
Acetab
Prox Ulna/Dist Hum*
Coracoid
D. Tibia 1/5
M. Hum 2/6
P. Fem 2/7
Prox Rad
Acrom 1/15
Isch Tub 1/9
L. Troch 2/5
M. Hum 2/4
Prox Fem
P. Rad 2/7
L. Troch 3/7
Med Hum
P. Fem 2/4
P. Rad 2/6
Isch Tub 1/4
L. Troch 1/3
Dist Tibia
P. Rad 1/5
Acrom 1/17
Isch Tub 1/7
G. Troch 1/6
L Troch
D. Tibia 1/3
M. Hum 3/7
P. Fem 2/5
Acrom 1/14
Isch Tub 1/3
G Troch
L.Troch 1/6
Acrom 1/13
D. Fem 1/14
Isch Tub
G. Troch 1/3
L. Troch 1/7
D. Tibia 1/4
P. Fem 1/9
Dist Fib
D. Fem 1/11
Prox Tibia
M. Clav 2/57
P. Hum 3/10
Iliac Crest 3/11
Acrom 4/8
Dist Fem
P. Tibia 1/11
Isch Tub 1/14
M. Clav 1/11
D. Rad 2/16
P. Hum 1/8
Iliac Crest 1/5
P. Fib 3/7
Acrom
D. Fem 4/8
Isch Tub 1/13
G. Troch 1/14
L. Troch 1/17
P. Fem 1/15
M. Clav 2/51
P. Hum 2/7
Iliac Crest 2/6
Prox Fib
Acrom 3/7
M. Clav 2/54
D. Rad 2/12
P. Hum 3/8
Illiac Crest
P. Fib 2/6
Acrom 1/5
D. Fem 3/11
M. Clav 2/53
D. Rad 2/10
Prox Hum
Iliac Crest 3/8
P. Fib 2/7
Acrom 1/8
D. Fem 3/10
M. Clav 6/53
Dist Rad
P. Hum 2/10
Iliac Crest 2/12
Acrom 2/16
M. Clav 6/13
Dist Ulna
Med Clav
D. Ullna 6/13
D. Rad 6/53
P. Hum 2/53
Iliac Crest 2/54
P. Fib 2/51
Acrom 1/11
D. Fem 2/57
*Sequence progression could not be determined

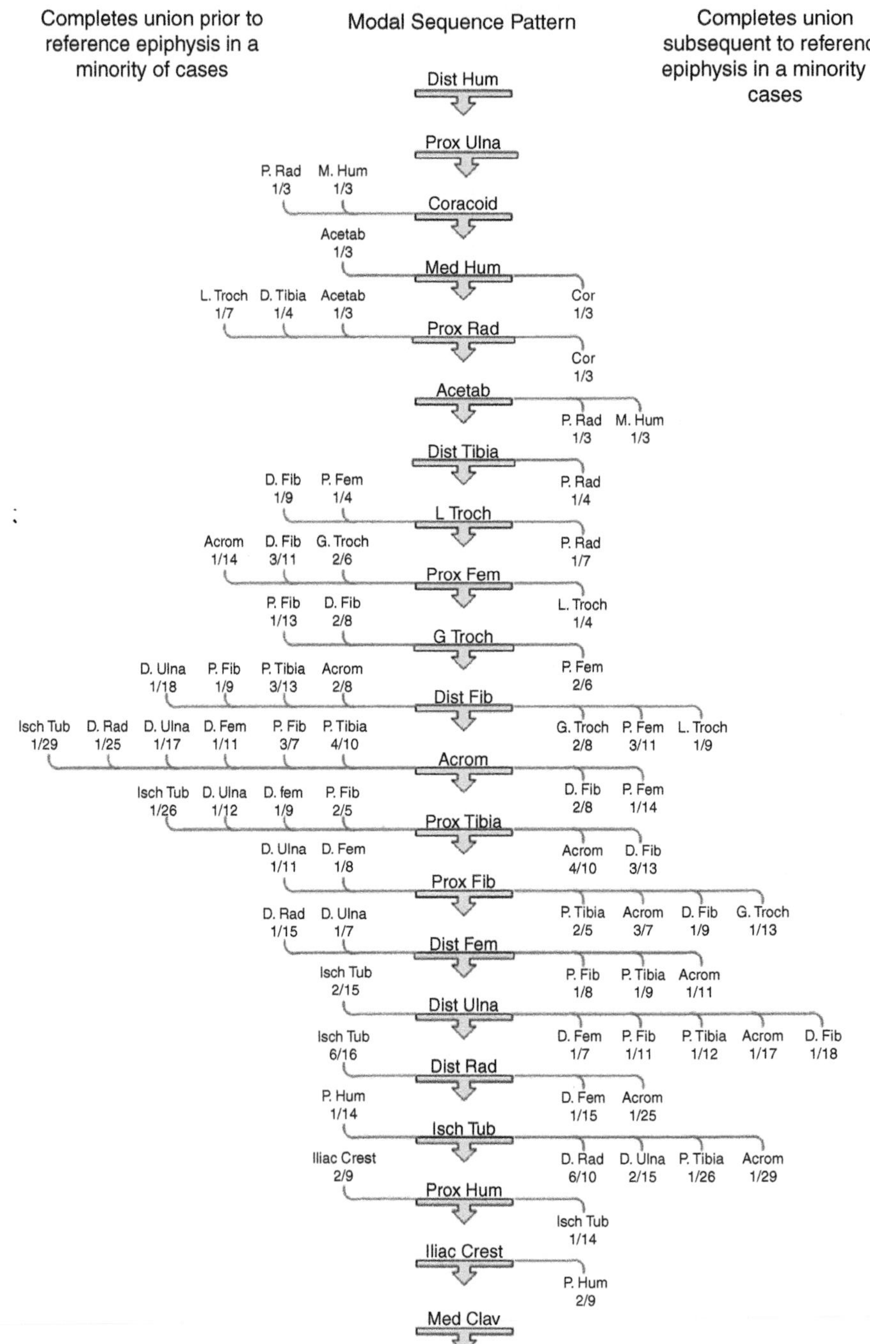
"Complete" Union
Completes union prior to reference epiphysis in a minority of cases
Modal Sequence Pattern
Completes union subsequent to reference epiphysis in a minority of cases
Dist Hum
Prox Ulna
P. Rad 1/3
M. Hum 1/3
Coracoid
Acetab 1/3
Med Hum
Cor 1/3
L. Troch 1/7
D. Tibia 1/4
Acetab 1/3
Prox Rad
Cor 1/3
Acetab
P. Rad 1/3
M. Hum 1/3
Dist Tibia
P. Rad 1/4
D. Fib 1/9
P. Fem 1/4
L Troch
P. Rad 1/7
Acrom 1/14
D. Fib 3/11
G. Troch 2/6
Prox Fem
L. Troch 1/4
P. Fib 1/13
D. Fib 2/8
G Troch
P. Fem 2/6
D. Ulna 1/18
P. Fib 1/9
P. Tibia 3/13
Acrom 2/8
Dist Fib
G. Troch 2/8
P. Fem 3/11
L. Troch 1/9
Isch Tub 1/29
D. Rad 1/25
D. Ulna 1/17
D. Fem 1/11
P. Fib 3/7
P. Tibia 4/10
Acrom
D. Fib 2/8
P. Fem 1/14
Isch Tub 1/26
D. Ulna 1/12
D. fem 1/9
P. Fib 2/5
Prox Tibia
Acrom 4/10
D. Fib 3/13
D. Ulna 1/11
D. Fem 1/8
Prox Fib
P. Tibia 2/5
Acrom 3/7
D. Fib 1/9
G. Troch 1/13
D. Rad 1/15
D. Ulna 1/7
Dist Fem
P. Fib 1/8
P. Tibia 1/9
Acrom 1/11
Isch Tub 2/15
Dist Ulna
D. Fem 1/7
P. Fib 1/11
P. Tibia 1/12
Acrom 1/17
D. Fib 1/18
Isch Tub 6/16
Dist Rad
D. Fem 1/15
Acrom 1/25
P. Hum 1/14
Isch Tub
D. Rad 6/10
D. Ulna 2/15
P. Tibia 1/26
Acrom 1/29
Iliac Crest 2/9
Prox Hum
Isch Tub 1/14
Iliac Crest
P. Hum 2/9
Med Clav

Index

Note: Page numbers followed by 'f' indicate figures, 't' indicate tables.

Printed and bound by CPI Group (UK) Ltd, Croydon, CR0 4YY

03/10/2024

01040319-0010